FRAILTY OF HUMAN AFFAIRS

CAROLINE ANGUS

Thank you to the four most important gentlemen in the world for their help – Grayson, Torben, Espen, and Lachlan, to whom I owe everything.

While locations and historical timelines are accurate, the characters and situations in this book are purely fictional.

For more information on the author and Cromwell period, visit carolineangus.com

FRAILTY OF HUMAN AFFAIRS

BOOK ONE OF THE QUEENMAKER SERIES

PREFACE

In 1509, King Henry VIII was crowned alongside his new bride, Princess Katherine of Aragon. Katherine had married Henry's brother, Prince Arthur, in 1501, only for him to die months later. After receiving dispensation from the Pope, the couple married and were crowned in a dual coronation, and would go on to have one daughter and lose another five children at birth. After having affairs with several well-known mistresses, King Henry set his sights on Anne Boleyn, lady-in-waiting to Queen Katherine, sometime in 1525. By 1527, Henry set his chief advisor, Cardinal Thomas Wolsey, Lord Chancellor of England, to the task of procuring an annulment of his marriage to Katherine, on the grounds that a man could not marry his brother's widow. After several failed attempts to persuade Pope Clement VII to agree to an annulment, a decision was made – an ecclesiastic legatine court was to be set up in London. Two cardinals, Cardinal Wolsey and Cardinal Lorenzo Campeggio, a chief confidant of the Pope, would stand in as papal legates (the Pope's representatives), and through a hearing, decide on whether Henry and Katherine's marriage was ever lawful in the eyes of God. The people of England loved Queen Katherine; she had ruled for twenty years, a kind, pious and beautiful Catholic queen all could respect. But Katherine was too old to give Henry what he needed – a son to inherit the English throne. Anne Boleyn was still in her twenties – pretty,   vi sophisticated, intelligent, and young enough to give birth to a male heir. After being in love with Anne Boleyn for four years, King Henry had become bitter towards his Queen, and also his sixteen-year-old daughter, Princess Mary, whom he considered too unnatural to inherit the throne, as she was female. Anne Boleyn was a mistress who would not share Henry's bed, and a combination of frustration, longing, and arrogance built in the 38-year-old ruler. Cardinal Wolsey, at Henry's side for twenty years, and credited with countless successes at home and abroad, and the wealthiest man in England, could not give the King what he wanted, an annulment from Katherine. With the witty Anne Boleyn and her family taking Wolsey's place at Henry's side, and the Protestant reformers beginning to eat into England's Catholic soul, the King could be easily swayed in any direction. Enter Thomas Cromwell – lawyer and advisor to Thomas Wolsey, a commoner with a smart mind and vivid history throughout Europe, educated in England and Italy, who had ideas on how to create an annulment, and destroy Pope Clement's power in the process. By 1529, no one, noble or common, knew what would happen in their realm, and with the anger of the Holy Roman Emperor also weighing upon the annulment issue - the King's 'Great Matter" – the threat of war was real, all to gain a male heir for the kingdom. King Henry needed a new queen, and Katherine would never give up her crown.

England's royal inner circle by 1529

King Henry VIII All-powerful, well-educated and athletic ruler of England for twenty years. Aged only 38 years old, a religious, volatile, arrogant man. Father of one legitimate heir, Princess Mary, and a bastard son, Henry Fitzroy, Duke of Richmond and Somerset

Queen Katherine Catholic Spanish princess married to Henry for twenty years - pious, respectable, intelligent, and mother to the only legitimate royal heir, Mary, Princess of Wales

Anne Boleyn Highly-educated former lady in-waiting to Queen Katherine, daughter to successful courtier Thomas Boleyn

Charles Brandon Duke of Suffolk, and Henry's best friend. Married to Henry's sister Mary, Dowager Queen of France. Member of the Privy Council

Thomas Howard Duke of Norfolk, uncle to Anne Boleyn, close courtier to Henry. Member of the Privy Council

Thomas Boleyn Lord Rochford and Lord Privy Seal. Father to Anne Boleyn, along with popular courtier George Boleyn and the beautiful Mary Boleyn, King Henry's former mistress

Advisors and courtiers to King Henry

Cardinal Thomas Wolsey Common-born man raised through the church to become advisor to King Henry, elevated to Cardinal by the Catholic Church, and Lord Chancellor of England, the nation's most powerful ministerial role

Thomas Cromwell Advisor and lawyer to Thomas Wolsey. Member of parliament, wealthy merchant and money lender. Former soldier, Italian trader and banker and English-trained scholar

Sir Thomas More Chancellor of the Duchy of Lancaster, respected humanist, author and Catholic theologian. Loyal advisor to King Henry and champion of Dutch writer Erasmus

Thomas Cranmer Highly-educated theologian, humanist and ordained priest, and supporter of Martin Luther. Diplomat to both Spanish court and Holy Roman Emperor on King Henry's behalf

Archdeacon Stephen Gardiner Trained in canon (religious) and civil law, and master secretary to Cardinal Wolsey. Well-travelled diplomat, Master of Trinity Hall and expert at Cambridge University

William Warham Archbishop of Canterbury and leader of the Convocation of Canterbury (religious parliament). Bound to Pope Clement and the Catholic faith

Eustace Chapuys Imperial Ambassador to England and champion of the cause of Queen Katherine on Charles V's behalf

Powerful Italian figures in 1529

Pope Clement VII Pope of Rome and leader of the Catholic faith since 1523. Member of the powerful Florentine Medici dynasty. Imprisoned during the sacking of Rome by Charles V's soldiers in 1527

Cardinal Lorenzo Campeggio Powerful and well-travelled cardinal, left in charge of Rome during the Pope's absences, and Cardinal Legate of England. Representative of Pope Clement abroad

Charles V of Spain King of Spain, Holy Roman Emperor, King of Italy, King of the Romans, Lord of the Netherlands and Duke of Burgundy, ruler of the German and Austrian states controlled by the Roman Empire. Nephew of Queen Katherine of England

The Medici dynasty Multi-generational family in control of the Republic of Florence. One of the wealthiest families in Europe, creator of two Popes, including Clement. Ousted from Florence in 1527 during a siege, only to be reinstated with full control and wealth, especially **Alessandro de' Medici** The last senior member of the original Medici generation, illegitimate son of Pope Clement, set to rule Florence. His 'sister', Catherine de' Medici, is set to become a French princess

Nicóla Frescobaldi Effeminate bastard son to the late Francesco Frescobaldi, a wealthy Florentine merchant and banker. Reclusive favourite courtier of Pope Clement, highly- educated man of business and theology

Nicóletta Frescobaldi Only living daughter of Francesco Frescobaldi. Pre-contracted in marriage to Alessandro de' Medici

Well known figures in Europe in 1529

Erasmus of Rotterdam Dutch Renaissance humanist, Catholic priest, social critic, teacher, and theologian. Creator of the Latin New Testament bible based on Greek texts

William Tyndale Creator of the English language bible, translated from Greek and Hebrew texts. Supporter of Protestant reform. In exile from England and against Henry's annulment

Martin Luther German theologian, excommunicated priest and creator of the Protestant Reformation and the German language bible

Niccoló Machiavelli Recently-deceased Florentine diplomat, politician, historian, philosopher, humanist, and writer. Creator of political science

King Francis I of France Popular young King of France. Well-educated writer and patron to Leonardo da Vinci. Signed the peace treaty at the Field of Cloth of Gold with England

Stephen Vaughan English merchant, royal agent and diplomat, and strong supporter of the Protestant Reformation

Popular English courtiers in 1529

Ralph Sadler Ward and master secretary to Thomas Cromwell
Richard (Williams) Cromwell Nephew to Thomas Cromwell
George Cavendish Writer and faithful attendant to Thomas Wolsey
Edmund Bonner Faithful friend and chaplain to Thomas Wolsey
Sir Thomas Audley Barrister and Speaker in the House of Commons
Richard Rich Popular lawyer and member of parliament
Thomas Wriothesley Lawyer serving Thomas Cromwell and Stephen Gardiner, clerk of the royal court
Sir Henry Norris, Sir Francis Weston, Sir William Brereton, Sir Francis Bryan Members of the privy chamber of King Henry
Mark Smeaton Talented young English composer and musician
Sir Thomas Wyatt Diplomat, politician, poet, loved friend of Anne Boleyn
Hans Holbein the Younger Popular German artist, given royal favour for his extraordinary portrait talents

NOTE

While all the world knows Thomas Cromwell, the man himself spelled his name 'Crumwell' and it was pronounced 'Crumell' during his life.

This book, like others in the series, uses the term "Protestant" when talking about the Reformation and the reformers, even though the terms was rarely in use in Germany until 1533, and in England from 1539. The term "evangelical" was in use during this period, however, I have avoided this term as much as possible, as the meaning has changed significantly over the centuries. For clarity, most mainstream Protestants are referred to as reformers, while the fully committed Protestants are named Lutherans. Calvinists in southern Germany and Switzerland are referred to as Calvinists, and the extremist Protestants of this time period are referred to as Anabaptists and/or Sacramentarians. I use all of these terms in the book series, and are kept separate for ease of reading. The term "Protestant" remains throughout the book as a catch-all phrase, to distinguish reformers from Catholics, who are also referred to as papists.

I have used only pounds in England, as the English currency of the period was complex. Approximately, £1 in Cromwell's period is £350 today.

'The first method for estimating the intelligence of a ruler is to look at the men he has around him.'

Niccoló Machiavelli The Prince, 1513

'And shall I name one who hath been in our age, and wish him now to live to cure so great a canker? Would God England had a Cromwell: I will say no more.'

Thomas Wilson Discourse on Usury, 1571

Chapter 1 – May 1529
York Place, London

The most wondrous seecryts art hydden coequal from thyself

Nicóla could not master the sound of the powerful male footstep. As men ambled together along echoing halls, Nicóla made a gentle tap, even if wearing heavy riding boots. Every person who met Nicóla regarded him up and down, questioning his every ability. Today proved no exception.

London seemed such a grim place. Many people on the muddy streets appeared near death, and Nicóla knew death well. Rain fell constantly, cold when driven into his face, as if God despised all. Yet was it not spring? The decorated walls of York Place provided scant relief; the hallways appeared bleak and shadowy, candles constantly snuffed out by endless drafts of chilled wind. Weeks at sea, to arrive hither? Nicóla feared death might seize him atop the crest of every wave of the journey. Now, after muddy roads tortured the horses, finally, London, the fabled York Place. A potential new plot with Cardinal Wolsey beckoned. Nicóla could not think of those left behind; Nicóla knew enough grief to stop any heart.

Two guards, dressed in dark blue with golden adornment, stood at the arched doorway. Both relented their positions when the party of three approached. Their master entered first, followed by Nicóla and purple-clad Bishop Alessandro, papers in hand, ever the attendants to the powerful man who allowed them his patronage, who needed them to endure England, far from Rome.

'His Eminence, Cardinal Lorenzo Campeggio.'

Nicóla acknowledged the short gentleman-usher who announced their presence, and glanced up and down his livery, the same as the guards; imported blue fabric, a decent price per yard of cloth. Following their master's lead, Nicóla and Bishop Alessandro shuffled, faces forward, towards the end of the extraordinary room. No view presented through the broad windows; early evening darkness blotted out the world. Yellowing candles flickered in their numbers in the dusty but richly decorated room, which smelled so strange. Someone named the smell to be mould, something which seldom grew at home in Florence. The damp weather caused it here, the way it made cheese in cellars in Italy. Little yet made sense in this foreign land, yet the opulence of this office, golden tapestries, Turkish carpets, gold and silver plate laid out said much. Only fit for the richest man in England.

'Lorenzo.' Cardinal Wolsey did not stand as he addressed his long-time colleague, his face as grim as his tone. The old Cardinal appeared harmless enough, at least in Nicóla's eyes. Ageing, a gift not bestowed to many, his fingers fat, jeweled rings constricting and bloating his hands. He wore the red robes of a cardinal, which Nicóla despised, the same as Campeggio. The Catholic faith gave Nicóla no comfort, even after going all the way to the Pope in need of salvation. Now, another cardinal with his furlined red robes and ugly red biretta cap sought to control Nicóla's life.

Cardinal Campeggio took the offer of a seat across the grand desk of Wolsey, and Nicóla stood, head down, a few steps behind him with Bishop Alessandro. The others had visited the palace of the English Cardinal Thomas Wolsey, not so Nicóla.

'Most thanks for seeing me before I need to address the King.' Campeggio spoke in accented English, his age evident in his voice. He stroked his long white beard, grown to commemorate the sacking of Rome eighteen months earlier, just as the Pope had done.

Wolsey sighed. 'The King will delay no longer. The court's decision on His Majesty's annulment from Queen Katherine has been considered enough. Perchance God made me so unwell for the winter, a way of giving Henry a chance to reconsider. But now it is my job as both papal legate and Lord Chancellor to hear, in your words, what you think before we start proceedings. Henry asked for an annulment two years ago, and the tide of favour is starting to turn against me.'

Campeggio gestured to Nicóla for his papers, which Nicóla happily dropped on the desk. The correspondence on Wolsey's desk sat in a neat pile, with perfect handwriting, next to a solid silver ink quill. A fastidious man. A lone orange sat on the desk; it was said Wolsey carried the orange at his nose, so not to smell commoners on the street.

'So few papers for such a burden,' Wolsey sniffed. 'You are a man of well over fifty years, Lorenzo, yet you seem to have let your long years of experience fail you.' His tone told Nicóla that Wolsey considered himself well superior to his Italian counterpart.

'Thomas, you would not believe the state of Rome,' Campeggio sighed and took the first page into his hands. 'The sacking of Rome was extreme and prolonged. I got left behind as papal legate to Rome, and I lost everything. My own palace got destroyed, robbed of its jewels, its art. I was almost killed.'

'Oh yes, we heard of Rome's sacking. You have told me several times this past year. Remember our own envoy got assaulted when hoping to see the Pope,' Wolsey replied, and the clean-shaven old man, his double chin shaking as he spoke, appeared bored.

'The Holy Roman Emperor's soldiers assaulted the palace. Almost all were killed in broad daylight. If not for my friend …' Campeggio paused and gestured at Nicóla… 'I would be dead.'

Nicóla tilted his head enough to see beyond his brim of the soft cap of Campeggio's servants' livery, to witness, beyond the wooden throne of the great Cardinal, another man dressed all in black, and most tall. He took a few steps forward out of the darkness of the corner, closer to Wolsey. Nicóla caught his eye and the pair stared at one another, the man refusing to look away. He stood older than Nicóla by more than ten years. Power sat in the hands of old men in England. How did the young bear it? At home in Florence, the generations all fought for power.

The man's wide golden eyes continued to stare with the slightest of frowns, and Nicóla remained still. Everyone regarded Nicóla up and down, took a second glance, but this man seemed the most threatening in his golden gaze. It was if he knew a secret so hidden that Nicóla felt faint at the thought of being discovered. This man wanted to recognise Nicóla but struggled. Secrets were Nicóla's trade and currency, and Nicóla could never lose his biggest secret of all for no special reason. The dark man's golden stare held remembrance, not secrecy.

Campeggio had seen the man in the shadows the whole time. 'If it was not for my friend, I could not have talked with the Pope during his capture or his time in Orvieto after His Holiness' escape. Nicóla delivered messages back and forth. Even then, it took months before the Pope decided to allow me hither, to come and decide on Henry's future.'

'Yes, but that is without relevance. You reached England eight months ago. If only your friend had brought us the papal dispensation we need from Rome,' the dark man spoke with only mild curiosity on the subject, one hand now on Wolsey's throne. His golden eyes continued to study Nicóla, but Nicóla refused to bow or look away. 'Who are you? I have not seen you in the Cardinal's envoy.'

'A total stranger could you believe,' Campeggio answered for Nicóla and coughed, the sound of a chronically ill man. 'You know, with my poor eyesight, I am in need of young men. During the sacking, this young boy found me cowering as my palace burnt, and took me to safety, a home already sacked, but safe. I promoted him to the Pope, and His Holiness brought Nicóla into the Church, to live in the Apostolic Palace. Nicóla is not consecrated with holy orders, like my son Alessandro here. Nicóla has just arrived from Rome with supplies needed for this extended trip.'

'You are here to rule on an annulment for King Henry and Queen Katherine, Your Eminence,' the man continued in a smooth, even tone, and switched his gaze to Campeggio in the chair. 'Anything less is a failure. I do not care why the Pope will not rule on the proposed annulment. We have the facts. No more delays; my master Cardinal Wolsey needs this completed.'

'And we know how desperate King Henry is to marry Lady Anne,' Wolsey added with a sigh. 'They are involved in a three-year love affair. The King's conscience is in a state of great suffering.' The old Cardinal threw a gentle smile to Nicóla. For being known throughout Christendom as the most powerful cardinal of them all, and known as a corrupt tyrant, he certainly appeared placid. Just another heavy-waisted old man.

'Before we continue, does your friend speak English?'

'Parli inglese?' the dark man asked, his voice suddenly as sharp as a blade. Nicóla glanced up at the sound of Italian. 'I speak fluent Italian, English, French, Spanish, Flemish, and Latin.' At once, Cardinal Wolsey and his man showed surprise at Nicóla's soft, lilting voice. 'But I prefer that remained private. Bishop Alessandro beside me speaks Italian, English, with Greek, German, Portuguese and Latin, so we can deal with any duty.'

'Gracious!' Wolsey exclaimed. 'What did a delicate man such as yourself do before entering the Church?'

Campeggio laughed; people often commented on Nicóla's short and modest frame. 'We call Nicóla 'il reietto' in Rome.'

Wolsey glanced to the dark man for a translation. 'It means one who is an outsider, outcast, left over, abandoned. In this instance, based on the appearance of this man, petite, delicate, gentle, I believe they are saying like "the Waif", someone small and useless.' His voice growled deep, strong as his golden gaze.

Nicóla could not look away, something about the man drew all eyes to him. 'I have spent my life as a banker's and merchant's apprentice in Florence, Your Eminence,' Nicóla replied to Wolsey.

Again the dark man had his gaze fixed upon Nicóla, enough to make any strong heart skip a little. 'Who are you?'

'Hush now, Thomas,' Wolsey snorted. 'He is Campeggio's well-dressed, dashing, if not petite, hero of Rome.'

But the dark man would not so easily abate. 'What is the make of your doublet and hose, Waif? Is that pale blue damask from Brussels? Are not churchmen bound to poverty, not opulence?'

'Thomas,' tumbled from Nicóla's lips and he covered them with a hand, guilty of speaking out of turn.

'We are both Thomas,' Wolsey replied with a smile and gestured to himself and his attendant. 'We know Bishop Alessandro Campeggio standing beside you, but tell us about yourself.'

'You are Thomas Crumwella,' Nicóla replied, his voice light and surprised, hands clasped together again. His sweet Italian accent added a vowel to the surname.

'Everyone in Europe knows Thomas Crumwella,' Campeggio commented from his seat.

'You have an admirer,' Wolsey jested to Crumwell. No wonder the King's annulment could not be settled; these two cardinals loved small talk which delayed work. But Nicóla wanted to speak to Crumwell personally, had come all this way in search of the man whispered of as "The Prince."

'Master Crumwella, you once worked as a servant in the Frescobaldi household in Florence. You worked as an apprentice to my father, Francesco. He spoke of you often.'

Crumwell's golden eyes flared but he uttered nothing. 'Do you know the name, Thomas?' Wolsey asked, the old man finding it all rather amusing.

'Perchance we ought to discuss the papal decision,' Crumwell cut in with a cough.

'Indeed,' Wolsey sighed. 'Lorenzo, your attendants can leave for your chambers downstairs.'

With a silent bow, Nicóla and Bishop Alessandro turned and left the cavernous room. Alessandro shuffled ahead of Nicóla in his purple bishop's vestments, Nicóla's calf-leather shoes making no sound on the wooden floorboards. But no sooner than the heavy doors closed behind them, they reopened, sending a short burst of light into the white stone hallway. There was Crumwell himself, following after Nicóla. Bishop Alessandro carried on along the hall, ignoring the Englishman.

With not a word spoken, Crumwell pulled Nicóla by the arm towards a window seat and pulled a great red curtain around the discussion. All done with his intense golden stare fixed upon Nicóla. But his touch sent a spark through Nicóla's body, and it mattered none who this man thought he was; Nicóla pulled away in defiance.

'You are the son of Francesco Frescobaldi?' Crumwell asked in a whisper as they sat together against the cold glass laced with black lattice in diamond patterns, the Thames dark below them.

'You knew my father,' Nicóla began.

'Most well!' Crumwell's golden eyes lit up, suddenly an angry face becoming a smile of pure happiness. 'Your father saved my life when he took me off the streets and into the Frescobaldi household. I remember your father being well furnished with daughters.'

'I am the bastard child of my father's annulled first marriage. Father had five daughters by his second marriage.'

'What year were you born?'

Nicóla resisted the urge to cringe. Crumwell remembered so much detail, too much. 'The year 1500.'

'I see, before my arrival in Florence. How is your father now?'

'My father went with God almost two years ago. Sadly, 1527 was not a positive year to be working in banking in Florence.'

'Francesco did not meet a natural death?' Crumwell swallowed hard at the thought.

'No, in the chaos of the Holy Roman Emperor's army rebelling in Rome, many took the chance to rise up against the Medici family and their power in Florence. My father got killed while visiting the Medici home at Poggio a Caiano. The palace got ransacked in the uprising.'

Crumwell dropped his gaze and shook his head, and slowly made the sign of the cross. Dark curls laced with silver hid his eyes for a moment. 'It is uncommon for an only son to join the Church, especially since your father's estate would be most prized. Your stepmother and sisters? The recent War of the League of Cognac was not kind on the Republic of Florence.'

'They cannot be harmed now.'

'So why have you come hither as part of Campeggio's envoy?'

'Did you not wander Europe once yourself?'

'I did. Your father helped me learn Italian. I see he has passed his English skills onto you.'

Nicóla smoothed the pearl buttons on his blue doublet and took a deep breath. 'There can be opportunities far and wide for a man who has seen war, who lives well and is educated. After Rome got sacked by the Emperor's army, I decided to travel.'

'Yet you found time to save the life of the papal legate of Rome and be praised by the Pope?' Every word Crumwell spoke brought back memories of him in his youth, working at Frescobaldi manor during Nicóla's childhood.

'Luck. One day I saw a group of men fighting, and an old cardinal lying on the ground in agony. I went to his aid, and in return, Cardinal Campeggio kindly offered me a position in his household, at a time when I had lost my place with the fallen Medici family. Leaving for England was a final moment offer, so I grabbed hold.'

'You have your father's look about you. The rose-gold hair, and green eyes, though very dark skin. Not a large man like your father, though your English is as fine.'

Nicóla made sure no shoulder length rose-gold strands strayed from under his black cap. 'It is said I am more like my mother, though I knew her not.'

19

'Your father used to call me Tomassito, little Thomas, when I was young and homeless. I was privileged to work in the Frescobaldi household. I had no clothes on my back, and starving when your father saved me. Your father worked for the Medicis?'

'Indeed, when seeking loans for clients, you always seek the help of the Medici family, one of the richest in Europe. I am sure you agree, Tomassito.' Nicóla suspected Crumwell would not take kindly to the informal title, but instead, he gave a trifling smile, a tiny insight into Crumwell as a man. As a master of secrets, every detail brought prized information to Nicóla. Crumwell's eyes did not leave Nicóla's, a gesture which stirred nerves. For the last few years, Nicóla had sought to remain silent, behind a new master, out of sight as much as possible. Now a man, one known throughout Christendom as a common blacksmith's boy who had risen above his station beside a cardinal, with a golden gaze ready to read the markings on one's soul, had Nicóla cornered.

'Cardinal Campeggio came to England unwelcome by many,' Crumwell continued. 'Campeggio is seen as weak by the King, and a natural ally to the Queen, and her nephew, the Roman Emperor. Campeggio may find his head departs his neck before long. Perchance we could be of assistance to one another.'

'How, Master Crumwella? I am just a humble attendant.' Yet Nicóla knew, as the child of the beloved Francesco Frescobaldi, Crumwell wanted collusion at once. Francesco had often spoken to Nicóla about Crumwell's undying fealty to the family many years ago.

'You may be a short man, a delicate man, but I am in need of people in all kinds of roles. I am sure you know how far the reach of Cardinal Wolsey extends.'

'You are a wealthy man. Everyone knows that.'

'Please, let us be friends. I shall do anything to be of service to the son of Francesco Frescobaldi. I loved your father, and I feel ashamed I knew not of his passing. We lost touch a while ago now, but I shall forever think upon him dearly.'

'How could I be of service to you?'

'Does it matter?' Crumwell asked.

Nicóla smiled. 'No, Master Crumwella. I suppose not. But Cardinal Campeggio is my master.'

'And Cardinal Wolsey is my master. The King's patience is at an end, and loyalties are being tested. Our masters must work together, and so must we, if we are to remain in success. It may be that someone with your accent has wandered into this palace at just the right moment. Go about your work for Campeggio, I will send for you when I am ready. A decision to claim scant of the English language is a wise choice. As I say, anything for the son of the kindest man I have ever known.'

'Men speak of you, Master Crumwella. They say you are a fierce lawyer, a masterful accountant, a skilled orator. Men say you are corrupt; that you profit by Wolsey's plots, with honest men's money flowing into your pockets. Bribes are constantly accepted by you. You are not noble, just base, common born, and called "the double-minded man".'

'Mr. Frescobaldi, I play unfairly in an unfair world. Your father taught me how to survive. If you have worked for your father, and the Medici family, then you understand.'

Corruption. Bribery. Lies. Nicóla understood perfectly. Falling into Crumwell's favour proved so easy. 'Let us be friends, Master Crumwella.'

Chapter 2 – May 1529
York Place, London

The moor thee hydes in seecryt, the moor words can reveale

Crumwell simply could not help himself; any time he left the private rooms at York Place, he searched for the Italian. He smiled when he saw the young Nicóla at dinner; eating out of hunger, but taking a second glance at the food served in England. So often he spotted the well-dressed young man in the neatly tended and balanced gardens, reading on his own while the others hunted or chased girls. Nicóla spent limited time in the chapel; Crumwell knew because he sent his secretary Ralph and nephew Richard to follow Nicóla. When Campeggio's men got left out of important meetings, Crumwell occasionally excused himself and found the Italians loitering in wait, except for Nicóla, who would be reading in Wolsey's library. Since Campeggio and his group arrived in England, little on the King's divorce got achieved and Crumwell despised every one of them and their lack of diligence. But not this late addition, the precious bastard son of Francesco Frescobaldi, a person who excited Crumwell's mind, something out of character for himself. Everyone else had qualities easy to read. But not petite, delicate Nicóla, in dashing fabrics, long rose-gold hair bound at the base of his slender neck. Dainty hands with dainty movements, nimble feet, a gentle laugh and soothing green eyes. Nicóla stood with a straight back, both hands rested on his right hip, so perfectly a wealthy Florentine. All things Crumwell admired from afar.

In Crumwell's mind, if the King wanted an annulment, he should get an annulment. Damn his conscience, damn the rules. The King could have what he liked. But the Catholic Church stood in the way of ending the royal marriage. Wolsey, Crumwell's greatest friend and companion, did not want to give the King an annulment, and Campeggio did not either. The Pope kept dispatching envoys, ambassadors, and now a papal legate to decide the conclusion of Henry and Katherine's marriage. With the Boleyn family constantly talking in Henry's ear, the tide of favour had finally slipped away from Wolsey, and Crumwell by association, after nearly twenty years of trust. Crumwell never abandoned his friends but wanted the King's favour at the same time. The line Crumwell needed to stride continued to shrink.

The detailed and blooming gardens of the Cardinal's York Place palace filled with people keen to hear rumours from the new legatine court, the proceedings held at the nearby chapel at Blackfriars. With Wolsey and Campeggio as the Pope's representatives, both the King and Queen needed to testify over their marriage's legal standing. A cool but bright early summer's morning had dawned when Crumwell spotted the young Italian wandering alone, as usual, in the gardens.

As a guest at York Place, Crumwell spotted Nicóla most mornings when he arrived from his own home, Austin Friars, not too far east along the Thames. Crumwell watched Nicóla from a distance, each casual footstep taken along the quiet pathway between the hedges. Not the face of a man at prayer, instead a face of thought. He felt a strange pull for the young man, but not the affection he felt for his own son, nine-year-old Gregory. He felt a pull that no man should feel towards another man, not in God's eyes. Crumwell was not usually a man prone to lust.

'Mr. Frescobaldi,' Crumwell called as he caught up the man wandering between the hedges. Oh, to call that name again after all these years, even if to the son, no longer the father. Nicóla turned and gave a sweet smile to Crumwell, a smile not so unlike a graceful woman's, at least in Crumwell's mind. They both seem to think so at the same time, and the smile quickly faded.

'Master Crumwella.'

Crumwell smiled for what felt like the first time in a week. Not much gave him cause to smile in the past year. 'I hope you are enjoying your time in London, il reietto.'

'Well enough, I suppose. Is that to be my name, the Waif?'

'If you like. No, if I like,' Crumwell replied in a smug tone. 'I suspect you find London a world away from Florence.' He clasped both hands on his black journal.

'Indeed, though, perchance that is not negative. I expected to hear from you much sooner. Perchance you do not need me, for you have an abundance of men under your command.'

'I had no idea my infamy travelled so far.'

'Yes you did,' Nicóla replied sharply. 'I have noticed you have sent two men to follow me. One young blonde man, and another a little older, a rougher man with a long dark beard.'

Crumwell revelled in the comment; his spies had been seen but he cared not. He noticed the Italian's hands appeared so small, smooth-looking, a world away from his own, now showing the age of his forty-plus years, withered with scars of sins past. 'I see you have joined us in the legatine court a few times this week.'

'I join whenever my master requests. It seems every nobleman in England wants a seat, and the commoners up in the gallery, all Queen Katherine supporters, are so eager. Though on the days where we debate solely religious texts, the noblemen seem distant. Discussions on the Queen's first marriage to Prince Arthur, and whether he bedded her, seem to attract a larger audience.'

'I am a lawyer, a money lender, Mr. Frescobaldi; I know these men. What they want, where they spend, how they repay. It bestows a window into any man's life. I am surprised none that the noblemen of the court like the intimate details of the Queen.'

'I am also a money lender, and know the law; I understand to perfection. Still, so demanding for someone as great as Katherine of Aragon. After twenty years as a queen, her privacy is that of a common whore. Is this how the English treat their women? Their betters? The mothers of their children, the guardians of their heirs?'

'Are you a champion of women, Mr. Frescobaldi?'

'More a champion of those who have fleeting power. I am the son of a banker. You are the son of a blacksmith I believe.'

'I am, and not ashamed to say so.'

'Nor should you be. Though the way I hear people speak, they resent both you and the Cardinal, whom they call "the butcher's boy".'

'The lords of England dislike those who are new to the circles of power. I know I have never had any acclaim.'

'I also hear Cardinal Wolsey is the most corrupt cardinal in Christendom. The lords hate him for rising so high, for running the country on religious and secular fronts while the King plays away his days. The people despise Wolsey for the high taxes he imposes, and then he personally keeps their hard-earned money. And now, it seems, after twenty years in power, even your King is ebbing in his love for the Cardinal. I have not heard a kind word whispered since I arrived.'

'Does anyone know you speak English?'

'I have spoken to some people, in order to learn, but mostly I stay silent.'

'Did Cardinal Campeggio bring you hither as a spy?'

'No, Rome sent me. The Cardinal made no objection; he is generous to me.'

'So who is your real master, if not Campeggio?'

'I am my master.'

Crumwell paused for a moment. Not many people held secrets Crumwell did not yet know, but Francesco's son was one of them. 'You sound like your father.'

'Do you remember him that well?'

Crumwell found himself staring at Nicóla's pink lips. 'Yes,' he replied, distracting himself.

'Did you learn the method of Ioci from my father?'

'We trained in the art of memory together, yes.'

'My father also trained me in the art of memory, in my younger years.'

'In that case, can you tell me why I remember my friend Francesco only having daughters?'

'Even a great man can be wrong.'

'A curious observation from an Ioci master. As one of Campeggio's men, should you not be a priest?'

'I have not taken holy orders,' Nicóla replied as the pair continued to amble through the gardens in the bright sunshine. 'I am still a layman, studying religious thought and theology, at the behest of my patron, the Pope. As for your lapse in memory, Master Crumwella. My mother, Nicóletta, died in childbirth. My father remarried a few years later. That would be the Signora Frescobaldi you remember. She had five daughters, and I was, how you say, superfluous, to her family and hidden from sight. My father's first marriage was in defiance of his family's wishes and was annulled. I'm a bastard.'

'Even as the only son of Francesco?'

'Even then, Master Crumwella. You may call me just Nicóla if you wish.'

'Do you have a quick answer for everything I question, Nicóla?'

'Every time.' The young Italian smiled a clear white smile, one which suggested an upbringing surrounded by wealth, as Francesco would have wanted. 'Why do you feel the need to question me? I am merely a member of an envoy hither to assist the Cardinal from Rome.'

'You sound as if the dual papal legate hearing of a monarch's divorce is no vast issue.'

'Oh, it is a vast issue. Pointless in its entirety, but important.'

'Why do you think it pointless?'

Nicóla stopped and smiled, and Crumwell regarded the sweet man's face with the sun directly beyond the pair. It felt pleasant to have an object such as the Italian to play with; people so often bored Crumwell.

'The Pope will never issue an annulment,' Nicóla reasoned. 'A smart man such as yourself surely recognises this. This "trial" if you will, with Campeggio and Wolsey at the head, has suffered enough delays. Are the English so foolish to believe there shall be a legitimate conclusion?'

'Yes, they are.'

'And you, Italianate Englishman?'

'I am loyal to my master. I do as he bids.'

'As do I.'

'You never told me who your master is, il reietto.'

'One ought to assume God is my master.'

A pain deepened in Crumwell's chest at every sound of the young Italian's Florentine accent. It reminded him of a simpler time in his life. Perchance that was why he kept searching out the Italian, despite having little need to do so. The conversation paused as someone neared them on the path, and Nicóla turned straight to Italian.

'Non c'è bisogno di avere paura me, Maestro Crumwella.'

Crumwell felt another crooked smile on his lips. No need to fear Nicóla? He did not fear Nicóla and told him so. 'Non ti preoccupare, non ho paura.'

The man wandering the gardens laughed as he approached the

pair, in the red and white livery of the old Duke of Norfolk, one of the King's allies and uncle to Anne Boleyn. 'I see you have not lost the language you found as a mercenary in Italy,' he muttered.

Crumwell saw the face of the Italian darken a little, only a subtle change, as Nicóla continued to hide his English. 'Some of us value our education.'

'Fighting for the French is hardly admirable,' the tall man mumbled as he sidled by, his foul breath lingering slighter longer than himself.

Crumwell turned his attentions back to Nicóla. 'Are you to chide me for my past, too?' he mocked.

'I know about you, Master Crumwella. I know you fought for the French against the Spanish in Italy. I know you fought at the battle of Garigliano, and lost. The ends justifies the means.'

'Words straight from the mouth of Machiavelli.'

'Machiavelli was a great man. His funeral two years ago,' Nicóla paused and shrugged, 'sombre, melancholy.'

'You attended the funeral of Niccoló Machiavelli?'

'I did.'

'Even though you worked for the Medicis, the same family who fought him out of the Florentine government?'

'I worked for my father on private business, and also we worked together for the Medici family. In that time, we had reason to meet Machiavelli on several occasions. I greatly admire his writings. Have you read much of Machiavelli?'

'Yes, of course.' Crumwell came into contact with the highest men in the land all the time as Wolsey's man. Life so often had the sensation of talking to solid walls, all closed minds. Now somehow, the Waif invoked a feeling of actions long past, of sights, and teachings, experiences, and learnings, all buried deep in Crumwell's mind. Life was a constant swirl of the King's "Great Matter", all of the fighting and jostling, of money and arguing, and here stood a graceful young Italian, tapping away at forgotten thoughts.

'Have you read Machiavelli's 1513 work, De Principatibus?' Nicóla probed.

'About Principalities? Naturally, I have.'

'There are plans to print a new version if the Medici family agree.'

'The Medici?'

'The Pope is a Medici, and the Medici family is the Pope, the power. We are not talking of England, with your kings and your rules. We in Florence are different – councils, committees, high-ranking families make the laws. Everyone has a side.'

'And Machiavelli and the Medicis were enemies, and equally duplicitous.'

Nicóla shrugged again, a sweet smile on his lips. 'The work of De Principatibus is dedicated to Lorenzo de' Medici. Do you know the book has another name? Il Principe?'

'What is that to me?'

'The work does not pay heed to a man such as Lorenzo de' Medici. Some say Cesare Borgia inspired the works. But do you know what some say?'

Crumwell held out his hand, palm up, for the answer.

'Some say Machiavelli met an Englishman in the first years of this century, who lived in Florence, and he inspired Machiavelli to write his book. Are you Il Principe?'

'Am I the man of The Prince?' Crumwell coughed.

'Do you possess a copy?'

'It is not printed, only handwritten.'

'I have a handwritten copy. You can borrow it if you so wish, in case you are, how you say… dim… in your memory.'

'My memory forgets naught.'

'Neither does mine.'

'From the moment I met you, Nicóla, I worried you were a spy, hither to watch Wolsey. I also thought you spied on Campeggio himself. But now I fear you could be something else entirely.'

'I am a simple advisor on theology.'

'You are none of the sort. You have revealed yourself so quickly.'

'Or so you think.'

'Who is your master, Nicóla Frescobaldi, a man of the Church, even though first sons never enter the seminary?'

'Who is yours, Master Crumwella?'

Crumwell crossed his arms, his journal against his black doublet. 'I serve Cardinal Wolsey only.'

'Not the King?'

'Sometimes the King. Wolsey always.'

'Wolsey runs this country. But power, real power, so often lies in the people behind the public face.'

'Meaning?'

'Meaning you are watched. You know this.'

'Are you spying on me?'

'I am a humble attendant, Master Crumwella.'

'As you are a guest at York Place, the home of my master, I must ask you, as a matter of safety, who is your master?'

'A man named Giulio.' Nicóla stood defiant, hands now behind his back. His soft chin tilted upwards a fraction, a man of confidence, a man used to being above others. How very Italian.

'And what is Giulio to you?'

'We have been… how to put it… intimate, for some time.'

Crumwell almost choked. 'Be careful with your words, Nicóla. Intimate can mean many things.'

'I know this, which is why I used it.'

'Are you confessing to buggery?' Crumwell scoffed. 'To me, the legal advisor to Cardinal Wolsey? That is frowned upon, and as a foreigner, you have no rights.'

'I am sure I could escape such a charge,' Nicóla replied.

There. The moment all was made plain. Nicóla's secret opened up wide, but Crumwell held his tongue. From the first glance, Nicóla stood so like his father; smart, composed, a fine mind and calm soul. But not yet as skilled as Francesco, and Nicóla had shown his hand too early. Time to quote Machiavelli. 'No enterprise is more likely to succeed than one concealed from the enemy until it is ripe for execution.'

Nicóla grinned, recognising the words. 'Well spoken, Master Crumwella. Allow me - the first method for learning the intelligence of a ruler is to regard the men he has around him.'

'You have come hither to spy on Wolsey.'

'Not Wolsey.'

Crumwell swallowed hard. 'Me? No one cares for me, much fewer people as far away as Italy.'

'You, Il Principe.'

'I am no prince, I am a self-made, self-educated man.'

'As am I, Master Crumwella.'

'You have revealed yourself too easily. I have watched you for weeks, Nicóla. Now that I am close to you, I see you for what you are. Your father's apprentice, certainly. It is so like standing alongside Francesco, yet with youth clouding the image.'

'I feel you speak out of familiarity, not confidence.'

Crumwell held his words. There was no name for this scenario, for all motives remained still unclear. If he were just spying, reporting, Nicóla posed no threat. One accepted spies; they lived everywhere.

'This Giulo…'

'You know him as Pope Clement. I only tell you this, as a friend to my father. It is not for public knowledge.'

'And your motive in London?'

Nicóla brought his delicate hands together before him. 'That is up to me. I am here officially as an advisor to Cardinal Campeggio, to give your King his annulment.'

'Will the King gain his annulment?'

'Should you like the King to succeed, Master Crumwella?'

'You sound as if you have reason to speak thus; as if you have some say in the matter.'

'I have all the say in the matter. I think you know this already.'

'If I think you are a threat to Cardinal Wolsey, I can have you tortured.'

'If you saw under my doublet and hose, Master Crumwella, you shall see I am well versed in the cruelty of men. Cardinal Wolsey needs not fear me, nor anyone in Rome.'

Nicóla turned away from Crumwell, his short steps crunching the pebbles on the path. Crumwell skipped up to Nicóla and touched his slender shoulder, and the Italian paused.

'You almost had me, il reietto. Your father has made you a charmer; the Medici have made you a liar. Do you know what gave you away? Your earlobes.'

Nicóla pulled his shoulder from Crumwell's much wider hand and sped away, the wind catching his long hair as he moved. The man who sent Crumwell's heart singing no longer had the power to make him feel like an ashamed man.

Chapter 3 – June 1529
Blackfriars Monastery and Westminster, London

Sum seecryts can only beest entrusted to straayngers

'If a man shall take his brother's wife, it is an impurity; he hath uncovered his brother's nakedness; they shall be childless.'

Leviticus Chapter 20 Verse 21 was stated so many times that every voice sounded the same to Nicóla. Sitting in the far corner, not far away from Cardinals Campeggio and Wolsey, Nicóla heard every voice echoing up to the arched white ceiling. Rows of men sat either side of the Blackfriars chapel, the witness being heard before the long table of the leaders, all there to hear proceedings. Today another bishop quoted Letivitus yet again.

'Your Grace,' Wolsey addressed Archbishop Warham from his prominent seat, his red robes flowing around him, 'last November, the King stated at Bridewell, that he felt he lived in detestable and abominable adultery.'

The Archbishop nodded his bald head, and his purple vestments swayed over his weight. Age took its toll on the Archbishop of Canterbury, yet his resolve remained fixed.

'Queen Katherine is a virtuous and noble woman, a perfect queen for twenty years. Yet, if the marriage is not real, not blessed by God, then how can it be legitimate? God has not bestowed a son on the King, an heir for England. But God gave the King a daughter and time shows him to have a legitimate marriage.' Warham, an old man, sounded as defiant and confident as a man a third his age.

'Your Grace,' Cardinal Campeggio interrupted, his words hard to hear over his accent, and his age making him eternally weary, 'the King received a papal bull from Pope Julius, declaring him free to marry his brother's wife. Do you believe the Pope right to issue such a bull?'

Nicóla sighed and blinked away sore eyes. Every witness called to give evidence in the King or Queen's defence said the same thing, answered the same questions and statements.

'The papal bull was brought forth under illegal circumstances,' the Bishop boomed, and everyone lowered their gaze, a sign they agreed and submitted to Henry's rule, though the commoners whispered in the gallery. 'But, as I claimed, time has made the marriage honest. I believe the King and Queen have a lawful marriage. Queen Katherine declared herself a virgin until the night of their marriage.'

'Yet,' Wolsey rebutted, 'we have heard witnesses swear to the fact the King's brother, God rest his mortal soul, spoke of bedding Katherine. Prince Arthur said the words, "last night I was in the midst of Spain" in the very doorway of his wedding bed! It pains me to repeat such harsh words, honourably spoken before this ecclesiastical court, but alas, that is a fact.' Hatred ran through Wolsey's words. 'The royal couple of Spain, Katherine's parents, ordered the papal bull, worded carelessly, leaving virginity from the equation upon marriage to Henry. But God's law cannot be changed.'

'However, the Queen is pious and honest. But… but, perchance the King is right.' Warham swallowed hard after his declaration. The voice of a lenient old man, a weary voice too tired to argue with a man such as Henry the Eighth.

Nicóla watched Cardinal Wolsey sigh. For all the reputation he had as a corrupt tyrant, he appeared scant more than a puppet to the King. The King always got his way. If he wanted a divorce, Henry assumed such would come from Cardinal Wolsey. Rumours suggested Wolsey had already promised the King a divorce; Crumwell would know for certain. As everyone nodded in silence, agreeing with the Bishop's words, the twitch of Crumwell's quill never ceased. He wrote everything in his book on the tiny desk in the front row, filled no doubt with the words spoken, the actions expressed. He only glanced up for a moment, and every time he did, he threw a quick glance at Nicóla across the narrow court. Nicóla knew the language of the body spoke more than the voice, and Crumwell had learned to observe his enemies in the same manner as Nicóla. Just the slightest flutter of an eyebrow showed his disagreement at comments spoken; Crumwell appeared not as guarded as he thought. Every so often he put his hand over his mouth, a gesture which suggested Crumwell heard a lie.

'God has taken three sons from the King,' Cardinal Wolsey argued. 'And two daughters. Only the Princess Mary survives. It is a sign, bishops of England. We have power from the Pope, and the King must do the right thing, and be married properly, honestly, before God. The Pope needs the support of every monarch in Christendom, especially King Henry. I suggest you choose your side of this debate wisely.'

By the time the legatine court finished for the day, Nicóla followed Cardinal Campeggio, to aid the gout-ridden old man back to his rooms at Westminster to rest before dinner. They had left York Place to instead reside at court with the King at his request, but never out from under Crumwell's gaze.

'Nicóla,' Campeggio said, his voice raw and croaking after the long day, 'all of this is sometimes too much to bear. These people seem to enjoy the opportunity to end a royal marriage.' Tears appeared in old Campeggio's eyes.

'Indeed, Cardinal,' Nicóla sighed as they edged towards Campeggio's room, Bishop Alessandro already opening the chambers. 'But do you ever think perchance the Archbishop Warham is correct in his wording?'

'Pope Julius himself gave dispensation for Henry and Katherine to marry,' Campeggio smiled. 'The Queen has the original papal bull in hand, and the King does not. The country defends Queen Katherine. God is on her side. Not for one moment shall we ever rule in favour of the King. Never shall we rule at all.'

They paused in the doorway and Campeggio touched Nicóla's arm. 'Please, can you go to Wolsey to summon him after dinner. Let us not have dinner in the main hall, rather take it privately in my rooms, and I shall see Wolsey afterward.'

'Certainly, I shall take the invitation to him now, Your Eminence.'

Everyone at the palace seemed curious when they saw a brightly dressed Italian stalking the halls. They smiled and nodded good day, something Nicóla always took the time to reply to in heavily-accented English. After so many years of being forgotten about, expected to step aside, stand in the shadows, now Nicóla roamed as freely as any man. The power of looking wealthy in new clothes could change a status in a heartbeat. The doublets of blues, greens, yellows, they made Nicóla stand out in terms of outward appearance, but no one wished to know any more detail or background, a perfect way to never be questioned.

The lavishly decorated hallways became jammed with a blockage of people. Nicóla squeezed between strolling men, being far lighter than the average man, and peered around the stone wall. Past the gardens to the river, there stood King Henry himself, beside his barge parked outside Westminster. King Henry, dressed in a magnificent golden doublet, appeared deep in conversation with Thomas Crumwell, as the King's guards in their Tudor forest-green livery stood close. Others attempted to appear casual as they waited their turn to speak. But the moment Henry finished with Crumwell, the King rushed past the waiting courtiers and into the palace, not another word stated. Henry's dark red eyebrows showed scorn, his stance stiff and unmerciful. The various important members of the court started to disperse now the King had departed. Nicóla noticed Wolsey's master secretary, a long-nosed man with shaking hands named Archdeacon Stephen Gardiner, who looked as angered as ever.

In the narrow side doorway, Crumwell needed to pass right by Nicóla. 'Mr. Frescobaldi.' The strong voice of Thomas Crumwell bit at Nicóla's stale nerves as his golden gaze hit upon Nicóla's more concealed look. 'What did you think of deliberations today?' Crumwell stood with his hands behind his back and rocked back and forth on his heels.

'It is the same arguments going around in circles,' Nicóla shrugged and noticed Crumwell's two young attendants, secretary Ralph Sadler and his nephew Richard Crumwell, hovering, an ear near the conversation, all three dressed in black as always. The pair made no attempt to hide the fact they followed Nicóla at Crumwell's behest any longer.

'How does your Cardinal receive the information, though? Is Campeggio feeling compassionate towards the King?'

'It is not a matter of compassion, it is whether God's will is being upheld. I see you and the King appear to be friends.'

'The "Great Matter" of the King's divorce is not the sole issue debated in the kingdom,' Crumwell replied and the pair started to wander the halls again, footsteps in time, Crumwell leading the way. Ralph and Richard followed close in silence. 'I can only be of service where the King desires.'

'A foot in each court, Master Crumwella.'

'The King's desires and Cardinal Wolsey's desires are the same. My master is the favourite of the King.'

'Making you a favourite of the King,' Nicóla added.

'My business is of no one's worry.'

Nicóla gestured the conversation away with a dismissive wave. 'I have to deliver a message from Cardinal Campeggio to your master.'

'You can give the message to me.'

Nicóla paused; they stood close to the court's rooms of Cardinal Wolsey, filled as ever with people wishing a moment with the man himself. All week, Crumwell had eyed Nicóla but not approached. And for the last week, Nicóla made hiding earlobes a top priority, large hats and long hair. 'Cardinal Campeggio wishes not to attend dinner in the main hall tonight, but wonders if Cardinal Wolsey will visit upon him in Campeggio's rooms after dinner.'

'Are we to take wine together?' Crumwell mocked Nicóla's gentle tone. 'That does sound appealing after a day of sitting together. I would much rather drink than go home and attend to my own business.'

'I failed to take the measure of your poor character, Master Crumwella,' Nicóla bit back.

'You failed in much, il reietto,' Crumwell grinned. 'Yes, little Waif, tell your master that Wolsey and I will see Campeggio, but in Wolsey's rooms. Perchance you could tarry, make the conversation a drop more... effeminate?'

Nicóla spun away from the taunting man and made the trek back to Campeggio's rooms. There might be no way to appeal Crumwell's order. But effeminate? Being short, thin, with long hair and a smooth complexion was not mocked so back home.

~~~

'How long have you studied in Rome, Mr. Frescobaldi? Or have you always heard the calling?' The words croaked through Wolsey's worn tone. The two Cardinals sat opposite one another close to a short fireplace, Nicóla and Crumwell each behind their master, like waiting dogs. Nicóla sat in silence, listening with eyes cast to the floor, while Crumwell continued to put himself into the conversation.

'Ah, Thomas, you are looking at my young friend again,' Campeggio replied for Nicóla through a tired smile. 'I met Nicóla in Rome two years ago; only then he came to live within the Church's embrace.'

'Tell us the tale of your meeting during the sacking of the holy city; bestow us a break from this annulment,' Wolsey replied.

'Terrible,' Campeggio moaned, throwing his hands in the air at the memories. 'I was at San Giovanni in Laterano, on my knees in the basilica, right at the altar. Before I knew it, the place got sacked and I was hit over the head and thrown out on the street. People were dying, thieving, so many went to the church for sanctuary, but the church was not considered sacred any longer. I lay in the dirt on the street, blood pouring from my forehead when a young man appeared and lifted me to my feet. Among the fighting, the swords hitting guilty and innocent alike, God allowed Nicóla to pull me to safety inside the modest building he sheltered in, safe from the wild soldiers. I easily could have died if not for Nicóla. As soon as we saw it safe to travel, we fled Rome for Orvieto, where Pope Clement sheltered. My Nicóla stayed in the Pope's care and entered the seminary. Then I received word Nicóla would be joining me hither, in London.' Beads of sweat ran down Campeggio's neck as he spoke.

'You also saved my life, Your Eminence,' Nicóla said discreetly behind the Cardinal. A glance to Crumwell showed him staring straight back, no doubt remembering each word for a later time. Crumwell dared not give away his thoughts with any expression.

'Dear loving and compassionate God, giver of all gifts, we pray especially today for the mercy and love You give us. Amen,' Wolsey said and gave the sign of the cross.

'Amen,' everyone repeated, crossing themselves.

A loud bang echoed through Wolsey's privy chamber and the heavy door opened to Stephen Gardiner, Wolsey's secretary. Nicóla had seen him daily at the ecclesiastical court, and everywhere near Wolsey on any given day, but Gardiner made it plain he bore no civility. Constantly dressed in his black robes overlaid with white linen, he had the ugliest hooked nose between deep-set eyes. He had a large level of confidence, and someone such as Nicóla did not even warrant so much as a glance.

'Your Eminences,' Gardiner began with a slight bow, 'I beg you to pay heed for a few moments.' His hands shook just a touch; not nerves, perchance illness? Nicóla noticed a sharp look between Gardiner and Crumwell; the unspoken words between the pair suggested an intense rivalry, a detail to recall later.

'You can leave us for the night, Thomas,' Wolsey murmured to Crumwell at his side.

Campeggio turned stiffly to Nicóla. 'You also, dear Nicóla. I shall see you at Mass in the morning.'

Nicóla rose from the warm comfortable seat and left the room without another word. Gardiner did not even seem to notice. Following Crumwell out of the room, the door shut behind them by the gentleman-usher, a plain man by the name of George Cavendish. Once through the antechamber, they passed through the main doors, with guards who stood sharply over the entrance in protection of their charges once more. The warm fire and wine had almost put Nicóla to sleep and Crumwell looked just as weary. His shoulders drooped, creating a posture better suited to an older man.

'Why does Archdeacon Gardiner loathe you so?' Nicóla asked as the pair strode away from Wolsey's private rooms.

'Is it so plain to see?' Crumwell scoffed.

'I have met few who like one another.'

'We are close to power, and everyone wants to rise higher still.'

'And you?'

'I want as much as everyone else. Gardiner dislikes my influence with Wolsey. Gardiner studied canon and civil law at Cambridge and is Master of Trinity Hall. He is a conservative archdeacon. I am a lawyer and have sat in parliament, yet Gardiner sees me as a threat. Plus, several years ago, Wolsey allowed the dissolution of thirty monasteries, to collect monies to build Wolsey's new schools at Oxford. Gardiner opposed such behaviour. Gardiner supports Wolsey's theory we should get a French princess on the English throne, as both have spent much time in France, and are in the pay of the French. I claim no French bribes, and have no such dreams of a French princess.'

'You agree not with their ideas, Master Crumwella?'

'Some nights, I know not what I believe.'

The pair wandered in the dark hallways alone, just a few candles lighting the way. Crumwell straightened himself and somehow appeared even taller than normal in the dark, his face thinner, his golden eyes brighter. Crumwell was one of the few men at court with no beard, freshly shaven every morning. He smelled a great deal better than most men too. His body suggested middling years had not yet claimed his waistline, only a few silvers in his dark curled hair.

'May I ask a question, Master Crumwella?'

Crumwell sighed, his shoulders sinking. 'I suppose, little Waif.'

'Will Wolsey give the King his annulment? Surely he wants to if he favours a French princess.'

'Wolsey favours the French because the French pay him to favour them. Wolsey has promised the King an annulment. The King always gets his way. Once a spoiled child, then a jealous brother; when Arthur died Henry married his brother's widow and took the crown. Henry gets whatever suits him.'

'But now it is the Lady Anne which suits him.'

'I know not why.'

'Wolsey does not expect the King will actually marry Lady Anne?'

'Lady Anne and the Boleyns hate Wolsey with a fervent passion, and everyone knows.' Crumwell kept his voice low, only their footsteps echoing. 'Anne wanted Henry Percy of Northumberland and Wolsey refused the match. Now she has the King in her sights and hates Wolsey. This alone could be the reason Wolsey favours a French princess.'

'But will Wolsey give the King an annulment? Especially if he suspects Lady Anne shall be on the throne after Katherine is set aside? Has not the King been with Lady Anne for years now?'

'The King's gaze rests on Lady Anne, for three years now. The King had little intention of gaining an annulment, but the pressure is so profound now. The King could explode with sexual discontent, with Lady Anne not sharing his bed. Wolsey and I need to keep the King contented, and the people want their Queen Katherine. But Wolsey has no allies to rally.'

'There are few as hated as Wolsey,' Nicóla mused. 'If Wolsey falls, he will fall a long way, and no one will be there to catch him. I thought perchance the commoners would rally to their commoner cardinal.'

'The people hate Wolsey due to his heavy taxation laws,' Crumwell explained. 'You know this.'

'Laws you write on his behalf?'

Crumwell just smiled. 'Wolsey is seen as noble by the commoners, yet still baseborn by the nobles.'

'You have a difficult master.'

'And Cardinal Campeggio? Is he any better?'

Nicóla shrugged this time. 'Campeggio is in the Pope's favour but he has secrets which could hurt him.'

'Secrets you know?'

'Well indeed. Mistresses and money; it always is with the clergy.'

'Is that why the Pope sent you? To spy on Campeggio or Wolsey?'

'I am no spy.'

'You are no subtle spy, Nicóla.'

Nicóla stopped their gentle pace and stood by a window, the Thames in the darkness below. 'I need not be subtle, Master Crumwella. There is no plot against you. All I need to know is whether you favour annulment or not. The Pope knows Wolsey can be bribed; he is even more corrupt than the Pope himself. Gardiner is strictly a papist; despite working to secure an annulment, he does not like the notion. Rome considers Gardiner a weakling. But you, sir, are the one the Pope cannot understand. You are the one who needs to be studied.'

'Why send you?' Another scowl accompanied Crumwell's words.

'The Pope trusts me.'

'Why?'

'History is why. In Italy, as you know, we honour families, we place trust in each other. My father once trusted you, so Rome assumes I could trust you.' Nicóla found Crumwell easy to study; Crumwell loosened in his privacy when tired.

'Are you here to influence the papal legates?'

'I am here to make sure Campeggio sticks to the requirements of the Pope, that is all.'

'And what be these?'

'The Pope will not grant an annulment. Never. Jesus could return to Earth before Pope Clement changes his mind on an annulment. He needs the backing of Spain and the Emperor. Queen Katherine will never be unseated in England. Campeggio has no intention of granting an annulment. I am here to make sure Wolsey stays true to his Catholic faith. But you, such an ally to Wolsey, needs to be watched and listened to, and no more. I am no spying assassin.'

'Just a spy who is the son of my former master. You are the blood of a man I considered a father to me. They used you, Nicóla, to get to me and to Wolsey.'

'I am just studying and learning under the Pope for several years, and can take holy orders if wished.'

'We both know you cannot take holy orders.'

'I am enjoying a life the best way I can, Master Crumwella. If your master gives the King a divorce, the Pope will ruin Wolsey.'

'The King will ruin Wolsey if he does not grant a divorce.'

'Then prepare for disaster, Master Crumwella, because your master is about to fall. You are the man that Machiavelli wrote of, so you know what you must do to survive.'

Chapter 4 – June 1529
Austin Friars, London

A sir is not what that gent thinkest he is, that gent is a seecryt

Crumwell sighed and peered up briefly from his desk. The square garden at the back of his private home at Austin Friars seemed so still now. In the distance sat the home of his friend John Cavalcante, a wealthy merchant from Italy. To the west, the Augustinian Friary which owned the land Crumwell's fourteen-room home sat upon. The wide and private garden, once glazed with the voices of his daughters, always with their mother close, now silent. The first anniversary of their deaths loomed, taken by God from these very halls, and the garden now home to nothing but birds. Austin Friars was still a beautiful, luxurious manor, but no longer a home, not without a family.

Crumwell watched the gentle sway of treetops from his ground floor window and forgot the pile of work to attend on his desk. Work for Wolsey so often took Crumwell from his home, and he liked it that way; he could try to forget the loss of his family when at the bustle of court or at York Place. While Crumwell had an office, and smaller offices for attendants like Ralph and Richard, Crumwell often worked in his library, where he seldom let anyone enter.

A brisk knock took Crumwell's wistful stare from the window to his nephew Richard, who came into his library, all four walls covered in books, Crumwell at his desk in the centre of the room.

'Uncle, you have a visitor,' Richard said, his brown curly hair messed by the cap now in his hands.

'Get Ralph to deal with them in the office.' Crumwell clicked his fingers twice to dismiss his nephew, as he did to all of his servants. No one but Wolsey or the King himself could interrupt.

'Ralph tried, and while most charming and delightful, this Italian is much persistent.'

Crumwell jumped from his seat, the woeful feeling dismissed. 'The Cardinal Campeggio?' No one used the phrase "charming" on Campeggio.

'No, not Campeggio, the young one, the short fellow you had us follow these last weeks.'

'Frescobaldi? Please, send him in at once.' Crumwell straightened his black doublet, shrugging to get it looking perfect. No, instead he sat back down, to look busy and important behind his desk. Why did he feel so eager to look important to the Waif?

'Mr. Nicóla Frescobaldi.' Richard announced the Italian and Crumwell bounded up from his chair again. With a polite nod, Nicóla entered the room and Richard shut the door.

With a smile, Nicóla removed a soft black hat from smooth rose-gold hair, now cut shorter, now more in the style of London, not Rome. Still much pinned back, but to everyone, the style belonged to a strange foreigner with strange foreign ways. 'Master Crumwella. Thank you for seeing me.'

'Good morrow and well met. I hoped to leave the divorce behind me today.' Crumwell sat down and gestured for Nicóla to do the same across the desk in a tall chair with thick armrests.

'I admit to the same. I come in need of a lawyer, and I admit to no English acquaintances. It has become immediately apparent you are the most intelligent man in London, and, as a friend to my father, the only person I wish to speak with on a delicate subject.'

Nicóla's tone seemed a brief tight; anxious? 'Ah, you need money. Half the English court has come hither with money requests. As you know, being a money lender is an endless stream of business.'

'I require total discretion.'

'You come to London to spy on me and my cardinal, and want my help?' Crumwell scoffed and leaned back in his chair. He took a moment to admire how soft and beautiful Nicóla's hair was, the colour of mid-summer straw tinged with pink, a thought he regretted; it released an uncomfortable sensation in him. The thrill of Nicóla's company gave Crumwell a sinful feeling.

Nicóla leaned forward but moved as if constricted, despite a loose-fitting silver doublet and hose. 'You know much of banking and finance in the Low Countries. I too have much experience, but you have knowledge of the law also; my legal knowledge is more suited to Italian banking. I want to know how it might be possible for someone to claim money from a bank account not in their own name.'

'Be more specific.' Crumwell laced his fingers together.

'How should I claim an inheritance? My father had accounts in Antwerp in his name. The money is owed to me. Likewise, his accounts in Florence and Venice and Rome. His will specifically states for me to inherit all. I cannot gain access to any money in Italy, as I do not have the copies of his will directly. I thought perchance I could try to access the money in Antwerp.'

'Where could there be a problem?' Crumwell asked. 'Knowing your father, his money and lands must be great. Where are the copies of the will?'

'A third party holds them.'

Crumwell scoffed with a crooked smile. 'Are you being blackmailed, little Waif?'

'I think we both know I am not destined for the Church.' Nicóla's tone showed how little patience could stretch. 'You know Florence; you know how... fluid the laws can be at times.'

'You worked with the Medici family, did you not?'

'Yes, that is true...'

Crumwell raised his eyebrows so high they almost reached his hair. 'Are you being blackmailed by the Medici family? If so, I am not touching the situation. We shall both be knifed in our beds.'

'Devi scegliere un capo.'

'You have to choose a captain. Si deve prendere lati?'

'Yes, I did take sides. I picked a master and I have paid the price.'

'Your father...?'

'My father was much involved in my life, as I was in his. My father entrusted his fortune to a man, to hold the money so it could be paid to me on my marriage. Only... only I find myself not ready to enter into the arrangement.'

'And you want your inheritance.'

Nicóla's gaze graced the Turkish carpets and nodded. 'I have moved in the same powerful circles my entire life. Due to the trouble

I find myself in, I am short of someone to trust. But you, a friend of my dear father, God rest his soul…' Nicóla sighed and looked up again. 'I can be of service you in return, anything you want. Perchance I could aid you in an endeavour, perchance you need information gathered, money collected, someone killed, and I shall also pay for your time.'

'No need,' Crumwell shook his head. 'Francesco was one of the greatest friends I have ever had. Without him as my master, I would be long dead by now. As he said to me, tu sei parte della famiglia. He made me a part of the family, so I can advise you on getting money out of Antwerp. Are you burdened with acting legal in your extraction?'

'I have no problem breaking laws, Master Crumwella.'

'Thomas. Perchance all we need is a dash of creativity. Let me write to a friend in Antwerp.'

'Thank you.' Nicóla paused and admired the well-appointed library, windows abound, sun pouring over the room. The tapestry on the wall showed rolling hills reminiscent of Tuscany. 'Is this where people come to borrow money from you, Tomassito?'

'Many a man has begged me in this room. Are you in need of a loan until your inheritance is paid? I could give you a comfortable interest rate.'

'No, no, I am compensated for my work with the Cardinal. Probably not as well as you from your Cardinal, but still. You still work as a lawyer, a money lender, a merchant, and work for the Cardinal?'

'A man needs businesses of his own.'

'Quite true, Tomassito, quite true. But you have a son, no?'

A gentle brush of those rose-gold curls tucked behind an ear made Crumwell shiver. 'Gregory. He is but nine years old. He is away, studying. A pleasant boy, a lively boy.' Crumwell paused; he did not see his son often enough, and when he did, it often reminded him of the loss of the rest of his family.

'Make sure you have a will for your son and a plan for him when he comes of age.'

'I do my best. For now, his education is much to me.' Had he paid Gregory's tutor? He so often forgot; it sat always at the bottom of the pile of work.

'I had the benefit of being born into a family wealthy for hundreds of years,' Nicóla said and wrung his hat with thin hands. Crumwell needed to lean forward to hear such a soft voice. 'Though, in recent years, learning has changed. Not so just an education of religious devotion, numbers, and languages. I also studied law and economics at Pisa, where the Medici moved the university. Now one can gain humanist insights such as the writings of Erasmus, or the word of Martin Luther. The world is making changes,' Nicóla conveyed. Such a keen tone of voice.

'Even in a deeply papist nation such as Italy?'

'For those with an ability to travel and trade, anything is available.' Nicóla finally smiled again, and Crumwell's heart gave a deep thud. A familiar look, like his old friend Francesco, the man who pulled him literally off the street and changed his life.

'Nicóla, perchance I could break with you on the subject of why you are in London for the legatine court.'

'I am here to observe, as I have stated; we have discussed thus. But your enemy, Stephen Gardiner...'

'Not enemy; we were close once.'

'Still, he is Cardinal Wolsey's master secretary and is known to be conservative. The Pope views Gardiner as an ally.'

'And me as an enemy?'

'Not an enemy, more an opponent,' Nicóla explained and shifted in the chair.

'I take no sides in the annulment case.'

'That is why you are such a threat,' Nicóla returned. 'Perchance I could bring you to our side, to the side of the Church, ensuring no divorce for Queen Katherine?'

'Did you come hither to bribe me?' Crumwell smiled.

'Not with money. I could be of service to you in some way. You help me get no divorce, and I help you gain another seat in parliament. I know all men enjoy power.'

'The last time I addressed parliament, I made an enemy of the King.' Crumwell thought back the six years since parliament last sat in session. It seemed forever ago now. 'How in the world could you get me a seat in parliament?'

'You need not worry about the details, my new friend.'

'I do not accept bribes.'

'Everyone accepts bribes, Tomassito. You think your enemy Gardiner does not?'

'Are you bribing Gardiner?'

'Gardiner is not my target,' Nicóla replied. 'He visits Rome often, talking, pleading with the Pope for an annulment. I cannot show my face around Gardiner, for fear of recognition from my place in the Pope's household.'

'The King wants a divorce. Is there any way to change Campeggio's mind, so the King can prevail?'

'And get you in favour with the King, Tomassito?'

'I am already in favour with the King. It is my master, Wolsey, who is in danger of falling, and that is something I never wish to see.'

'Everyone knows of Wolsey's behaviour. For example, I hear he overcharges people in their rents and pockets the difference. Or is that you?'

'It is me, but Wolsey keeps the money, not I.'

'The trouble with being a commoner is, as a commoner, we are expendable. Bonds with loyal houses are not broken when a commoner is cast aside. I suspect that is the same hither in England.'

'That is the most truthful fact I have heard in quite some time, Nicóla.'

'It is time I left you, Tomassito. There is always work to be done.'

Crumwell rose from his seat as the young Italian extended a hand. Nicóla's skin was so soft and gentle; the smell of rosewater, very feminine, like all of his natures. 'I am to dine with my neighbour, an Italian man, John Cavalcante. Sir Thomas More is also attending. Would you like to come?'

'Me? Dine with Sir Thomas More, the great Catholic humanist, a champion of Erasmus, and a lawyer? I am well to remain silent and observe. That dinner may go against my envoy,' Nicóla smiled.

'Of course.' Crumwell shook his head. Why invite the young man to be his companion? That might raise too many questions.

'Thank you for your indulgence. You are strikingly brilliant, just as my father said.'

'We have barely spoken, Nicóla.'

'I know all I need.'

Chapter 5 - June 1529
Westminster, London

With a seecryt liketh this, at some pointeth the seecryt itself beecomes
irrelevante. The fact thee hath kept it doest not

No matter what time one sought Queen Katherine, the answer remained the same; she was at prayer. No woman could claim piety like Katherine. But with her crown and marriage at stake, Katherine prayed even more than usual. Campeggio had already got down on one knee and begged Katherine to enter a nunnery, to divorce herself from public life, and allow Henry to remarry. Katherine would never relent. She was the child of two anointed sovereigns in Spain, she had fought a life in both wealth and poverty to become Queen, and married two brothers to secure the throne. She stood by as mistresses came and went, mourned over the deaths of her royal babies. Katherine battled the Scots at the head of an army, and fought every diplomatic issue in England over her twenty years on the throne. No one could compare to the magnificent Queen Katherine.

The halls of Westminster sat silenced late in the night, almost devoid of life. Katherine needed to appear before the legatine court at Blackfriars the following day. Would she attend? Could such a thing ever happen? The Queen on trial for her marriage?

Passing only guards along the candlelit hallways, Crumwell glanced ahead of his master Wolsey as they approached Queen Katherine's antechamber. To his astonishment, there stood the old Campeggio, his face ashen with worry, a contrast to his red robes. There, as always, stood Nicóla, and Campeggio's son Bishop Alessandro.

'Ah, Thomas,' croaked Campeggio's tired tone, breaking the silence of the dark hallway. 'I see you have the same thoughts as I on this warm night.'

'I have waited to see the Queen all day,' Wolsey replied and handed his journal to Crumwell, a heavy black book where Wolsey had Crumwell make many notes, his mind never forgetful, rather constantly hatching new plots. 'I see you seek a place in Her Majesty's presence late this evening.'

'To counsel Her Majesty only. To give her strength and perchance guide her on what to say if she attends the court tomorrow.'

'She must, and I am here to tell her what to say,' Wolsey sighed. 'The court has progressed despite her distaste. Her Majesty's testimony is crucial now. The tide has turned against her.'

The conversation paused as the main doors to the Queen's rooms opened, and there behind the guards stood Maria de Salinas, Baroness of Willoughby, the Queen's longtime Spanish lady-in-waiting. The stern woman eyed the two Cardinals, along with their men. 'Her Majesty is not receiving visitors,' Lady Maria barked, her Spanish accent showing hatred at the meeting.

'Mi señora, vengo en nombre del Papa. Vengo para dar comodidad en privacidad,' Nicóla burst forth. The Spanish threw everyone off guard as Nicóla knelt before Maria de Salinas and took her hand. Lady Maria, surprised by her native tongue, took something from Nicóla's hand and peered at it; Crumwell could not see the trinket exchanged, nor understand the words used. But Maria's wide eyes said it all.

'Sí, entra, la reina te verá,' Lady Maria replied, and the door shut in the face of the waiting Cardinals, young Nicóla gone from sight.

The Queen's guards stood over the door, their eyes on the irate Cardinals, and saw Crumwell's mouth hang open. That was not the gentle Italian man which had come to Crumwell's office just yesterday; that was a master at work.

'What a disgrace,' Campeggio spat as he sat on a nearby chair, which creaked under his weight. His son Alessandro placed a hand on his father's shoulder to console him. Wolsey sat across the hallway, against the window, and Crumwell stood to one side, gripping the black journal in his hands.

'That is your attendant, a virtual child,' Wolsey spat. 'You must be greatly offended by that... that... Waif. Crumwell, what did Frescobaldi say to the Lady Maria?'

'I must confess I did not understand, Your Eminence,' Crumwell replied.

'Open those doors,' Wolsey wheezed with anger at being second best. He poked a finger towards the guards. 'Open the doors, we must see the Queen at once! Crumwell!'

With the guards still over the doors, the men ready to strike, Crumwell pounded his fist on the door over and over until someone came. There stood Lady Maria again, this time furious at the interruption. 'The Cardinals must see the Queen at once!' Crumwell threatened, though the imposing Spaniard frightened him, not that he would admit so. Both the guards relented, unwilling to fight old cardinals as the men in red forced their way into the Queen's chambers. Crumwell and Bishop Alessandro followed on their heels, and then burst into the Queen's private room, where she sat by the dead fireplace, every bit the picture of grace and dignity, her auburn hair pulled under a hood, back from her pale face, her blue eyes so light they looked almost reflective in the candlelight. Nicóla knelt before the Queen and held Katherine's hand. They prayed together in Latin, the Queen's eyes wet with tears. Whatever could this appealing Italian have to say to the Queen? Campeggio seemed struck dumb by the scene. He did not utter a word to his young advisor, who stood in time with the Queen and they hugged, kissed one another's cheeks, something no one could do with the Queen. Crumwell felt his own eyes as wide as the Cardinals' before him.

Queen Katherine turned to the intruding group, as did her ladies scattered about the room. She gave Campeggio no emotion in her gaze, but Wolsey met an angry sigh. In the peace of her privy chamber, the Queen remained strikingly beautiful, even at the advanced matronly age of five and forty years.

'I shall excuse myself from your presence, Your Majesty,' Nicóla murmured and bowed low to the Queen. Without a glance to Campeggio, Nicóla floated on silent footsteps from the room.

'Follow him,' Wolsey snapped in Crumwell's ear as he grabbed the journal. As discreetly as possible, Crumwell trotted from the Queen's chambers and followed Nicóla, now already back in the hallway of silence. The guards slammed her door shut, cutting off the light and exotic feminine smells of the Queen's chambers. Crumwell grabbed

Nicóla by the arm and felt just how small the Waif was under heavy clothes.

'I pray you did no harm to our annulment suit,' Crumwell derided as he pulled Nicóla along the hallway.

'How do I offend, Tomassito?' Nicóla asked, a gentle voice attempting to sound innocent. 'I thought we could be allies.'

Crumwell could not speak in any room other than Wolsey's office. Nicóla followed Crumwell, or rather got pulled along, all the way to Wolsey's rooms at court. The night, already warm, needed no fire, even in the palace's interior. The single candle left lit on Wolsey's desk had now shrunk to a third of its size, wax caked on the edge of the paper-covered desk, beside a knife for opening letters. Wolsey's office reeked of wealth and privilege. A common man who rose to rule a nation, with an office which reflected that rise.

Now in the closed space, Nicóla pulled away from Crumwell's grip, displaying a strength not shown just moments ago. Crumwell reacted on instinct, startled by the fight, and pulled away Nicóla's hat. Rose-gold curls fell from under the hat almost to Nicóla's shoulders.

'I ought to have you thrown in the Tower!' Crumwell cried, angry at his own outburst, which came from nowhere.

'On Wolsey's authority?' Nicóla fought in return and tried in vain to hide the rose-gold curls. The scent of the freshly-washed curls seemed so feminine.

'On mine!' Crumwell scoffed at the suggestion he would need anyone else's authority.

'On my master's authority, I would be out again in hours!'

'You forget you are foreign, Waif. You have few rights here.'

'Is it true?' Nicóla goaded him.

'What?' Crumwell's heart pounded at being so close to a spy who he thought could be an ally, but also because this spy owned the temper of a serpent.

'That you, Master Crumwella, are a Lutheran. You are a heretic! We could be friends, but we could also be enemies!' Nicóla cried the insult aloud, echoing around the room and no doubt outside as well. 'You are the servant of a Catholic man in public and a Lutheran in private. People love to talk about the heretic commoner they loathe.'

'Whispers made by enemies!' Crumwell cried. He held Nicóla against him, his hands crushing the thin arms of the Waif. Their faces met, and Crumwell could not contain his anger at being so stared upon. It happened every day; everyone in his circle thought him beneath them. But this Italian made his blood boil. As he felt the body of the angered Italian against him, all his suspicions were confirmed. They stared at one another, Nicóla's green eyes strong, refusing to back away from the much older and taller man. The pair stood still as they caught their breath.

'Who are you, your real name?' Crumwell whispered, his words barely uttered before they landed on Nicóla's pink lips, just a fraction from his.

'I told you, the day we met.'

'You accuse me of being a heretic, yet here you are, lying in such a manner? What would the Queen say if she knew you disrespected God's laws so?'

'The Queen knows all.'

Crumwell let go of Nicóla, but neither of the pair moved away. 'The Queen is a kind woman, wise, virtuous, pious, honest...' he said.

'And threatened.'

'Why say you are the son of my former friend?'

'My father was Francesco Frescobaldi. That is no lie.'

'Do I need to have your doublet and hose pulled from your body?'

'To what end?'

'To prove you a liar and a spy in the court of Henry the Eighth!'

'And what good will that do you, Tomassito? Campeggio will be brought low, his credibility in tatters. This legatine court will be tarnished and abandoned. Your King will not get his annulment.'

'You claimed Campeggio will never give an annulment. My King has no chance either way.'

'You are naught more than a puppet for the cruelty of Cardinal Wolsey.'

Crumwell shoved the Italian to the ground and leapt on top of him before Nicóla had a chance to make any move. Crumwell fought with Nicóla's doublet, pulling it in a blind anger, wondering what he would do if he was wrong. But under the doublet and linen shirt laid a woman's shift made of pure white Valencian silk. Only noblewomen wore silk.

Nicóla fought like a woman too. She jammed her knee deep between his legs and Crumwell fell onto the stone floor with a thud. With a deft movement, she grabbed the thin knife on the desk and held it tight in his face, with her elbow hard on his throat. While the woman had the light weight of her body, she knew how to knock down a man. With the pain between his legs still aching, she almost choked him with her elbow, the knife an inch from his mouth.

'Who are you?' Crumwell choked, dizziness taking hold.

Nicóla released the agony from his throat, and she sat up on him, a knee on the floor either side of his body, the knife still gripped in the direction of his face. 'I told you, the son of Francesco Frescobaldi. I have been Nicóla for fifteen years.'

Crumwell watched her chest rise and fall as she panted over him. With her shoulder length hair, the face of a woman appeared far clearer. The worries that he found a man attractive over the last few weeks melted away, God be praised. 'Your name?' he swallowed.

'Nicóletta Frescobaldi. My father was only graced with daughters. He needed an apprentice, an heir, and his second wife did not give him one. Father mentioned I appeared smarter than half the men he met in his life. Boys clothes, binding cloths, a well-rounded education, a change in mannerisms and no one questioned anything. I say my name is Nicóla instead of Nicóletta and my math and accounting skills make everyone assume I am my father's bastard son. I can still be Nicóletta if I need, but I have fifteen years of pretending to be a man.'

'A woman pretending to be a man, that is an abomination!'

'Only to a man! A woman can be a mother or a maiden. If she does not fit that, she is a harlot or a witch.'

'Which are you?'

'None of those things, hence my choice to be a man.'

'That is why you cannot access your father's money. Women cannot inherit. Did the Medici family know the truth about you?'

'They did. Remember my father took you off the streets, dressed you, educated you when he did not have to, Englishman. You know Italians have the cunning to be kind. They also understand this woman's need to learn and trade.'

Crumwell caught his breath, but the knife stayed close to his face. The woman who sat on him had blood on her lip, cut from the entanglement, but she seemed not to notice. 'Will you let me up now?'

'Only if I can trust you will not run out crying that I am a woman. A woman dressed as a man? I shall be raped and dead before sunrise, even hither within the "noblemen".'

'I swear.' And he truly meant it. Crumwell was face to face with one of God's greatest accidents; a man's mind trapped in a woman's body, just like Queen Katherine. Crumwell kept his eyes locked on Nicóla as she let him inch out from under her. He had not touched a woman in any way in a year and was not ready to start anew. They sat on the floor together, Crumwell against the wall, his assailant surrounded by billowing hair, knife in hand.

'Piacere di conoscerti, Nicóletta Frescobaldi.'

A faint smile traced her lips. 'Charmed to meet you too, Master Crumwella.'

'You are Francesco's eldest daughter?'

'Yes, that is indeed. His sole child from his brief first marriage. All of my sisters and my stepmother have since passed into God's hands, as my mother did when I was an infant. Plague and childbirth, the fates of so many women.'

'I am sorry. I have learned to remember you; you were young when I left Florence, perchance thirteen.'

The classic Italian shrug of the shoulders. 'My father spoke so well of you, Tomassito.'

'Francesco died during the sacking of Florence, is that part true?'

'My father died for being a Medici employee. I escaped and sought out the Pope for safety.'

'Did you well indeed save Campeggio from ransacking soldiers?'

'I did. Pope Clement, as everyone calls him, sat not in Rome, with Campeggio as papal legate in the Pope's place. I saved Campeggio because I needed him. My father had taught me to fight, how to use a sword, and I lived in Rome as a man. I offered my services to get Campeggio to Orvieto, though in truth, he helped me get to the Pope's Orvieto palace. I dressed as a man at all times, and no one questioned my appearance. If I had been a woman in Rome, I would have been raped and flung out on the street.'

The fact Nicóla dressed as a man made more sense as she spoke. No woman could hold an official post, in England, or anywhere. Women were the spoils of the battle for the soldiers who destroyed Rome and helped the Holy Roman Emperor Charles take the Pope prisoner.

'Why go to the Pope?' Crumwell asked.

'Why should I trust you now?'

'I already know so much of your secret. I have suspected for some weeks. Your earlobes, remember? I can see they are pierced with a needle, for heavy earrings, unlike a man would have. I could have confronted you earlier.'

'Why did you not?'

'I had no reason.' The secret was too delicious to reveal.

Nicóla nodded and slowly dropped the knife from Crumwell's direction. 'My father and I worked for the Medici family. They ran Florence, and two Medici men have sat as Pope, this Pope included.'

'You have a family connection with Pope Clement?'

'I do. I have known Giulio my whole life. To me, he was Cardinal Giulio de' Medici, Archbishop of Florence, since a young age, and Pope Clement the Seventh for the last six years.'

'And he recognised you dressed as a man?'

'At once. The notion was Giulio's idea in the first instance. He suggested it to my father, as both men knew of my intellect. I have been a man for half my life.'

'And the Pope sent you here to spy on the Cardinals. To spy on me.'

'Be not offended, Master Crumwella.'

'Thomas.'

'Tomassito.' She smiled and dropped the knife to the floor. 'Cardinal Wolsey, he says he will not grant an annulment in private, yet tells the King he will. The Pope wanted a close eye on him, and cannot trust Campeggio. Campeggio is charged by the Pope to not grant an annulment, but he is not a smart man; he can easily sway.'

'And me?'

'You are unknown in your allegiances. I am meant to watch you. Not have my life discovered.'

'Try being less beautiful if you want to pass as a man.'

She laughed and Crumwell smiled. They could both understand the absurdity of the situation. He watched as Nicóla crawled around the room, picking up her hair pins, and he watched her pin back her curls. Indeed Nicóla did not have the body of a woman, but Crumwell had heard of women who bound themselves to take the appearance of a man – like Joan of Arc, who died for it.

Crumwell picked up the knife as he stood up and put out his hand to help her to her feet. Minutes earlier, she looked prepared to kill him. Nicóla was Francesco's daughter, a man known as gentle, kind, smart, a man pleased to make friends with an Englishman who had fled the French army and wanted to become an Italian merchant. Crumwell brought his fingers to her chin and wiped the dribble of blood from her lip, and she did not move. Doubtless, the woman had seen far more than most.

'I suppose you will have me on the next ship back to Italy, Tomassito.'

Crumwell swiped her black hat from the floor and handed it to her, to complete her disguise. 'If I do that, the Pope will have the papal army after me in no time. A woman who is family to him, a daughter to him.'

'Not a daughter,' Nicóla scoffed. 'How I wish our relationship was so simple, so pure.'

'But Campeggio and Wolsey shall feel annoyed by your rush into the Queen's chambers. Does Queen Katherine know of you, the truth of you?'

'Giulio – Pope Clement – gave me a jeweled ring to hand to Her Majesty personally, and said she would recognise the ring as something the Emperor once owned, a family heirloom. I revealed myself as a woman hidden in the guise of a man. The Queen understood.'

'And the Imperial ambassador?'

'He has no idea of my identity, well indeed no idea I live in any form, as far as I am awares. I am here to report to the Pope. That is all.'

'I had an intelligent daughter. Two daughters.'

'I heard you lost your wife and daughters last year. I am sorry.'

'Sweating sickness.'

'The Tudor curse.' The pair both crossed themselves. 'I can return to Rome. Pope Clement will understand.'

'You wish to return?'

'Not yet. I am not ready to take on my obligations to the Medici family. I like it here. No Medici disapproval hanging over me. And it is fortunate to meet a friend of my father, the Italianate Englishman my father liked so much. Even if you are despised here.'

'You have gathered idle talk at court.'

'The English like idle talk,' she grinned. 'They think I do not understand and speak freely.'

Crumwell could not help himself. He liked this Italian. She had a dislike for rules, was intelligent like her father, and trained in the art of power and control by the Medici family. Impertinent, brazen and daring, just like himself. And best of all, a spy in the camp of the unpredictable Campeggio. Crumwell enjoyed keeping strange pets, and Nicóla would make a lovely addition.

'Never fear, Nicóla. We can still both achieve the conclusions we need for our Cardinals.'

'What is your goal, Tomassito?'

'To be honest, I am sure not.'

'Then I suggest picking a side in this war. The battle is about to reach its height. Whatever the Pope decides will see the conclusion of power in this country, and the Pope will do anything I say.'

Chapter 6 – June 1529
Blackfriars Monastery and Westminster, London

A seecryt's wyrth depends on the peepel from whom it beest hath kept

Crumwell felt cold in the middle of summer. His body froze in position in his chair, not far from the King in the long hall at Blackfriars. Some cheered when King Henry entered the legatine court to give evidence about his marriage. Crumwell sat between the Duke of Norfolk and the Duke of Suffolk, both men who despised him, and each other. Wolsey sat the end of the room at a long table bearing his coat of arms of four blue leopards, plus the Tudor rose and dragon. Cardinal Campeggio sat next to him, totally expressionless. The King sat on a throne to the right of the long table, in front of everyone else, under his gold damask cloth of estate. The court packed with the nobles seated and the commoners' gallery above. Crumwell could barely move, not for lack of space, but for the true worry of what could happen to the country he loved.

The bowed, rose-gold head of Nicóla Frescobaldi moved slightly, catching Crumwell's eye across the aisle. The young Italian sat at the end of the rows against the wall, so he could go to his master if needed. Her master. His master. How to even think of the young Nicóletta Frescobaldi, living life's greatest lie? She responded to Nicóla, considered herself male. Her green eyes locked onto Crumwell, and his body grew warm again, creating a shiver under his black clothing. Oh, how he wanted to remain fair in the matter of the King's divorce, but one look from young Nicóla and he would do anything she wanted. He thanked God in morning prayers Nicóla was a woman under the guise of a man, or the feelings within him for the last few weeks would have sent him straight to hell. Had it been any other, Crumwell would have crowed her news to the world. This time, however, it served no purpose – yet.

A roar erupted outside the chapel. The crowd, the commoners lining the streets outside Blackfriars, had a glimpse of who they wanted – Queen Katherine. Cheering, clapping, endless cries of "God save the Queen!" all the while getting louder told the court the witness they needed had arrived. The King had already spoken; he spoke of the Queen's devotion, her pious and loving nature. But he also spoke of his burdened conscience, of how he had taken his brother's wife, not just his crown. How, at the time, all was blessed by the Pope, but now, Henry believed he committed a true crime against God and he could no longer remain by Katherine's side. His new love, Anne Boleyn, of three years, was wise enough to stay far away from Blackfriars. The people of London might have torn Anne to shreds if the sounds of the English men and women outside judged their devotion to Katherine.

A sound in the main doorway, at the opposite end of the court, pulled everyone to standing, to respect the great Queen. Katherine walked along the aisle of the court alone, her hands clasped together, her rosary laced between her fingers. She regarded no one until she passed her ally, Bishop John Fisher, close to the head table and the King. Katherine stopped before the Cardinals and said nothing. Not a single man took a breath. From his seat to the right, Crumwell looked past the Queen to see Nicóla's gaze fixed on the perfect Spanish Queen, almost lost in her stare. Whatever Nicóla spoke to the Queen last night, it must have worked; a token from the Pope and Emperor told Katherine she had allies in her quest to remain the Queen of England, the role she played since betrothed at age three, over forty years ago, still a princess back in Spain.

Queen Katherine, dressed in the most elaborate black and golden gown, jewels dripping from her, sparkling against her plump skin, took a few tiny steps towards the King on his throne and sank to her knees. Everyone gasped in collective shock, and Henry reached to pull his wife to her feet. But Katherine, firm yet discreet, fought his hands and forced him back onto his throne as she tarried on the ground, and clasped her hands together in prayer up at her husband of twenty years.

'Sir, I beseech you for all the love been between us, and for the love of God, let me have justice. Give me pity and compassion, for I am a poor woman, and a stranger born out of your dominion. I have no assured friends and fair counsel…'

Henry again tried to pull his pleading wife from her knees, and again she fought him, Henry unable to pull Katherine from the ground. They shared such an intense stare for a moment, and a pain struck Crumwell's chest. The woman intended to use the moment in court to full advantage. Henry let go of his wife and sat down, unable to look into the pleading blue eyes before him, her begging hands just a fraction away from his knees on the throne.

Katherine's voice, fueled by passion and agony in one, sounded like the tone of a woman cruelly harmed, constantly in pain through her destiny to be Queen. 'Alas! Sir, how have I offended you, or what displeasure have I deserved? I have been to you a true, humble and obedient wife, bowing to your will and pleasure, and never said or did anything to the contrary, and always contented with your delights and dalliances, big or small. I never argued or showed a spark of discontent. I loved all those you loved, only for your sake, whether I had a cause or not, whether they were my friends or enemies. These twenty years I have been your true wife and we had many children, although it pleased God to call them out of this world, which is no fault of mine.'

The pause in the pleading Spanish accent brought the full problem to pass; six children born to them, three sons. Only one baby alive, the Princess Mary, who lived far away in Ludlow. The joy and agony of their first born son eighteen years ago, who lived just a few weeks. It mattered none how grand Katherine was, her noble birth, her piety, her intelligence, her charm, her strength. With no son, Katherine could not gain Henry's true desire; an heir to hold the kingdom. He wanted his family to raise a dynasty, and as the second of his line to hold the throne, Henry needed an heir. A male heir. Not only that, Katherine's most prized "gift" to give Henry, her virginity, was now questioned. But the strong Queen had the strength to speak.

'When you had me at first, I take God as my judge, I was a true maid, never touched by a man. And whether is true or not, I put it to your conscience. If there is any just cause by law that you can allege against me, I am content to depart to my great shame and dishonour. And if there no just cause, then I beseech you, let me remain in my former estate… Therefore, I most humbly require you, in the way of charity and for the love of God – who is the just judge – to spare me the pain of this new court, until I can be advised on what action to take. And if you cannot extend me this, then only to God, do I commit my cause!'

Only now did Queen Katherine rise to her feet. She curtsied to the King and again they shared an intense stare, one only a husband and wife could share, one with twenty years of trust behind it. It told Crumwell all; the Queen had won over the court, without question. Henry knew it, too.

With a graceful sweep of her gown, Katherine turned and headed back along the aisle in which she had just entered. A hush of shock fell over the rows of men, awed by a woman's power. Wolsey pulled himself to his feet so fast he all but tripped on his own red robes.

'Your Majesty, I must implore you to return and take your place at the head of the court,' he called to Queen Katherine.

Campeggio too rose to his feet, as surprised as Wolsey. 'This court represents the Pope of Rome and we must ask you to return, Queen Katherine,' he spoke, as desperate as Wolsey.

Queen Katherine only half turned and eyed the flustered Cardinals. 'Carry on, for it matters not, for this is no fair court to me, so therefore I will not tarry. Go on.' She turned and carried on to the door of the chapel, a small army of ladies-in-waiting and guards to escort her through the crowds outside.

Crumwell stood, like so many in the court, unsure of what would happen now. The King sat with his face in one hand, his elbow balanced on the throne's arm. Wolsey slunk back into his seat, confused as Campeggio next to him. Still perched on the row of seats, Nicóla sat with a smile on her face. She sat there to make sure the Queen remained the Queen, and today, Katherine had made sure she would not be ousted by a woman of younger years.

~~~

The King's face still stuck in a horrid expression. When Katherine walked head held high from Blackfriars, the King did not show the face of a man upset he had pained a wife of twenty years. To Crumwell, Henry's face told of humiliation, the worst emotion to stir within the King. Now, after dinner, as everyone talked and mingled at court, the King sat at the head table, the same fixed expression; his mouth pursed, his eyebrows curved to a stern brow, his eyes blank. The blankness frightened Crumwell. Henry was an excitable man. A confident man. A man quick to be amused by the latest new trick to appear at court.

The King jumped from his chair, and everyone rose, the room filled with the sound of men and women called to pay heed. The Queen had not appeared at dinner, and no one had filled her place, not even the Lady Anne. With just two fingers, the King beckoned Cardinal Wolsey, who left Crumwell's side at their table. A wave of hushed tones followed the weary Cardinal as he and Henry disappeared behind a closed door. The moment they left, the room sighed in relief, many eyes falling on Crumwell.

'Here, butcher's servant,' the Duke of Norfolk called to Crumwell from his own table close to the King's, 'how long before the c-c-common Cardinal's head is on a s-s-spike on London Bridge? After today's vast fireworks display, I see not how y-y-you expect to be anywhere near this court.'

Crumwell wiped his mouth with a cloth and stood again. He could not give Thomas Howard, the old, ever-foul Duke of Norfolk, the satisfaction of growing his temper. The wide old man smelled of stale sweat and horse, crumbs caught in his long grey beard. Old Norfolk's stutter could never be mocked, for he held too much power.

'The Cardinal's desire is the King's desire. We seek to do God's work here, Your Grace.'

'Regard the unproper m-m-man, walking away,' the Duke called as Crumwell headed from the hall.

There could be no advantage in provoking Norfolk, or any of the lords, into an argument at dinner. Wolsey might not need him after a private audience with the King. So many people crowded about, wanting to hear Henry yell at Wolsey for his humiliation at Blackfriars, leaving no room for Crumwell to help. Better to wait until Wolsey limped out from his fight with the King.

As Crumwell crossed the dark courtyard to ready Wolsey's barge for the ride back to York Place, a dark figure came in the other direction of the entrance gate. Nicóla was brave to exit the grounds of court at night alone. She had her arms wrapped around a modest package, head down, gaze hidden under her ever-present hat. Crumwell stopped to watch her cross the courtyard; it did not seem such a surprise she passed for a man. Even though she was petite for a man, she had mastered walking like a man, her gestures betrayed the feminine. Crumwell could not imagine what possessed Francesco to dress Nicóla as male when she was just fourteen, to cut off her hair and give her hose and doublet instead of dresses.

Crumwell skirted along the wall of the courtyard towards the hurrying Italian, headed towards the hall where Campeggio would exit after dinner. He caught up to Nicóla as a guard pulled open a heavy door, and went in behind her. Only when they bathed in the darkness of the candle-lit hall did she turn to see the person behind her.

'Wherever I turn, there you are,' Nicóla muttered under her breath and pressed her package closer to her chest.

'Good evening to you also, my Waif.' Crumwell fell into line with her brisk pace. 'Do not tell me that you took to the streets of London in the dark, all alone,' Crumwell uttered. 'Certainly, you are smarter than that.'

'I survived Rome without being raped; I can handle London.'

Crumwell brought his eyes to hers, a solemn pooling of pale green. In the distance, he could hear the laughter of the great hall where the court sat at dinner.

'It is a confused matter,' Nicóla continued. 'Think no more of it.'

'For what do you usher yourself out into the night?' Crumwell asked, desperate for any occasion to break with Nicóla on any subject. 'We have pages and ushers who could run errands on your behalf. You are a guest of the court.'

'My affairs are my own, Master Crumwella, so please, none of your worries must be bestowed upon me. My person conceals many things, one being a dagger I have trained to use. I simply went to fetch a book.'

With each word from Nicóla, her rhythmic accent reminded Crumwell of a different time, of days spent learning besides Francesco Frescobaldi. Once more, his old friend walked alongside him, but this time as a woman. An engaging, intelligent Italian hidden under layers of fabric which hid an enormous lie.

'Might we talk in private?' Crumwell probed.

'Are we not doing so now?' Nicóla replied, her voice still slightly deepened compared to a woman, no doubt learned with time and practice.

'Nowhere is safe in this court.'

'Nowhere is safe in this country.'

Crumwell escorted Nicóla all the way to Campeggio's private rooms at court, two Italians guarding the main entry. Did they know the truth of their countryman? How did the secret stay so hidden? The details and opportunities to be caught as a woman surely appeared everywhere.

Campeggio's privy chamber room sat empty, the Cardinal no doubt enjoying the company and free-flowing wine. Crumwell watched Nicóla head off to a small side room, and he peered through the door. A tiny bedroom. Nicóla had her own room off Campeggio's chambers? That was how she kept her secret – she did not sleep with the other men. Crumwell watched Nicóla place her book, wrapped in a white cloth, on the bed, and pulled off her black cloak, tossed over the book. She came back, hat still perched upon her head.

'How do you keep yourself so hidden?' Crumwell asked as Nicóla gestured for him to sit by the empty fireside. The room had no windows, and the summer heat hung in the air.

'I write to the Pope weekly, in code.' Nicóla sat down and smoothed her rose-gold hair behind her ears. 'Campeggio was instructed to treat me as if I was Pope myself, and he knows he must abide. The Pope could destroy Campeggio easily enough. So I have my privacy and anything I desire. Which is slight, truth be told. I lived an opulent life in Florence, but since my father was murdered, I have learned to get by on little. It is far cheaper to be a man than a woman, also.'

A dainty smile flickered. Her smile showed Crumwell femininity. It explained the constant hauntingly pensive expression Nicóla showed in the daylight; she hid a woman's smile.

'Master Crumwella?' Nicóla asked, her voice lifting a fraction higher in pitch. 'What did you wish to discuss?'

Crumwell cleared his throat; she could stop his mind just by being present, such was her mystery. 'Your matter with the Antwerp bank. I have sent word. I have written, stating the money ought to be sent to you, as is your legal right. Cardinal Wolsey wrote a letter, stating of your marvellous character. The banker who has your money, he has holdings here also, so I expect a fair answer.'

'I expected my issue to be held until after the legatine court finished,' Nicóla replied, her face radiant with surprise. 'Wolsey spoke for me? Did you tell him of my secret? My real name?'

'I did not. I explained your father's death and how you require discretion.'

'I…' Nicóla left her chair and paced in a circle before locking eyes with Crumwell. 'Do you suppose it may work?'

'We have a solid case. If we can convince Antwerp, then perchance we can also release your father's money in Italy.'

'You did not have to work so soon; you are a busy man.'

'A busy man with many staff. My nephew, Richard, is most helpful. You can trust him, Nicóla.' Crumwell hoped his meandering smile gave Nicóla confidence over her identity's safety.

'How do I repay such assistance? I shall pay your fee, naturally. What percentage do you expect to gain from me?'

'If there is one character fault in me, and I am sure the court says I have many, it is my loyalty. Always to your father, so my fealty now extends to you.'

'Forgive me, but I have no reason to feel safe in anyone's hands.'

'Even Pope Clement's?'

'If the Pope knows we have gone behind his back, he will be furious. Trust me.'

'How grave is your situation with the Pope?'

Nicóla sat again and took a deep breath. 'It depends on one's opinion. Some argue I have a home and guardian for life. Some may see it as a death sentence.'

'And what do you see?'

'I see enough money in my father's Antwerp account for me to run away to Spain and pray the Inquisition never finds me.'

A heavy sound poured from the antechamber; the main door opened. The sound of quick-fire Italian beckoned; the Cardinal had returned from dinner. Crumwell jumped to his feet, half a dozen excuses for being there flooding his thoughts. But Nicóla pushed him, and he let her guide him to the bedroom. She shut the door, shielding him from view, and Crumwell froze. He heard Nicóla speaking with Campeggio in Italian; though muffled, Crumwell heard of common conversation. He glanced at the bed. Simple curiosity abounding, Crumwell lifted Nicóla's cloak and pulled the cloth from the hidden book. Tyndale's English Bible. He covered it again, the smell of Nicóla on his hands from her cloak. She purchased an illegal heretical bible? A new Protestant Bible? From where? The Germans? The Low Countries? She had worked in banking and trading; she knew how to gain such items. But Nicóla worked for the Medicis, practically one of the family, had the security of the Pope himself. Why would a Catholic like Nicóla need Tyndale's Bible? Crumwell, of course, owned one himself, along with Martin Luther's illegal German translation.

The door flung open and Nicóla gestured to Crumwell. 'Campeggio is in his room,' she whispered. 'Go now, and speak no more of this.' Her voice spoke of the haste she expected.

Crumwell took her olive-hued hand and Nicóla frowned a confused look. He brought her knuckles to his lips and kissed her temperate skin. Nicóla did not understand, nor did she pull away.

Crumwell turned and left the main room without another word, and the Italian guards shut and manned the main door, not at all watching comings and goings.

The daughter of Francesco Frescobaldi. A man you considered a father. You are damning your soul to hell, Thomas.

Chapter 7 - June 1529
Blackfriars Monastery and Westminster, London

Twas learned we're all entytled to hast our seecryts

'Quos Deus conjunxit, homo non separet. What therefore God has joined together, let no man put asunder. And, for as much as this marriage was made and joined by God to a good intent, I say that I know the truth; which is that man cannot break the bond of marriage.'

John Fisher, Bishop of Rochester spoke each word with a passion unseen until now. He stood before Wolsey and Campeggio in the hall at Blackfriars, his hands clasped together, sweat rolling from his bald head down his face and neck onto his purple vestment, such was his fervent support of Queen Katherine. The room hung in silence, concern twinkling in the summer heat. But as Bishop Fisher spoke, all listened. Nicóla noticed shaky-hands Stephen Gardiner constantly nodding his head in agreement. How Gardiner must have felt conflicted; to be a favourite of the King and yet determined against divorce.

Adjusting his purple mitre, Bishop Fisher continued. 'After careful study of the Fathers and Sacred Scripture, I am totally convinced there is no prohibition against a marriage between King Henry and Queen Katherine. The precisely worded papal bull by Pope Julian is in Queen Katherine's possession, and it states plainly the Catholic Church's position. I feel the King has not lived in sin these past twenty years.'

'You seem so convinced, Bishop,' Wolsey stated with a slight cough. Wolsey looked terrible in Nicóla's eyes. Sleep alluded him, the heat did no favours. Worse, he looked beaten, defeated, as if his patience had deserted him. "He that marries his brother's wife does an unlawful thing . . . they shall be without children." The King hears those words when he speaks to God. What makes you, Bishop Fisher, any better than the King, better than myself, or any other man who has carefully studied in this great matter?'

'I have no grievance with the study of this issue,' Fisher spat back at the Cardinal, much to Campeggio's surprise. 'However, I do not benefit from one conclusion or the other. The Pope knows the King worries about his marriage's lawfulness because he wishes to take a new wife. Marriage is a sacrament which can never be broken! Our King Henry is the Defender of the Faith, titled such by the Pope eight years ago; we know his piety and grace. Yet, in this matter, I cannot be swayed. I speak thus for Queen Katherine and her complete innocence. Her Majesty did not have carnal knowledge of Prince Arthur, the King's brother. Why not? That is between her and God. This matter is so serious due to the nature of those involved. I have never given an issue more thought than this, a royal divorce! I shall not fail in this matter, for my diligence shall speak the truth. I have fulfilled all of my responsibilities to King Henry, but I shall never pull away from my support to Queen Katherine. When my name appeared before this court, in support of an annulment, I felt abhorred by the lie. The King may pray speak against me if he must, but my opinion must be known to the court, and to the Pope himself.'

Nicóla saw Crumwell look across the court at the mention of the Pope. They locked eyes but neither made any expression. She could still feel his lips on her hand.

'Saint John the Baptist himself suffered death for violation of marriage. Nothing can be considered more sacred,' Fisher continued.

'Saint John the Baptist languished in prison, trapped under the will of a despot, and then got beheaded. Are you prepared for such punishment, Bishop Fisher?' Wolsey asked.

'I do naught to warrant such treatment! King Henry is the anointed King, and surely he would not do such a thing to a man for speaking God's word.'

~~~

How raw the evening air felt after the oppression of the legatine court in the day. Nicóla stood in the garden of the palace, and closed her eyes, to just feel the gentle breeze. Although the stench of the Thames flooded in, the air moved just enough to let Nicóla feel a bit cooler. The binding of her breasts was a constant constriction and made her body hot all summer long. The loose clothing she constantly wore, helpful to hide her body shape, grew sticky throughout the day and she yearned for the open air of Tuscany, where she could wear so little, and let the breeze over her skin. Those nights, long ago now, of lying in bed, no clothes to be seen, in the arms of the man who had seduced her at fourteen. How hurt they felt when the Church stopped their love. How Nicóla's heart hardened, how he became a broken man. How much their alliances had changed.

Footsteps pulled Nicóla from her daydream. A group of women approached, most unusual in the evening, but the heat offered a simple explanation. Nicóla had seen the Lady Anne Boleyn from a distance; but now here she stood, flanked by her six ladies-in-waiting, including her beautiful blonde sister Mary, heading along the same path where Nicóla found solace. The women walked at a delicate pace, their dresses sweeping the gravel path lit by the occasional torch alight in the garden. Several guards followed the Lady Anne, so she could stroll in the evening air, out of sight of Queen Katherine.

Nicóla stepped far to one side, the sharp branches on the perfectly trimmed shrubs digging into her lower legs. But with her head bowed, her hands clasped around her book, William Tyndale's Obedience of a Christian Man, pulled close to her chest, she did not immediately see the Lady Anne stop right before her. Nicóla glanced up to regard the amused smile of the bewitching Anne Boleyn. Lady Anne was pretty, not beautiful, but pretty. Her hands were hidden beneath long dark red sleeves, a colour which looked lovely against her swarthy-coloured skin. Her black eyes stared right at Nicóla while her long dark hair blew in the gentle breeze of the garden.

'And whom do we have hither?' Lady Anne commented, half to Nicóla, half to her ladies. Her voice, gentle and elegant, gave Nicóla the sense to stand up straight and smile in her presence.

'I think this is one of the Italians arrived with Campeggio,' one of the ladies-in-waiting replied. Nicóla recognised her as Jane Boleyn, married to Anne's brother George. George seemed an intelligent and engaging man, his wife a simple woman whom no one ever spoke of, though she seemed a pretty thing. Nicóla now felt well-versed in pretending to have slight English. It made listening far easier at court.

'Nicóla Frescobaldi, attendant to Cardinal Campeggio,' Nicóla said in her accent, with a bow.

'Quite the dainty handsome fellow,' one the ladies commented.

'Are you not busy enough being my Uncle Norfolk's mistress, Bess?' Anne giggled and the ladies followed.

'Yes, Mr. Frescobaldi,' Anne continued. 'You do wear your hair long in Italy, do you not? It is almost as if it is pinned like a woman's.'

Nicóla regarded the pretty Anne. Not a strong beauty, but the way she held herself elevated her looks. She had an instant sense of grace in her movements. Her dark hair looked long enough to be caught under her when she sat. Her black eyes danced as she held Nicóla's green gaze. Anne had olive skin, like Nicóla's, and her accent almost sounded as if it carried French blood. 'A pleasure to meet you, my Lady, you are very well met.'

'Do you speak much English, my good sir?' Anne enquired.

'A little.'

'French?'

'Oui, madam.'

'Est-il prêt à accorder une annulation?'

Anne's perfect French and sweet voice caught Nicóla off guard as she asked Nicóla's opinion on the annulment. 'Toutes les preuves doivent encore être entendues,' Nicóla stumbled.

'Yes, the evidence still needs to be heard,' Anne translated for her ladies, except for her sister, who surely had attended the French court also. Mary Boleyn was a blonde beauty; no wonder the King had once made her a mistress. The rumours at court said her two children bore red hair, like the King, not like her husband.

'Say something in Italian,' Mary said with a grin.

'Si tratta di una bella donna che vedo davanti a me questa sera,' Nicóla said. 'It is a beautiful woman I see before me tonight.'

'Well, are you not just so sweet,' Anne giggled. 'My sister Mary is single now, her husband died of the sweating sickness last year. I almost died also.'

Nicóla did not respond; to do so would make her grasp of English seem too advanced. 'You spend time with the Master Cremwell,' Anne continued, Crumwell's name getting caught in her accent. 'I hear they call you "the Waif" at court.'

'Master Crumwella, yes,' Nicóla nodded. Suddenly, that seemed unwise; how did Lady Anne know? The spies Crumwell spoke of… who spied not in this court?

'And what do you read?' Anne asked, and peered at Nicóla's book.

'Nothing, my Lady,' Nicóla uttered and tried to hide it. Too late; Anne read Tyndale's name on the front.

'You read the heretical Tyndale? In English?' Her black eyes widened. 'You know the book is banned in England? How can your master allow such a thing? How can you read such an edition, in English?'

'I learn English,' Nicóla brokenly replied on purpose. 'Cardinal Campeggio needs heresy learned…'

'Perchance people need to learn Tyndale's teachings so they can arrest heretics, having full knowledge of their behaviour,' Mary Boleyn suggested to her sister. She repeated in French to Nicóla, assuming she did not understand the words.

'Yes, Lady Mary,' Nicóla replied.

'I have a Tyndale English Bible. Would I enjoy the Obedience of a Christian Man?' Anne continued, ignoring her sister's comment.

'If you wish, Lady Anne,' Nicóla ventured.

'I cannot take your book, surely. I am well cared for here at court, but you appear to have little.'

'Please, Lady Anne, if you wish.' Nicóla handed the text to Anne who looked upon the banned book with keen curiosity.

'Your Henry will not like this,' Jane Boleyn muttered.

'I do not like that he keeps myself and Queen Katherine in the same court,' Anne commented, to the astounded giggles of the women. Nicóla kept a straight face, and Anne noticed.

'Thank you, Mr. Frescobaldi,' she said, pronouncing the name to perfection, something rare for the English. 'And fear not, heresy is always punished hither in London, my Henry makes certain.'

~~~

Nicóla sped the hallways of the palace in search of Crumwell. He likely left to return to York Place or his own Austin Friars for the night, with no court proceedings for a few days. One thing about Henry's court; everyone knew everyone's business. If someone had not seen Crumwell, then they knew who to ask in finding him. Dashing in the direction of Cardinal Wolsey's rooms, Nicóla had to find him before he left the court. Wolsey had returned to York Place, in a fiery mood, so several courtiers claimed. One guard sat at the door to Wolsey's rooms, a young man who looked ready to sleep, though the time had not yet gone midnight.

'Excuse me, sir,' Nicóla panted, feeling beads of sweat under her clothes.

'Cardinal Wolsey has retired for the night,' the young man said, his voice cracking, no doubt the scourge of his young age.

'I seek Master Crumwella.'

'Who asks after him?'

'Nicóla Frescobaldi, counsel to Cardinal Lorenzo Campeggio.'

'Ah…'

'Just say the Italian. Please, sir, it is most urgent.' Nicóla pulled a coin from her pocket and handed it over.

The young man pulled himself to his feet, smoothing his dark blue Wolsey livery. He entered after a brief knock and Nicóla heard arguing voices, one being Crumwell's. The moment the young boy came back, Stephen Gardiner appeared behind him, his dull face reddened with annoyance. He regarded Nicóla up and down for a moment, taking in Nicóla's elaborate black doublet, and grimaced. Shaky-hands Gardiner appeared most disturbed. 'I suppose you bring trouble from Campeggio? What is it now?' Each word from Gardiner's mouth toiled with exasperation.

'No, Archdeacon Gardiner,' Nicóla replied, still catching her breath. 'I have need of Master Crumwella.'

'I hear the two of you are seen together most days.' Gardiner's dark eyes pointed straight at Nicóla, as if looking for more than he spoke.

'Master Crumwella, he speaks my native tongue,' Nicóla argued. 'He is helpful to me.'

'At least he is useful to someone,' Gardiner sniffed his hook nose as he headed away from Nicóla and disappeared in the darkness of the hall, it swallowing him in his dark vestments in moments.

'Sir,' the young guard murmured. 'Please, follow me.'

Nicóla trotted in behind the boy and took off her hat, careful to keep her pins in place. By now, no one thought anything of the Italian who needed to pin his hair, rather it was just a fancy from where he hailed from, making Nicóla's lie a little simpler.

'Nicóla, my Waif,' Crumwell said with a weary smile and waved the guard from the room. Crumwell stood in the privy chamber of Wolsey's rooms, the fire gratefully out, the room instead lit with candles circling the lavish golden room. 'Are you well?'

Nicóla waited until she heard the guard shut the main door through the antechamber. 'I fear I have lost myself tonight, and I could be in danger. Please, do not that clicking of the fingers you do when you send people away. I have trouble.'

'The court does take some getting used to,' Crumwell jested and gestured Nicóla to sit in a plush red chair across from Crumwell's. On the floor lay piles of paper, no doubt a casualty of Stephen Gardiner's temper. But Nicóla could not sit for her annoyance.

'Master Crumwella, I am no fool. I have worked alongside my father to close many serious deals in my time. I have assisted the Medici family in their finances. I have served at the chambers of the Republic of Florence, and the court of the Pope. I have even met Charles, Holy Roman Emperor and King of Spain. Even, once, as a woman, I slapped the ruler of Venice when he touched me in a way not becoming of a gentleman. I speak six languages. I have worked on my studies in business, trading, finance, banking, civil law. And yet tonight...' Nicóla paused and took a breath, fighting the urge to fall back into Italian.

Crumwell took her pause as a chance to bestow a smile on her temper. 'We all have sorry days, Nicóla.'

'Tonight, I met Anne Boleyn. Not only did she ruin my game of lacking English by using French, she took my book!'

'What is that to me?'

'It was a religious book.'

'Old Testament or New?'

'Neither.'

The colour drained from Crumwell's face as wrinkles appeared around his eyes. 'You mean the Tyndale Bible you hid under your cloak the other night?'

'You looked through my possessions?' Nicóla cried.

'You compressed me into your room in a hurry, like some improper harlot.'

'As it happens, the book was Obedience of a Christian Man.'

'Lady Anne Boleyn took your heretical Tyndale text?'

'Yes, took it from my hands, while I stood there, like some young babbling fool.'

'Sit, Nicóla, please.' As weary as Crumwell looked, he inched forward in his seat to be close to Nicóla across from him, but he did not touch her. After his kiss the other night, it was probably for the best. Nicóla's reputation with her father's friends was not a proud one. 'Does Campeggio know you read Tyndale?'

'Of course not, Campeggio is of an age where he rejects all he does not call traditional. He has no stomach for new learning. I had a Tyndale Bible in Rome, the Pope allowed it, for studying heresy, but Campeggio forbids me any Tyndale in London.'

'So you procured new copies hither.'

'Yes. And now it is in the hands of the King's mistress.'

Crumwell's mind already worked over the problem, Nicóla could tell by his mellow gaze. 'My question is, Nicóla, why would you need a Tyndale Bible or other books by him?'

'Does it matter?' Nicóla shrugged.

'Perchance.'

'What happens to those who are caught with heretical texts in London?'

'You will be charged with heresy, by Wolsey or Gardiner, and thrown in the Tower.'

'The Tower of London? The famous one, where they torture everyone and cut off their heads?'

'The very same. Though you are not noble, so you would be burned at Tyburn,' Crumwell dismissed her.

'Comforting.'

'Why did the Pope allow you to read Tyndale?'

'Giulio – Pope Clement – regards kindly on my many fancies. In Rome, I study heresy to better understand the minds of those who turn against the Church.'

'Is that why you read it?'

'I cannot read Luther's works in German, so Tyndale is my only choice to read Protestant thoughts on God's work. William Tyndale's English translation comes from Erasmus' three Greek translations, the received text. It derives from Hebrew and Greek texts which are older and with more authority than the Latin Vulgate texts of St. Jerome. It is taken from the same Greek texts as Martin Luther's German texts, no? I can read neither German nor Greek.'

'The new English translation suggests any man can pray to God, to read God's word, not just a priest in Latin in a church, among other issues. You are a man… woman… close to the Pope. Yet you want to read things against the Pope himself?'

'No, just contrary to Catholic and Latin teachings.'

'Such as there being no purgatory for our souls to endure after our Earthly sins are held against us?'

'Yes,' Nicóla said and paused for a moment. 'Have you read Tyndale's work? When I accused you of being a Lutheran a few weeks ago, I did it out of anger only.'

'A cheap assault at a man's reputation, as the English would say. I have a copy of Tyndale's Bible, likewise Luther's Bible. I have had much correspondence with William Tyndale. I have the protection of Wolsey, though, and you do not.'

'Might Wolsey be of service to me?' Nicóla asked and inched forward in her seat. Her knees almost touched Crumwell's now.

'We could suggest you study all manners of texts as we dwell on the King's divorce. Wolsey is in a difficult state, I must say. The King is furious with him and this legatine court. The whole palace knows of their arguments. Gardiner may not look too kindly on your reading, especially as you gave it to the King's mistress.'

'I can handle Gardiner,' Nicóla replied and put her hands on her lap to compose herself. 'I saw Gardiner in Rome last year. By all accounts, he does not remember me with the Pope. Gardiner made such a mess of his time in Rome, petitioning for the King's divorce. I do not think the King knows how horrid Gardiner performed there.'

'Will you tell me? I do enjoy information against Gardiner, the spiteful, confident man he is.'

'If you help me and my lost book, then certainly, Tomassito.'

Crumwell smiled at Nicóla and she returned it on instinct. Yes, there lay an age difference of fifteen years between them but that never made an impression on Nicóla's choices. Trapped on this awful little island, Crumwell was the only person she wished to see. He had pledged loyalty upon their meeting. Nicóla told herself she could expect no more than fealty, no matter her desire for Earthly delights.

'We shall say the book is mine,' Crumwell replied. 'You simply borrowed it from me, in order to help your learning. I will take the issue from there. It may go unnoticed, given the anger of the King towards Wolsey at the moment.'

'Perchance the anger could be Wolsey's saving grace,' Nicóla suggested.

'How?'

'If the King of England read from Tyndale, it would upset the Church, the Pope himself. If King Henry turns against Wolsey, the Cardinal who runs England, that would also worry Rome. If Wolsey were to be seen as falling from favour, perchance the Pope will relent on his annulment stance. Rome does not want to lose England the way they have lost the Germans to the Protestants.'

'We turn Henry to Protestant readings and fake the downfall of Wolsey to anger the Pope into giving an annulment?' Crumwell asked. 'You have one ambitious plan.'

'Mayhap my Tyndale book, or your book as we will call it, falling into Anne Boleyn's hands will create the world where we can get Wolsey what he needs to survive and make the King merry.'

'Are you not hither to ensure no divorce can go ahead?'

'True. The Pope and the men of Rome want no divorce because it shall upset the Emperor, the Queen's nephew. They want Charles' favour, his money, his power. Greed drives Rome, not religion, not the guidance of royal souls. I am personally hither as a sign I am committed to Rome, and in turn, will receive my inheritance. If my mission fails, I still get my money. And Anne Boleyn is a kind woman, not beautiful, but she is gentle, elegant, sweet. You can see why a man might fall for her.'

'The Queen is strong but dull, and Henry cannot cope with her any longer. He needs a charming woman who will breed. Anne meets enough of his needs; she is young, fair, probably fertile, plus virtuous and intelligent,' Crumwell sighed. 'The Lady Anne does not like me, and she hates Wolsey.'

'Campeggio will never issue an annulment. I am hither to ensure that, by any means necessary,' Nicóla said, her voice firm again. 'If you are as loyal to Wolsey as you were to my father, I suggest you come up with a plan to save him because the King's wrath will rain upon us all sooner or later.'

Nicóla watched Crumwell nod, deep in thought. She wanted to reach out, touch him, but knew she could not make such a lapse again, with another man who did not deserve to be shamed by her. Plotting together was the total of their partnership, unlike she and Giulio, so long ago.

Chapter 8 - July 1529
Blackfriars Monastery and Westminster, London

Some seecryts art meanteth to beest learned - but once learned thee cannot forgete

Crumwell heard the calls of the common man as he entered the legatine court for the final time. The people of England wanted their beloved Queen Katherine to stay as their ruler's wife. If the highest wife in the land could be tossed aside, what of the rest? No woman felt safe. No man knew where he stood. Why on Earth should a gracious Spanish princess be cast aside because a younger English girl caught the King's eye? The crude comments tossed at Cardinal Wolsey as he entered the court caught Crumwell's ear but he never glanced up from the dusty ground beneath his feet. The coming moments inside the court would shape his life – and as a man of wealth and new-found status, Crumwell should have had some power over his life by now, yet he found himself lost as ever in the game fought by masters.

In their seats for another session, Wolsey and Campeggio sat at the head of the room, the King again under his cloth of estate, to one side. Crumwell shifted in his seat as the heat of summer hung over the nobles on the floor and the commoners up in the gallery. The final day in court, which King Henry longed for, burned with worry. Wolsey appeared in extreme discomfort, his gaze on his hands on the long white table before him, never meeting the King's dark looks. The King almost trembled in anticipation. Wolsey knew not the reasoning for the special convening of the court, only Campeggio.

Crumwell had not spoken with the young Nicóla for a week, the Italians tucked away in meetings of their own, unseen at court. Crumwell stole a quick glance across the court to Nicóla, sitting opposite him once again. Perched on the end of the rows of seating, her expression looked impossible to understand. Her expression spoke of positively nothing; something Crumwell noticed frequently. Her years of pretending to be someone else was so ingrained in her; her look, her stance, her steps, her voice, all crafted to fool and she never slipped or gave away the tiniest hint of her secret. Even now, at a crucial moment, between the hushed whispers and the overwhelming heat.

Campeggio rose to his gout-ridden feet and held the table before him for support. His long white beard brushed the tablecloth, his hunched back unable to straighten out. 'Your Majesty, Your Eminence, Your Graces, my Lords,' Campeggio addressed the group in his lyrical accent, and the King straightened on his throne. Crumwell noticed Nicóla do the same as if bracing herself.

'We came hither one calendar month ago to decide on whether the King of England is truly married in the sight of God, or whether he burned his soul with sin. The Queen Katherine herself applied for an appeal to His Holiness Pope Clement, dismissing this legatine court. We have heard naught of such a decision from Rome, and so must continue to assume this court is the highest office which shall break the subject of this annulment. However, it is now July, and in Rome, the time of reaping and harvesting. During this time, no court sits or makes any decisions. As this court is set up on the behalf of our Pope Clement, God's voice on Earth, I must decree this court is adjourned until October in accordance with the laws of Rome.'

The words of the ancient Cardinal gave way to a mixture of shock and fury as the lords sprang to their feet in surprise, Crumwell in among them. Above in the galleries, the commoners openly showed their loathing for the lack of news while the lords talked of their impatience between one another.

'This is beyond the pinnacle of injustice!' King Henry boomed as he jumped from his throne. Such was his mood the jewels sewn to his green doublet shook with his rage, his face as flushed as his red hair. 'Must my soul remain as trapped as my body in a marriage not right by law or by God? We care none for the reaping and harvesting done by the wastrels of Rome!'

A single-fingered gesture from the King in the direction of pompous Charles Brandon, Duke of Suffolk, and he clambered from his seat and towards the King. The Duke, a man easily as tall as the glorious King himself, stood before the Cardinals' table, both Campeggio and Wolsey back in their seats during the commotion. The Duke slammed his angry palms onto the table before Campeggio. The fierce bang silenced the hall for a moment. Not only did Wolsey and Campeggio defy the King, it showed anyone could defy the laws of England. One angry slam reminded the Cardinals they could not deny Henry.

Nicóla slipped between jostling lords and made her way to the table, coming to a stop behind her master Campeggio. She looked humble in comparison to the huge Suffolk, a monster among men at over six feet in height, his ageing shoulders still as wide as in his youth, now with a waistline to match. King Henry's heavily-bearded best friend and brother-in-law never got questioned, a loyal man and soldier of record in the court. Yet Nicóla stood there, one hand on Campeggio's shoulder, ready to defend him should the Duke lose all his sense at the request of the King. The stare between Suffolk and Nicóla lasted a few moments in which Crumwell felt unable to move. He should have gone to Wolsey, to stand beside Nicóla, yet did not have the strength to do so; yet Nicóla could stare down the monster before her.

The Duke scoffed at the sight of the tiny Italian and took a few steps back, not foolish enough to strike a cardinal in the halls of a monastery, no matter the mood of his King. Everyone fell into a hurried bow as King Henry swept from the hall, the Duke of Suffolk right behind him. The room flowed with voices coated in shock, and Crumwell stumbled from his seat to his master, in shock over the King's rage. Campeggio, however, had the smile of a much calmer man.

'That was all rather foolish, would you not say?' Campeggio said, almost a skip of laughter in his voice.

'Well played, Your Eminence,' Nicóla replied as Campeggio's other courtiers came to his side.

'I fear our welcome in London shall be ever more strained,' Campeggio said as his son helped him from his seat. 'Standing up to Charles Brandon like that, Nicóla, entertained us. I truly believed he would strike me.'

'It is all part of the masque we perform hither,' Nicóla smiled.

'Masque?' Wolsey spat as he jumped to his feet beside Crumwell. The lords and commoners leaving their respective spots glanced at the raised voice from the head of the hall. 'My favour with the King hangs by a thread, and you, Campeggio, with your dank, cavernous tooth-hole consumes all truth and reason! What folly do you seek, Campeggio? Do you seek my downfall, my very place within our society?'

'I seek a fair and honest conclusion for this most serious of discussions,' Campeggio scoffed. 'I seek to preserve marriage as God wishes.'

Crumwell threw a look at Nicóla, looking so smug. The Pope would never allow a divorce. She succeeded in her master's quest, the Pope's request to have the court rule in his desire.

Wolsey fell back into his throne of a chair, his eyes closed. 'Thomas,' he said, his eyes hidden behind a limp hand, 'perchance it is best I retire to Hampton Court tonight, rather than York Place. There can become space between the King and myself.'

'I can request an audience with King Henry, to explain the situation while you cross the Thames to Hampton Court,' Crumwell offered.

'And explain what?' Wolsey squawked as he threw his hand into his lap. 'I fear there can be no more to be said on this matter.'

As the final men shuffled from the hall, the bang of heavy footsteps echoed. 'Oh, what is this?' Crumwell muttered to his master and the Italians.

The Duke of Suffolk returned, four of the King's black-clad guards behind him, all marching in time to the grinning Duke. 'Celebrating your victory, Cardinals?' the Duke said as he approached. 'You have unleashed a fury even the Lady Anne may not be able to soothe.'

'There is no victory for anyone today, Your Grace,' Crumwell said for the group.

'But there must be some satisfaction. You,' the Duke pointed at Nicóla, 'what is your name?'

'Nicóla Frescobaldi.' Nicóla stood tall, chin high, her green eyes directly on the gaze of the bejeweled plump man before her.

Crumwell saw the flicker of pride in Suffolk's eyes. 'Your Grace, may I ask over the issue?'

'I care nothing of your opinion, common Crumwell,' Suffolk dismissed him. 'Frescobaldi, you are under arrest, by order of the King.'

'On what charge?' Crumwell spat out as the King's guards surrounded Nicóla, who did not move a muscle.

Crumwell jumped forward as the first guard grabbed Nicóla by her thin arm but Crumwell got shoved away. 'Please, Mr Frescobaldi speaks little English,' Crumwell lied.

'It is his actions, not his words, which gives the King trouble,' Suffolk scoffed. 'You ought to know better than to stand up for those the King despises.'

'Your Grace,' Campeggio interjected and made to rise on his own, 'my man hither has done no wrong.'

'He shall have to speak thus to the King himself. Henry wants to see you, Frescobaldi.'

'What folly,' Wolsey interrupted. 'Surely I can calm any of the King's burdens.'

'No, the King asked specifically for the young Italian.' The Duke of Suffolk paused as the guards brought Nicóla to him before the court's head table. Suffolk punched Nicóla's stomach with the force of his meaty fist, enough to knock Nicóla to the ground with a groan.

'Please, Your Grace,' Crumwell begged, 'allow me to accompany the Waif. I can speak his language.'

'He can speak for himself.'

'I am a lawyer.'

'And I am a duke. Get to your feet, Waif.'

Nicóla pulled herself to sitting and Crumwell cringed in agony as Suffolk kicked her hard in the mouth, enough to throw her back and knock one of the guards from his stance. At once, everyone else in the room rose to their feet.

'Your Grace!' Campeggio admonished, his voice finding its strength, 'this is a monastery, and Frescobaldi is a man of the Church! You cannot come hither and do such things in a house ordained by God. You would injure a man in the sight of our Lord to satisfy your own vanity?'

Crumwell knelt down to Nicóla as the guards tried to pull her upright. Still awake, blood gushed from her mouth and nose. Her hat had come off, her bound hair still tucked back into her collar. Her eyes fell on Crumwell's with pure strain as she fought the pain. She seemed calm, probably due to the fact she knew there was no escape.

'What shall the King say when you pull a scholar before him covered in blood, spilled in a house of a Benedictine Catholic religious order?' Crumwell said as he helped the guards pull Nicóla to her feet, with brief success. She hung in the steady arms of the guards, men no doubt prepared for these occasions.

'You think Henry shall even notice?' Suffolk scoffed. 'Well indeed, a servant boy of a corrupt Italian cardinal. But very well, you can come before the King if you wish, commoner.'

A quick look to Wolsey gave Crumwell permission to leave. Campeggio, unsteady on his feet, held his son Bishop Alessandro's arm, filled with worry. The old Cardinal crossed himself as Nicóla got dragged away, her blood dribbling between Crumwell's fingers as he attempted to cradle her face.

They rode the Thames on Suffolk's private barge, the smell of the warm city in the breeze abhorrent at this time of day. People paused on the shore and watched the barge go by, the Duke at the front, stiff as a statue, the guards posted on either side. Crumwell sat on the damp floor of the barge, the soaked wooden surface dampening his black clothes. Nicóla had her head on his lap, her eyes closed as Crumwell held a dirty cloth to her face, in an effort to stem the bleeding. They had gone for the weakest person and lashed out. The King raged and could not bring in a cardinal covered in blood, but instead, a helpless advisor could bear witness to Henry's rage. The golden days of Henry the Eighth seemed long over. No longer the tallest, wisest, most handsome King in Christendom, now an ageing man with a desire for young girls, the only detail unchanged in his personality.

Crumwell wiped sweat from Nicóla's brow, her skin so soft. Her eyes opened, and focused on the face above hers. Crumwell caught a moment of tenderness, something she inherited from her father, a gentle calm where another man might show fear.

'I shall be of service to you,' Crumwell muttered, the guards' eyes upon the pair. 'You will not have to speak, not after what Suffolk has done. Let me speak for you.'

With a gentle hand, Nicóla took Crumwell's hand away from her mouth, the bloodied cloth with it. She spat into her own hand and produced a tooth.

'Oh…' Crumwell's words stuck in his worry. 'How could…?' He took the tooth from her and tossed it in Suffolk's direction. The man himself noticed nothing, but the guards did, eyebrows raised at the level of defiance in the common man on a noble's barge.

'I could have sold the tooth at a profit,' Nicóla mumbled and Crumwell brought the cloth back to her chin.

'I shall collect it for you. Shh, you must not speak.'

'Abate, Tomassito, for I will be well.'

'Can you see, Nicóla?'

'It is istupidire…'

'Befuddled,' Crumwell translated with a smile.

'Odd word,' she mumbled, her lips swollen. 'Odd country.'

'Yes, this is what happens to people who defend the safety of an old man of the cloth,' Crumwell scowled.

'These men … do wrong… for it is men like us… who rule.'

'What do you mean?'

'Kings do not rule... bankers rule.'

Crumwell smiled again, this time bringing an actual satisfying sensation. 'I would mumble those words in a quiet tone, Nicóla.'

'I trust you,' she whispered and closed her eyes again.

~~~

The King's rooms at the palace seemed oddly devoid of life. The antechamber, where men stood into their hundreds, all in need of the King's favour, now sat empty. No fool dared to ask the King for even a word this afternoon. Crumwell walked behind Suffolk, the bloodied cloth still in his hands as the King's guards pulled Nicóla along, her feet shuffling and tripping in her dizziness. The blood had stopped but the tell-tale signs of black eyes already formed on her olive skin. Through into the presence chamber, with just a lone guard inside, the King was nowhere to be seen. The gold cloth of estate hung over Henry's elevated throne, but despite the emptiness of the space, the King's voice echoed from his privy chamber through the side door. Crumwell felt sweat at the back of his neck and he pulled his black hat from his greying hair but could not straighten it as blood stuck to his fingers.

The Duke of Suffolk burst through a door as a chamberlain announced him to the King, the guards and then Crumwell close behind them. The King's privy chamber, a room decorated in gold and black, had candles surrounding every space. A wide fireplace sat in silence, underneath a portrait of Henry's father. A large table, big enough to seat ten lined the centre, and a desk at one end, where Henry no doubt did his private correspondence. Several men of the privy chamber stood at the opposite end, all clad in black, and their eyes lowered, none meant to see or hear a thing. Large windows behind them showed the fading light of the day. There stood the admirable Henry, still dressed in his ethereal green and white Tudor colours, the red and white Tudor rose in jewels pinned to his chest. His red hair saw scant of the top of his head, most gathering around his ears. His face, puffy at the best of times, look as red as the devil. He tore his eyes from the window to Nicóla and frowned deeply.

'How do I interrogate a man who is barely alive, Charles?' Henry asked the Duke.

'The young Italian had an accident.'

'With a boot?'

Both men grinned, momentarily soothed. Henry, one hand leaning on the fireplace mantle, looked about the room. 'Everyone, get out!' he cried, and his attendants quickly turned, no doubt relieved to escape.

The guards let go of Nicóla and bowed to exit, and she swayed but stood alone, clutching her punched stomach. Nicóla, eyes down, bowed uneasily before the King as a meagre drop of blood rolled down her lip. Crumwell dashed forward and dabbed her before blood spilled before Henry.

'What on God's Earth are you doing hither, Crumwell? Ought you to not be celebrating with Wolsey over my downfall?' Each sound from Henry's mouth sounded so bitter, so disheartened.

'Crumwell wished to handle the little Waif,' Suffolk mocked.

'Leave us,' the King sighed.

'Your Majesty?' Suffolk responded with confusion.

'Damn you to hell, Charles!' the King bellowed with rage, enough to make Crumwell and Nicóla cower in preparation for pain. 'Why must the entire world question my authority? What must the people of my own realm think; that they can do as they please? You have vexed me many a time, Charles. Leave me!'

The Duke exited the room after the smallest of bows, and Crumwell froze. The King's anger was legendary and sounded dangerous enough to ignite a great fire. But to leave Nicóla standing there, still bleeding?

'Excuse us, Your Majesty,' Crumwell mumbled and pulled Nicóla's arm; perchance this was the chance to take her with him.

'Not so fast,' the King said, wiping his top lip as he tried to quell his mania. 'I must speak with the spy.'

'Perchance I could be of assistance, Your Majesty. Mr. Frescobaldi is… unwell, and speaks much in Italian and not English.'

'Please, leave me, Master Crumwella,' Nicóla mumbled and tried to stand straight, her hands clasped before her. 'I must be of service to the King in any way I can.'

The King gestured for Crumwell to step back and he did, until he reached the wall, leaving Nicóla to stand there before the King. 'The court is all talk for the handsome Waif creature from Italy,' Henry began, taking a few paces back and forth before Nicóla, who had her eyes cast downwards. 'The effeminate young man who seems to have won Thomas Crumwell's favour, and yes, that is apparent.'

'Master Crumwella is a friend of my father, Your Majesty.'

'Perchance the Waif does speak our common tongue!' the King jested, ignoring Nicóla's mumble. 'In any case, if you are a spy in my court, Waif, perchance Mr. Crumwell is too.'

'Lies, Your Majesty.' Nicóla turned her eyes straight to the King, who stopped his pacing in surprise to her defiance.

'Then tell me why you write to the Pope every week? Is that not excessive? The Pope and the Emperor both have ambassadors in my court, so why weekly letters from you?'

Crumwell watched Nicóla take a moment to choose her words. He felt nervous before the King, but Nicóla did not. Perchance because she did not understand the terror of being sent to the Tower.

'The Pope requires my reports in order to have full information on the legatine court and the matters of London. It soothes His Holiness.'

'I am the one in need of soothing!'

'Then allow me to soothe His Majesty.'

The words stopped the King again. 'How?'

'In your wisdom, Your Majesty, you chose to see me in your time of dire need. The court has left your soul burdened by the questions of your marriage. If you have chosen to see me at this time, it surely means I can be of assistance.'

The King looked to Crumwell and then back to the cowering Waif. Nicóla wobbled on her feet, and Crumwell stepped forward on instinct to help, but the King threw him an angry look. 'I can be of service to the Waif,' Henry protested. 'I am a man of the people.'

'Oh indeed, Your Majesty. Please, excuse my appearance, my speech. The Duke of Suffolk did not like the conclusion in court today,' Nicóla said as the King held her hands for a moment, to steady her. It seemed such an out of place moment of kindness.

'Nobody enjoyed the conclusion, except that simpering wife of mine, no doubt! Katherine shall be dancing in the halls, planning a party I suspect. But what of me, of my needs? A kingdom needs an heir. My soul needs peace.' Nicóla did not reply and the King continued. 'Why do letters from you soothe the Pope?'

'It is a private matter.'

'Tell me, or you will bleed with more haste!'

Nicóla wiped the blood from her chin and took a deep breath. 'My family has worked with the Pope's family for almost twenty years, Your Majesty. The Pope and I are known to one another, ever since he was just a cardinal. His Holiness places trust in me.'

'Is it true Queen Katherine has asked to appeal the decision of the annulment even before our court has made a decision?'

'It is, Your Majesty. I wish I knew His Holiness' mind.'

'All the reaping and harvesting business. Is it true Italian courts cannot sit in the summer?'

'Well indeed, Your Majesty. The weather in Rome is much hotter, and work in the city is difficult. And pestilence is rife.'

'I myself shall leave London on progress with the Lady Anne immediately,' the King agreed.

'In truth, Your Majesty, your great matter has given the Pope much sorrow. Whenever he is asked on the matter, he is prone to fits of sobbing tears. The turmoil of his reign has taken a high toll. Your sister's divorce two years ago was hard enough, and she is only a Dowager Queen of Scotland. This matter has the courts of Europe taking sides and Pope Clement is nervous.'

'What is your opinion?'

'It is too dangerous for the Pope to give you an annulment. He hoped Katherine may see the light of God and leave for a nunnery.'

'What will the Pope do if Campeggio gives me an annulment when the court reconvenes in October?'

'The Pope may excommunicate you. He may render Cardinal Campeggio's decision unlawful. He may hear Queen Katherine's appeal and grant her still wed. The Pope… he is not of sound mind, Your Majesty.'

'He is well? Healthy?'

'In the body, yes, but a head injury has given him much difficulty.' Nicóla paused again to wipe the blood off her chin. Crumwell noticed she looked even paler; she could faint in the King's presence at any moment. 'And with reformation occurring in Europe…'

'Yes, which is the issue I wish to discuss. Why did you give my Lady Anne a heretical book?'

Here came Crumwell's chance to help. 'Your Majesty, the book belonged to me, and…'

'You?' The King asked. 'The Cardinal's man?'

'I am also my own man, Your Majesty.'

'I am awares; I remember you telling me I was wrong about war in France, in your first speech in parliament six years ago.'

'First and only, Your Majesty. I am a man of business. I read things, find things, am given things. Mr. Frescobaldi simply borrowed the book to study heresy in English, to help with the case of your annulment.' Perchance these words could soothe the heavy heart of the King.

'Lady Anne most enjoyed the book. The world of Luther excites her, now Tyndale too. The book says I can be the leader of my people, in matters of Church and State. The Pope could be only a bishop of Rome, and I would be the leader of the Catholic Church in England.'

'It is a fine idea, Your Majesty,' Nicóla replied. 'You could make a level-headed decision on your own marriage.'

'And stop sending money to the corrupt Church of Rome,' Crumwell added.

'That is heresy to just utter, Crumwell. I know you closed monasteries for Wolsey for years, but, all the same.'

'Your Majesty, the Church is rife with corruption. Without the Pope in Rome, you could be the richest man in England, and run your nation in all matters.' Crumwell could not believe the words pouring from himself. But everyone knew you told King Henry what he wanted to hear.

'Is there any chance we can get the court back in session?' Henry asked. 'You are the man for Wolsey, and you, Waif, are the man for Campeggio. Make it happen!'

'I find it unlikely, Your Majesty,' Nicóla replied and closed her eyes for a moment. 'Even the Pope himself shall not discuss the matter for the rest of the summer. He is grievously burdened with the issue.'

'I am the one burdened!' the King said and grabbed Nicóla by the shoulders, shaking her. 'Will Campeggio ever give me what I need?'

'No,' Nicóla muttered and wiped Henry's spit from her sore face. 'Cardinal Campeggio is under strict orders to never give you an annulment. The Cardinal arrived in England a year ago with a papal bull decreeing no annulment shall ever be issued.'

Crumwell felt shocked Nicóla gave up her master so easily. But weakened and before the King himself, who knew what people would do to save themselves?

The King pushed Nicóla to the floor, and she fell with scant fight against the King's hand. 'You will write to your precious Pope, and convince him to give me an annulment, or I shall lock you in the Tower,' the King seethed. 'Do you hear me?'

'Your Majesty,' Crumwell said and stepped forward. His heart ached for Nicóla. 'Perchance Mr. Frescobaldi could be under house arrest until the Pope grants an annulment,' he offered and watched Nicóla turn and scowl at him. 'The Waif could tarry with Cardinal Wolsey at York Place.'

'Never.'

'Then perchance at my home, at Austin Friars? Frescobaldi can write to the Pope under my supervision.'

'No letters can go to Rome without me reading them first, and no seals may be put upon them.' Henry took the idea as his own. 'We shall convince the stupid old Pope one letter at a time. And you shall never let the Waif from your sight.'

'As you wish, Your Majesty,' Crumwell said. Anything to get out of the King's privy chamber.

'I cannot stand any more of you today, Waif,' the King said, anguish suddenly in his tone. 'But at least I have learned more. Campeggio and Wolsey cannot be trusted. You, Waif, are my direct line to the Pope. I shall marry my Lady Anne. I care not for what any person says, not even Anne herself.'

Chapter 9 – August 1529
Austin Friars, London

The graytest seecryts art at each momente hydden in the most unlikely
playces

Nicóla smiled as she felt the warm summer sun on her face. She laid back in bed, her eyes still closed, the day not yet beginning. Her skin still felt fresh from her bath the night before, the air filled with the scent of rosewater. Crumwell could not do enough for her. A request for her own bathtub – done. How the servants complained having to heat water nightly and fill the tub, only to have to empty it again an hour later. A maid complained that shaky-hands Stephen Gardiner had pronounced daily bathing sinful vanity. Nicóla overheard the girl but said naught. Crumwell already knew the girl spied for Gardiner and allowed her to tarry, for the amusement. Someone else in the Crumwell household was spying for the King, but who, neither Crumwell nor Nicóla could tell. All the servants lived under the instruction of Mercy Pryor, Crumwell's mother-in-law, the detail of Crumwell's wife being deceased not relevant; they were family.

How a month of being under house arrest at Austin Friars soothed Nicóla. The last two years – the death of her father, the sacking of Rome, the hidden life under the Pope's instruction, all needed to be purged. Being assaulted by the pompous Suffolk was the most unlikely gift from God. Nicóla was a curious woman, but a woman all the same – the weaker sex needed to take the time to console her weak mind and soul. Pope Clement advised so. Her injuries, the sore ribs in her chest, her broken nose, her split lips and bruised eyes, all now healed under the careful consideration of a physician Crumwell hired, and nursing by gentle Mercy. But no one touched Nicóla, in order to maintain the secret of her sex, but all the same, they offered advice on making sure her face returned to normal, unlike so many damaged noses Nicóla had seen in her time. With luck or God's grace, perchance both, the tooth lost from Nicóla's mouth sat further back, more or less hidden when she smiled. Crumwell gave her a wondrous gift – a short brush made for teeth. The brushes came through Venice for years now, from lands far in the east, the home of so many spices and silks, and Crumwell made sure he got these brushes to help Nicóla's mouth as it healed. Already Nicóla started plans to trade these short brushes in London – easy profit from people who loved new and cheap items. Between Nicóla and Crumwell, they had enough contacts to gain supply, perchance even have them made somewhere in Europe.

The knock on her door opened Nicóla's green eyes to the start of the day. She peeked out from beyond the covers, her eyes hurting in the weak dawn sunrise. Only one person would be awake so early, wanting to come in even before the servants.

'Come in if you will,' Nicóla called with a yawn and sat up in her bed. She no longer covered herself with the bedcovers in Crumwell's company, for he visited early every morning for the past month now.

'Buongiorno, signora,' Crumwell said once he made sure the door closed behind him.

'Buongiorno, maestro.' Nicóla loved the smile which came to Crumwell's face when she called him master. Crumwell had such skill in hiding his thoughts and feelings, but always too eager to let his guard down in her presence. Crumwell came in, dressed in black as always, never anything but black, with his wavy hair combed and tucked behind his ears. His barber had already shaved Crumwell for the day, and his hair appeared trimmed also, the silver threads cut down to appear younger, as he did more often these days.

Crumwell sat perched on the edge of Nicóla's bed, careful not to ruffle the golden bedcovers. 'Come stai questa mattina?'

'I am well, my prince.'

'I am not the prince Machiavelli wrote of, Nicó.'

'The new ruler must determine all the injuries that he will need to inflict. He must inflict them once and for all,' Nicóla recited.

'Yes, I know that is a quote from Machiavelli's works. I am not a ruler; a mere servant to a master. I am not "The Prince" by Machiavelli.'

'It sounds like something you would say, Tomassito.'

'You must stop, for I am not "The Prince."'

'I must stop being so lazy, though, and be up as early as you.' Nicóla paused as she noticed Crumwell's gaze at the white ribbon tie at her throat, the neckline of her nightgown undone. She decided to leave it untied. 'I am more than recovered now and wish to return to work.'

'You are my guest, Nicóla; you need not do anything. You are under house arrest, so all you need to do is write reports to the Pope.'

'And report what?' Nicóla asked with a shrug. 'That I am in the height of luxury at Austin Friars? I have every need tended, and I live not as a man of the Church, but as a rich man once more? Tomassito Crumwell, the smartest man in England, treats me like a prince.'

'Shall you ever allow yourself to be addressed as a woman, even in my presence?'

'It is a habit, Tomassito. I must never slip. I am a man; I see the world through the eyes of a man. This way works, has for fifteen years.'

'Even so…'

'Even so, being caught could do me no end of trouble. I know what is at stake, so I shall not falter. Have you come to take away my letter to the Pope? I write only what you advised me to write.'

Crumwell helped Nicóla with her letters to Pope Clement. There seemed so little in the way of news of late. King Henry had not sent a single word to Austin Friars; Nicóla was in exile. But she could be sure Henry's spies would read every letter Nicóla sent to her old ally the Pope. All the letters said King Henry needed an urgent settlement of his "Great Matter." Crumwell looked down at the delicate stitching of the bed cover, his ageing hands brushing the needlework.

'You think of Wolsey,' Nicóla stated.

'Wolsey is at York Place on his own. Stephen Gardiner no longer works as his secretary. Many people have left Wolsey's household, knowing King Henry no longer favours him. Wolsey refuses to speak to Campeggio, who sends his prayers for your recovery, as always. I shall take today's letter to be sent to Rome, but this morning I come with news.'

'Please, do share. Until you relent on me being a patient and let me work on my idea of trading those eastern mouth cleaners…'

'I think a toothbrush might be a better title.'

'News, Tomassito!'

Crumwell's smile reappeared on his lips. They spent so much time together this past month, with these early morning talks before Crumwell started work for the day. Long dinners, walks in the garden as Nicóla's recovery went on, and always long nights over wine. They spoke of trading, of merchants they knew, the business they had dealt, their families, their ideas, the state of England in this fragile time. Religion so often reared its head, with Crumwell such a keen supporter of reformation and the growing Protestant principles. Nicóla was a Catholic safe in the bosom of Rome.

Crumwell licked his lips, reluctant to speak. He always prepared his lips this way for news he disliked, put this hand over his lips when he lied. So easy to tell his thoughts. 'The King is going away on progress, as late in the season as it is for such an occasion. He plans to visit many estates between now and the start of autumn.'

'Whether King Henry is in London or anywhere in this island kingdom is no matter. I am still imprisoned in Austin Friars, no?'

'Is it such a prison?' Crumwell said with a light laugh.

'Until there are peacocks in the garden, yes, well indeed,' Nicóla jested back to him and saw him shine a weak open smile, which made his golden eyes sparkle in return. This time, the sparkle quickly faded.

'King Henry is summoning both Cardinal Wolsey and your man Campeggio to Grafton House. Henry and Anne Boleyn are there to go hunting.'

'And this Gafton House?'

'Grafton House,' Crumwell corrected her accent. 'A manor, the home where King Henry's mother Elizabeth was born, and her mother before her, both English queens. It is special to Henry, who adored his mother as a boy. To call both Wolsey and Campeggio there is strange. Grafton House is some sixty miles from London, and the King is moving away from his troubles, not inviting them along the journey.'

'The King means to unsettle his two opponents.'

'Precisely what I feared.'

'Why fear, Tomassito?'

'Because Wolsey has my loyalty, and I am afraid for him, going to a king who is constantly surrounded by the Boleyn family.'

'You need to be careful, Tomassito, I have said this many times. Loyalty is the fullest measure of a man's honour, but it must be bestowed upon the deserving. Take it from me, I got pushed before the King and I betrayed the Pope, a man who would hold off the fires of hell in my name. I can but pray for forgiveness.'

'Wolsey has requested I accompany him to Grafton House, Nicó.'

'And you wish to accompany him?'

'I honestly must go to Grafton. I must know what the King plans.'

'You must stay in the good graces of the King and your Cardinal, a tricky line you must walk, Tomassito. Be careful.'

'Still, I must travel to Northamptonshire soon.'

'I shall tarry hither, no? Who will be my jailer?'

'The King said I must never let you out of my sight.'

'Is that the reason we are together so often, Tomassito? I hoped you enjoyed my company.'

The slightest of pinks flushed Crumwell's cheeks. 'I thought perchance you could accompany me to Grafton House.'

'I can ride at last?' Nicóla said, sitting up straight in her bed, and leaned forward towards Crumwell. 'Do you think it possible? Shall you ask King Henry?'

'Wolsey is the King's Lord Chancellor; without Wolsey, the King is in disarray. I cannot trouble the King with such a simple request.'

'Then I shall ride to this north… Northhemp manor and we shall spy on the situation together.'

'Northhamptonshire. Mr. Pompous, the Duke of Suffolk, shall be in attendance, though he is no ample lover of an annulment or Anne Boleyn.'

'Perchance we can upset the delicate pride of the Duke with our presence,' Nicóla replied, thinking of what a delight it could be.

'Word quickly spread that the Duke assaulted a humble attendant inside a monastery. It is not a sweet testament to any man's character. He is hurt by all the judgement placed on him at court.'

'Then we shall travel to this Grafton House and see if we can help our Cardinals.'

'Even though we no longer even know what our Cardinals require?'

'Mine needs to never grant an annulment, yours needs to do whatever suits his personal situation best,' Nicóla shrugged. 'I will one day return to Rome and inherit my fortune but you, Tomassito, need to live hither. I can be of service, even if it prevents your Cardinal from falling from his high place at court. In the end of all this, I matter not.'

'You matter, Nicó.'

'Let us have an adventure,' Nicóla replied and she shuffled toward Crumwell on her knees, and sat close to him. She placed a hand on his, still warm from her bedsheets, and felt him impress his fingers firmly against her skin. 'When the time is right, let us go with our Cardinals and resolve this matter without the meddling of so many judges, both on Earth and in heaven. Allow me to be of service, Tomassito, before I return to Rome forever.'

Nicóla stared at Crumwell, who held her gaze for a long while, the silence of early morning London ringing in her ears. She knew she needed to leave him soon, but Nicóla could feel safe in Crumwell's care a little longer.

Chapter 10 - September 1529
Grafton House, Grafton Regis, Northhamptonshire

I want to beest with those who knoweth seecryt thyngs, orelse be alone

Two full days' ride to Grafton House felt easy in the zest of summer, even for the Cardinals. The night's accommodation seemed welcome enough, but Crumwell's mind leaned not on the journey, nor its destination; only upon Nicóla. Dressed once again in her Italian finery, Nicóla rode with the Italian envoy around Cardinal Campeggio, a group of about twenty including guards. Crumwell watched her ride, sturdy in her saddle, deep in conversation. After a month of being confined to Austin Friars under house arrest, the Italians were quick to fill Nicóla with all their conversations.

The roads were hard and dry as they neared the town of Grafton. The fresh air of the surroundings, the trees green, the fields ready for harvesting, or filled with labourers doing just that, lifted a weight from Crumwell's shoulders. Every so often, he dropped back from his place in the train to where Nicóla rode, under the guise of still being her guardian, still under house arrest. But he could only find so many reasons to take his horse to hers; the risk of seeming foolish or suspicious settled around every discussion.

'Am I to be scolded for my movements?'

The voice took Crumwell from his thoughts of Nicóla into reality. There she sat, out of her place in the casual train which ambled through the shade of tall trees. She rode up alongside Crumwell and young Ralph Sadler, who also enjoyed the young Waif's company. Ralph was a young man of two and twenty years, and Nicóla was just nine and twenty; the pair made Crumwell feel his age at four and forty years of age. Ralph had lived with Crumwell for fifteen years; he saw Ralph as a son. He should have felt the same way for Nicóla, dear Francesco's child, but he could not confess to such simple thoughts.

'I shall not reprimand you this time,' Crumwell said and did not hide his soft smile as Nicóla trotted alongside him, her knee close to his.

Nicóla returned a grin, born in an expression which suggested revelry.

'How do we not know you shall try to escape as soon as the moment arises?' Ralph jested. 'You are well treated as our forced house guest, hither, riding the wild lands of England.'

'If I galloped from you, would you follow me as I made my escape?' Nicóla teased in reply. 'And where precisely would I go?'

'You Italians are slippery even when we trust you,' Crumwell commented.

Nicóla pursed her sweet lips together for a moment and spurred on her horse. She charged forward, past the guards at the front, and off the roads onto a lush green field surrounded by tall trees. In a heartbeat, Ralph charged after her as he laughed. Nicóla had better skills on the horse than Ralph, able to outrun him as he circled around on the field, moving back and forth, their laughter echoing back to the amused riders in the travel party. As they galloped the length of the field again, Nicóla's hat flew from her head, her lengthening rose-gold curls left flying in the wind. Ralph caught the hat as it flew past him and held it up to taunt her as she doubled back in his direction. Crumwell felt jealous; he wanted to be the one who caught her hat, held it in his hands.

'Curious,' Crumwell heard one of the guards, dressed in Wolsey's navy livery, say to another. 'Hair almost as long as a woman's but no woman can ride as well as the Waif can.'

'Italy is different,' Crumwell said as he watched his charges coming back in his direction. 'Pay no notice to Mr. Frescobaldi's outward appearance. There is surely a man's mind upon those slender shoulders.'

Ralph and Nicóla slowed their tired horses as they rejoined the group, the pair laughing to one another, almost as breathless as their animals. Crumwell felt a pain in his chest; jealousy. Crumwell felt jealous Nicóla laughed with young Ralph. How absurd to feel such a way. They looked young and merry, and Crumwell could not deny them a moment of fun. To feel jealous Nicóla laughed not with him made Crumwell chide himself; though the feeling would not so easily abate.

Within the hour, the party arrived at Grafton House, where so much of the court stayed with King Henry and his Anne. Crumwell needed to resist the urge to help Nicóla from her horse. A man to the outside world, Nicóla needed no assistance. She jumped from the horse as steady as Crumwell did, and gave the beast a pat as a servant took the reins from her gloved hands. She at once turned to help Campeggio and Crumwell needed to do the same and see Wolsey inside to rest before seeing the King. Only the Lord knew what the visit may bring.

'Oh, thank you so much, Tom,' Wolsey croaked as he got from his horse. 'I do so need to rest a while and change from my riding clothes at once.'

'Whatever is your wish,' Crumwell said, not taking his eyes from Nicóla, who walked just behind Campeggio as they disappeared inside Grafton House's large front door, led by the manor's steward. Crumwell took a step back behind Wolsey, who had a burst of energy as he entered the manor. Crumwell felt a thousand eyes on them, staring down from the windows above, heard whispers as they walked the stark grey stone halls in search of the Cardinal's rooms. To no avail; as they walked the enormous manor no servants arrived to serve Wolsey. Crumwell searched to find an answer and grabbed an older man carrying linens to rooms.

'I am sorry, Cardinal,' the stark, a middle-aged man dressed all black, the Tudor rose at his breast, said with his eyes cast downward. 'I am afraid there are no rooms for you hither at Grafton House.'

'I am Lord Chancellor of England!' Wolsey retorted, his feeble chest puffed under his red velvet robes. 'I am the advisor of the King himself! These lapses do not happen! The Italians are furnished, so why not me and my party?'

'We have simple lodgings for your companions, but alas, no such room for Your Eminence.'

Wolsey and Crumwell stood alone in the hallway as the man backed away, not an ounce of integrity in his tone. 'Do not burden yourself,' Crumwell assured his longtime friend. 'I shall assert you.'

A dark wooden door opened close by, and the curly brown head of Sir Henry Norris, the King's Groom of the Stool, appeared. 'Your Eminence,' he said in his typical gentle voice. 'Please, have my rooms, for I shall be in the King's rooms for most of my time, or else I can find room with Thomas Wyatt. It would be my honour to allow you into rooms assigned to me.'

Cardinal Wolsey rested his hand gently upon the slim shoulder of the middle-aged courtier. 'God willing, the King shall be as kind of heart as yourself, Norris.'

The Cardinal strode into the well-appointed, sunlit room and Crumwell stood at the doorway with Norris. 'How shall we find the King?' Crumwell muttered to Norris under his breath.

'You will find him impatient and in complete despair over the annulment, for he cannot wait a moment longer. I dare say Lady Anne shall tear Cardinal Wolsey into narrow pieces if she gains the opportunity.'

Crumwell poked his head into the privy chamber, a modest but well-lit room, windows overlooking tall trees along one side of the garden. But Wolsey stood front and centre, his hands thrust in the air as if expecting Jesus himself to walk in from the bedroom.

'Cardinal?'

'Do you not see?' Wolsey implored as he turned and dropped his ageing hands. 'Honestly, Tom, after a dozen years with you at my side? You do not see what is happening to us?'

'Your Eminence, I believe accidents happen.'

'But never do they involve me. I am God's man in England. I have ruled this country on Henry's behalf for twenty years. No one could forget I need a place to rest my head after the ride all the way from London. This is a deliberate act, one to humiliate me. Already all of Grafton House shall know of this. They shall know I was not expected as a guest, not expected to be comfortable, not at all on the King's mind. This is a deliberate and precise humiliation. The King means to throw me down.'

'Please, Your Eminence,' Crumwell replied with a sigh.

'You think I do not see when a man's time has come? Do you think I have not seen men cast out of the court, out from the King's affections? We may serve the wisest King in Christendom, but I also know when you are cast from the sunlight which is Henry's presence, you are never to be forgiven.'

'His Majesty forgave his sister Mary when she married Charles Brandon.'

'After considerable punishment! The King has brought me hither to humiliate me. You must leave me at once, Tom, before you too have the shadow cast upon yourself.'

'I am ready to bear all your burdens.'

'Only God can help now.'

Crumwell sighed again. 'Perchance I shall take care of your Earthly needs.' Crumwell left the tired Cardinal in his rooms, to seek out the chests of clothing Wolsey needed for dinner with King Henry. He trailed the long halls of the home once occupied by Henry's mother and her envied Woodville family, wondering where Ralph and the others had gone. But a booming voice echoing along the stone hallways made him stop in his tracks.

King Henry turned around a corner, a gesture thrown behind him to dismiss whoever irritated him with their questions. Crumwell bowed as the King approached, and expected Henry to pass. Instead, the King stopped before Crumwell, and Crumwell raised his eyes to the King's, surrounded by red cheeks, and an ermine-lined coat which clipped tight around his neck. The King gave a smell of fresh sweat, the smell of horse still upon his clothes.

'Mr. Crumwell,' the King said and brought his hands together around his stomach, his wide ruby ring contracting a thick finger. 'You are unexpected at Grafton House.'

'I am accompanying Cardinal Wolsey now that Archdeacon Stephen Gardiner has left the Cardinal's employ, Your Majesty.'

'I wanted Gardiner for myself,' Henry said. 'I receive the letters your Waif writes and read them all before they are sent to the Pope.'

'And are you content with the current situation, Your Majesty?'

'I am pleased the Italian is doing his part. Lady Anne is pleased we have the ear of the Pope now, in having the Waif under arrest. But as always, the delay in receiving mail from Rome is causing me endless pains. Where is the Waif now?'

'Lodging with Cardinal Campeggio, Your Majesty. Gathering information as we speak, I do not doubt.'

'Wise of you to lodge him with Campeggio!' Henry replied and slapped a heavy hand on Crumwell's shoulder.

Crumwell smiled, relieved the King did not mind the presence of Nicóla at Grafton House.

'I shall speak thus with both Wolsey and Campeggio tonight. I understand the Italians will return home?'

'His Eminence Cardinal Campeggio has come to say good morrow and shall head home to Rome.'

'But the Waif cannot leave.'

'Your Majesty?'

'Do you think I am going to relinquish such an asset back to Rome, Crumwell? Not for a moment do I believe so. We shall have to come up with a way of keeping the Waif without alerting the Pope to his situation.'

'I can assist you, I am certain, Your Majesty.' Nicóla to stay in England! Crumwell's heart jumped with joy.

'You are finding yourself to be a comfort to me, Crumwell, and I thank you for it,' the King continued. 'I can assume you think an annulment is possible in the near future?'

'I am hither to serve my master,' Crumwell replied. Whether Wolsey's rooms got forgotten, by hate or malice, did not need to be asked. 'You are my King, Your Majesty, and I shall assist wherever I can be of service.'

'Do you have any idea how it feels, to be in love with someone but denied their love? Have you ever looked at a woman and wanted her for love, even if it provides no advantage for your family? Do you have any idea of the pain it causes my heart and my immortal soul to be denied the right to marry legally?'

'I have some idea, Your Majesty.'

The King cast a stern brow. 'I do not enjoy lies, Crumwell. How could anyone know my pain?'

'I am widowed, Your Majesty. My wife was a favourable woman, and I was well-married. Elizabeth garnished my life with a son, and also my daughters, God rest their souls. But …'

'Ahh…' the King broke into a smile. 'There is a new lady in your life, Crumwell. Can you not have her? Not even as a mistress?'

'She is not the type to be a mistress, Your Majesty.'

'Young?'

'As is your Lady Anne in years.'

'Beautiful?'

'Captivating,' Crumwell sighed; it felt so relieving to say it aloud.

'Why can you not marry her? Is she noble?'

'Well, no, Your Majesty. She is not from a noble house.'

'Wealthy?'

'Yes, a very wealthy family. With considerable connections. But foreign, Your Majesty.'

'Foreign? It is not like a commoner such as yourself to marry a foreign bride. I see your dilemma. Does she know of your love?'

'I have wrestled to hide my affection, Your Majesty. Not always as well as I would hope.' God in heaven, why start such conversation? The entire court would know of the affair by dinner! At least no one would suspect Nicóla as the object of his affection. Surely even God himself thought lowly of Crumwell's feelings.

'Love denied is a blight upon the soul,' the King said and looked through the window out onto the gardens below. 'I swear my heart burns.'

'Hearts burn when thoughts drift to love. Even a mere thought of a woman talking to another can hurt your heart, your mind.' It was all true; Crumwell did not know Nicóla's location in the manor and he needed to know, like a lovesick fool.

'Yes!' The King grabbed Crumwell's shoulders again. 'It is almost as if my vision is impaired at times, such are my denied affections.'

'You find yourself thinking of when you shall see or hear from your love, and it meddles with daily activity.'

'You do understand, Crumwell! If you can help me with Lady Anne, perchance then I can assist you in getting yourself a foreign bride. I am the King, and I can command anything I wish, and abroad I have much power also.'

'You are too kind, Your Majesty.'

'I shall let you continue with your day, Mr. Crumwell. Always pleasant to break with you. Perchance your skills can be useful again soon.'

Crumwell remained bowed until the King had departed, his guards marching in time behind him and his dragging coat. Once again in silence, Crumwell skimmed the hallways back downstairs to the carts which carried their supplies, parked in neat rows beside the stables. What an ill-starred moment in time. The last thing Crumwell needed was court rumours about him and the obtaining of a foreign bride. Nothing could be done which could uncover Nicóla's identity. Crumwell felt suddenly halting, dispirited. And the King's meeting with Wolsey had not even yet begun.

Chapter 11 - September 1529
Grafton House, Grafton Regis, Northamptonshire

Seecryts art errours for lyars

Nicóla closed her eyes as she leaned against the stone doorway into the main dining hall of Grafton House. The room glowed before her, more from the wine than the candles. She opened her green gaze again and refocused on the festivities. The dinner heralded a sumptuous affair, and the drinking and dancing afterwards wondrous and lavish, normal for a king like Henry. Henry welcomed Wolsey with open arms as if nothing had ever occurred, and the acrimony which flowed from Lady Anne could be seen – her hatred for the Cardinal possessed such rage. Now, hours had passed, and with the King drunk, his hand firmly on Lady Anne's leg as they sat together at the head table. Henry's laughter became loud enough to fill the room with gaiety. It seemed easy for a foreigner to shy away from the party, too lavish and vain to attend.

It brought back memories for Nicóla in so many ways. The sweet smell reminded her of the wine back at Austin Friars, nights sipping with Crumwell in her private rooms. The smell of the spices reminded Nicóla of her father, their trips to Venice to purchase shipments to trade, saffron, cloves, rosemary, and pepper. The smell of the roast meats reminded her of the summer parties once held in Florence, as a member of the Medici inner circle, filled with ruthless men only kind and generous to those they admired, such as Nicóla and her father. The joy of the party, the melodious music made her think of times even further gone now, when she still dressed as a woman, a true young woman, caught up in the frivolity and appetite of those around her. As ever, Nicóla appeared as a member of a party standing on the sidelines as the noblemen took up with beautiful women.

She watched the important people in the room. She knew the King was well and truly distracted, likewise the Lady Anne. Her father and brother sat close by, eager to whisper into the King's ear. Wolsey sat at another table, holding his goblet as if nothing had ever gone wrong in the world, a smile which reminded everyone how much the King loved him. Campeggio sat beside him, quiet, too old to enjoy anything more than eyeing the young girls. As always, Crumwell sat near Wolsey, talking to someone Nicóla did not know. Crumwell constantly looked in her direction, but she never returned his gaze. Shaky-hands Gardiner appeared deep in talks with the pompous Duke of Suffolk in the far corner, their heads bowed in conversation. Mark Smeaton, one of Wolsey's young musicians, played his lute by the windows with the other musicians, and every so often Nicóla threw him a wink in reply to his own. Plenty of men like talented young Mark preferred the company of those whose gender seemed a little confused. They mistook Nicóla as an object of affection, something she could never be for them. Chastity was Nicóla's companion.

With all the major players accounted for, more or less, Nicóla sighed to herself, unable to enjoy the party. She longed to go home to Rome, where her identity rested as Frescobaldi, the man of female favour. No one spoke of it; they simply accepted it and no one uttered a word. Hither, while no one questioned Nicóla – why would they? – the whole secret took more effort to maintain. The bindings around her chest tugged and irritated her tonight; they had moved constantly during the two days' ride, with no chance to remove them or bathe, and Grafton House offered no opportunity either. She shared a room tonight with Campeggio's son Alessandro. Young Alessandro knew not the truth of Nicóla, the secret also not extending to conservative Campeggio. At least she felt safe with Alessandro, who would never meddle with a man of confusing origins, the ultimate companion of the Pope.

A crude hand thrust itself upon Nicóla's shoulder, and she spun around on one foot, ready to face whoever accosted her from the darkness of the hallway. There stood three young men dressed in the red and white livery of the man who stood behind them, Thomas Howard, the leathery Duke of Howard. How had he come up behind her? He usually sat close to his niece, the Lady Anne, and appeared as if he could barely stay awake on all the wine. All four men stood in semi-darkness, only the Duke himself with any facial expression.

'Your Grace,' Nicóla bowed. The man in the late fifties, a round man with pasty weathered skin and a long nose, regarded Nicóla up and down, the sparkles of his embroidered doublet catching the minimal light in the hallway.

'Why s-sstand hither in the doorway, Waif?' No one could mock Norfolk's stutter; his rank protected him from such shame.

'I am in need of air, Your Grace,' Nicóla bluffed and stood up straight, though no match for any of the men of the group. 'I feel sorrow if I have somehow troubled you with my presence.'

'Take him,' Norfolk said to his men. Two of them grabbed Nicóla by the shoulders and they started down the hallway behind the round Norfolk, the third guard so close behind that Nicóla felt his breath on her neck. They entered the first door off the hallway, a narrow barely-lit room, the party still echoing into their ears through stone walls. The guards shoved Nicóla and she fell, her black hat coming from her head.

'You are a s-s-strange little Waif,' Norfolk growled as he stood over Nicóla, the guards all stepping back on command.

'I am hither only to serve my master,' Nicóla said and held her hat with both hands, determined not to seem troubled by the accosting.

'I know you s-s-speak English, s-s-so do not even try the pretense of confusion.' Norfolk must have had a spy in Austin Friars. Smart.

'Your Grace, I am humble in your presence.'

'You sh-sh-should be stomped on in my presence, like when that bastard S-S-Suffolk took a s-s-swing at you!' Norfolk's face had already started to change from pink angered cheeks to a constrained red face, inflamed in anger.

'How do I offend, Your Grace?' Nicóla tried to sit as comfortable as possible and tried never to respond to anger; that so often unsettled people.

'Who are you, distinctly, W-W-Waif? We know you are no attendant for C-C-Campeggio.'

That caught Nicóla off guard. 'Your Grace, my name is Nicóla Frescobaldi. I am a scholar in Rome, and no, I am not a priest, as I have not taken holy orders. I am still studying the word of God before I commit my life to the Church.'

'Why would the P-P-Pope himself take such care with you? Why sh-sh-should you live with the Pope in Rome, in his palace? The King thinks you a sp-sp-spy!'

'The King knows of my behaviour, Your Grace,' Nicóla replied. 'His Majesty knows of my movements and beliefs.'

'Yet he calls me hither to accuse you of heresy.'

'Heresy?' Nicóla choked on the word. Heresy; punishable by death. 'Your Grace, I am a scholar in the Pope's embrace. I am no heretic.'

From underneath his fur-lined cloak, the Duke provided a letter. At once Nicóla saw the broken seal of Pope Clement. All the bland letters sent to His Holiness in the last month now received answers, and the King had obviously read such before Nicóla even knew of its existence. The Duke unfurled the paper and his beady brown eyes scowled over the wide lettering. 'Why would the P-P-Pope write to you, requesting your immediate return to R-R-Rome now the King's marriage is s-ssecure? Since when did the Pope become assured of such security?'

'I wish I knew his mind.' Nicóla kept her words calm and measured, as she no idea what the letter contained, she could mount no defence for her safety.

'It says here the P-P-Pope has received an appeal from Queen K-K-Katherine and he has granted Her Majesty an appeal! Never sh-sh-shall Wolsey or Campeggio decide on an annulment! You, his trusty young spy, surely knew of th-th-this all along!'

Norfolk kicked Nicóla, catching her off guard. He struck her in the jaw; much like Suffolk had done a month prior. She fell back and steadied herself on her elbows, tasting blood in her mouth. Norfolk's spittle landed on her face as he leaned over her again, the smell of a long-unwashed man wafting over the pair. 'Wh-wh-what brings you?' Norfolk spat on Nicóla's doublet.

'To assist ageing Cardinal Campeggio in his mission to advise on God's will.' Nicóla's words sent blood down her chin, her eyes watering from the pain.

'Then why does it s-s-say, in this letter, your inheritance sh-sh-shall be granted upon your return to Rome? Why does this letter s-s-state you have completed your s-s-so-called mission to such great effect? And why does it state you can be married as s-s-soon as you go home to Rome? Why would a Pope care for an inheritance?'

Giulio must have not yet read of Nicóla's house arrest at Austin Friars. Giulio had written thinking Nicóla safe and well, and had not written in code. That suggested His Holiness was having a bout of ill-mindedness again. 'Pope Clement instructed me to aid Cardinal Campeggio,' Nicóla said again, wondering how to get away from Norfolk and his men. They barred the door with their stiff stance. 'Your Grace, I am an only son, and when my father passed…'

'Who lets an only s-s-son enter the Church?' Norfolk scoffed. 'That is folly.' Without warning the door behind the guards opened. 'Leave us!' Norfolk cried the words so angry they must have burned in his throat.

'I come directly from the King, Your Grace.'

The voice changed everything for Nicóla. Crumwell's voice sounded like pure music. Crumwell edged into the dark room and away from the angry-faced guards. 'May I ask why you have laid a young man on the floor, Your Grace?'

'Ah yes, I knew you w-w-would be hither in a moment, Thomas Crowmell.'

'Crumwell,' he corrected the Duke.

'These past months y-y-you and the Waif have appeared m-m-much intimate.' Norfolk curved his thin lips into a dirty smile as if to suggest much of Crumwell and Nicóla's time together.

Crumwell looked past Norfolk at Nicóla, their eyes meeting in a moment. 'Stai bene?' he asked about her well-being.

'Si,' she muttered back, though not sure if she spoke the truth. Blood smeared her teeth.

'Curse your st-st-stupid language no one l-l-learns,' Norfolk interrupted.

'What is your business with Mr. Frescobaldi?' Crumwell asked. 'He is under my protection, by order of King Henry.'

'And I am under order from H-H-Henry to question the foreigner,' Norfolk replied, his anger cooling. He had obviously faked his temper to frighten Nicóla. It began to work, too.

'Perchance I can be of assistance.' Crumwell snaked his way around Norfolk before the Duke could object. He bent down to Nicóla and took her hand, be damned how it may appear to the already suspicious Norfolk. For the first time, she looked weakened, more so than when pompous Suffolk beat her, but Nicóla could not help herself. Once Crumwell read the letter, he might hate her. Would hate her. The look in his eyes when he disliked someone could reduce a man to stone; being on the receiving end of his anger induced faintheartedness.

'Is there a reason why I should worry about a commoner being so familiar with a foreign spy?' Norfolk tossed the letter from the Pope at Crumwell.

Crumwell swiped up the letter before Nicóla could, and he helped her to her feet. 'Your Grace,' Nicóla replied, a last attempt to remain calm, 'it is as I told you. I am an only son. I only entered the Church as a layman after my father's passing, so there was never a problem with being the only son entering the Church. I am to care for my inheritance and pass it to my sister upon her marriage. I know the Pope did not write in English, he does not speak the tongue. I pray you, while reading Latin, Your Grace, perchance you mistook my sister's marriage for mine, as it is I who shall need to pay her dowry?'

At once, Crumwell's head snapped towards Nicóla but she did not respond, her eyes fixed on Norfolk. 'I can read L-L-Latin,' the old man sniffed and moved from one foot to another.

'Of course, Your Grace, but all the wonderful wine at this celebration can force confusion, even from a king,' she replied.

'Why would King Henry ask you to question Mr. Frescobaldi on such a subject?' Crumwell asked the Duke with a timid voice, probably to soothe him.

'You know the King,' Norfolk replied and tucked his thumb into his belt, his codpiece looking grossly oversized. 'Henry can n-n-never let just one person deal with an issue. He knows the Italian Waif is a spy for the Pope and lets you w-w-watch him. Yet, s-s-sometimes you need to be tested. You are just a commoner. One bloody solid with m-m-money, but still a commoner, C-C-Crowmell.'

'Crumwell. But I shall take the compliment,' Crumwell corrected him and squeezed the letter tight in his hand. 'I shall return the letter to King Henry if you wish. You can report you frightened a foreigner into speaking with you about his family thousands of miles away. Quite the noble act.'

'Do not pretend to tell me what is n-n-noble.' Norfolk looked Crumwell up and down for a long moment. With a simple hand gesture, he commanded his men to leave the room. In a heartbeat they disappeared, Crumwell and Nicóla left in the dusty space, a single candle in the far corner, presumably lit in preparation for her interrogation.

'Once again, I must thank you,' Nicóla said and looked down at her hand in Crumwell's. 'How did you know to come hither?'

'I noticed you disappear, and I followed. Norfolk's voice is easy to hear through walls.'

'You know the King sent him. The King will have seen you come after me.'

'What of it?'

'Henry is testing you. He knows you and I spend much time together. Henry knows of the Tyndale book I accidentally gave Lady Anne. And clearly, he suspects something in the words from the Pope.'

'We all wonder of your connection to the Pope.'

'If you knew, you would wish you did not.'

Crumwell let go of Nicóla's hand and picked up her hat from the floor, not taking his wide golden eyes from hers. He placed the soft cap on Nicóla's head and brushed her rose-gold hair behind her ears to complete the costume. But one hand lingered on her throat. Crumwell would be able to feel the pulse in her neck, pounding despite her outward calm. Nicóla did not want to him to move away, but she wanted the letter. They stood together, in total silence, total stillness in the room where he could kiss her. She was the child of his best friend. She still possessed her youth. Despite all the facts, she still felt for Crumwell, the double-minded man with the golden eyes. Her Machiavellian prince.

'Dear God, you are the doctor and physician of my soul. You are the salvation of those who turn to You,' Nicóla prayed. 'I beseech You to make powerless, banish, and drive out every sinful presence which shall make me commit my soul to evil.'

'What shall make your soul committed to evil?' Crumwell whispered.

'I am under no protection from God,' she muttered as his mouth came closer to hers.

'My past sins must not grow inside me again to hurt those around me.' Crumwell rested his forehead against hers, his eyes closed. He should not kiss Nicóla, she knew it, and he knew it.

They stood against one another for the longest time and Nicóla wanted to cry. Tears stung at her eyes. She came to England to use her influence over Crumwell to get to Wolsey, to make sure no annulment went through. Nicóla needed to manipulate Crumwell, not feel impure, sinful thoughts for the man.

'Hear, Lord, the prayers we offer from contrite hearts. Have pity on us as we acknowledge our sins. Lead us back to the way of holiness. Protect us now and always from the wounds of sin. May we ever keep safe in all its fullness the gift Your love once gave us and Your mercy now restores,' she recited.

'Amen,' they repeated together, and Crumwell stepped away.

'What shall you do with the letter from the Pope?' Nicóla asked, blinking tears from her eyes. She pulled a cloth from her pocket to wipe the blood from her lips. Perchance that was not wise to move; the blood acted as a barrier to sin.

'I shall keep it, I suppose, until such time the King wants it back. What did Norfolk mean by your sister's marriage?'

'It is confusing.'

Crumwell unfurled the crushed letter and Nicóla moved forward to cover the Latin with her fingers. At once she saw Giulio's hand on the page. Once a strong and virile man, now damaged by time and injury, Giulio produced wide scrawling letters on the page. Crumwell's stern brow clouded in judgement, as he did not like Nicóla trying to shield the news. 'You are to return to Rome at once,' Crumwell read. 'But King Henry commanded you tarry in London.'

'When?'

'Henry said those true words just this afternoon, to me personally.' Crumwell kept reading, his eyes despising the words beneath an ever-increasing frown. 'You will receive your father's inheritance on the return for ensuring the King did not gain an annulment.'

'It is not simple.'

'Deny it no more! You are a spy of the Pope!' Crumwell clapped a hand over his mouth, shocked by his own words.

'I am no spy,' Nicóla implored and reached for Crumwell but he took a few steps back. 'I came to make sure Campeggio stuck to his task of blocking an annulment! I told you so! He needed some little whispers in his ear. But Campeggio agreed to no annulment from the beginning – I did nothing. I am hither to soothe Giulio's fears.'

'His name is Pope Clement the Seventh. Why must you call him by his Earthly name?'

'I know him as Cardinal Giulio de' Medici. We were close once, long before his head injury. None of this is news to you. Our families are close…'

'But they are the Medici family,' Crumwell said, pleading in his eyes. 'They are not virtuous people.'

'They are ruthless and they are men of business. I am one of them, cloaked under a good family name. I am a liar when I say I wish to be a man of the Church, but…'

'You are not even a man!' Crumwell replied. 'Dear God, please, let me not lust for a man.'

'You lust for me?' Nicóla asked, starting to feel more control again.

'You know I do, and I should not.' Crumwell now cared not for the letter between his fingers. Nicóla knew she should never use Crumwell's feelings against him, but she had no choice.

'No, you should not. Lust is a sin which will lead us to hell.'

'I am already marked for hell, I do fear.'

'I was marked for hell from the first moment the Medici suggested to my father I become a man of business. I should return to Rome and my original plans should be maintained. My life is in Rome; my life is owned by the Medici Pope. You must tarry hither and be of service to your Cardinal.' Crumwell returned to the letter, and Nicóla knew there was no point in distracting him any longer. 'The Pope writes… he writes you can receive your inheritance money. If all you had to do was complete your envoy to London, why ask me to funnel money from Antwerp?'

'Because the Pope holds conditions over the money.'

Crumwell turned back to the letter. 'You are to be married on your release back to Rome.' Now Crumwell would not look at her. 'You are to be married immediately on your arrival in Rome, as stated in your pre-contract.' His voice enacted a strange calm. Nicóla swallowed hard. She did not wish Crumwell to hear these words, in any way. The letter from the Pope made a pre-contract, the betrothal practically bound by God Himself. There was no way to explain it; no words could soothe the heart breaking before her. 'You came hither months ago,' Crumwell whispered as he screwed up the letter again. 'You could have mentioned this at any opportunity.' The paper slipped from his forlorn hands. 'How? You are a man, and yet you are to marry, what… a man? Are you to live as a man married to another man? A woman living as a man? Or marry a woman? Does this betrothed know you pretend to be a man?'

'He knows,' Nicóla confessed. 'He has known me for much of his life. We are to marry in private and I can continue to live as I do. I am simply Nicóla Frescobaldi, merchant and accountant for the Medici family. With the Pope's blessing, one can do as they wish. The marriage is solely for my inheritance to go to my future husband. I asked you to see if the money from my father's Antwerp accounts may be released so I could take the money and run from the Medici family.'

'You used me all along. The Pope sent you to attend me, did he not? I lived as a friend to your father, a man known for loyalty, fealty. You have used me since the moment you arrived in London.'

'Oh, Tomassito, please do not say such things. I am not entirely honest, but I never wished to use you! You are the most intelligent man I have ever known. You inspire something egregious within me. I have not met a man such as you in my entire life. You bewitch people in a way I have never seen in a man, you captivate with your words; even the King is wrapped up in your presence. You wield an invisible charm even you may not understand.'

Nicóla's pleading fell on deaf ears. Crumwell's face hardened, his eyes on the floor. 'You are the Pope's mistress, are you not?'

'No, I am not.'

'The Medici dress you as a man to hide the fact the Pope has a mistress.'

'Giulio has not had a mistress since he became the Pope. That condition was plain, both by the Church and by his family. They wanted a chaste, pious Pope in Giulio. The last Medici Pope liked to keep company with other men. Giulio needed to be a wise pope, and the Church has suffered so many outside scandals, like reformation all over Europe, and the sacking of Rome. If the Pope has a mistress, I have no knowledge. Giulo is not a healthy man; I doubt he has the power to do his duty by a woman.'

'You are an expert liar.'

'I have spoken nothing but truth.'

'Yes, by being intelligent. There is no other woman like you. You are intelligent on a scale no woman should be able to achieve.'

'A mystery of God. I can assure you that I suffer all the other frailties of being a woman.'

'You tell the truth by speaking in riddles. Were you Giulio de' Medici's mistress? Not Pope Clement's mistress, were you Cardinal Giulio de' Medici's mistress?'

Nicóla could not subdue a man like Thomas Crumwell. The man had a mind unlike any she had met; he understood so much. He listened, instead of spoke. His mind stretched so far he had discovered her darkest secret in a dusty little room behind the gaiety of a royal party. 'I spent a year as the mistress of Giulio de' Medici,' she whispered. 'I had just turned 14, and Giulio was already your age; thirty years older than me. But I was seduced by him; I could not help myself. When my father discovered the secret, he felt mortified. I could not be married to Giulio de' Medici, no matter how much money my father had amassed. Giulio already held the seat of Cardinal of Florence, in line to be the next Pope. I am damaged; I am sullied in the eyes of God and man. But my father had put so much time and energy into my education, his favourite child, the daughter of his first wife. That is when it was suggested, by Giulio, that I live as a man and work for my father. I could never marry; I have no virtue, no honour. In return for holding the secret of Giulio's meddling with a girl, the Medici helped my father's business thrive in Florence, Rome, Venice, Antwerp, London. I have kept far away from Giulio. I did not see him for twelve years, until I went to him after the sacking of Rome. Giulo is not the handsome and powerful man he used to be, not after being imprisoned and beaten by the Emperor's soldiers. He is weak, feeble. He can barely remember me some days.'

'So who is this husband you will take?'

'Alessandro is one of the Medici bastards. Being a bastard is not frowned upon in Italy as it is hither. The Pope himself is a bastard child. Giulio lay with one of the household's maids at a young age, a Moorish girl from Africa. She bore his child, but with Giulio destined for the Church, his nephew Lorenzo took the child into his household. Lorenzo's family raised the child as a bastard son alongside Lorenzo's bastard daughter, Catherine de' Medici. Giulio is seeking a good marriage for Catherine, a royal match. Once the family takes back control of their home city, they shall install the son, the young Alessandro, known as Il Moro, the dark-skinned Moor, as Duke of Florence, and I am wealthy enough to help him.'

'You are to be Duchess of Florence.'

'Alessandro is only nineteen; to him I am old and I am a monster from God. He is a spiteful young man and he wants to marry me as little as I wish to marry him. But it means I have no access to my inheritance, which father left the Medicis to care for, as I am merely a woman. This is the best solution; the Medici get my father's wealth and I get to marry into the family which cradled me, despite me being so sullied.'

'You fornicated with the Cardinal destined to be Pope, and now you shall marry his son. The Pope has given his mistress to his bastard son. No wonder King Henry thinks of breaking from Rome, the way the Germans have done. All of you are loathsome.'

'Tomassito, please…'

'Master Crumwell! I will tell Henry you must be returned to Italy with Campeggio immediately. You can leave at dawn! You can go back to your sinful Florentine life. Your father would be truly angered by you, Nicóletta. How could you be so sinful and wicked, born of a father so pious? You dress as a man and yet you are a whore!'

'I agreed to all of this until I met you!' Nicóla cried as Crumwell reached for the door. 'I want away from the Church, I want away from the Medicis, but they will never let me go, and as a lowly woman, I have no rights. I cannot pose as a man forever.'

'None of this is my worry, Mr. Frescobaldi.' Crumwell had turned colder than a Venetian winter. Only minutes earlier Nicóla had briefly imagined him undressing her; now he would never look at her again.

'I am under house arrest, by order of the King, under your protection.'

'Either you leave with Campeggio for Rome, or can go to the Tower in London, neither way shall burden me. I shall not help in getting money out of Antwerp. If the King questions any of this, I shall tell him you are a papal spy. They shall burn you on account of handing a heretical book to Anne Boleyn.'

'Just like that, you can have me taken away?'

'You will do things our way in England.'

Chapter 12 – September 1529
Grafton House, Grafton Regis, Northhamptonshire

Sylent seecryts sitteth in dark palaces, wayting for dethroning

Crumwell considered begging to God, to make sure he would not vomit in the chapel. In the dead of night, hours before Mass would begin, but long after the party of the evening, he walked towards the altar. His heart, sagging deep in his chest, burned with anger and longing.

The tiny candles lit beneath a golden statue of Jesus guided the way, to a God who held the answers, the salvation that Crumwell's aching soul needed in the dead of night. But as Crumwell moved towards the front of the dark chapel, the shape of another praying soul appeared from the darkness. A woman, her head against her hands in prayer, a tiny voice deep in a begging whisper to God. Even in the tiny tone of her voice, Crumwell could hear her agony, hidden under her long auburn hair. He considered backing away to instead sit at the back of the Grafton House chapel, but it was too late. Her head tilted up and her black eyes spotted him. Anne Boleyn.

'Master Cremwell,' she whispered and sniffed through her tears.

'Beg your pardon, Lady Anne.' Crumwell crossed himself and turned to leave Anne to her prayers.

'What brings you hither at this hour, when even the priest cannot see you?' she murmured.

Crumwell turned back to the sullen Anne who remained on her knees. Her face, red from crying, her eyes puffy from lack of sleep and her constant worries about Henry's divorce.

'The salvation of God, the same as you, no doubt.' Crumwell did not move from the altar or any closer to the King's mistress.

'Can you not just go to your most beloved Cardinal for that?' Anne said, her voice angry in an instant. 'Your Cardinal, who can do no wrong in Henry's eyes, who always gets his way.'

'A meeting and an invitation to dinner does not mean the King is reconciled to the legatine court decision, Lady Anne. It would be too early to suggest Cardinal Wolsey is in the King's good graces just yet.'

'You are just another one of his henchmen,' Anne spat.

'His best henchman. Tonight, my Lady, I have never felt further from God than any man alive.'

Anne frowned a touch. 'Should you not be happy, drunk on the knowledge Henry is taking Wolsey's counsel again?'

'A calm and friendly evening does not solve all the ills of the court. If the sun comes up tomorrow, not one of us knows what the world will look like.'

'If? It is God's will that the sun rises every morning,' Anne said, her voice just above a whisper now.

'I would not mind if we never saw the sun again.'

Anne gestured to the seat next to her, and Crumwell took the invitation. Rather than sitting, he knelt down next to the Lady Anne and clasped his hands in prayer, the same position as she. Anne held her right sleeve between her fingers to cover her tiny sixth fingernail, even though darkness covered all. 'Henry tells me the Pope writes to your Italian Waif, instructing all to return home to Rome.'

'Yes, they will leave tomorrow, with the King's blessing.'

'Henry also whispered to me that you wished to take a foreign bride.'

'The King is far ahead of me on the subject of any marriage.'

Crumwell almost smiled at the thought of Henry and Anne thinking of a Crumwell wedding. 'I cannot take a wife, Lady Anne. To love anyone would be a betrayal of my Elizabeth, the fine wife she made for me.'

'Henry said you are desperate for love, though.'

'His Majesty loves to love,' Crumwell murmured and rested his chin on his hands, his eyes on the altar candles. 'It matters none now, for that woman… she is pre-contracted.'

'A pre-contract can be voided,' Anne replied. 'Wolsey himself made sure I could not marry Henry Percy when I fell in love.'

Crumwell turned to face Anne, and she bit her bottom lip. Anne Boleyn wanted to marry the Duke of Northumberland five years ago and pre-contracted herself to Henry Percy. Wolsey had forbidden the marriage, Anne too lowly for the young Duke. Oh, what an error to turn Anne Boleyn away from Percy, to make an enemy of her. The realm would be a different place had the King not got his chance to love Anne. But she just admitted to real love with Henry Percy, something she had denied to the King, Crumwell knew so. Wolsey hushed the pre-contract with Henry Percy, under threats Crumwell personally delivered. Anne had retracted any notions of wanting Percy. But here she sat, on her knees in the chapel, unguarded with her secrets in the middle of the night.

'Love wanders the gardens the way a blind man might, my Lady,' Crumwell said, to soothe the worry she had in her moment of admission. 'Love knows there are sweet smelling flowers about, but, like the blind man, love cannot see the flower. Love could smell a rose or a poisonous weed, too blind to know the difference.'

'It is most definite, Master Cremwell,' Anne's French accent catching his name as always. 'But what if you are the rose, caught by the blind love? The blind love, as the blind man, may be able to escape his wrongs, but what of the flower? How does the flower escape?'

Anne Boleyn cried in the chapel because King Henry wanted her, not because he could not gain the annulment. Crumwell knew so little of Anne, for no one but her family and their allies could get close to her. But her professed love for King Henry was known throughout England, and she was hated for it. 'My Lady, are you the blind man, or the flower?'

'I want to be neither some nights.'

'I must agree.'

'Love causes nothing but trouble.'

'Amen.' The pair crossed themselves and Anne sat in silence for a few moments.

'The whole country is waiting for me to fall from my place beside the King,' Anne said, and Crumwell noticed her eyes wet with tears again. 'I can do no right in anyone's eyes. I want to be the Queen. I want to be by Henry's side. I have made my choices, my sacrifices, but all these delays… Henry has loved me for years already and yet no end is in sight with his marriage. Meanwhile, I age and have not given a husband a son. I shall never gain the chance.' Anne broke down in tears, but Crumwell did not move a hand to comfort her. He was only a commoner and Anne, while not much higher than him, would not like to be touched, he felt sure.

'My Lady,' Crumwell stumbled, uneasy in her anguish, though grateful it alleviated his own. 'My Lady, the King loves you very much, your time shall come.'

'Everyone calls me a whore, a concubine, or "that woman". Your Cardinal calls me "the night crow". I am no whore. My sister, she is a whore, but not I. My virtue is one thing no man will take from me; I shall grant it.'

Crumwell believed Anne at that moment, she so unguarded and in pain on her knees at the altar. She would not lie at this moment. Anne had not yet slept with the King, as many thought. Perchance if she did slip into Henry's bed, then he would have won the hunt, enjoyed the thrill of the chase, and forget Lady Anne Boleyn. She appeared strikingly pleasant, not a beauty destined for artworks perchance, but eye-catching all the same, her auburn hair, her black eyes, even her skin darker than many. She walked with such confidence, spoke with such intelligence, jested as if only she could make a man laugh, and danced like a feather in the breeze. A woman as charming and poised as Anne Boleyn, raised in the French royal court, would not slip into the King's bed, like her sister did all those years ago, left with two bastard children.

'When a woman gives away her honour, she gives away part of her soul,' Crumwell said, his eyes on Jesus before him, shining above the candles. 'When a woman is without virtue, she could succumb to any number of foul ideas.' Like Nicóla and her decision to marry her former lover's son. Just the thought of her sweet face made Crumwell's stomach turn, his pain returning three-fold.

'You speak with anger, Master Cremwell.'

'I speak with sadness.'

'Life is much filled with sadness. Only my dear brother Georgie can make me smile some days. If I could, I would be in his bed now, talking with him as he soothed all my worries. Alas, Georgie has another bedfellow this night.'

Crumwell imagined Anne and George, a man so alike his sister, sitting on a bed together, perchance laughing, talking together. Perchance as merry as Crumwell felt with Nicóla while she recovered at Austin Friars.

'George is with his wife, I am sure,' Crumwell mumbled.

'Jane? Gracious, no. The woman is so quiet, and never enough for a knave like my Georgie. What a choice to pair a prize like Georgie to Jane Parker, a nobody. No, my Georgie likes the company of many others. A man's needs must be met. This night I also tried the room of my dear Thomas Wyatt, but he is sharing with Henry Norris tonight, and Norris, he can never keep a secret, bless his sweet heart.'

'You spend time with Thomas Wyatt also?'

'Oh yes, Thomas and I have known one another for many years. He writes me the most beautiful poetry in all of Christendom. I can trust him with my secrets.'

'I heard Wyatt fell in love with you.'

'In times past, but he knows I belong to the King now. I am fortunate to have men like Georgie, like Thomas, and even chatty Henry Norris as my close friends.' Anne seemed comfortable in the company of all the men of Henry's privy chamber, surrounded by people who supported her. And yet, she still sat in the chapel, in the middle of the night, in tears, fighting to be recognised as more than the King's latest whore. Perchance Nicóla once did the same, as a cardinal's whore.

'You are in much luck to have so many companions, my Lady,' Crumwell sighed.

'Who is your companion, Master Cremwell? Cardinal Wolsey, I suppose?'

'Even some things cannot be shared with the Cardinal.'

'Your foreign love?'

'I have no foreign love, Lady Anne, I assure you.'

'In that case, you have lied to the King of England.'

Crumwell turned to face Anne, his hands no longer resting in prayer, and she did the same. 'I have done no such thing.'

'Then you do have a foreign love.'

'No longer.'

'Love does not just disappear.'

'But Lady Anne, things can break love. Love is blind and fickle, like all women.'

'I know all about your friendship with the Italian Waif sent from the Pope.'

'I do as the King commands with Nicóla Frescobaldi.'

'Henry told me, before dinner, he suspected you fell in love with the Waif.'

'The King thinks me a sodomite?' Crumwell croaked and then crossed himself for saying such a word in Church.

'Half of the court suspects the same. Worry not, for Henry spoke that wish to marry the sister of the Waif. That is why the pair of you are spotted together all the time.'

'I shall remedy that when the Italian envoy leaves tomorrow.'

'But Henry wants the Waif to remain in our protection. Henry finds the man curious like he finds you curious.'

'Then the Waif can do so in the Tower on return to London.'

'You do so turn on your friends quickly, Master Cremwell. I expect you to be my ally or perchance you shall turn against me.'

'I am nobody, Lady Anne. Nobody shall ever fear me.'

'My father feared you when he owed you a great deal of money and struggled to repay.'

'But repay Lord Rochford did, so all is well. I am a banker, not a devil who comes for people.'

'Do you suppose the Italian Waif shall like his Tyndale book returned to him?'

'No, Lady Anne, the book is yours if you want it.'

'I much want it. I adore The Obedience of a Christian Man. It says the Catholic Church is a imposture affecting every department of English life. We should obey our sovereign Lord, and not the Pope of Rome.'

'It could be the future where we thrive, my Lady,' Crumwell uttered, knowing neither should speak such heresy in a chapel. 'I closed monasteries on Cardinal Wolsey's behalf. All greedy and riddled with filth. With the money from the monasteries and the taxes they no longer pay to Rome, King Henry could be the richest man in England. I swore I could make him so, given the chance.'

'Mayhap all you and I need is a chance,' Anne replied. She wiped the last few tears from her eyes and stood up. Crumwell copied and the pair crossed themselves before the altar. 'I feel strikingly well,' Anne said as Crumwell moved so she could leave the chapel. 'You provide a surprising amount of solace, Master Cremwell.'

Crumwell bowed goodnight and Anne swept away, the sweet smell of her rosewater-washed hair trailing behind her. She quickly disappeared into the darkness and Crumwell looked again to the altar.

His own words rang in his ears; love was as blind as a man smelling the sweet scent of a poisonous weed. He had no choice but to oust Nicóla completely.

~~~

The world changed yet again by sunrise. As soon as Mass ended, Wolsey tried to get an audience with the King but got denied. Wolsey waited in the main hall for hours in search of King Henry, Crumwell at his side, in case his master needed him. When he heard voices outside, Crumwell's stomach turned once again; this time with another sickening thought. 'Cardinal, I do believe the King is outside,' Crumwell said with all reluctance.

Wolsey moved through the manor with all the haste an old man in cardinal's robes could, and found King Henry and Lady Anne on horseback, readying themselves to go hunting, which the King so loved at Grafton House. 'Please, Your Majesty, I must speak with you,' Wolsey called to him, a friendly voice and cheerful wave from the doorway.

Two of the King's black-clad guards barred his way, holding the Cardinal in the doorway. 'Please step aside so His Eminence can speak with King,' Crumwell called from behind Wolsey, without reply.

'Your Majesty,' Wolsey called to the King, who acted as if he heard no voice at all. Wolsey cried out again and the King simply turned his horse and rode away. Lady Anne followed, now looking as graceful and composed as ever, and she caught Crumwell's eye for a second, a smile on her lips. At that moment, Crumwell knew all he needed. Lady Anne Boleyn was caught up in the King's love, and her hate for Wolsey over the Percy affair would never end. All the meetings the night before with Wolsey well received by Henry meant nothing. The King had turned away as if Wolsey and their twenty years together never happened. Wolsey, as shunned as Queen Katherine herself. The old were out – the young could take over. A golden age of royalty had changed its generation and the King would not let his annulment go. All it took was for the King to turn his horse away from Wolsey for Crumwell to see it.

Chapter 13 – October 1529
The Tower, London

The seecryts we all hast shall never byd fairwele

Nicóla stretched out her shoulders and they ached from the wound which bruised its way across her back. Weeks now in a damp cell in the Tower of London, after being repeatedly hit by a guard upon arrival. Crumwell may have sworn to imprison her or send her back to Rome, but she had not believed him. But the day Campeggio and the Italian envoy left Grafton House – just a day after arriving – Crumwell dismissed Nicóla from his care. He reasoned the Pope's orders; Nicóla must return to Italy with Campeggio. But as hard as it felt, to ride away without speaking to Crumwell, or even young Ralph Sadler in his place, more lay ahead. No sooner than the party arrived back in London to prepare for a sea voyage to Rome, the King's guards met the party at the city gates and arrested Nicóla. The "King's orders". Campeggio and the others tried to argue on her behalf, to no avail.

Now, Nicóla, hidden away in a tiny cell, lit only by a square window too high for her to look out of, bore no hope of escape. The bed was no more than a pallet stuffed with hay, which rats regularly came to nibble upon. The bucket to be used in the corner for private business would be of no help once her courses arrived. For years she had always travelled with strips of linen to put inside her hose, balanced to prevent menstruation from being noticed. She would have to use her chest binding cloths, but then she would distinctly be discovered.

Everything she owned was long gone; all her books, her letters from the Pope, her clothes, her spare binding cloths. They even took the ring from her finger, the delicious red ruby set in gold, given to Nicóla by her father. Long days passed, and while Nicóla knew many prisoners sat there months or years without any salvation, any attention or care, settling into this waiting felt too hard to bear. During the sacking of Rome, with the streets filled with killers, rapists, thieves, Nicóla at least could move about in secret, try to seek out a kind of survival. But this waiting, long painful days with the sound of endless footsteps passing her wooden door, the night passing with the cries of men in other cells, weeping in pain from torture, weeping for their loved ones. It frightened Nicóla on a level she never understood before. Her whole life, Nicóla's father supported her, with the Medici family always close by as protection. Nicóla strode the streets of Florence as if she had an army at her back; such was the power she had on her side. Now, countless thousands of miles away on this wet, filthy little island, all that power lay useless. Nicóla should have accompanied old Campeggio, to keep an eye on him, make sure he did not choose to side with Henry, only side with Katherine. Report back to Rome, as a spy would do. Be invisible. She had gained too much of the confidence of Wolsey and his advisors. She was presupposed to use Thomas Crumwell only if Campeggio swayed in the wrong direction, not become his constant companion, not fall... fall into something with him. No one was meant to know Nicóla was secretly a woman.

But bloody Thomas Crumwell had to go and be too intelligent! Had he never learned, perchance they never would have become as close as they had. Now Nicóla waited for Crumwell to appear in the Tower and find a way to get her out. If anyone could come up with a plan, it would be Thomas Crumwell. But after weeks staring at the old dark bricks of the walls, with something foul dripping between their cracks, the door opened, and Nicóla did not move. The only person who entered would be a guard with bread and ale. Nicóla had known hunger during the sacking of Rome; she had no need to chase down food like a dog just yet.

'Nicóla Frescobaldi?'

From her place on the floor, beside an unlit fireplace, Nicóla turned in surprise. The guards never spoke. But rather than a dirty and rough man, there stood a priest, dressed all in black, his square biretta hat in his hands. He seemed middle-aged with dark hair, nervous brown eyes, perchance fearful of whom or what he would find in the cell.

'I am he,' Nicóla said, and stood slowly, her legs a victim of heavy blows during her arrest.

'You can speak English?'

'Indeed, well enough. Who are you?' The light which poured in behind this stranger burned Nicóla's pale eyes.

'I am Thomas Cranmer. I am one of the Cambridge scholars who work for Stephen Gardiner, and on occasion, the King.'

'You are not a priest?'

'I am ordained, yes. I study theology, though, as well as the teaching of divinity. I used to live in Spain as an English ambassador.'

'And who do you study?' Nicóla could not get an immediate impression of this quiet man. Who could spar with an enemy or side with an ally, without knowing him?

'I have studied much of Erasmus' views, though of late, I have also come to understand the teachings of Martin Luther. I also enjoy the works of Tyndale, as well as many other humanists.'

This Cranmer appeared a Lutheran, a secret Protestant. But he said he worked for shaky-hands Stephen Gardiner, now out from under Wolsey's grip and into the palm of the King himself. 'Jacques Lefèvre d'Étaples?'

'Yes, he is one of the best French theologians. But I have not come to discuss humanism with you, Mr. Frescobaldi.'

'Well, I would offer you a chair, but I am not permitted a seat.' Nicóla gestured around her sparse room, nothing but the pallet bed and the bucket in the corner.

Cranmer glanced about the tiny cell and held his hand to his small nose for a moment. He had the skin of a man who spent so much time indoors, exceedingly pale. He appeared sick in comparison to Nicóla's olive skin. Everything about him seemed tepid. 'Mr. Frescobaldi, I came hither to discuss several matters with you.'

'Who sent you, Dr. Cranmer?'

'Does it matter?'

'I am afraid it matters to me. Perchance I am not as well travelled as yourself, but I am no fool, either.'

'Not at all. I hear you are fluent in six languages,' Cranmer continued.

'I had a life before entering the Pope's instruction.'

'Yes, I am told you live in Rome under the guidance of the Pope.'

'All is true, sir. But I must ask who sent you?' Nicóla pressed him.

'I come by the word of Stephen Gardiner.'

'A man who thinks little of me.'

'A man who knows about your imprisonment hither.'

'Perchance then Archdeacon Gardiner can tell me with what I am charged.'

'Heresy, I am afraid, of reading heretical texts.'

'No more heretical than what you must read as a scholar. Can a Florentine not be a scholar?'

'I come not to condemn. I do swear. Your envoy, including Cardinal Campeggio, has left for Rome. It will only be a matter of time before Pope Clement hears you are not with the envoy. Gardiner is worried the Pope will be angered by your imprisonment and wishes to speak, perchance get you freed, to help the King seem kinder in the eyes of the Pope. Also, you have a friend at court, someone who has taken a liking to you, and wants you released.'

Nicóla suppressed the urge of a smile. These Englishmen had finally worked out her value; the Pope would be furious to know she stood in a cell when she should have gone home, ready to marry and become Duchess of Florence.

'I need you to tell me first; did you give a Tyndale book to Lady Anne Boleyn?'

'Is it important?'

'Lady Anne and her family are friends. I can assure you safety. However, those at court in your corner are ardent Catholics.'

'No one can assure safety.' Nicóla took a breath. She would have to give his man some trust or she would gain none of his. 'Yes, Dr. Cranmer, I did give Anne Boleyn a Tyndale book, Obedience of a Christian Man. I possessed the heretical text and Lady Anne saw it and wished to take it. I allowed such; for whom would deny Lady Anne Boleyn? I have read these so-called heresies for years now, Dr. Cranmer, back in Rome, as part of my quiet time in the Pope's palace. Why are English priests not permitted to study the heretical bibles?'

'Some are permitted to certain extents, only under the wishes of King Henry.' Cranmer brought his hands together and paused, hesitant to trust as Nicóla. 'Some of us do read the texts, and we discuss them at length. I spent much of the summer at Waltham, to avoid plague in Cambridge. My friends, Stephen Gardiner and Edward Foxe, joined me. We spent much of the summer talking, that if the Pope and Rome will not make a decision of the King's annulment, instead the scholars of Europe could bring up ideas and solutions to His Majesty's "Great Matter".'

'Why tell me, Dr. Cranmer? I have studied divinity and humanism for less than two years. I am a merchant, and banker by trade. To be honest, that is where I belong.'

'I am told you are quite the scholar. No one talks with Thomas Crumwell for days and weeks without being exceedingly intelligent.'

'I thank you for your compliment, Dr. Cranmer, though I seek no such praise.'

'I come to you, Mr. Frescobaldi, to ask your opinion. What would Pope Clement say to the King adopting the opinions of scholars, rather than the religious minds of Rome?'

Nicóla paused. She thought of Giulio in Rome, how he cried with stress whenever someone mentioned King Henry's annulment. After his head injury two years ago, when he was tortured in prison on the Emperor's orders, he became unable to make a strong decision. He needed everyone around him to hold the throne of Christendom. 'I think this choice would not anger him, Dr. Cranmer. I believe the Pope would brush off any notions of this search for scholarly opinion. The Pope believes he is God's being on Earth; as do all wise, pious Catholics all over Christendom. The opinions of scholars would not cause His Holiness to have any thoughts at all.'

'You truly think so?'

'You want to put your scholarly pursuits to the King, and at the same time, not anger the Pope? You expect me to help you?'

'Only advise, Mr. Frescobaldi.'

'I can assure you, when Cardinal Campeggio's envoy arrives back in Rome and I am not with them, Pope Clement will have a rage unlike anyone might expect. He is almost a father to me.' It was almost true, had he not also seduced her. But post-injury Giulio was a different man to the younger, virile man she once loved.

'Perchance we could get you moved back to Austin Friars.'

'I am sure Thomas Crumwella will not have me back. I am nothing but trouble for him.'

'On the contrary, I have heard reports Crumwell is at court every day since he returned to London, hoping to see the King. King Henry requested Crumwell to do some business and Crumwell returns each day, and everyone is certain it is to speak on your behalf.'

'I am sure Master Crumwella is more burdened with the needs of Cardinal Wolsey and his works for the King. Crumwella has no time for trivial things such as an Italian Waif once his house guest.'

'I fear Cardinal Wolsey is not in a considerable position at present. Wolsey is Lord Chancellor of England. He has run this country on King Henry's behalf for most of his reign. But now it is the Lady Anne who is in charge of our kind prince.'

'There are worse things, Dr. Cranmer, than a woman being able to lead.'

'A woman leading is against the word of God. Women are inferior to men in every way and seek to change the natural order of the world.'

'Forgive me, Dr. Cranmer, but I am under arrest. To me, the world is already out of its natural order. Things are different where I am from, and to be honest, I am completely lost in England. Perchance I have enjoyed too much freedom in life, perchance I received too much of everything. No one can question the wealth and corruption of the Church, and the power of Rome, or well indeed the Republic of Florence, which is my home. If the King wishes to not anger the Pope, His Majesty should put me on the first ship which leaves this island. All this could be at an end.'

'If you go back to Rome, would you have influence over the Pope?'

'The Pope is trapped. His Holiness shall never go against the words of the Holy Roman Emperor. Your King shall never gain an annulment from the Pope. Our envoy hither came to ensure such. You cannot harm Cardinal Campeggio, who is just a pawn in this game, that I can say. Have me tortured if you wish; I hear the screams coming from the rooms below. Am I spying for the Pope? Yes. Am I important? Yes, the Pope wants me back, needs me back. I am not sure why you have come hither today, Dr. Cranmer.'

'I am trying to help my friends, such as Stephen Gardiner, come up with a way to allow the King to gain his desires. I want to find a way to rid the world of all the faults of the Christian faith. But I cannot pose a suggestion to King Henry without knowing what may happen. Sending scholars to Europe can only be suggested if it does not anger the Pope.'

'I have told you all I can, Dr. Cranmer. I doubt you will anger the Pope; I doubt he will give it more than a passing glimpse. Pope Clement the Seventh is the embodiment of God on Earth; destined to be such for years, perchance even before he became a cardinal in Florence. His Holiness has so many problems, but his faith is not one. Pope Clement is a man; he has flaws, like all men. But he believes a marriage ordained by God can never be pulled apart. If His Holiness felt in mind to annul Henry and Katherine's marriage, he would have done it years ago when he annulled Henry's sister's marriage up in Scotland. That issue abused him much grief, and this, of Henry and Katherine, is so much worse. Pope Clement will never rule in the King's favour.'

'How can I believe you, Mr. Frescobaldi? Forgive me, but we have never spoken until today.'

'How can I trust you, Thomas Cranmer? We have never spoken until today.'

The pair stood, their eyes locked as the moments passed. 'I come seeking only to understand faith and the King's "Great Matter",' Cranmer said, his voice calm and quiet since he entered the room.

'I have nothing to offer, nothing to lose.'

Cranmer looked around the tiny cell again. 'Is there anything I could bring you?'

'If it pleases you, could you deliver a message? Would you be able to speak to Thomas Crumwella, for I cannot write a letter.'

'I can try.'

'Please tell him that my sister, who is due to marry in Florence, would goodly give up her inheritance and future titles if she received another offer.'

'That is a strange message.'

'Tom... Master Crumwella once lived as close friends with my family, many years ago, lived in our home, and was taught by my father. He has curiosity for affairs in Florence, out of friendship. Please tell him, my sister does not wish to marry. She wishes to break her pre-contract.'

'Your sister is in need of guidance, of both a spiritual and moral preference.'

'Indeed, and if I cannot be of service to her, perchance Master Crumwella can.'

'Your sister's name?'

'Nicóletta.'

'I shall pass the matter of Mistress Nicóletta to Master Crumwell if I see him.'

'God be with you, Dr. Cranmer.'

'And God be with you.' Cranmer gave the sign of the cross and Nicóla returned it. 'May our souls find the truth in all spiritual and moral matters.'

'I pray for this day and night, both hither and wherever I go, Dr. Cranmer. Will you tarry and pray a moment more?'

Cranmer bowed his head in prayer, and Nicóla copied, relieved to hear solace of God in another's voice. 'May Christ support us all the day long, till the shadows lengthen, and the evening comes, and the busy world is hushed, and the fever of life is over and our work is done. Then in His mercy may He give us a safe lodging, and holy rest and peace at the last. Amen.'

Nicóla crossed herself and Cranmer did the same. There as a benevolent soul inside this man, easy to understand, easy to trust. Even God knew such was hard to find in this corrupt land named England. 'One thing, Dr. Cranmer. You say I have Catholic supporters at court? Who wishes to see me released? Who is this?'

'The Queen and her court,' Cranmer replied. 'Queen Katherine supports you.'

'I delivered Her Majesty a token of affection from the Holy Roman Emperor.'

'The Queen is as powerful as the King. Between them and the Pope, you are much fixed in danger, Mr. Frescobaldi.'

'Trust me, I understand.'

Chapter 14 - October 1529
York Place, London

Seecryts consoome what is valorous and leaveth behynd dystruction

'At least the Italians are gone.' Wolsey spoke with such bitterness as he stared from the window behind his wide desk at York Place. 'How we ever expected to get an envoy from Rome to decide on the annulment is beyond me.'

Crumwell stood firm on the other side of the desk, his hands behind his back. Countless times a day Wolsey would either break down in tears or rage in anger. He sat a broken man, fallen from the King's favour, having not spoken together since the farce at Grafton. He held the post of Lord Chancellor of England still, but surely the role would fall from Wolsey's endlessly vainglorious grip. The Cardinal was no longer the man he imagined. Wolsey forgot he was well through his fifties already, such an old man to carry such weight on his bones. With every cry, his second and third chins shook with a sickening wobble. His eyes, reddened from lack of sleep failed to fix on any task. A lifetime of work had come to nothing, and Crumwell knew not whether to pity his master or run in fear of falling far himself.

The King had called Crumwell to court at Greenwich several times in the past weeks to do various tasks, with Wolsey banished from attending court now. Wolsey wanted every detail of court chatter after Crumwell's visits, wanted to know how the King looked, how he acted. But King Henry looked calm and composed every time Crumwell saw him, not troubled by his annulment. Henry, Katherine, and the Lady Anne all moved to Greenwich, a strange threesome separated by the palace's size, yet the hundreds, thousands who made a life at court could send every detail between them with speed.

'Perchance we should regard more pressing matters hither, Your Eminence,' Crumwell said, his voice without soul. Since his fight with Nicóla at Grafton, everything he experienced seemed stone-cold. People commented on the double-minded man's new demeanor, a confident man frozen in anger.

'Such as?' Wolsey said with a wave of his ring-laden hand.

'I heard at court that the King will call parliament to sit. They have not done so in six years now.'

'And?'

'And I thought perchance I should try to gain a seat in parliament again.'

Wolsey turned from the window and smiled just a fraction. 'You think we should extend your reach into parliament? I am already on the Privy Council, and there are only six members now.'

Yes, because Wolsey himself cut it down to make sure his influence was the only one heard by royal ears. Crumwell wanted to extend his own reach. He had so little in life. He wanted nothing but work. 'Honestly, Cardinal, I wish to make something of myself again.'

'You are an advisor to one of the most powerful men in this country, Thomas. What more could you need? Are you ready to flee so you are not harmed by me?'

'Thomas,' Crumwell spoke plainly, 'you have given me so much. I had little in England when I returned from Europe. Thanks to working for you, I have gained so much. I can never repay such a debt.'

Wolsey smiled, fuller this time. 'I can see about having someone's seat in parliament handed over to you.'

'I did not mean to use connections to gain a place.'

'What good is power if we cannot use it to our advantage?'

'To advance the King?' Crumwell ventured. After all, it was not Wolsey's kingdom, though he so often acted that way.

'Of course, our precious prince, who shall one day see this mess with the legatine court is not my fault.'

The room felt stuffy; at the slightest suggestion autumn arrived in London, Wolsey refused to open the windows. Crumwell's life had become too overwhelmed with the King's business that his own business fell into neglect. His nephew Richard could only do so much on his own at Austin Friars. Crumwell had become something of a nurse for Wolsey and his ailing emotions.

'With Rome agreeing to hear Queen Katherine's appeal, we shall never see a decision,' Wolsey said, as if forgetting the entire conversation about parliament. 'Now Pope Clement expects Henry to appear in Rome to explain the annulment. Never shall the legatine court hither or in Rome make a decision. My life shall be over soon enough. The Italians have ruined everything. If only your Waif did not reside in the Tower. Perchance young Frescobaldi could shed some light on the situation; tell us the best way forward, knowing the Pope so well.'

'Nicóla Frescobaldi got arrested for heresy and for colluding with the Pope during the legatine court hearings. He is a spy. We shall not enlist his help.'

'Even though he is the son of your former master? Why have you become cold to the Waif? I thought him quite pleasant indeed.'

Half the court thought so, too. They rejoiced in talk of how Crumwell's new foreign friend sat in the Tower. Every aspect of this damned annulment slowly undid Crumwell's life. He could never be unfaithful to his dear wife Elizabeth, God rest her soul. With his past connections now questioned, some thought him in an affair with a man. At least the King asked for nothing but assistance on business matters. "Ah, Crumwell, you understand me", King Henry said after every meeting concluded. Wolsey used to say the same thing.

'I have taken to wearing a hair shirt, Thomas,' Wolsey muttered as he looked out of the window again, the trees already starting to fade from luscious green, the river dirty and low. 'I must have penitence with the pain of the rough fabric on my skin.'

That deep, nagging thud in his chest, which accompanied Crumwell, as if followed by a demon, hit him again. Cardinal Wolsey was his closest friend and ally. 'A hair shirt? Why would you wear such a thing? You are in no need of penitence, of mortification or self-sacrifice.'

'I could not give my King what he needed. I must be punished. The King is as if my own son and he is denied his greatest desire. Henry's desires are my desires. I feel as if I have walked this Earth and achieved nothing. God has forsaken us all.' Wolsey turned away from the glass and rested his hands on his desk. The pair locked eyes and Crumwell saw real, true contrition from the Cardinal, something no one believed him capable.

A loud bang came from the heavy door at the other end of the long room. Wolsey's gentleman-usher Cavendish came in with a panicked face. 'The Duke of Norfolk and the Duke of Suffolk, Your Eminence.'

Stuttering Norfolk and pompous Suffolk; Nicóla's nicknames for them both stuck in Crumwell's mind. Both men entered the room, smug grins abound. Norfolk, a wide and difficult man at the best of times, had not crossed paths with Crumwell since the night at Grafton, hitting Nicóla in that tiny room. Suffolk had passed Crumwell at court several times and saw him not, as if not even present. Neither men even looked at Crumwell, instead made straight for Wolsey. 'Jesus, do thou lock my heart into thine, and let my body and my soul be commended unto thee,' Wolsey muttered as they approached.

'C-C-Cardinal Thomas Wolsey, Archb-b-bishop of York, Lord Chancellor of England,' Norfolk said, his head tilted slightly upwards, 'b-b-by the order of King Henry, you are charged with praemunire. You have asserted your p-p-papal jurisdiction against the supremacy of the monarch of England. You are to appear in c-c-court to hear the charge upon you and be tried according to the law.'

'And you have proof of this?' Wolsey scoffed at the ageing Duke.

Suffolk thrust a piece of paper at Wolsey, but Crumwell snatched it from his chubby hand. Sure enough at the bottom of the message rested the seal of Henry, his signature beside. Sir Christopher Hales, the attorney-general at the Court of the King's Bench in Westminster had drawn up the papers eight days ago, on October 9. It was official now; the King had turned forever against Wolsey after twenty full years, an ally whose will and cause would change with Henry's mind. Praemunire, a most serious offense, and one as vague as treason or heresy; easy to use on someone and almost impossible to be denied.

George Cavendish came in the room as calmly as he could. Not just one of Wolsey's gentleman-ushers, Cavendish was also a friend and ally to Wolsey as much as Crumwell. He panted from his run, his face pale against his dark clothes and worried heart. 'Your Eminence,' Cavendish said and tried to catch his breath, 'there are men hither, who accompanied the Dukes of Norfolk and Suffolk…'

'Leave them be,' Norfolk barked at Cavendish, who smoothed his dark hair behind his ears. 'Cardinal Wolsey, under these charges, you are s-s-stripped of your title as Lord Chancellor of England and all your p-p-possessions become the property of the King. You are to leave York P-P-Place, and everything is to be g-g-given directly to King Henry.'

Wolsey tightened a grip on the red robes he wore, now his only possession on Earth. 'But where am I to live?' he squeaked. 'And what of my mistress, Joan, or my 500 servants?'

'Everything is in the keeping of the King,' Suffolk said, ever ready to enjoy being in charge of another. 'You butcher's boy, are to go to your palace in Esher, by order of the King, while the charges and evidence are prepared for your court date. You are welcome to remove all your jewels from your person now.'

'But Esher is a minor palace, and far away in Surrey. It must be fifteen miles from London,' Crumwell said. 'It is ill-equipped and unprepared.'

'Your golden age is over, Wolsey,' Suffolk said, a seething grin on his bearded face. 'You are to leave by barge at once, and you are instructed not to take anything with you, as you no longer own a thing. Everything the King has given you, now he shall have it all back.'

'I shall travel with you, Cardinal,' Cavendish offered, perchance not seeing the seriousness of the situation.

'As will I,' Crumwell added in a hurry. While many jumped to be on Anne Boleyn's side, Crumwell could not simply leave his master.

'All you need to do is s-s-surrender the Great Seal of England,' Norfolk continued. 'You w-w-will never need it again. It is time you return to the l-l-lowly existence from which you came.'

'You must stay hither,' Wolsey stuttered to Crumwell. 'Stay and attend as they go through all my silver, my linens, my treasures from a long life.'

'Everything is to be given to Lady Anne Boleyn, including York Place,' Suffolk said. 'You have no need for worry. Lady Anne will take care of all your treasures and servants.' He and Norfolk shared a satisfied smile.

'I will not leave without you, Your Eminence,' Crumwell said defiantly. In a moment his broken heart seemed lost; he needed to be the strongest man in the room, for the life he worked for, for Wolsey, even for George Cavendish. 'The weather is terrible for travelling to

Esher and there is little help or food,' Crumwell said. 'I shall ready all at once.'

'You are to take nothing!' Suffolk barked.

'I shall pay every penny from my own pocket,' Crumwell bit back into the Duke's face. 'I shall pay, I shall do the work, and I shall never defy the Cardinal. You can hide behind the cloaks of your King all you please but I am not a man like you.'

'No, I am ennobled.'

'You would not have your head on your shoulders if not for my past help, thanks to all your foolery,' Wolsey rose up to Suffolk. 'Can I not take a coat for the journey, not as a cardinal in search of possessions, but as an old man in need of warmth?'

Norfolk threw him a dismissive wave and Cavendish led the startled Cardinal away. Norfolk turned instead to Crumwell. 'You c-c-could do well for yourself if you left the Cardinal.'

'I have already done well, Your Grace.'

'All on the back of being b-b-beneath Wolsey. What shall you do now?'

'Never abandon a friend in his time of need.'

'You shall b-b-be seen as nothing m-m-more than a creature of Wolsey's making,' Norfolk said. 'The man with the g-g-golden eyes which make money appear. Forever th-th-the double-minded man, so intelligent but c-c-cannot be trusted.'

'I will get into parliament and we shall talk again.' Crumwell's heart felt frozen and in need of power.

Chapter 15 - November 1529
Esher Place, Surrey

Pretendeth there art nay more seecryts

The only thing which made the lengthy, soggy ride easier to bear was being on horseback again. After over a month in the Tower, one day Nicóla's door flew open to the sight of shaky-hands Stephen Gardiner. A few words on his order and she got released from the fetid cell, out into the cold of the London autumn. A bed at court, in a room given to Gardiner's attendants, in return for information given about the Pope. Nicóla took up Gardiner's offer, of being on hand to provide information on His Holiness. With no money, Nicóla had no other options than to take a place in Gardiner's household.

Austin Friars told the story of Crumwell's move away to Esher. A trip to York Place saw Nicóla beholding the sight of the Cardinal's life stripped and put into chests. If she could not go home to Florence, then Nicóla needed to do something. Work for shaky-hands Gardiner? Never. Nicóla needed to make things right with her Crumwell. In the plain black livery given to her by Gardiner, Nicóla again became the man from her father's side years ago. After the years of wealth and comfort the Church had provided, Nicóla had to close that time of life away. She should have never distinctly enjoyed the embrace of the Apostolic Palace as much as she did. The chatter of the Italian layman becoming Gardiner's underling spread like the plague. The Waif had become even more outcast. None of it mattered now.

Worn and weary, sore and thin, Nicóla rode on a horse borrowed from Richard Crumwell at Austin Friars. But the ride, the mud, the rain which fell like a sign Nicóla rode the trail to hell, felt like an abject punishment. By November 1, at the broken and unworthy "palace" at Esher, surrounded by mud and withering trees, Nicóla ached, unsure her body could take much more. No one came when she led her horse around the back to the stables. Nicóla tied up the poor beast herself under shelter and made sure he had food and water. The only sound other than rain was the sodden noise of her black riding boots, which stuck in the mud with every footstep.

She trekked around the palace to the front entranceway, and tried to scrape the mud off her boots against rocks in the empty garden. She raised a hand to knock for attendance when something caught her eye. There sat Crumwell at a large window a level above her. Even with the rain on the glass, she could see him crying. Thomas Crumwell was crying, and she was not the only one who noticed.

'Is that you, Mr. Frescobaldi?' asked Cavendish, in the now-open doorway of the palace, a warm draught of air floating from behind him.

'It is.' Nicóla took another look at Crumwell in the window before heading out of the rain. 'I have much to report. Please, Mr. Cavendish, refer to me as just Nicóla.'

'You have much news to report?'

'I have seen all the destruction of Wolsey's life this past week in London. I have come to do penance and implore the chance to offer my service.'

'There are few of you hither,' Cavendish said as he closed the door. 'Cardinal Wolsey's position is much changed. He is dressed in the simplest vestments of white and purple. We have no money in which to pay any of his servants and there is little money for food or even firewood. Wolsey is a man quite humbled; he does little but pray with his personal chaplain Edmund Bonner, or his mistress, Joan.'

The palace felt not much warmer than outside, but thankfully dry. Without any more heed, Cavendish led Nicóla through the old red-brick building, all the hallways dark and damp, nothing like the opulent York Place. It spoke more of the sacked building in Rome where Nicóla hid for safety in the wake of the Emperor's soldiers. Of all the darkness, the cold ache of her body, the pain of her time in the Tower, the sound hurt the most. Only sobbing could be heard. Deep, raw pain. She stopped in the doorway behind Cavendish and looked across the wide but bare room to Crumwell sitting in the bay window which looked out upon the front door.

There sat Crumwell, tears running down his cheeks as he held a Latin primer in his shaking hands. He muttered the Te Deum in Latin as he read. 'Miserére nostri, Dómine, miserére nostri. Fiat misericórdia tua, Dómine, super nos, quemádmodum sperávimus in te. In te, Dómine, sperávi: non confúndar in ætérnum.'

Nicóla took a step back, shocked by the sight from the enduring Thomas Crumwell crying and praying. O Lord, have mercy upon us: have mercy upon us. O Lord, let thy mercy lighten upon us: as our trust is in thee. O Lord, in thee, have I trusted: let me never be confounded.

'Master Crumwell, what is the means of your sorrow?' Cavendish interrupted and Nicóla stood back from the doorway, in wait for an answer.

'It is my own unhappy adventure, as I am about to lose all I have after spending all my days working for my master. I am hated due to the dislike everyone has for Wolsey. Once a man has a bad reputation, it can never be changed,' Crumwell sniffed. Such pity did not seem like Crumwell.

With a stern brow, Nicóla stepped forward, showing herself. 'May we have a moment of privacy?' she muttered to Cavendish.

Without a word, Cavendish abided and closed the door behind her as Nicóla took wet, muddy steps on the bare wooden floor. Yet Crumwell said nothing as she slowly approached him, drips falling from her black clothes, her simple black riding cloak so wet it hung almost to the floor under its own weight. None of her rose-gold hair peeked from under her large black hat; she probably looked nothing like herself in his eyes. Though, he looked nothing like himself in hers, tears on his cheeks, pink from his anguish. They stared back at one another for a moment, no idea what to say.

Crumwell closed the prayer book, not taking his wide golden eyes from her. He did not look angry, but not pleased, not surprised, nothing. For a man filled with pain, he showed no emotion on his face at all. Clearly, the news of her release from the Tower had not reached Esher.

Nicóla ran to Crumwell's side and sunk to her knees, water falling from her hat as she pulled it from her head, showing her rain-soaked curls. 'I broke your trust and my sins have punished me with a separation from your side. I am sorry, Tom. I do not wish to return to my sin-filled life. Jesus Christ died for the sins of men, and with my heart filled with His love, I beg you to forgive me, for I have angered you, and beseech you to let me repair the burdens which I have caused. I want to gain your trust again, and I want to be of service to you and your master in a time of such need.'

Seconds stretched out in silence as Crumwell continued to stare at her without a word. She longed to wipe the tears from his cheeks. To have anyone, much less someone a masterful as Thomas Crumwell, think of her as a baseborn whore, sullied by father and son alike, blighted her soul.

She gasped in fright as he lunged towards her, thrusting his lips on hers. The shock did not abate as he took occasion to kiss her, a deep, forceful, enfolding kiss on her mouth. The sinful urge of longing pulsed in her blood as she kissed him back, the pair almost seeing out their anger at the world against one another's lips. His hands grabbed at her body, lost and confused as he touched men's clothes, not the shape of a woman. He fell from his seat, throwing her onto her back against the floor as he kissed her, his hands fighting to undo her doublet and hose, not caring about her wet clothing. His angry lips never left hers as he fought to pull her clothes from her body, a whole range of feelings caught up in lips and hands.

But just as Nicóla felt him free her from her wet clothes, Crumwell pulled himself from her body with an angry cry. Nicóla struggled to pull her clothes over her body again as he stood over her, one hand clapped over his mouth. Nicóla sat up, a sudden shock of shame running through her body. No woman should feel this way, let alone act this way. She could work as a man, dress as a man, but she could never have the lustful appetite of a man. For fifteen years, she lived as male; never once had she touched anyone. Even a kiss felt raw and foreign.

'I have lost everything,' Crumwell snarled as he paced before Nicóla, still in a shamed heap on the floor. 'I have lost all and yet you come here as if you matter! You are just a curse upon me, Nicó! You distracted me with love since the moment you came to London, and my life is ruined! I should be capable of seeing my way through all this menace, and yet I only thought of you!'

Nicóla opened her mouth to speak but Crumwell cut her off with his anger. 'I have worked to be something and now I find I am nothing and nobody once more! My master, my friend, is thrown in the mud, all the money gone, all the deeds forgotten. You mean nothing to me any longer. How could you come hither, to where Wolsey's disgrace is so obvious, yet should be so private?'

The question went unanswered as Crumwell continued with his rage. 'You must go! You cannot tarry a moment longer. You should never have come. If you are free from the Tower, for whatever reason, I am sure it is devious. Go far from hither, take your lies, take your enchantments, take your wickedness and your deception and leave this place!'

Nicóla stood without a word, her face still hurt from Crumwell's kiss. She left the room and followed the staircase and hallways, out of sight of Cavendish. She went from the front door unseen by any servants and sped into the rain to fetch her horse. The poor animal had barely time to relax before getting on the road again, but London lay not too far away.

Without looking around, Nicóla mounted her horse and took off at high speed from Esher, dreading the thought of Crumwell watching her from his window of despair. Nicóla had done enough crying and pitying, best suited to a woman in the Tower. She would not sit and pray and weep. Nicóla would go back to London and gain all she needed to get home to marry and become the Duchess of Florence. No man would ever love Nicóla, and she would never love anyone in return. Just as Crumwell lived as a creature of Thomas Wolsey, Nicóla lived as a creature of the Pope. No time for tears when there was money to be made and positions to be sought.

Chapter 16 – November 1529
Greenwich Palace, downstream London

A seecryt's worth depends on from whom it myght beest kept

The closer Crumwell got to court, the more the stares lingered. It was true, he knew it; he was now the incarnation of Wolsey. Nicóla's arrival at Esher had changed everything for Crumwell. Seeing her sparked anger in him, and he needed to stop wallowing in his misery. Crumwell got Wolsey's house in order as well as he could within one evening; giving money from his own pocket to pay for household expenses, he left for London. A short stop at Austin Friars was all he had time for, before heading directly to court to be as ruthless as his cold heart would stretch. Luckily in this instance, he was ready to do anything it took to get into parliament. It was the stuttering Duke of Norfolk who needed to be his new ally, and he had seemed amenable in the past, so mayhap there was a chance.

Yet, as he stalked the halls of Greenwich Palace, people stopped him with their stares of curiosity and contempt, and Crumwell was in for the fight of his life. Parliament would sit in the House of Commons in just two days' time, not a lot of opportunity to obtain such a posting. Crumwell found himself facing Charles Brandon, the pompous Duke of Suffolk, instead of Norfolk. There Suffolk was, surrounded by his constant companions while Crumwell stood alone in a hallway. Even Ralph was missing, off to speak to a friend. Suffolk stood imposing in a thick black fur coat, his billowing sleeves perfectly white underneath. Crumwell wondered if the white collar of his own shirt looked anything near white. He did not even have time to check such things on a day like today.

'The double-minded man, much surprised to see you at court,' Suffolk said with a smile, a few wayward crumbs still in his greying beard. 'The court has much wondered on your whereabouts.'

'Everyone knows my whereabouts, Your Grace.'

'Banished to Esher; tell me, how is the Cardinal? Still praying with old Edmund Bonner, in the hopes of restoration?'

'Do you care?'

Suffolk snorted with laughter. 'God is not shining on your conversation skills, Crumwell. If you expect to survive hither, you need to learn to speak properly to those ennobled. Everyone thinks you a henchman for Wolsey. Do you think the King wants to see you?'

'The King is not my master. Neither is Wolsey any longer.' An ache for his life lost stung through, but Crumwell had no time for fealty now. 'I am my own master, and a wealthy man, Your Grace.'

'Have you come to fetch your little Waif? All are talking of the Italian who is no longer a man of the cloth, but with Gardiner.'

'Gardiner?' Crumwell choked on the name. Nicóla, usher to Gardiner, master secretary to the King?

'You know not? Crumwell, surely not so! Rumours abound the Italian went to see Wolsey at Esher. Everyone who comes or goes from Esher is reported to the King. Surely you have seen the Waif.'

'I am hither to speak with the Duke of Norfolk,' Crumwell replied, to keep rumours at bay. 'Is the Duke wandering about the halls today?'

'I thought you might see Sir Thomas More, now he is appointed Lord Chancellor in Wolsey's place.'

Crumwell refused to even open his mouth at the attempt to anger him.

'You ought to spend some time in the company of your Italian. The Waif is the one who can bring a smile to many a face hither.'

Crumwell could not resist. 'What do you mean?'

'This past week the Italian has been at court, even I have spoken with him. Frescobaldi has made friends in such a short space of time. I must admit, for a foreigner, he is rather witty. Even if he is the spy for a corrupt and dim Pope.'

'It was not long ago I was tending the wounds you inflicted on…'

Crumwell almost uttered her, ' Nicóla Frescobaldi.'

'You? Tending the wounds?' Suffolk laughed. 'The Waif has gotten under everyone's skin. I would imagine you have the bedside manner of a wolf.'

Crumwell stood on the spot as Suffolk's laugh dimmed while he wandered away, his followers trotting along behind him.

'Master Crumwell!' Crumwell turned to see Ralph running towards him, having to hold his hat upon his light-coloured hair. He almost skidded to a stop in his damp black shoes. 'Master Crumwell! Such news.'

Crumwell clicked his fingers twice, to order Ralph to speak. 'What happened, Ralph?' he worried, wondering if something had happened to the boy. 'I spoke with my friend, Sir Thomas Rush, a Yeoman of the Guard. Sir Thomas was once a politician, and his stepson Thomas Alvard is the member of parliament for Taunton in Somerset.'

'What is that to me?'

'Rush knew already of your needs, and said his stepson Alvard is prepared to step down for you to take his seat in the Commons.'

'How did Rush know?'

Ralph paused for a moment, and would not answer. 'Rush was once a friend of Cardinal Wolsey, and will see his son give the seat in return for your favour, while you are in parliament. Rush seems to think you are to do well in the role.'

'What does he distinctly want?'

'I hear Rush is in some financial trouble, so I would imagine a loan on simple terms would suit him,' Ralph grinned. 'Mayhap just an easy bribe. But there is more. Rush said he spoke with William Paulet, the Master of the King's Wards. Paulet wrote to have you registered as the member for Taunton in time for the opening of parliament in two days. The paperwork is paid for and awaiting you.'

'On what terms?'

'Paulet wants a reduction in the interest rate he pays you on his debts. But as I say, the fee has already been paid on your behalf.'

Crumwell smiled, that self-righteous judgemental smile, more often seen on Wolsey's face than Crumwell's. But there was no time to play pious, docile. Crumwell had to gain a place for himself, or face a life of ruin back at Esher.

'I have scheduled a meeting, between you and Paulet, so the papers are ready for your signature.'

'You have outdone yourself, Ralph! Why, you have achieved such a conclusion I feared even I could not put together.'

'I fear I ought not take the credit, Master Crumwell. It seems while my speaking with my friend seems so fortunate, someone else had discussed all this with Sir Thomas Rush before me.'

'Who would do such a thing?'

'Nicóla,' Ralph replied, his eyes downcast. While Ralph had no idea of the situation between Crumwell and Nicóla, he knew of some grand dispute and wanted to steer well clear of any such intrusion.

'What did Rush say of Nicóla?'

'It seems Nicóla is poking around court, looking for opportunities on your behalf, well before we arrived back in London, Master Crumwell. It seems Nicóla is now under the patronage of Stephen Gardiner. Nicóla has gone through something of a change. He is no longer in preparation to take holy orders, much to everyone's grand diversion; such is the spectacle of the witty Waif. Nicóla tells tales to the Lady Anne. A rumour stated Nicóla visited the rooms of Queen Katherine! He has been to see Richard at Austin Friars. Nicóla bargained all over court on your behalf, talking of your virtuous name.'

Crumwell shut his eyes tight for a moment. He thought of the look on Nicóla's face when he pushed himself off her half-dressed body at Esher. The shame he felt, the hurt he caused. Crumwell spent hours on his knees, begging God for forgiveness. Nicóla had caught him at a distraught moment, his passion overwhelming his fragile state. She had gone, just as instructed, but not far. They could not be together, anywhere. Nicóla needed to return to the Holy See of Rome. Crumwell could not lust after the daughter of his friend. The Pope's future daughter-in-law. The whore of Christendom, just like Anne Boleyn. If Nicóla needed money to get home, Crumwell would goodly pay. Whatever the reason, Crumwell would take this fortune. He opened his eyes again.

'Thank you, Ralph; we shall be celebrating at Austin Friars tonight! Come, we have much to do.'

'There is more,' Ralph said as they began along a hallway together, to head out through the courtyard to the river. 'The rumour is Gardiner was with the King, on the matter of a dispute over monies owed to His Majesty. As they discussed the difficulties they had with a lawyer, Nicóla, who had gotten himself in the room, spoke quite out of turn. Nicóla spoke up and suggested to His Majesty himself that you, Master Crumwell, should be the man to service the King's financial troubles!'

Crumwell shook his head, unable to think straight. How dare she wander around London, thinking she had a right to break with anyone on any subject! And to think of all the deeply private things they had discussed. Crumwell divulged so much information to Nicóla about people he worked with and for, the people he lent money to, the contacts he did business with, and all told over wine at Austin Friars. And Nicóla's memory was as trained as his – she would forget not a single word.

'Master,' Ralph interrupted Crumwell's internal tirade, 'shall I arrange for tomorrow…'

'No,' Crumwell cut him off. 'We must have everything prepared today. I shall return to Esher in the morning to speak with Wolsey. If all goes well, we shall be back in London for the opening of parliament. There is much work to be done.'

'Of course. I was simply asking, since my lucky talk with my friend has saved us so much time, that I might be permitted to speak with Nicóla before we return to Austin Friars?'

'What?' Crumwell spat at his secretary, and stopped in his tracks.

'I know Nicóla was detained in the Tower, Master, but he was a pleasant friend to me, and Gardiner dropped all of Nicóla's heresy charges… I only ask because he is just there…'

Crumwell followed Ralph's pointed hand, and saw Nicóla, standing the centre of the courtyard among the perfectly arch-shaped plantings. Her expensive Italian clothes gone, Nicóla stood in a plain black doublet and hose, with the riding boots she wore when she arrived at Esher. Only now, instead of claiming to be penitent, she laughed and danced on the spot, while she spoke with the poet, 'engrossing' Thomas Wyatt, and the musician, 'delightful' Mark Smeaton. The nicknames she gave everyone stuck in Crumwell's head. The three stood in the weak November sun, and played some sort of game involving dance steps. They acted as if the world shined a wondrous place; perchance it was for the young. A group of ladies stood nearby watching the three imitating each other's dance steps. Crumwell headed straight towards Nicóla and Ralph trailed behind, no doubt unawares of Crumwell's curious anger towards the Italian.

The contented threesome did not notice their presence until

Thomas Wyatt looked up from their laughing circle and saw his patron almost right beside him. 'Master Crumwell,' he said with harmonious surprise, his blonde hair bouncing around his pale face. 'I heard someone mention you had just arrived back in London! Good morrow and well met. You have been missed!'

Crumwell regarded his friend, a strikingly handsome gentleman well over six feet tall, excellent as an ambassador abroad, just for his presence alone. Wyatt was an educated, quick-witted man, and obviously Nicóla had tapped into his friendly nature. Everyone got along well with Nicóla. She had the trick of being able to charm, with her quick assumptions, her ability to read people, her perfect memory and knowledge of the world. Damn all her qualities! She was the Pope's whore!

'Master Crumwell,' Mark Smeaton said, and bowed a fraction. Smeaton was about only eighteen years, but a gifted musician and composer, who played for Wolsey as well as at court. With his dark curls and large brown eyes he could be a ladies man, but Crumwell had already noticed Smeaton preferred the company of men. No wonder the slender and uncommon Nicóla Frescobaldi attracted his curiosity.

Crumwell looked to Nicóla, stood in total defiance of him, as if the incident at Esher never occurred. The sun shone on her rose-gold hair, cut shorter than Crumwell had ever seen, far more of a man's haircut, barely even covering her ears now. Nicóla seemed slimmer than ever, perchance due to starvation in the Tower. Their time at Esher was so raw Crumwell barely had time to take her in, but now he had the chance. Nicóla stood in total reticence, not even daring to utter his name. The others in the group stood back a fraction, unnerved by the sudden silence.

'Nicóla!' Ralph stepped forward, cutting Crumwell's line of sight. Ralph took Nicóla in his outstretched arms and the pair embraced, friends since the moment they met. As they spoke, Crumwell noticed Smeaton throw a look to Wyatt; acknowledging the demeanour between the money lender and his Italian counterpart.

'We must go,' Crumwell announced, his voice louder than he expected. 'Come, Ralph, we have much to do before our party tonight. Thomas, Mark, you must come to Austin Friars tonight, for one of my dinners.'

'Splendid, thank you,' Smeaton replied. 'I will bring my lute.'

Crumwell took in Nicóla one more time and left without uttering a word to her, only clicking his fingers for Ralph to follow. It was only once they crossed the courtyard completely Crumwell turned in the cold London shade, and saw Nicóla again. Wyatt and Smeaton laughed once more, but Nicóla stared right back at him. Why would she be talking of him around court when she plainly hated Crumwell with a passion? What was the end Nicóla wished for, with the odds so stacked in his favour? She was a foreigner, an usher now to shaky-hands Gardiner. Crumwell was about to enter parliament again and had the upper hand, but only due to her efforts.

'Are you well?' Ralph asked, noting Crumwell stuck hard on the spot.

'As well as I can be, in the times we live in now.'

Chapter 17 - November 1529
Westminster and Austin Friars, London

We danceth round a cyrcle but the seecryt sits in the myddel

Nicóla sat drooped in her chair at the table in the court's dining hall, running her fingers around the rim of her wine goblet. She felt a touch dazed by the vast amount of wine taken with the evening meal, which was so loaded with roasted meats it made her long for the fresher, lighter meals of Florence. The room hummed around her, people up from their seats after the end of the meal, talking and laughing with one another. Bits of cheese sat stuck to the wooden table top before her, half bitten pieces of bread scattered about, spilled next to empty plates and dirty knives. Nicóla caught the laugh of Thomas Wyatt, and glanced up for a moment, seeing him across the room, talking with the Lady Anne and some older courtier whose name eluded her… Brereton? Nicóla made sure, as her gaze cast back to her half-filled cup, she did not look in Crumwell's direction; he too caught up in conversation after the first session in parliament. Why was he even at court tonight? For a moment, Nicóla considered marching over to him, asking him for a loan, enough to set sail for Rome. No need to earn enough from shaky-hands Gardiner to go home. After all, Gardiner could only interrogate her for information on the Pope so many times before there was no more to tell. Nicóla's place at court was only temporal.

A hand rested on Nicóla's shoulder and she blinked a few times and looked up to see shaky-hands Gardiner, his beady dark eyes showing his ever-present disdain for her presence. Gardiner was an odd man; he seemed as if he disliked all human company, yet kept a large web of spies in his employ, keeping him busy, someone always in his ear.

'Archdeacon Gardiner,' Nicóla sighed. 'As always, I am ready to serve.'

'Then drop the sharp humours and get up at this instant because the King wishes to speak with you.'

That forced Nicóla into sobriety. She leapt from her seat and straightened her black doublet, a few crumbs swept away. Nicóla followed Gardiner; his black fur coat was so long that her heavy boots almost stepped on its fabric. That coat would be expensive by the yard; French certainly. At last with her shortened hair, Nicóla had less need for her flat cap to cover her appearance. The court had plenty of delicate men anyway, making life rather simple, considering all the obstacles she could have faced. Still, seeing the King was never serene.

Nicóla followed Gardiner through the rows of tables and dancing courtiers, and past guards through a hallway she had seen no one use all night. Darkness filled the archway space but Gardiner seemed to know precisely where to head. They turned and arrived at the heavy wooden door where guards and attendants awaited. With a simple nod from Gardiner, the usher opened the huge door and pronounced their arrival.

'The King's Master Secretary Stephen Gardiner.'

Now Nicóla recognised the room, the space in which the King assaulted her and Crumwell took her into his care – the King's privy chamber. A quick glance around a bookcase showed another entrance, the one they must have used that horrible afternoon. The King stood by the fireplace, the fire so huge it roared like an animal. Henry stood with his hands behind his back, his gold and black doublet speckled with white pearls. Gold thread trickled along the ruffles of his hose, sparkling when the fire caught their shine. His lips pursed closed, his dark red eyebrows in a frown as the King took in Nicóla, a step behind Gardiner. She observed Henry's desk had moved closer to the windows, no doubt to catch the winter light.

'Your Majesty,' Gardiner said with a bow, and Nicóla copied him, but kept her mouth shut.

'Gardiner, thank you for bringing me your new attendant,' Henry said, and brought his hands together in front of him. 'Mr.

Frescobaldi, I understand from talk you are no longer a Church layman.'

'I have yet to take holy orders, Your Majesty,' Nicóla replied, careful to keep the tone of her voice low and steady. 'I was under orders, as part of the Campeggio envoy, to act as a Church layman, and now am absolved from that requirement.'

'Do you not think it an affront to God to act as a man of the cloth when you are none of the sort?'

'I seek to do naught but live by God's laws, Your Majesty. The Pope is God's voice on this Earth and I obeyed his orders, as a pious servant.'

'Gardiner told me all about your knowledge of the feeble Pope Clement. It was I who had you released from the Tower, did you know?'

Nicóla stole a glance to Gardiner, who nodded in response. She assumed it was Queen Katherine. 'I was unawares, Your Majesty, and I thank you.'

'You ought to thank me. The letter which the Pope wrote to you made me pay heed. You and Pope Clement are clearly close, and you are a spy. Do you know why I let you go free into Gardiner's care?'

'In order to extract information from me, Your Majesty.'

'You are of much use to Archdeacon Gardiner, as he has reported much of your musings back to us. However, we could have, as easily, had you tortured for that information, still in the Tower.'

'Your Majesty is much gracious to offer me such kind and considerate treatment.'

'I noticed from letters between you and the Pope that he values you, and hurting you would only damage our case for annulment, so consider yourself lucky, Mr. Frescobaldi.'

'His Majesty is widely known to be the wisest and gentlest prince in Christendom.'

'Is that so?'

Nicóla had Henry wanting abroad rumours. Nicóla glanced to shaky-hands Gardiner again, who gestured she continue speaking.

'Italy does not have a monarchy as elaborate as yours, Your Majesty. As you know, the Republic of Florence, where I was born, has ruling families, prominent and wealthy, not ennobled rulers. While the system can have success, it lacks the experience of your great family.'

'Archdeacon Gardiner relates to me that you mention Pope Clement is much diminished in his health after a head injury?'

'While imprisoned during the Roman sacking, Your Majesty. It is not a well-known story, and I only told Archdeacon Gardiner and also Dr. Cranmer the truth because I trusted them as scholars and men of God.'

'I am glad you chose to tell us. It brings much cheer to hear the Pope is not of sound mind. It goes some way to explain the huge delays in our correspondence. Pope Clement is quite mad and unable to make sound decisions. Tell me, Mr. Frescobaldi, is it true you claimed to both Archdeacon Gardiner and Dr. Cranmer that the Pope shall never submit to an annulment?'

'It is my personal opinion, Your Majesty. Rome may not be the best way to secure such a decision.' Nicóla swallowed hard. Henry's face changed not in demeanour but was known to change mood as quickly as a coin flipping game at a seaside trickery stall. It hurt to tell such truths about Giulio and her "family" back home, no matter the circumstance.

King Henry wandered away from the fireplace and sat in a nearby chair, his thick legs crossed. Henry leaned back and eyed both Nicóla and Gardiner, who stood stiff and ready for more questions. 'Mr. Frescobaldi, I understand, since your release from the Tower, that you launched an attempt to win a seat in parliament for Crumwell. I was unawares you worked for him.'

'I do not work for Master Crumwella, Your Majesty. I simply knew of his desire to re-enter parliament and I sought to look for an opening on his behalf, as he was with…' Nicóla froze, not wanting to speak of Wolsey, 'business in Esher. Master Crumwella has been kindly to me and I wished to repay the favour.'

'You must have done something right, because I know Crumwell sits in parliament now. I spoke to Crumwell just tonight, and he is quick to help me in any legal matter I have.'

'He is a notable lawyer, Your Majesty. You shall be well served by Master Crumwella.'

'You speak awfully high of Crumwell, who is just a commoner. I hear you asked Dr. Cranmer to give him a message from the Tower. Did you expect Crumwell to visit you there?'

'No, Your Majesty, I did not. I would not any arrest of mine to harm Master Crumwella; I only wished to let him know certain facts.'

'Trust me, we hear all. Tell me, why would Crumwell care for your sister's intention to marry in Florence? Does Crumwell mean to have the heiress Frescobaldi for himself?'

Nicóla paused; she could not for her life understand what the King wanted. 'Master Crumwella was in my father's household in Florence when I was born, Your Majesty. He became close to my father over about ten years. Master Crumwella cares for our family, which is now only myself and one remaining sister.' Such a bold lie to a king.

'You are no ordinary family, so let us not pretend, Mr. Frescobaldi. You are the spy for His Holiness in Rome. You and your sister must be held in high regard.'

'Family ties are strong in Italy, as is loyalty. Once you are in the keep of a family, or your houses are in alliance, you stay that way for generations. These alliances in Florence allow me to be in the care of the Pope's family, along with my sister. Our father was murdered and my stepmother died in childbirth many years ago. My other sisters all died of the plague outbreak in 1520. I only escaped when my father took me to the Low Countries as his secretary on a trading mission. As Master Crumwella knows of this, he wished to know more of my sister's prolonged marriage arrangements. I wanted to update him on proceedings.'

'But not your condition in the Tower?'

'I do not wish to harm Master Crumwella by being associated with me, Your Majesty.'

'Master Crumwell is a friend of Gardiner here, as well as Thomas Boleyn, and even old Norfolk seems to think highly of his skills. I am glad to know Crumwell is on my side, and not conspiring somehow with you or the Pope.'

'Absolutely not, Your Majesty, I swear on God's grace.'

'But I bring you hither on another matter. The Pope writes to you, but the letter was opened. His Holiness wants you back in Rome with all haste.'

'I do wish to return home, Your Majesty.'

'You see, Mr. Frescobaldi, as a friend to the Pope, you are a valued commodity, so why should we release you to Rome?'

'I have naught left to offer, Your Majesty.'

'I did wonder if perchance you could return to Rome and write back to us hither, to keep us abreast of all news on the annulment.

But if your loyalties in Italy are as strong as you say, perchance that cannot happen. Perchance we cannot allow you to travel.'

With the right words, the King would pay for travel to Rome and Nicóla could get away from the poisonous English court immediately. Away from Crumwell's hate. 'My strong loyalties could work in your favour, Your Majesty. Master Crumwella may not bear my family's name, but he was tutored by my father, taken in as one of the family.'

'What is that to me?'

'Perchance if I was to leave London, knowing Master Crumwella was being well regarded and well utilised for his skills, it would make it far simpler for me to provide him any information you may need. I could pass information freely, knowing Master Crumwella was at the other end of my letters.'

'Are you asking for a bribe from the King of England?' Henry asked and stood in a heartbeat.

'No, Your Majesty,' Nicóla replied, unable to maintain her low tone. 'I am simply saying my family loyalties are as strong hither as they are in Rome. I am saying you can trust me. If I wanted to be bribed, I would do so to gain the ruby ring taken from me when I entered the Tower, as it belonged to my father.'

'Why should I trust you, Mr. Frescobaldi? For all I know, you shall go back to the Pope and betray us.'

'The Pope shall well indeed wish to know of my time here, but to simply discuss matters would not have any effect. The Apostolic Palace does not run as your court. In Italy things are done differently.'

King Henry sat down again and threw his hands in the air, not heeded by Nicóla's words. 'What does that mean? We are efficient hither, we are educated.'

'Well indeed, Your Majesty. But in Italy we are ruthless, and we have webs at play, which can have as much power and influence as any ruler. I have the Pope's ear, but so do many others. There is a whole web of men who run the Apostolic Palace in the Pope's place when His Holiness is unable to do the work dispatched to him. It is through these webs that wealthy men see to their well-being. If you ever wish to have any influence, you need to be part of the web.'

'I am the King of England! I am no pawn in some foreign game!'

'You are a pawn, Your Majesty. All men, kings or peasants, are pawns; that is how the Catholic Church continues to control

Christendom. You shall never gain what you need by fighting the web; you could win by using the web to your own advantage. You need someone who understands how the Italians work, how they think.'

'And you are that person? I ask again, why should I trust you?'

'I fear, Your Majesty, I shall not remain in Rome for long, by the Pope's side. I am ordered to return to Florence, the home of the Pope's family. The man who knows the Italians is already hither at court; Master Crumwella.'

'Why speak so highly of Crumwell? What is the secret?'

'There is none, Your Majesty, however, I do believe I am indebted to Master Crumwella, for all the kindness he has shown me over the summer, when he had no need to do so. I have, in turn, become somewhat dazzled by his presence, his intelligence, his ambition.'

Gardiner burst out in a coughing fit, and Nicóla threw him a look, knowing he was simply scoffing at the statement in vain jealousy.

'Crumwell is still Wolsey's man,' King Henry replied.

'There is a way that could be acceptable, Your Majesty. I believe that could work in your favour, even if Wolsey was unable to make an annulment.'

'I cannot talk of Wolsey,' the King replied and wiped his sweaty top lip with his hand. 'I simply cannot. Mr. Frescobaldi, I shall have Gardiner arrange to have you sent back to Rome immediately. You shall need to leave London in the morning. I want you back where the Pope can see we did not harm his "family".'

'I shall do as His Majesty commands, and leave at dawn, in whatever manner is deemed best.'

Henry dismissed the pair with a simple wave of his hand, and Nicóla and Gardiner quickly left the room. All at once, Nicóla had procured a way back to Rome without delay, away from England. It was time to stop all this madness, and rejoin her real life, helping the Medici family rise again as rulers of Florence, and take her place as the wealthy wife of its leader. Not once in fifteen years had she looked at a man; being a man was far more important than any romance. Nicóla simply could not even be in the same country as Thomas Crumwell; the connection between them made no sense and would bring only trouble. As soon as Nicóla was free of the meeting, she stood for a second in the dining hall; there seemed only a few people to speak to before she prepared her few meagre possessions for travelling. Gardiner had already gone to get money and a list of ships which could take her to France and then beyond at the King's command.

Plenty of eyes followed Nicóla after being pulled aside by the King. Thomas Wyatt scurried towards her, Mark Smeaton falling in closely behind. 'On Lord's mercy, what happened?' Wyatt whispered. 'Smeaton and I were about to leave to play cards but noticed you missing. Are you well? We worried you were headed for the cells again.'

'Quite the opposite,' Nicóla sighed. 'I am heading back to Rome. At dawn.'

'Rome?' Smeaton repeated, his angelic face filled with surprise. 'So soon? What happened?'

'The King does not wish to have a papal spy living at court, even under the gaze of Stephen Gardiner. I am being ordered home. My time has come; without an annulment there is no reason to have me hither. With the new ambassador to the Holy Roman Emperor, Eustace Chapuys, arriving a few months ago, there is no need to also have another representative for the Pope at court. I sail in the morning on the first ship that can leave England.'

'What a shame, and just as we started becoming all such strong friends,' Smeaton said with a sweet pout of his lips. The wine and party had gone to his head. 'We are not the only ones looking for you. Master Crumwell saw you disappear towards the King's chambers. He gave me something for you.'

'I am not in Master Crumwella's good graces. What did he give you – a knife?'

Wyatt laughed as he handed a note to Nicóla. She unfurled the paper to just a few hasty words. Se hai bisogno di me, io verrò. If you need me, I will come. Nicóla folded the note again. 'Let us have another wine, gentlemen, and then sadly, I must farewell you forever.'

~~~

The bitter London rain lashed the city as Nicóla trekked along the edge of the city walls, less than a mile's walk in the dark to Bishopsgate. No one was out on the London streets tonight, not even the whores. At least while Nicóla followed the walls with the King's guards placed along the way, she felt a touch safer, but only just.

Wyatt had given her a knife to carry, surprised the Italian wished to leave court that very night, long before dawn. With her long black cloak with hood, Nicóla could disappear along the edge of the inner city unnoticed, a wise choice for someone carrying a large sum of money. Nicóla left the sanctuary of the wall's comfort and dived down dirty Broad Street, past the Augustinian monastery's wide entrance, and was soon upon the front gate of Crumwell's home. She pounded the heavy hook on the wooden gate, and hoped, close to midnight on a freezing night, that the steward would open up. It had to be luck; Peter, the young boy who manned the gate appeared soon after, letting Nicóla in with the sight of Crumwell's note. A single candle lit a window on the third floor, which was Crumwell's bedroom, the only room used on the third level now his family had passed away. Nicóla's heart began to beat a scant faster as she crossed the courtyard towards the front door. But his note had said se hai bisogno di me, io verrò, so mayhap he would speak to her.

One of the maids answered the door and let Nicóla in, recognising her from her earlier stay. She stood alone in the austere entranceway, dripping and shivering, longing for the fireplace in the parlour. It took several minutes before she heard footsteps again. A door from the stairway opened and there stood Crumwell, still dressed if ready to go outside, boots on, even a cloak. Crumwell regarded Nicóla up and down but did not say a word.

Nicóla held up the note, now ruined by the rain. 'If you need me, I will come,' she repeated his words. Crumwell looked lost for words. Nicóla just stared at him as his face softened with each passing moment, as if her presence in his home made him more comfortable as the seconds ticked past. Nicóla swallowed hard and brushed a few drops of water from her face with her black gloved hand.

'Do you need me?' he asked, his voice deep and so tender, a hint of a worry in his tone.

'I am leaving for Rome in the morning.' Crumwell's face did not give any answer to the news. He took a few measured steps towards her, their eyes never parting. 'I wanted to say to you, Master Crumwella, before I sail; if you need me, I will come. So much has happened in the past few months…'

Nicóla's voice trailed off as Crumwell reached to her throat and undid the tie of her wet cloak. Crumwell carefully took it from her shoulders and dropped it on the floor with a wet slap. With slow precise movements, he then took the slight bag from her hands and placed it on the floor beside a long cabinet which lined the detailed wooden wall. All the while he kept his intense golden stare on her. Crumwell stood before her again, not a word uttered. Nicóla copied his actions and pulled at the string which fixed his cloak around his shoulders. Had he dressed, ready to be of service late at night? After the fierce anger he displayed? One by one, he carefully pulled her fingers from her plain wet gloves, drips of water running along his hands as he took them from her. His scarred hands felt so warm against hers, frozen from the walk in the London night. Being touched by Crumwell was unlike any other person; everyone in Nicóla's life was family, friends or business partners. There was no man to love her, to show affection, to be a husband. But she had vowed never to dishonour her father again, as she did as a girl. Nicóla never even talked of the notion of love; think what love was doing to the entire nation of England! Marriage, virtue, honour, all things too precious to throw away on love. But the touch of Crumwell's hand against hers threw Nicóla into a world she had longed to avoid.

One hand enclosed in his, Crumwell guided her towards the stairs and Nicóla followed, willing but overwhelmed. Up the stairs to the silent third floor, Crumwell did not face her again until in the sanctity of his enormous bedroom. The roar of the fire seemed angry like a beast as Crumwell led her to the warmth, chairs placed close to the fire, wine on the table beside them. Nicóla shivered with the sudden change in temperature, and again as Crumwell ran his hands through her short wet hair, one hand resting on her back of her bare neck.

'Hai bisogno di me?' he whispered, his mouth so preciously close to hers, his golden stare on hers. Yes, she did need him. Nicóla nodded just a little and Crumwell brought his lips to hers, nothing like the frightening moment at Esher. His kiss flowed over her lips, gentle at first, careful and wary of the moment. Nicóla knew too much of life to be meek as a normal woman would, but love was still a new concept. She kissed him back, deeper, slow and probing and Crumwell instantly picked up on her need. His mouth began to drift from hers, kisses raining down her neck and Nicóla sighed, relieved to have Crumwell to herself at last. She could feel him undoing the buttons on her wet doublet, her clothes getting lighter with every button unfastened. He slipped the doublet from her shoulders and it fell at her feet.

Crumwell brought his eyes back to hers and Nicóla tried to catch her breath, cold in her white shirt. Crumwell smiled and Nicóla copied; Crumwell was checking to make sure she consented. None of this was ever meant to happen. Nicóla was to marry Alessandro, a man, more a boy, who made it plain he would have mistresses, no desire for legitimate children. This was Nicóla's one and only chance to express love. Nothing mattered any longer, not the will of God, or the men on Earth who instructed God's will.

~~~

My dearest Tomassito

The King has let me go home, and you must use this to your advantage, as the King shall no doubt attempt to use you. I told King Henry about the use of Italian family honour to establish power and influence, but told him you are the only man in England who understands how Florentine politics work. The King is going to look to you for advice, and, if you are willing to forgive my sins, I am happy to write to you and guide you with information. I know how torn you are, to be caught between your fealty to Cardinal Wolsey and your need for survival. If Wolsey is cast down, the Pope shall feel as if he has no power in England any longer. If Wolsey is returned to favour by the King, the Pope will soften towards England again. Be the man who saves his longtime friend and brings the King back into the Pope's favour. The reformation is coming to the Papal States, to Naples, to Venice, to Savoy, Genoa, even the Republic of Florence. The pressure in Rome has never seemed more intense. As long as King Henry is a source of pressure, he shall never gain the Pope's favour. Henry must be seen as moderate. Be the man who understands the need to tread lightly, Tomassito. Be the man who is gentle, even if you wish for the Protestant reformation to proceed in England. Nothing is forever, not even marriage, any longer. The King is lost and Sir Thomas More is a man fixed in his love for the Catholic faith. An extreme view will be a man's downfall at such a time. The faster changes are made, the faster changes fall apart.

The moderate man shall inherit the kingdom. That man needs to be the Queenmaker.

Chapter 18 – December 1529
Austin Friars and Greenwich Palace, London

Weare thy seecryts as if they be mayde of armour

Crumwell burnt the letter from Nicóla. He did not wish to see it go, but the information never needed to be seen by other eyes. Parting with the letter was not hard; waking up to find Nicóla gone from Austin Friars caused a break to his heart. Crumwell woke well past dawn, but the sky still hung dark, rain lashing the city. He lay naked in his bed and reached out for Nicóla's soft body, to find only cold bedsheets, the fireplace almost as cold across the room. Nicóla's wet clothes left to dry by the flames had gone, nothing but the note, written on damp paper from shaky-hands Gardiner's office. Crumwell could still smell her against him. Had a woman ever truly wanted him, even in his youth? He was young once, a soldier, then found success and became moderately wealthy. But love? He cared deeply for Elizabeth for their entire marriage, but there was never lust. Last night's comparison made it obvious. Mayhap the beguiling Anne Boleyn could love the ageing King, because a beautiful Italian passionately loved Crumwell, for at least one night.

A few strands of rose-gold hair remained on the bed's pillows, and Crumwell gathered them, all evidence taken away. Nicóla must have known he would beg her not to go home, not to marry. She was to inherit her father's fortune, to be removed to her new husband. Nicóla was set to be married to the man who would run the tiny nation of Florence. Nicóla would be the wife of a Medici. Another man would have her extraordinary mind by his side. Another man would lie with her, touch her olive skin and find rose-gold hair on his pillow. Nicóla was a woman of another world, and chose to return to the land of Crumwell's youth, ready to claim her power and wealth. But for one night, Nicóla lay in Crumwell's arms at Austin Friars.

~~~

A month passed with indifference, Crumwell impassive to the world around him. He swore not to wallow when he left Esher, but the pain of his life made his soul turn cold. One benefit was he looked utterly serious in the House of Commons, not willing to enter into any frivolous discussions. Surely God taking so much needed to have some lessons, some tests, some conclusion. The main item of business in parliament was the Bill of Attainder against Wolsey, now called the Book of Articles, as the bill had six and forty charges laid against the Cardinal. There was worry Crumwell would favour the Cardinal, for the language used in the bills created by Norfolk and the other lords was outrageous with the claims it made. Wolsey was guilty of over-reaching in his decision-making, he took too many bribes, kept too much money for himself. Crumwell had long over-charged rents on Wolsey's tenants, and used the extra takings to line Wolsey's pockets. This was just one thing, and Wolsey had also skimmed money from the King for so long that he paid to build the extraordinary Hampton Court Palace. The Cardinal could hold court himself in rival to the King; such was Wolsey's lavish uses of royal favour.

Now was no time for Wolsey to be writing to Crumwell. Wolsey, so recently a haughty and assuming leader, had fallen to the bottom of the social order. His letters to Austin Friars asked Crumwell to come back to Esher, even though he knew Crumwell had to attend parliament. Wolsey begged Crumwell to come in every letter sent, as if he not yet understood the master-servant days were gone.

I need your good, sad, discreet advice and counsel but also need to express certain things to you.

Take some pains for me and forsake me not in my extreme need, and as I cannot, God shall reward you. Now is the time to show whether you love me or not.

For all love, leave me not now, lost of all comfort.

Crumwell felt no different; alone in the world, viewed by all as a Wolsey supporter, and nursing the ache of having fallen in love and then lost it, something which happened to lesser men. Crumwell had no choice but to care not for Wolsey's appeals. With all those important to him gone, Crumwell could work with surprising speed, no distractions from the business of making money, lending and collecting, buying and selling, solving disputes among the wealthy yet poorly educated.

A late night call at Austin Friars heralded guards demanding to take Crumwell to the King, currently still at Greenwich. A hurried trip along the Thames saw Crumwell taken through the quiet palace, its luxurious tapestries and golden detailing seen by no eyes but those of the servants, who seemed in the midst of decorating for Christmas. The guards who fetched Crumwell marched him into Henry's privy chamber.

There stood the King, dressed informally, a white linen shirt with wide sleeves, plain black hose. The toll of carrying heavily embroidered clothes, loaded with jewels and gold thread, warm ermine furs and delicate French detailing must have taken its toll on the red-haired King. Henry looked up from his desk as Crumwell was announced. The King stood at his desk and gestured for the door to be shut as Crumwell bowed and clasped his hands in front of him. The heat of the fireplace made Crumwell's cold fingers tingle.

'Mr. Crumwell,' Henry sighed and rested his hands on the edge of his desk, 'how kind of you to travel to court on this cold evening.'

'Always a pleasure, Your Majesty.' As if Crumwell had any choice!

'Tell me, what do you think of the Bill of Attainder before parliament? Of the charges relating to praemunire against Wolsey?'

'Honestly, Your Majesty, the parliament is having trouble in reconciling the paperwork, which appears hasty and poorly-worded.'

'No matter,' Henry sniffed. 'By royal command, I shall have the attainder dropped. You are only one who knows, so if that detail gets out, I shall know you betrayed me, Crumwell.'

'I have no need of chatter, Your Majesty.' Crumwell did not feel like speaking with anyone, on any subject.

'I hear Wolsey writes to you, as he writes to me.'

Spies again. It was time to purge some of the staff at Austin Friars. Crumwell already had his suspicions on several. 'Yes, Your Majesty, I am in receivance of letters. Cardinal Wolsey is most unwell at Esher.'

'I know, and I have sent my physician, Dr. William Butts, to attend upon him to cure his dropsy.'

'That is most gracious, Your Majesty.' That fact alone would soothe Wolsey's demands, surely. The demands for attention from Wolsey wore at Crumwell's already limited patience.

'I cannot have the Lady Anne hearing I sent my doctor to Esher,' the King said, and leaned away from the desk. 'She will be even more unforgiving. You know of Sir John Russell, one of Wolsey's supporters? He is to be in parliament, and I shall name him a Knight of the Garter. Russell spoke to me several weeks ago in support of Wolsey. Anne overheard and has not spoken to him since. I cannot have men at odds with Anne.'

London rumours raged with news on how Lady Anne wanted the throne, how she despised Queen Katherine, Cardinal Wolsey, and anyone else who stood in her way. Anne was done with waiting, and Crumwell blamed her not – almost four years now.

'Do you know my Groom of the Stool, Sir Henry Norris? He obliged Wolsey with a room at Grafton House in September. He also visited Esher for me recently. Norris is much affected by Wolsey's downfall. The Lady Anne is livid with Norris. Can you go to Norris for me, Crumwell? Can you ask him to ease the displeasure he has caused Anne? He needs to attain her favour. The Norris family has worked for myself and my father in roles of close privacy and I wish to have a more harmonious household.'

'You wish me to ask Sir Henry Norris to pay more heed to the pleasures of Lady Anne Boleyn?' Crumwell asked with much confusion. What in God's name did it have to do with Crumwell? But he eased his sudden stern brow. The King tested him, tested his confidence and his alliances. 'As you wish, Your Majesty.'

'Excellent.' Henry clapped his hands together and wandered over to the fireplace. The flames highlighted the redness of his hair and beard, though greys came through, much like Crumwell's own hair. 'I have given York Place to Lady Anne, had you heard?'

'Of course, Your Majesty, it is keen news. Cardinal Wolsey dearly loved his palace. It has always been in the hands of the Bishops of York for almost three hundred years. I hear the exquisite new Hampton Court Palace is now Your Majesty's palace.'

'Well indeed. Surely the King ought to have the most grand palace? Though, we shall be renaming and expanding York Place. I have also taken The More from Wolsey, and Tittenhanger in Herefordshire. I am sure you know.'

Crumwell nodded. He also knew the King had taken the Cluniac monastery of St Augustine in North Hampshire, the richest monastery in all England. The profits from the monastery had paid to build Oxford College. Wolsey's colleges now belonged to the King.

'If you wish, Your Majesty, I can write to Cardinal Wolsey and ask him to grant money to the Boleyn family, perchance to help attain their favour? A timely bribe can quell many an argument. Perchance the Lady Anne's father, Lord Rochford, could receive the income of the Bishopric of Winchester, and the lands at St. Albans Abbey in Hertfordshire. Both are favourable incomes, worthy of a man such as the Lord.'

'You remember the amounts from memory? That is quite a skill.'

'A method called Ioci, which I learned in Florence.'

The King nodded slowly, his mind bouncing between ideas. 'I shall tell Thomas Boleyn of your splendid idea. Boleyn will be best pleased. I am to make him the Earl of Wiltshire and Ormond, and his son, George, shall be the new Lord Rochford.'

A suggestion of bribery had just hitched Crumwell's wagon to an ever rising member of the court. Quite a bonus.

'You shall need to betray your former master to extend yourself hither at court, Mr. Crumwell. Do you understand? I cannot have men loyal to the dishonest ways of my enemies.'

'I am a lawyer, Your Majesty. I am loyal, but only to those who are honest and of sound mind.' That was extremely vague, but it made Henry smile.

'They say you are a Lutheran, Crumwell, that you want Protestant reform. My new Chancellor, Sir Thomas More, says so and he is my closest friend and advisor. More is never wrong.'

'I am a money lender, Your Majesty, a banker, a lawyer, worse than any heretic.'

Henry burst out laughing. 'I like you, Crumwell. Baseborn men are curious.'

'We are easily disposed of, Your Majesty.'

The King laughed again. 'You are loyal by choice, rather than ruled by family ties. I like that.' Henry paused and took a deep breath. 'At least we have the business of the Italians and the legatine court behind us now, Crumwell. I truly hoped God would place his decision in the court and give me freedom.'

'I too wished the court more success.' Crumwell was careful not to mention which conclusion he preferred; in truth, he did not care too much.

'And your Italian Waif, the ship which took him to Rome may have landed by now.'

'I am unawares of how Mr. Frescobaldi travelled back to Rome.'

'I have people who bring me news. I know none of my ships are harmed of late, so the Italian might have arrived back in Rome. Have you visited the nest of vipers, Crumwell?'

'Rome, Your Majesty? Yes, and I met the old Pope Leo, on Wolsey's behalf, many years ago now. The Holy See has the strong presence of God, but the country always has a sense of foreboding.'

'Agreed. They cannot get themselves together, not with the Emperor and his laws, the Spanish constantly invading southern lands, the French fighting in the north. And yet my realm is being pulled asunder because of the confusion of an ailing Pope!'

'May I suggest something, Your Majesty?' Now was the chance to act upon the words in Nicóla's letter. 'The Pope shall know now, surely, of how Wolsey has fallen from favour. Pope Clement shall hear of England's only cardinal living in poverty and illness, forsaken by all. As a man under pressure from all corners of Christendom, this insult on a man ordained cardinal shall not sit well.'

'What is that to me?' Henry frowned.

'Restoring Wolsey would soothe the Pope and his opinion of your troubles.'

'I cannot restore Wolsey, no matter how much I love him or miss him. Never. Anne would never forgive me, and it is for Anne and my country that I must marry and gain a son.'

'Perchance time away from court and his loss of the Lord Chancellor's office allows Cardinal Wolsey to spend more time with God. I suggest not to give Wolsey his life back, Your Majesty. That would not sit well with the entire court and all your supporters. But if Wolsey lived somewhere more fitting to his needs; warmer, drier, more comfortable, where he can tend to his soul, the Pope would think you a kind prince.'

'Am I not a kind prince?'

'Yes, Your Majesty, forgive my words. The Pope would see you caring for an old man, who has finished his time in the court and can now talk with God. It is time to appear friendly to the Pope, to gain his trust again.'

'How do I do such things, Crumwell? I have made my disdain plain.'

'Naught is solved with simple gestures, Your Majesty.'

'But I have no more time. I fight with Anne, I fight with Katherine... I cannot live with a queen who was never truly my wife, and also the woman who will soon become a queen. I am weary!'

'Love is tiring, Your Majesty.'

Henry nodded slowly and then snapped back to attention. 'How is your situation, Crumwell? The foreign woman you wish to love?'

'It is forgotten, Your Majesty.'

'Love is not easily forgotten. The Italian Waif, he is to see his sister married in Florence?'

'Indeed, Your Majesty.'

'Is it the Frescobaldi sister you wish to take as a wife? Were you not once part of their household?'

'I wish it forgotten, Your Majesty.'

'Crumwell, I have met many women in my time. A king must maintain a certain reputation. I know women; I know their games, their whims. In truth, I have not the success with women as many would think. I loved my wife with all my heart. But in truth, I had only three mistresses over fifteen years of marriage, not the dozens people like to imagine.'

'I know, Your Majesty. The women you gave homes and marriages to, after being your mistresses, are recorded in Wolsey's dealings. I know it is considered manly to have many mistresses, but there is no harm in just having a few favourites. Either way, your secret is embraced with safety.'

'But my Anne is an intelligent woman. Anne is different, even to her sister. Only a woman can understand a woman, do you think?'

'They are creatures not for the male mind, Your Majesty.'

'Anne has a certain feeling about Frescobaldi.'

Crumwell swallowed hard. At least Nicóla resided far away now. 'Your Majesty?'

'A feeling that the Italian is special. I too had many thoughts on him. I suspect you know the Italian far better than Anne or myself.'

Crumwell's mind had a flash of Nicóla, kissing him in bed. 'It is possible, Your Majesty.'

'Well,' the King smiled, 'let us not tarry on such issues. The Italian has gone from England and we can focus on the future. Please, Mr.

Crumwell, I invite you to attend dinner at court nightly from now. I wish to hear more from you, so we shall make sure you have rooms at court, for your own comfort.'

The King suspected Nicóla's character. Lady Anne suspected. It no longer mattered if Crumwell supported Wolsey; if Crumwell did anything except support Henry, he could be arrested over Nicóla's truth. Dressing as a man violated social conducts decided by the Church.

'Let us celebrate Christmas together, Crumwell, and then see what we shall discuss next. Perchance we shall figure a way to bring you an Italian bride. But have you heard the rumours? That Florence has been sacked by Imperial and Spanish men, as Rome suffered? The War of the League of Cognac has landed upon the Republic of Florence to restore one of the Medicis as ruler, making Florence part of the Imperial Empire.'

'Alessandro de' Medici, Your Majesty, one of the many bastards of the family shall be a duke when the uprising is over.'

'Be best pleased your time in Italy is gone, for no safety is to be had. God help your Waif in the battle. Someone so delicate is unlikely to survive a siege.'

Chapter 19 – December 1529
Austin Friars, London

Secynd chances art more poywerful than seecryts

Crumwell was well-accustomed to lavish Christmas and Epiphany occasions. Austin Friars always held an enormous feast; the yearly party for the Company of Merchant Adventurers of London, a way to show patronage and pay favour. Every merchant and scholar within travelling distance would come. Crumwell's longtime friend, Stephen Vaughan, often made the trip back from the Low Countries. But there was talk Vaughan was a heretic earlier in the year. Vaughan met regularly with William Tyndale, the infamous author of the English Bible, now favoured by Lady Anne and the Boleyn family. Crumwell begged Sir Thomas More, former parliament speaker and ever faithful advisor to the King, to leave Vaughan alone, and he had. But now, More was Lord Chancellor and Crumwell feared for Vaughan, the man whom he called a close friend for many years. Vaughan needed to tarry safe in Antwerp, and trade on Crumwell's behalf from there. If Vaughan was to be in voluntary exile, at least Crumwell could throw him work on behalf of the King.

But for the second year in a row, without his wife Elizabeth at his side, Crumwell felt no need to host Christmas, no Company of Merchant Adventurers of London feast. No meetings on prices abroad, of money trading, of scholarly pursuits or swapping the latest designs and fabrics. No dazzling people with the hawks and falcons Crumwell kept or archery competitions in the garden. This year, with the King in need of multiple celebrations, Crumwell attended a lavish party at court, a banquet for Henry and his beloved Anne Boleyn. It was more like a wedding than anything else. Everyone seemed so eager to shine their light on Lady Anne, who was glorious in gold at the King's side. The Boleyn family followed Henry wherever he went, and shifty Thomas Boleyn, the new Earl of Wiltshire, was merry to see Crumwell in their circle of friends and away from Wolsey. At least someone liked a commoner amongst the nobles.

One benefit of the season was Crumwell's only son, Gregory, coming home from his studies in Buckinghamshire, and Crumwell could have the King's artist, Hans Holbein paint his son as well as himself while the family came together.

'Are you much distracted, Master Cromwoll?' asked Holbein as he sketched the young Gregory, his accent unable to pronounce the name. Holbein was a portly German man, famed for his talents by all at court since Sir Thomas More first spotted him and raised him into lucrative favour. The man had a skilled talent, one Crumwell was keen to pursue once Holbein returned from his upcoming trip home to Basel.

'I am not distracted, Master Holbein,' Crumwell said, and looked away from the window where snowflakes patted.

'Father is much distracted of late,' Gregory replied. Gregory was so much his mother's son, with brilliant blonde hair, a sweet pink mouth, and delicate blue eyes. Gregory would turn ten on his next birthday, and each day Crumwell felt he never did enough for his son. Gregory's education could not be compromised though, hence his need to be away living with a close friend, Prioress Vernon in Marlow. Gregory grew up under the care of his tutor, alongside his friends Nicholas, William and Christopher, boys who enjoyed Crumwell's wealth in providing them an education. Nicholas Sadler was Ralph's young brother, and Ralph was such a trusted secretary to Crumwell. Christopher and William were Crumwell's youngest nephews, born to Crumwell's youngest sister Elizabeth. Crumwell wanted family about him, especially with his wife Elizabeth and his daughters with God now. But education always came first.

'My skill is seeing people,' Holbein continued as he stared at Gregory, seated by the fireplace in the main parlour in Austin Friars, dressed in black sewn with silver thread, bright like his hair. 'But to paint someone, I need to see their soul, not just their appearance.'

'And how do you do such a thing?' Crumwell asked with a

suspicious smile. 'Surely only God can see a man's soul.'

'The double-minded man with the wide golden eyes asks me how I see all? You understand me, I suspect, Master Cromwoll. For example, watching a distracted man looking out the window, he has something on his mind. That suggests intelligence, it suggests authority and control.'

'It suggests I am busy with work!'

'Perchance,' Holbein replied, and pulled a funny face at Gregory, causing a sweet smile, several front teeth still growing in. 'In your son, his smile, I see a boy of growing confidence, at ease with his own nature, and the way he sits suggests an athletic, healthy build.'

'Thank you,' Crumwell replied, his voice soft. He so loved his son, now his only child. Holbein pulled another face, this time sticking out his tongue and Gregory giggled again.

'The boy's pale blue eyes sparkle. I see a boy ready to learn.'

'I can do all my numbers and letters to much satisfaction,' Gregory replied, his voice ever more confident. The child wiggled in his seat to sit up straight, as if a king in his manor. 'I am learning Latin, Master Holbein.'

Holbein laughed inwardly. 'I have no doubt, my young friend. I am certain the King himself would feel proud to have such a child such as you.'

Well indeed Henry would. At this stage, Henry would perchance take a fool over his daughter. Henry was already well on the way to legitimising his bastard son he got on Bessie Blount ten years ago. Queen Katherine's daughter, the Princess Mary, was forgotten away in Wales. The bastard child, Henry Fitzroy, was already the Duke of Richmond and Somerset and Lord-Lieutenant of Ireland. Wolsey had once mentioned that Fitzroy could marry his half-sister, Princess Mary, and take the throne. Crumwell hoped Wolsey was just jesting, as the notion disgusted him. But young Henry was loved by his father's legitimate or not, and well-mannered and cared for.

'Tell me, Master Gregory. What does your father dream of as he watches the snowflakes?' Holbein asked, his eyes firmly on the sketch resting on the table before him.

'Perchance father thinks of the King,' Gregory said, his voice was high and delicate. A bit like Nicóla.

'Perchance.'

'Perchance Father thinks of my mother and my sisters, may the souls of all the faithful departed, through the mercy of God, rest in peace.'

'Amen.'

'Perchance Father thinks of all the parties he has attended at court this week, and how fat he shall become from all the feasting!'

'Gregory!' Crumwell admonished.

'I think it lucky I have finished my sketch of you, Master Gregory,' Holbein said, and put down his silverpoint rod. 'For now I can sketch your father in preparation for the paintings. We need to paint him before he is fat and remembered for all time as a plump old man!'

'Run along to your grandmother, Gregory,' Crumwell said as Gregory laughed at the jest.

'Can I go and play with Ralph?' Gregory begged. 'Ralph has new falconry gloves to show me.'

'Ralph is my secretary; he and cousin Richard have much work to be done.'

'Please, Father?'

Crumwell gave dismissive gesture and the boy ran off in search of Ralph in his office. He sat himself by the fire so Holbein could start his work on the second portrait.

'Master Gregory is a lovely son,' Holbein commented. 'I have a son, Philipp, the same age.'

'I thank God for Gregory. We had two more sons, Henry and Thomas, both taken soon after birth before Gregory was born strong and healthy. I do not think Elizabeth's heart could have coped with losing a third child. I am grateful to God that Gregory has journeyed well through the death of his mother and sisters.'

Holbein pulled out a fresh piece of white-coated paper, ready to start with his silverpoint impression. 'One thing a child cannot know; what his father is thinking. It takes an artist to know.'

Crumwell smiled again, just a fraction this time. 'And what do I think of, Master Holbein?'

'Women.'

'A grand assumption only.'

'Am I wrong, Master Cromwoll?'

Crumwell paused; of course he thought of Nicóla. A person may leave in presence, but not always in spirit. It would take a while to rid himself of Nicóla.

'Are you to marry again?' Holbein asked.

'No, that is not a plan for me.'

'Sir Thomas More told me of rumours you would marry again.'

'Sir Thomas More is now Chancellor of England; he should have more important works than thinking of my private life.'

'There are no private lives at court. Did you hear More had Thomas Hitton arrested? Rumours are Hitton is tortured in the Tower.'

Crumwell knew the name in a moment. Hitton was an English priest who lived in the Low Countries, a large supporter of Tyndale and the reformation. Hitton was also friends with Stephen Vaughan, the very friend Crumwell feared for. 'What charges will Hitton face?'

'Heresy. I am sorry, Master Cromwoll, I know you loyal to Cardinal Wolsey, but I heard you are Lutheran.'

'I have recently had cause to greatly dislike the Pope and the Church.' If not for Pope Clement, Nicóla may not be marrying Alessandro de'Medici. If not for the Pope, holding Nicóla's inheritance from her, due to her accidentally being born a girl, things may be different. Nicóla's father, such a gracious man, must have thought he put his daughter's inheritance in safe hands, unawares he would be murdered and his unnaturally intelligent daughter forced into marrying the Pope's own son. The corruption was endless. But Crumwell knew he could not let the situation cloud his judgement. In time, he could reconcile his thoughts.

'So it is a woman,' Holbein mused.

'What?'

'The way you speak, Master Cromwoll. You are suffering from the passion of a woman.'

'I was widowed not one year and a half ago. I lost my Elizabeth, little Anne and Grace. Also my sister Katheryn and her husband Morgan. The only solace was Richard, their son, who changed his surname to mine, and allows me to educate his young brother. My other nephews, Walter and Gregory, live far away in Wales.'

'Men have remarried in much less time. I fear your own King would remarry in minutes.'

'Please do not pretend to know me, Master Holbein.'

'Forgive me. I do feel for Thomas Hitton. Archbishop Warham and Bishop Fisher condemn him. Hitton was in England to distribute banned Protestant Testaments, letters written to him from many English exiles, all wishing to see the reformation come to England.

Luther's works, Tyndale's works and more are being printed. Hitton also had with him the English Primer translated by George Joye.'

'I wanted a copy for myself,' Crumwell mused. 'I hear Joye shall translate the Old Testament.'

'Rumour is, if found guilty of heresy by Sir Thomas More, Hitton will be burnt. He shall not repent.'

'Hitton believes in the supremacy of the Scriptures. He also wrote he thought neither marriage nor baptism needed a priest or a church. Hitton wrote if the word of God was printed in English, they would be better understood, which makes total sense to me.'

Holbein nodded as he began to sketch. 'Back home the reformation is already well underway. One day I pray we can all be saved from Catholic idolatry and of the false relics we must endure in church, all under the guide of corrupt priests.'

'You speak with such confidence, Master Holbein. I ought to warn you that we are a Catholic nation still, ruled by clerics.'

'Again, forgive me. I wish to know you, sir. I will return to England after my time in Basel. I expect by the time I return, the man with the golden eyes shall be the most powerful at court. I shall need a new patron. If Sir Thomas More is burning heretics, I will not find myself safe in his company any longer.'

'Fear not, Master Holbein.' Crumwell was already building an empire for himself. Over the Christmas period, powerful men returned home all over the country. Before they left, Ralph and Richard went to visit their servants, all people loyal to Wolsey. Now they became spies in Crumwell's employ. A spider web of confidence slowly built, powerful enough to protect anyone Crumwell wished to know, and each bribe given out was only a small sum, worth the ongoing costs. From well-placed secretaries, to humble delivery men, to cooks in wealthy homes, and ladies-in-waiting who cared for talkative noble wives. It was time to have his own web of allies, to grab those already proven useful, to gain new spies, and turn those working for others at court, just like Nicóla had back in Florence. Already brazen young lawyer Thomas Wriothesley, who worked for Stephen Gardiner, was in Crumwell's employ. Crumwell needed to follow Nicóla's advice; be the moderate man, be the Queenmaker. The only way to do that was play all sides and play nothing openly. Now, these Crumwell creatures spread across England for Christmas, gathering news.

~~~

The darkness had long arrived when Ralph appeared in Crumwell's library. 'Master,' Ralph said, and held out his hand. 'A letter has just arrived. It carries the seal of the Pope.'

Crumwell snatched the letter. If it carried the seal of the Pope, half of England would already know of its existence. Yet it was still perfectly sealed. Perchance it was a copy, the original already read by the King, or Gardiner or vicious More.

Ralph tugged his short blonde beard, his long oval face carrying a stern brow. 'Should we be worried?'

'We should be worried who knows of this letter's existence. I am certain this note's existence was known to the court just moments after its arrival on the English coast. There are eyes everywhere.'

'Surely the Pope has messengers who are subtle? Pity we had no eyes at the port, or we could have hidden the letter ourselves.'

'That is a task for another night.' Crumwell sat down at his desk again and regarded the heavy red seal, the coats of arms of the Holy See pressed into the wax. Few would dare damage the seal of the Pope, though they had ripped the letters recently sent to Nicóla when she sat in the Tower. Why had this gotten through? Perchance God himself saved the words for Crumwell's eyes.

'Why would the Pope write to you?' Ralph asked with a frown. 'I mean no offence, Master, but...'

'No, I understand. It will be from the offices of the Apostolic Palace, not the Pope himself, I am sure. The Pope does not simply write letters to all and dispatch them across Europe.'

'Could it be about Nicóla?'

'If anything has occurred with Nicóla, I will be sure to let you know. Pay the messenger handsomely for his silence in the delivery.' Crumwell clicked his fingers to dismiss Ralph.

The moment Crumwell tore at the letter, the red ribbons weaved through the wax fell away, to reveal the hand of Nicóla. The date was early December, a month ago now; she must have used the Pope's messengers to get a letter to London so swiftly.

Tomassito

My humble duty remembered, hoping in the Almighty of your health and prosperity which on my knees I beseech Him long to continue. I pray this letter finds you well, and you read the letter I left on my departure.

I am received back in Rome to much delight, and am staying at the Apostolic Palace, not hidden in the unused Borgia Apartments, but in the Raphael Apartments with His Holiness. The Pope is in fine health for this spiritual time of year. I am writing this in the Stanza della Segnatura room, where all papal letters are signed and sealed. The theme here is wisdom, though is there wisdom hither? I cannot be certain in a room meant to consider humanism and Greek theology as well as Christian faith. I am about to retire to the library and forget the politics. I am a woman after all, not smart enough to understand papal business. I am being judged by eyes in Raphael's painting of the Disputation of the Holy Sacrament.

The situation in Rome is smoother than when I left. The Pope and the Emperor seem to be on good terms after a meeting yesterday, and the French have given no indication they wish to support your King Henry and his decision to divorce. I have been hither but four days, but I can see Campeggio has provided the Pope much information about your King, and none of it speaks well to King Henry's character. His Holiness was furious I got imprisoned in the Tower, even if it was for only a month. Pope Clement is also well-versed in the sorry state of your Wolsey, and I have told him all I know of the situation. I urged His Holiness not to make any hasty decisions, but if the situation between Henry and Katherine, and well indeed Henry and Wolsey, do not improve soon, Henry risks excommunication. Pope Clement wants to appear a strong leader once more throughout Europe, so excommunication is not an empty threat.

War with the Turks is always a threat here. The Emperor Charles expects total loyalty from His Holiness in respect to protecting Rome from the invaders. I wish I could offer you a solution. I wish there was secret information I could provide, but as yet there is meager to report. Pope Clement seems confident in his decision to delay the annulment. I told His Holiness of Gardiner's and Cranmer's suggestion to probe theologians across Europe for their opinions, but His Holiness simply scoffed at the notion. It appears he thinks that, with God on his side, naught can bring harm. The best you can do, for now, is make sure your own position is safe. Tell the King to tarry until pressures on the Pope are lessened. It may not be long now, and I will write as soon as the time comes.

I am to marry in Florence in April, so I have months in the safety of the papal palace before I go back to join the Medicis while they rebuild their power. A siege plagues Florence at present, but all should be won for the Medici son. You should try to stay in favour while I attempt to do the same hither. Despite being so close to God, I feel my faith shaken beyond repair. God forgive me for such a notion committed by an already condemned soul. Thus indebted to you for your pains taken for me, I bid you farewell.

Holy See of Rome, XIII MDXXIX
Your friend, Nicó

Nothing but serious words. But what else could Crumwell expect – words of gushing love? The ink had blotted, as if she cried as she wrote her name. Was that too much to ask? Soon Nicóla would be another man's wife, and Crumwell needed to put her from his mind. And rising in favour in the court of King Henry was the way to do that.

Chapter 20 - December 1529
Greenwich Palace, downstream London

A seecryt is liketh a stone nowe too hevy to lyft

The palace at Greenwich had lost its Christmas cheer, even with the court all there to celebrate. The joyous celebrations cooled the moment Henry needed to be with Katherine instead of Lady Anne. There was no favour to gain being in an audience with the Queen; courtiers had less reason to smile, to give gifts, to laugh and dance and celebrate this sacred time of year. Crumwell took a boat to Greenwich with Ralph and Richard, the trip along the Thames filled more with fog and stench than celebration and good tidings. Trees, now leafless, hung over the water like fingers belonging to a creature of Satan. Only when burning torches appeared, showing the spot for the boat to stop, did the palace even appear from the dense white glaze lapping over London.

Crumwell raised his eyebrows at the lavish and detailed Christmas decor of Greenwich. Surely the Exchequer would be close to empty after paying for the celebrations for Lady Anne only weeks ago. Greenwich had its own incredible tapestries on the walls – each one more golden and elaborate, the detailing on the furniture intricate and luxurious. The King had his usual Christmas dish prepared - a coffin shaped pie, filled with turkey stuffed with goose, stuffed with chicken, stuffed with partridge, stuffed with pigeon. Crumwell sat at a long table in the dining hall, candles dancing around exquisite green table decorations, and sipped his spiced wine. Crumwell wondered what Nicóla would have thought of the hellish bird pie. She would celebrate Christmas with tortellini in broth and Canederli bread dumplings served in butter. Nicóla would choke at the sight of the coffin pie.

'Is that a s-s-smile on the face of Thomas Crowmell? Surely even G-G-God could not conjure such a miracle.'

'Crumwell.' Crumwell turned in his high-backed wooden seat and found Thomas Howard, the old Duke of Norfolk, still pronouncing his name wrong. 'You sound as if you do not believe in miracles, Your Grace, even as a man as devout as yourself. You should believe, for I think it is a miracle it is past dinner and you are still sober enough to stand up straight.'

'Be fortunate I am d-d-drunk enough not to punch your unproper face, Crowmell,' Norfolk laughed and slapped Crumwell on the back. 'I see you dressed up f-f-for the occasion!'

Crumwell glanced at himself, his usual black clothes, black velvet and a black fur-lined coat for the warmth against the winter. Norfolk on the other hand wore luscious reds and golds, a huge ruby on the cross around his neck, pearls sewn into his doublet. His fat fingers shined, adorned with golden rings, even his shoes sewn with golden thread. A pretty penny by the yard that costume, especially around a waist so thick.

'Shall we see you singing the c-c-carols beside the Yule l-l-log, Crowmell?' the Duke continued.

'Crumwell. Perchance we best leave that to the lovely young ladies of the court.'

'Those who came,' Norfolk sniffed. Many wished to be in Anne Boleyn's favour not the Queen's; many of those who had come to court did so because they were unable to find a decent excuse. After the blazing fights between King and Queen, and King and Queen-to-be, only a month previous, no one knew which way to turn. But with Katherine soon to be off to Richmond and Henry staying in inner London, perchance distance would settle some wounds.

'You must be on the l-l-lookout for a new bride at court,' Norfolk said, and nudged Crumwell again.

'No, Your Grace, I am not in the market for a bride. I have no need for one.'

'Even to c-c-close off the rumours between you and the Italian? Mind you, another r-r-rumour said you are after the W-W-Waif's rich sister!'

'I am delighted to be part of anyone's rumours.' The sarcasm in Crumwell's voice became so thick it almost hurt his throat, and he sipped his warm wine again.

'I came h-h-hither for a reason. The King wishes to s-s-see you, Crowmell.'

'Crumwell!' Crumwell threw a look to the main table, where Henry sat, his eyes set on Crumwell. 'Why did you not start with that, Your Grace?'

Crumwell jumped from his chair, the wine going to his head. He stumbled past the wide-waisted Duke and scattered his way around tables and cheering guests until he stood before the table of the royal couple and bowed low.

'Mr. Crumwell,' murmured the ever-flawless Queen Katherine, her deep-red hair laced with silver, curled and tied neatly beneath her crown. 'I hear you are much at court recently.'

Crumwell paused for a moment as the Queen's blue eyes stared at him. Her silk and damask gown, pale green laced with shining white pearls; Tudor colours. Katherine was a thing of another world, the daughter of a militant Spanish queen, a princess from birth, destined for England's throne; Katherine of Aragon was everything a king could ask. And yet she was old, almost as old as Crumwell himself, over forty! Her only crime was living long enough to no longer be able to bear a son. While Lady Anne had charm and wit to captivate her audiences, it was Queen Katherine that Crumwell far more admired; intelligent, experienced, calm, and patient. But Katherine was fervently Catholic; a system Crumwell wanted rid of in England, even if only to get his Nicóla back.

'Your Majesty, I am most blessed to be hither in your presence on such an occasion.'

'And how is your master, Cardinal Wolsey?' she asked, knowing all too well how fallen Wolsey was in Esher. Katherine would always consider Wolsey a grievous enemy.

'Wolsey is taking time to be with God, though ill with dropsy. I am unable to see him.'

'Never mind old Wolsey,' Henry dismissed the conversation with a wave of his bejeweled hand. 'Come, Crumwell, we must talk.'

The King came down from his table and ushered Crumwell away from the others, in the corner behind the royal table. Henry had a huge grin behind his orange beard, but it looked rather veiled, and something unpleasant was caught in his teeth. The smell of wine on Henry made Crumwell sway a fraction; Henry drank even more than himself.

'Crumwell, I hear you received a letter bearing the papal seal.'

Lord, have mercy. 'I did, Your Majesty.'

'I also; from your Italian. Frescobaldi wrote me to say all annulment business is delayed due to the festivities of the season. The Italian Waif says you have ideas on how to regain the Pope's favour, or else to break with Rome completely? Is this true? Do you have ideas on how I can resolve this mess?'

Crumwell licked his lips. To suggest a break with Rome was heresy, but to deny Henry his desires had equal consequences – treason charges. 'Your Majesty, I have knowledge of Italians and their politics. I also know the enemies of the Papal States. I understand the writings of the new religion, and the beliefs of the theologians you canvas throughout Europe...' Crumwell needed to be vague. He needed to pounce in whichever direction the King wished, otherwise Crumwell would find himself thrown down in favour and not earning again. 'You have ambassadors of course, but they have agendas, masters to obey. I do not have such limitations.'

'Crumwell, you once said you could make me the richest man in England.'

'You ought to be the richest man in England, Your Majesty! England is your kingdom!'

'Indeed! My Exchequer is totally empty after years of meddling by so many people. I am going to name Thomas Boleyn my new Lord Privy Seal, but I need your money-making ideas to help me.'

'Any way I can be of service, Your Majesty.'

'Finally, someone who understands how important money is to me! I know you are in parliament now. I know this time of year is rather laden with tasks, God knows my desk is charged with requests, and Gardiner is not coping. Come and see me in February. I wish you to be an advisor to me, a new role. I need an advisor for all parliamentary and legal affairs.'

'Your Majesty.' Crumwell sank down on one knee in gratefulness to the King.

'Come.' Henry rose him up again. 'You have skills I need. Together, we shall make me rich again, and at last solve the problem of my marriage. I have total faith in you, Crumwell. Why would I not want the double-minded man on my side? They say your golden eyes make money appear.'

This was what Crumwell needed. He had the ear of the King, an opportunity to rise in fortune and even save Wolsey from his perilous state, as long as it did not halt his ability to stay in favour and make a profit from working for the court. God bless Nicóla and the letter she wrote to the King. From thrown down with Wolsey, to parliament, to the King's legal advisor in just a few months, was a dream only God could make true.

'But of Wolsey,' the King sighed, 'he was faithful to me, and I was unawares of the heavy burden he took all these years. Perchance it is best to move him to The Lodge at Richmond after the Epiphany, and my physician, Dr. Butts, can treat his dropsy there. The Pope shall like that display of kingly kindness.'

'You are a king of such wonders, Your Majesty.' Crumwell was ready to use his intelligence – an ability not shared among many of his courtly peers – and to throw emotions aside and rise in power. Nicóla took Crumwell's heart to Rome with her, but Crumwell still had his life and his skills to make money, with her blessing. While the Queen, Lady Anne, the Boleyn family, and all the courtiers jostled for power and the love of the King, it was Crumwell who could remain open and rational. Money mattered, not feelings. The moderate man shall inherit the kingdom.

London 1530

Thomas Crumwell began work as an advisor to King Henry on February 10, 1530. After two days of negotiation, he secured Cardinal Wolsey a pardon from his charges of Praemunire, and the Bill of Attainder against Wolsey was dropped by royal decree. After another two days, Crumwell also had Cardinal Wolsey restored to Archbishop of York. By March 1, Crumwell secured Wolsey's move again, this time to a home beside the Carthusian monastery at Sheen, ten miles from London. Crumwell's incredible skills for negotiation and advisement saw other courtiers, such as the Duke of Norfolk ready to form an uneasy alliance, but Wolsey's restoration did not sit easy with the Cardinal's enemies, now most of the royal court.

The suggestion was made that Wolsey be moved to York, some 200 miles to the north, where the Cardinal had never visited, despite being its spiritual leader. The King gave Wolsey a massive £1000, the money entrusted to Crumwell directly. Soon after Crumwell personally delivered the money, Wolsey and some 160 servants departed on the long trek north. But less than month later, Wolsey wrote to King Henry, already complaining of the situation. Crumwell could advocate for Wolsey, and visited him prior to his trek north, but patience wore thin. Wolsey appeared increasingly arrogant, expecting a full restoration of his position within the court, an expectation he would run the country once more.

Letters of complaint kept arriving for King Henry, Crumwell, and Master Secretary Gardiner. In a series of stern writings, Crumwell had to turn on his former master, urging peace and caution so as to not upset the King, something Wolsey's greedy letters started to achieve. Crumwell worked night and day, making sure monies usually paid to Wolsey from his lands and holdings now went to courtiers close to the King, making more alliances as each penny changed hands.

With the enemies of Wolsey given extra coin, Wolsey seemed safe in York, as long as he stayed silent, grateful and pious. July brought even more favour for Crumwell as he worked daily by the King's side. The Cardinal's College at Ipswich was suspended and the glorious college at Oxford was renamed King Henry VIII College. Since Crumwell knew so much of the creation, being the overseer of construction under Wolsey, the immense and lucrative projects fell straight into Crumwell's hands. Already Crumwell had sold clerical chattels from monasteries for a personal profit, and now more profit could be made from the college projects.

By this time, the relationship with Crumwell and Wolsey became ever more estranged. Wolsey no longer thought Crumwell had his best intentions at heart, but Crumwell had no time for sentiment; he wanted to dedicate his life to his work.

"But I shall bear you only good will. Let God judge between us. Truly, in some things you overshoot yourself. There should be care given to the things you utter and to whom."

The Cardinal was right to accuse Crumwell of working for himself rather than his former master. Crumwell was an advisor to the King and a member of parliament. He was not Wolsey's man any longer, and the constant over-reaching of the fallen cleric became a constant pressure. Even Ralph and Richard knew Crumwell had to let go of Wolsey.

But Wolsey would not heed such warning words. He wrote Crumwell of how his state was not enough, about not enough money in his accounts, of his estates given to others, of the fact his colleges were taken. Everyone in the King's favour was merry, except for Cardinal Wolsey.

November 7 was chosen as a day to remember in York. Wolsey planned to have himself officially enthroned as Archbishop of York again. He summoned lords and abbots, priors, knights and their men to his manor in Cawood. That way as he entered York to be enthroned in the cathedral, all the nearby nobility could revel in his restoration. The King could not bear the arrogance of his Cardinal.

But all this aside, the fallen Wolsey then made his biggest lapse of all. Wolsey wrote to the Pope. Crumwell wondered if Pope Clement asked for Nicóla Frescobaldi's advice when he read the letter. Did Nicóla push the Pope to save Wolsey, or destroy him? Wolsey promised the Pope he could ensure Queen Katherine remained on the throne of England, as soon as the Pope ensured Wolsey's full restoration to court once more. Pope Clement, in Bologna, issued a papal edict, forbidding Henry from ever marrying Anne Boleyn. To do so would bring pain of excommunication. The news of the edict would be published and shared across the land, nailed to church doors, on the same day as Wolsey's enthronement at York.

Wolsey had conspired with Queen Katherine and Pope Clement, and now King Henry would not forgive him. Crumwell would not be able to either. Wolsey would be arrested for high treason. The punishment – death.

Chapter 21 - November 1530
Austin Friars, London

seecryts can attracteth sumthyng maygical

Nicóla could see the look of irritation on the steward's face as he answered her knock on the gates outside Austin Friars. All of London seemed soggy as tiny opaque snowflakes fluttered among the light, almost faded as the sun disappeared over the horizon. Peter at the window on the gate, clutched a candle which fought the icy wind that funneled its way down Broad Street. Peter recognised Nicóla, hidden inside a heavy cloak with hood, bags strapped to both her back and front.

'Mr. Frescobaldi!' Peter exclaimed as he pulled at the heavy bolt of the gate to let her inside. 'Master Crumwell did not say you would arrive tonight. You are in luck; Master Crumwell is home, something which is most rare these days. Master Ralph and Master Richard are both still out. We see much less of Master Crumwell these days; he is at court with the King himself most nights.'

Nicóla noticed many changes as she walked along the courtyard outside the main entrance; more horses in the stables, a new fountain built, gardens bigger than ever, everything immaculate. The main house looked as if it had a whole new roof, and wooden carvings of angels now encircled the new front door, its double wooden entrance fixed with huge shining handles. A new gentlemen-usher opened the door, the young man wearing grey velvet livery.

Nicóla stepped inside to a new tapestry on the wall, the green and red work shining with golden thread. It was the Old Testament story of Esther and Ahasuerus, Queen Esther bowed before her husband the King, begging him to stop the killing of Persian Jews. Nicóla pinched the tapestry between her fingers; wool and silk, perchance from Brussels. Exquisite. Was it one of Wolsey's tapestries? Crumwell preferred the New Testament to the Old; he could recite most of it from memory.

Several more gentleman-ushers passed her as she waited for Crumwell to be told of her arrival, and a few maids, in tidy green dresses with perfectly white aprons, stood in the main parlour off the entrance hall, stoking a fire. But when Crumwell's voice echoed from his offices, Nicóla's attention to detail disappeared, and her heart pounded. She unhooked the bag from her shoulder, and it fell to the floor but she clung to the bundle strapped to her front with anticipation.

'I expressly said I was not to be disturbed,' Crumwell grumbled to someone, presumably the usher who had to fetch him from his office. 'This is my one night off from court all month. I can only...'

Crumwell came to a halt both in steps and voice when he saw Nicóla, wrapped up from the snow, laden with so many items. The gentleman-usher bowed and disappeared into the parlour, closing the door behind him, unawares of the meeting taking place. Nicóla pulled her cloak hood away, and it pulled out her long damp hair, and she shook it from her face. Her smile could not be abated. Nicóla grinned with excitement to see him, with a healthy dose of nerves.

Before she could say a word, Crumwell sank to his knees and took her hand in his. He pulled her wet glove from her hand and held her cold skin against his rough cheek, his eyes closed tight. 'I praise you, Lord, Father of all; I thank you for calling us to be Your people, and for choosing us to give You glory. In a special way I thank you for bringing my love back to me,' he prayed, tears appearing on his dark eyelashes.

'I am still your love?' Nicóla asked, stunned by the sudden outpouring. Crumwell never wrote to her.

Crumwell climbed to his feet and held her face in his hands. 'You are my love and I swore to God if I ever saw you again I would be truthful in this.' He roughly kissed her lips, his hands still on her cheeks, the occasion to kiss desperate and rushed and it was all Nicóla had hoped. His heart could easily have hardened in the year past.

Nicóla put her hands to his chest, to hold him back from her for a moment. 'Tomassito, I need you so ardently to pause...'

Crumwell's eyes watched her, tears on his cheeks as he took in every inch of her. Nicóla pulled away her cloak to reveal a soft black sling across her chest. She unfurled the fabric to show Crumwell inside.

Poor Crumwell could not utter a word. Inside slept a baby, wrapped warmly in a white blanket, its head covered in a tiny hat. The baby had rich olive skin and thick black eyelashes but rose-gold eyebrows, a tiny pink mouth puckered. Nicóla placed one hand on Crumwell's chest again but did not say a word, feeling the pounding against her palm. His eyes flicked from the child to Nicóla and back again as he understood the sight before him.

'Her name is Giovanna, and she was born in July, the hot depths of the Italian summer. I know not what her name is in English.'

'Jane,' Crumwell said, his eyes fixed on the girl sleeping against her mother. 'Her name is Jane.'

'Do you despise me now?'

'No,' Crumwell replied, breathless. 'Nicó, no... I find myself...'

'She is your daughter. Giovanna is not a product of my husband.'

'You married?'

'Si, yes, I moved the wedding forward as soon as I discovered the baby. I was much ill after my return to Rome, and I requested the wedding moved in case of such a situation. As you can imagine, Alessandro did not wish to be a cuckold, but he wanted my dowry.'

The baby moved within her tiny swaddled haven, and Crumwell watched as she woke. The child was four months old and her golden eyes opened wide and she fussed with a whimper. 'I have fed her at my own breast,' Nicóla said. 'I had to leave my nurses behind in Florence. Please, might I be able to attend to my daughter here? She has suffered on the trip, on the boat for weeks.'

Crumwell went to the door of the parlour and his gentleman-usher stood ready, chatting with one of the young maids. 'Fetch Mistress Pryor at once!' he ordered with a double click of his fingers.

A few moments later, Mercy, who Nicóla remembered to be the mother of Crumwell's wife, appeared. Long grey hair hid beneath a black hood, she dressed still in a black mourning dress.

'Mercy, pray, I need your help. We have a visitor with a child in need of care,' Crumwell instructed.

Mercy raised her eyebrows as Nicóla pulled her crying baby from her sling, the child's clothes dirty and damp. 'This is no way to treat a child,' Mercy sighed and crossed herself. 'Is that you, Mr. Frescobaldi?'

'Yes, Mistress. Pray, this baby is my niece,' Nicóla said and felt a deep pain. If she were to be a man in London, she could not feed her daughter, not even acknowledge her. 'Jane is in need of a home.'

'Please, Mercy, take the girl and help her. Jane is to be given the best of everything. Send for whomever is needed. Wet nurses, physicians, anything, any cost at any hour,' Crumwell commanded.

Mercy took the baby in her wrinkled hands and regarded the child. 'She is a beautiful one, the rose-gold hair of her uncle, I see. And golden eyes?' She looked both Nicóla and Crumwell up and down. 'Jane, you say? Of course, Thomas, I can be of service to you.'

'Thank you, Mercy, I must attend to my friend who has come to see me. And tell the maids, I need the bath filled with hot water for Mr. Frescobaldi at once.'

'All the rooms on the second floor are full, Thomas.'

'Then have the bath taken into Elizabeth's old rooms, and prepare the rooms for Mr. Frescobaldi. All of Elizabeth's precious items are no longer in there. And prepare the nursery for the child, who I shall visit at once.'

Mercy disappeared with the child in her arms, and Nicóla ached with the loss. She had spent weeks on a ship as it made its way to England, weeks of just her and her daughter in a private cabin. Now Giovanna was whisked away. But at least she would have food, milk, a warm bath, a nurse to care for her, a comb for her thin rose-gold hair.

'I cannot have your wife's rooms,' Nicóla whispered as Crumwell took her bag from the floor.

'You can and you shall.' Crumwell took her hand and guided her up the private stairs to the third floor. Only Crumwell's rooms awaited up there, along with rooms for his wife and daughters, no longer of this world. Gregory must have been with his tutor, for no life stirred in the beautiful home.

The fire roared in Crumwell's room, candles dotted around the enormous bedroom. It too had much changed since Nicóla's last visit. Ornate green and red damask curtains hung around the bed, held by cords of gold. The frame was new, a dark wood carved in intertwining patterns. New furniture sat by the fire, green velvet cushions on the chairs, crystal glasses on silver plate set on the round table. Success was displayed all through Austin Friars, even in such a private room.

'Let me take off your cloak,' Crumwell fussed as he undid her cloak. He tossed it to the floor and started unwinding the fabric Nicóla wore to sling the baby to her chest. He paused on her doublet buttons. The family crest of the Medici, gold and red with a black hawk was embroidered on a white background. So too was Alessandro Medici's personal seal, a rhinoceros with the proverb, Non bvelvo sin vencer.

'What language is this? The old Spanish?' he asked.

'Yes, it means "I shall not return without victory". Tomassito, while I am pleased with your happiness to see me, you must relax.'

'Relax?' he scoffed. 'I long assumed this day would never arrive. It is like an angel appearing in my home! And you have come bearing a child!'

Nicóla let Crumwell guide her close to the fire, something she could not refuse. He sat her in a chair and knelt before her, her hands in his, each movement so smooth and gentle. He just stared at her and reached up to stroke her hair, now long past her shoulders. Oh to see a smile on the face of the double-minded man! 'I was ready for you to cast me away before I even showed you the baby,' Nicóla said and shivered from going from cold to hot so quickly.

'Why would I?'

'I never heard from you. I wrote to you, but you never wrote back.'

'All the letters are watched. I could not write anything to you without the King's spies seeing it before it left England's shores, Nicó. And to be honest, I had naught to say. What could be said? You left me here, sure of your life path. You needed to return to your home. I understand. I had to carry on with my own life.'

'I was not a wise spy for the Pope while here. I was not gentle with you, Tomassito. But I returned home and that has not worked either.'

'I... I do not even know where to begin, Nicó. Have you lived as a man or a woman?'

'I stayed in Rome upon my return, with Giulio – His Holiness. I was ill, and he is God's voice on Earth, so I could not lie to him. I spoke to him of my condition after the Christmas celebrations, when I was sure.'

'Was he angry?'

'The Italians, the Medici, do not act harshly to bastard children. Giulio himself is a bastard, as were his parents. Alessandro, too, is a bastard, his mother just a servant until she was married off. To the Medici, my child was a consequence I had to endure for my mission to England. They assumed seduction was part of my plan to become close to Wolsey. I was seen as a martyr to the cause of preventing King Henry's annulment. I was greeted warmly.'

'And Alessandro? Your husband?' Crumwell swallowed hard as he croaked the words.

'Of course, he was not merry; I was with child! I am thirty years old, his old bride. He is but twenty years now. No part of him wished for the marriage, but it was needed. I would never gain a good marriage anywhere, not after my virtue was taken all those years ago. Alessandro needed my dowry. We married right away in Rome so the baby might be considered Alessandro's. Giovanna is known as a child born of Alessandro. I lived as a woman in Florence and known as the sister of Nicóla, the Pope's counsel. Alessandro is building the incredibly sized Fortezzo de Basso, a fort within the walls of Florence, and I hid away. Few eyes saw my pregnancy and confinement. But I lived openly with my daughter, who was baptised in Rome by the Pope himself. The Pope knows you are the true father, Tomassito. His Holiness knows not of your desires to bring down the Church, and I shared not this detail. Alessandro, he is kind to his head mistress only, her name is Taddea Malaspina. Taddea lives nearby with her mother. Alessandro is not her only lover, so he does not keep her in our palace. Her sister, Ricciarda, is also one of Alessandro's lovers. They are the daughters of the Marquis of Massa, a well-connected family. Alliances are important now, more than ever.'

Crumwell took all the details in, memorising every word, every name. 'What sort of man is Alessandro?'

'Cruel. Incompetent. Depraved. He is a believer of force as a way to hold power in Florence. Alessandro is a man of lewd appetites, but families wish to be allied with him, so let their daughters fall into his hands.'

'And… does he…'

'Alessandro will not touch me. He considers me old and sinful. He knows not that I lay with his father in my youth. I was also with child for much of the year. My confinement was in Rome in July, the same month the Medici power over Florence was finally restored. The Pope bought the title of Duke for Alessandro from Charles the Emperor that month. Alessandro does not have power over Florence yet; he will take control next July, under peaceful terms. The Republic of Florence will be no more, instead, it will be part of the Papal States under the Holy Roman Emperor's rule, part of Italy. There are many people who do not wish the Republic to be held by the Emperor, and resistance is growing. Force may yet hold the transfer of power back into our family's hands.'

'Our family,' Crumwell whispered.

'My father was a believer of the Medici, and I have known them half my life. Married or no, I am on their side. I do not wish to see the Republic of Florence swallowed by Emperor Charles' might, but safety is also important. We do not want the French invading us yet again. We need an army; my dowry paid for one.'

'Spoken as the Duchess of Florence.'

'I am not yet officially ennobled, but the day shall come. Father wanted that for me, God rest his soul.'

'Eternal rest grant unto Francesco, O Lord, and let perpetual light shine upon him. Amen,' Crumwell uttered and they both crossed themselves. 'So, the Medici have access to the Frescobaldi fortune?'

'They do, and are in need of the funds. But they are good to me. They allow me to handle the finances of the household while Alessandro attends to his own needs. They allowed me to invest the money you could not get from Antwerp. While all of the money my father made in Italy is now swallowed by the Medici accounts, some of the Antwerp money is still there for me to use, to lend, to invest. I have total access, and I made sure I have all the papers necessary for that to continue. My father taught me well; the family has no idea what I have done. They have no access to some of the Antwerp money now.'

'I like it all, but you must be careful if you are to hide money from the powerful Medici dynasty.'

'You think me simple, Master Crumwella?' Nicóla teased.

'On the contrary, I believe your intelligence makes you a considerable threat.'

'Does this answer your questions about Rome and Florence?'

Crumwell paused and his gaze regarded his hands in hers. 'Does Alessandro recognise the baby?'

'Alessandro avoids the situation. Alessandro was not present at her baptism; he has never touched her. The Pope is her godfather. The baby is generally accepted, but it is privately known Giovanna is not Alessandro's natural child. Alessandro's mother, Simetta, was African, that is why they call Alessandro il Moro, for his dark skin. Giovanna is like me, but paler because of her English father.'

'I have another daughter,' Crumwell muttered and held onto Nicóla's hands tighter.

'I am sorry I could not give you a son. I worried you would not want a daughter. You had two daughters, legitimate daughters, and I do not wish to leave Giovanna here for you to raise as a bastard, not after the loss of Anne and Grace. May their souls, through the mercy of God, rest in peace.'

'Amen.'

'I wanted to write, Tomassito, I swear. I wondered if the child was safer as an English girl. Alessandro is a sinful man, a dangerous man. I have prospered in Florence only because I lived as a man for so many years. I can no longer do that now I have a child; the Pope decided I can no longer live as a man, as Nicóla. I am a wife now, a mother, and must be Nicóletta, a sister returned. Alessandro is angered; he wished to marry Margarete of Austria, the Emperor's bastard daughter, for the status. Without my father, Florence feels lost to me.'

'You are still in need of a home.'

'But His Holiness told me of a papal brief he wrote, demanding Henry return to Katherine and leave Anne Boleyn at once. I know Queen Katherine and Cardinal Wolsey have written to the Pope. I know Wolsey expects to be restored when Queen Katherine is by Henry's side again.'

'It shall never occur.'

'I assumed that all the way from Rome. I heard the Privy Council indicted eight bishops and three abbots on praemunire because they obey the law of Rome over the law of King Henry. I wondered if you had something to do with that.'

'I have everything to do with that. I am head of all Henry's legal affairs now. I have no intention of harming these men, Nicó, I swear.

It is blackmail. If we can hold these clerics on praemunire, it means we could hold any cleric on praemunire, all clerics; it is a threat. They must swear their allegiance to Henry, not Rome.'

'And break your country away from the power of the Church, away from the power of Rome?'

Crumwell sighed and looked up to Nicóla again. She could not help herself; she put her hand on his face, eager to be close to him. Nicóla ached for Crumwell, and he seemed to pity her more than adore her. 'If the King adopts the laws of the Tyndale Bible, with the opinion that the ruler of the realm is the leader on spiritual matters, he can gain an annulment. Henry can lead the Church in England, and not require the Pope's approval for anything. Already Thomas Cranmer has been sent to Rome, to be ambassador to the Emperor Charles, but I like not his chances of convincing Charles to allow annulment. Reform is the only way.'

'Tomassito, you are breaking up the Catholic Church, the only thing which binds all men and women together throughout Christendom. Other countries are in a spin. Look at the Germans! The violence is widespread. The uneducated only have the word of God, and you seek to take that from them?'

'No, I seek to be of service to them! The people of England shall preach in English, understand the word of God at last. No more Latin, no more corrupt monasteries. I am sorry, I know you are family to the Pope...'

'The Church is also what binds me to a man I never wished to marry. The Church held my inheritance from me for their gain. By their laws, I am without virtue and soiled goods, even though it was a cardinal, now a pope, who stole my virtue. I know the Pope, yes. I am in the heart of the Church, see it take bribes, see it dispense violence, see it defy the laws it makes for the people. I have always been immune to the pain the Church causes because they love me, but anyone cast out is destroyed. I want to warn you, Tomassito, if you wish to tear the Church apart, and make it seem like King Henry's doing, you must be careful.'

'I know this more now than ever. Wolsey is so difficult, indeed for some months now. He is returned to his arrogance, even though he is not fully restored. Wolsey makes demands, for money, for patronage. King Henry knows Wolsey has conspired with Queen Katherine. Wolsey is to be arrested and brought back to London.'

'Where is he at present?'

'In York, in the north.'

'Shall Wolsey be executed?'

Crumwell nodded, and his eyes cast down once more. 'I fear so. And, as a commoner, he can be tortured in the Tower. Pray the King spares him, for his love of Wolsey and the work Wolsey has done for God.'

'Do you think Wolsey shall beg for his life, or die a martyr? Do you think he will talk before his death?'

'I fear he will, yes. Wolsey had written me recently. Wolsey says he knows I no longer serve him, but rather serve the King. Wolsey accused me of profiting from his downfall.'

'Have you?'

'I profit more by the day from the patronage of the King. Supporting Wolsey now would have me out on the street. But in return, I secured Wolsey money, better lodgings, some titles restored. I did my duty by my old master.'

'Is there anything Wolsey can say to harm you when he returns to London?'

Crumwell took Nicóla's hand from his cheek and kissed her palm. 'I lied on his accounts, hid monies, moved the King's money to Wolsey's accounts, and my own, for years. Wolsey and I profited from breaking up monasteries to fund colleges, selling their chattels for personal profit. We kept the money for ourselves, spent lavishly. Yes, I have committed sins and profited where I ought not to have, all with Wolsey's blessing. It is no wonder the public wanted my head. I am guilty.'

'Then Wolsey is well to remain silent so you can continue to rise in the King's eyes,' Nicóla replied.

'God shall see what I have done.'

'God, I have found, will give any amount of forgiveness if the right amount of money has changed hands. The Church has no right to judge anyone.'

Crumwell sat up on his knees and kissed Nicóla. She slipped forward in her seat as he poured his lips over hers, letting him slide his body between her legs. Nicóla held him tight against her, relieved he still felt the same as a year ago. Nicóla buried her face against his neck and wanted to cry. She felt so utterly alone since the day she last set foot inside Austin Friars. Tears stung her eyes but she held them back, her eyes tightly shut as Crumwell stroked her hair. He was not angry about the baby, not angry about her marriage. Crumwell had not just forgotten her.

'I fear God shall never forgive me for my sins,' Crumwell muttered.

'We are products of the world which God thrust us into and surely cannot preach such hate upon us.'

'When shall you go back to Rome?'

Nicóla raised her head from Crumwell's shoulder. 'I have no such plans. I left the papal palace six weeks ago, claiming to be on the road home to Florence; they shall notice my disappearance. I have heard no word from the Pope, but I am certain he will find me.'

'They know not that you came hither?' Crumwell scoffed, surprised by her defiance.

'I felt a need to escape. I felt the need to return here, to finish what I started.'

'And what is that?'

'I am not sure of my mission. I could not leave Giovanna behind. I knew you could give her a better life in London than I can in Florence.'

'I shall take the child if you so desire, Nicó. But as I am rising at court, I am also taking down the Catholic faith. I have the full support of King Henry. I have the full support of Lady Anne and the Boleyn family. Lady Anne is more of a reformist than ever. She wants the deceit and corrupt natures of the Church eradicated. The King wants power in his own kingdom.'

'I care nothing for the Catholic Church and its use of me.' The distaste in Nicóla's voice surprised even Nicóla. 'They rise in power in Italy but not here. Here, I can gain revenge against the oppression the Church forced upon me.'

Crumwell smiled, the smug grin he so often displayed whenever he won a battle. 'In any case, never return to Rome.'

'What shall I do here? Raise my bastard daughter? Have a sinful love for a man who shall never marry me?'

'Of course you are welcome at Austin Friars. You can live as Nicóla if you wish, and I shall grant you all the protection you shall ever need. You can live as a woman, as Nicóla's sister Nicóletta, as the mother of Jane if you prefer. I would offer to marry you now if I could.'

'Perchance you can make the King leader of the Church and he can issue me an annulment also.'

'Never have I wanted to be of service to King Henry more,' Crumwell smiled. 'But Wolsey…'

Nicóla could see it all; for all that occurred, Crumwell still bore a love for the man who raised him high in England. Love and respect did not simply fade away. 'All you can do is pray for Wolsey.'

'And avoid Sir Thomas More,' Crumwell replied. 'More is Lord Chancellor; the King listens to him on every issue. More is a humanist, a scholar, but is a Catholic more than anything else. He lets his conscience guide him, and conscience is a fickle ruler. More is my biggest enemy at this time. More claims to be pious, caring naught for vanity, for wealth, yet lives as a rich man and tortures those who think unlike him. I know not where alliances shall be placed.'

'Allow me to find out.'

'I have my creatures, my spies in his household as we speak.'

'Let me join your creatures, Master Crumwella. Just never dispatch me home to Florence.'

Chapter 22 - November 1530
Austin Friars, London

Tis one of the most wyndrous seecryts in lyfe - yond thyngs most wyrth doing, we doth fore others

Crumwell closed his eyes for a moment and felt warmth on his eyelids, the fire in the dining room close by. He opened them again and heard nothing but the crackle of the flames. A quick gaze up saw everyone else at dinner staring back at him, each with a different expression on their face. Nicóla, dressed in the best black velvet doublet and hose Crumwell could get, sat with a look of patience as always. Nicóla's newly cut rose-gold hair was all swept back from her face, making her look thin. Not a muscle moved on her face as he regarded her.

Next to her, Thomas Wyatt, the tall man sitting straight in his seat, towered over Nicóla. He and Nicóla shared their tales of being trapped in Rome during the sacking by their Emperor's army in 1527. So too had the guest across from Nicóla, the Imperial ambassador Eustace Chapuys. The ambassador sat drooped in his seat, still wearing his grey fur over his puffed French doublet. Chapuys had his lips pursed as if his silence should spur Crumwell to speak. Next to Chapuys sat beady-eyed Sir Thomas More, who arrived unannounced at Austin Friars, a guest of the ambassador. Crumwell could never feel quite at ease with More, who considered himself far superior to everyone around him. Also, More had burnt men at the stake over the course of the year, and banned religious books printed outside England. A look into Crumwell's library would have More clutching the Tudor rose hanging from his golden chains of office, the mighty Chain of Esses. So much for not caring for Earthly displays of wealth. The chain could feed an entire city for a year, such was its value. Every book banned by More sat in Crumwell's library in peace, each considered a disease that needed to be cut from religion. But Crumwell knew he had to keep the cruel and efficient Lord Chancellor close. The two men could not be further apart in their beliefs but inched closer to the King's ear by the day. At least beady-eyed More had a mind not to challenge Crumwell too often. For now. More sat with his hands folded together on the table, dinner now cleared away, only wine remaining.

'Pray tell us, Crumwell, what does the message say?'

Crumwell again looked to the letter crunched in his hands. Everyone had seen the seal of Wolsey on the message. 'On November 4, Lord Henry Percy, Duke of Northumberland, arrived at Cardinal Wolsey's home at Cawood, twelve miles from York. Wolsey was at dinner with George Cavendish and Edmond Bonner, talking about Wolsey's coming enthronement at York Abbey. Percy burst in, the fickle man he is, and arrested Wolsey for high treason, by the King's command. Wolsey was taken to Sheffield Park, the home of the Earl of Shrewsbury. They will send Sir William Kingston, Constable of the Tower, north to bring Wolsey back to London, where he will be tried for his crimes against the King.'

'But the only possible sentence is execution,' More muttered.

'The King is sending a powerful message,' Chapuys added in his deep French accent. 'Henry is afraid of Wolsey, of his power and how popular he is with the people.'

'Wolsey has no more power,' Wyatt scoffed at the two older men across from him.

'Wolsey is discreet. He will never rise in favour again.' Crumwell looked to Nicóla, who still remained silent, her expression still not giving anything away. 'Wolsey is increasing in his favour with the people,' he said to the group. 'They say the streets of York are lined with people eager to see Wolsey when he passes. Wolsey asks constantly for more money, for the chance to be in favour with the King again. Just weeks ago, Wolsey wrote to Henry, asking for money so he may live in the comfort he was accustomed to when being in divine office. Wolsey thinks time has healed the rift between himself and the King.'

'Shall you have the chance to see him, do you think, when he gets back to London?' asked Wyatt. Wyatt too knew Wolsey well, had worked for him in France for several years.

'The question is, should you see him when he comes back to London?' Nicóla asked, her voice low, not out of her act to be male, but instead for the grave situation at hand.

'Wolsey is a man of the Church, and he answers to the Pope, to God, not the King,' More said.

'Wolsey is also a man who seems to think himself above the law of England,' Nicóla replied. 'He thinks himself all conquering. Wolsey has not spent all his time in the service of God. Pope Clement's constant praise of Wolsey, for standing up to Henry and the annulment issue, does naught but inflate Wolsey's confidence.'

'The Pope is still firmly on Wolsey's side?' More asked.

'Completely on Wolsey's side. As you know, Ambassador Chapuys, the Emperor in Rome wishes for no annulment and the Pope will do whatever the Emperor commands. Wolsey is seen as a martyr to the cause of the annulment, even though it was Campeggio who denied the King all along. But remember, we are not in Rome, we are in London.'

'I think Wolsey would give Henry anything he wanted in return for the trappings of office again,' Crumwell yielded. 'Wolsey thinks not of what is right, but what is proper for his station in life. I am woeful to say this about my former master, a former friend.'

'Wolsey acts like any man of his age who finds himself under pressure,' Nicóla sighed. 'He is closer to meeting his maker than any of us, and thus sees life in a different light.'

'You know, Wolsey had a story. Many years ago, he went to a fortune teller, a foolish thing, a trifle. The woman told him that he would meet his end in Kingston. That small area in Surrey? Wolsey always avoided the place. But it is Sir William Kingston who shall take Wolsey to the Tower,' Crumwell told the group.

'If the Cardinal is brought back to London in chains,' More shook his head as he spoke, 'paraded through the streets to the ordinary man, tried in the Tower, and God forbid it, executed, who knows what ordeal it could unleash upon England. God may take his revenge on us all. It is but two years past since God washed England with the sweating sickness, killing countless thousands, all as punishment for Henry's annulment.'

'Why does Wolsey write to you direct?' Nicóla asked Crumwell.

'It says if I should find myself a member of Henry's council, I ought to be careful what ideas I put in his head, because once in relevance, Henry will never put the idea from his mind again.'

'There is a difference between what a king can do, and what a king should do,' More replied, to a ripple of nodding through the group.

'Wolsey states he is to send me more letters and a parcel as soon as he can,' Crumwell said.

'You had better be careful, Master Crumwell,' Wyatt said as he lifted his silver cup, 'for to defend Wolsey in this is to blacken yourself in the King's eyes.'

~~~

Crumwell sat on his bed, unable to even undress for sleep, such was the weight on his heart. He heard a gentle tap on the door which went from his rooms directly to his wife's, now Nicóla's. She appeared a moment later, dressed only in her white nightgown. Even with her short hair, she looked feminine to him. The sheer fabric showed Nicóla had removed the bindings from her chest, something which Crumwell despaired her wearing. The fabric, tethered to her for so many years now, caused grooves in her skin to appear, her body so used to binding.

'May I?' she murmured, despite the fact no one would hear her. The nursery where baby Jane slept down the long hallway was shut, the nurses unable to hear any conversation.

Crumwell gestured for her to come, and she scurried, bare feet over carpets to the bed and sat down next to him. Crumwell took her hand tight in his own and kissed it.

'Tell me what you fear,' she said, her green eyes on the fire across the room.

'I know nothing.'

'Such folly, Tomassito,' she replied and gestured for him to speak.

'I knew Wolsey's time would come. I thought by making him move to the north, all the way up in York, he would be from the minds of Anne Boleyn and her family. Even stuttering Norfolk could forget the Cardinal. But they fear Wolsey's influence on the King so they have pursued an old man hundreds of miles away. Henry Percy, who wanted to marry Lady Anne years ago, was the one to arrest Wolsey, years after Wolsey denied Percy the right to marry. All this was inevitable. The Boleyns will not rest until they have power. There is no stopping them. I can see no conclusion but death and disgrace for Wolsey now.'

'The trouble is, Tomassito, you are so immersed in the emotion of this, you are not seeing the practical issues at play. There is a chance you will be dragged down with Wolsey, and we must prevent that. Wolsey must not write to you, must not speak to you, and mostly importantly, never speak about you to anyone. If the axe does fall upon his neck, it must be in silence.'

'But how can such a thing be done? Our relationship has broken over these past months as I have worked for the King. Wolsey will not seek to spare me, only save himself. Perchance even blame me for all wrongs, as I was his legal advisor.'

'You must be ruthless, Tomassito. You know this.'

'Aside from killing Wolsey now, before he gets to London, what can I do? If I wrote to him, asking him to be silent, the letter will be read by the King's men, and I will find myself in the Tower.'

Nicóla did not respond and Crumwell turned to face her. She looked back with a cold reply and he could see her thoughts. 'No, we are not like the Medici family, Nicó. We do not just kill people.'

'Of course you do. Tonight we dined with a man who burns men for reading books he does not approve. Books we read. More sends tortured men, tortured by his own hand in his own home, to their efficient deaths. Beady-eyed More is a man with power and he dispenses it. Do not pretend England is better than Florence or Rome. We are simply more advanced in corruption back home. Our alliances to one another are stronger than those hither, which makes England ever more dangerous. Everyone must be seen as your enemy. You know all of this.' Nicóla was entirely precise.

'What can I do? Ride north and hope to meet the Cardinal's escort? And do what? Send a sword through his heart? Wolsey is a fool but I still love him. Even the King loves him.'

'No, you cannot be seen to do a thing,' Nicóla replied, dismissing his malice.

'I was not in seriousness, Nicó.'

'Tomassito, I could go north. I do not have to see the King every day. I do not have to be at court or parliament. I could ride north and meet the escort. I could see about speaking to Wolsey, taking whatever action I can, whatever is necessary.'

'It is winter,' Crumwell dismissed his love. 'You cannot ride that far. York is two hundred miles from here. Snow is falling, and the roads are not safe.'

'What is halfway between London and this York city?'

Crumwell imagined the map in his mind. 'Leicester. There is a large abbey in Leicester and the escort would stop there without question.'

'How many days' ride is it to Leis... Lasci...'

'Leicester,' Crumwell corrected her pronunciation. 'It is hard riding from York in this weather. That is assuming the trip goes to plan. Mayhap four days hard riding.'

'Solid roads?'

'Some of the way, with the papers necessary to let you pass through the King's lands.'

'Papers you could gain on my behalf?'

'Nicó, you cannot go to Wolsey.'

'Why not, Tomassito? Why not? I am an accomplished rider. Is it that I am a woman?'

'It is dangerous on your own.'

'Send some of your men with me, you have over 200 servants. They need know nothing of the plan, only that they take me to this Leitis...chair... Abbey.'

Crumwell forced a smile and kissed Nicóla's soft cheek. 'Leicester,' he repeated again. 'But what would you do when you arrive? How would you get past Sir William Kingston and the guards? There are perchance as many as two dozen men in the escort.'

'That matters little,' Nicóla replied. 'I shall worry myself with the facts when I arrive. This might your last chance to give a message to Wolsey.'

'I cannot ask such things of you. You arrived in England only weeks ago.'

'Precisely; few know of my arrival. Jane is embraced in safety here at Austin Friars. We must ensure Wolsey's silence for your benefit.'

'Why would you help me in this most dangerous pursuit?'

'I love you! And of course fealty; you trusted me the moment I first came to this godforsaken island. Non tornerò senza vittoria.'

'I shall not return without victory,' Crumwell repeated. 'But at what price?'

'Leave that to my soul, one already condemned to hell.'

Chapter 23 - November 1530
Leicester Abbey, Leicestershire

Seecryts are as dark and colde as wynter's nyght

No matter how cold, how dark, how much mist covered the roads north, how much the grey expanse sucked the life from every corner, Nicóla rode on toward Leicester. With two of Crumwell's men with her, they made the steady trek north, every day cradling less sunshine than the last. Where the people hid, Nicóla knew not. The early winter seemed to have driven all away from the roads, inside near warm fire. Rain fell when snow did not, and at the end of each day, the horses shivered despite their hard riding. Their breath in the mist was sometimes the only movement around the threesome as they rode through windless towns, across empty plains, through silent forests. Every night they slept in simple taverns, beds no more than straw pallets on the floor, rats looking to huddle up for warmth, fleas inside everything. Staying anywhere grander was not an option; their journey did not need to be seen.

The abbey filled the centre of the town of Leicester. The town, ample with cramped wooden buildings huddled together for safety, had mud-filled streets, and people suspicious of the group as they arrived. The journey was right on time; it was obvious the town had plenty of strangers in it; every public house Crumwell's men ventured inside brought them a frosty stare. Captain of the Guard and Constable of the Tower Sir William Kingston had an escort of two dozen men also in town.

Dressed in plain black, no livery markings to show, Nicóla had no problem finding somewhere for Crumwell's men to tarry without attracting any attention; just two more men up from London. Nicóla rode to the abbey entrance on her own. She approached at nightfall, fog covering so much she followed the edge of the abbey's grey walls along the east side until she found an entrance, the stone covered with overgrowing vines around a large wooden gate. Just as the last of the feeble sun set, she pounded on the gate and waited, her horse finding it difficult to stand still in the cold. Nicóla stroked the animal's wet brown mane as she waited for someone to come.

An angered face appeared, a fat man with red cheeks which suggested he was already drunk. He scowled at the hooded rider still on horseback. 'The abbey is closed,' he barked, and coughed several times, upsetting Nicóla's horse.

'I come for Abbot Richard Pescall,' she said, not pulling her hood from her face.

'This is an Augustine abbey, sir. While the canons are committed to the pastoral care of the community, people cannot come and go from the abbey at will.'

'I saw several of your canons in town, drinking, which makes me assume the rules of this abbey are somewhat loose.'

Nicóla watched the man scowl again; he did not wish to help someone with an accent, but there was no way to sound English. This far north, the accent was so difficult Nicóla had trouble understanding simple English words. 'Fine sir,' she said, as slow and clear as she could, 'I come to see your master on urgent business.'

'We have Cardinal Wolsey with us, so we can permit none into the abbey, sir.'

'I come on behalf of my master, Thomas Crumwell. From the accounts I have seen, your abbot pays vital bribes to my master to keep his job at this abbey. I will not return to London without seeing the abbot.' She watched the drunken man peer at her. 'Sir,' she added.

'We are under inspection again so soon?'

'Yes, and I must be allowed in at once. I know the abbot only holds this abbey due to my master's favour. Pescall's monks will no longer go hunting, drinking and whoring in town if they do not submit to inspection.' Just as Crumwell said. The constant inspection of Leicester Abbey found it a place of sin. The bribes paid seemed so large that Crumwell permitted sin to continue, but as he gained favour with King Henry, the need for bribes from the abbeys became less important to him.

The drunken steward pulled open the gate and Nicóla jumped from her horse, her legs almost frozen in place in her saddle. A young man dressed in black robes came and took her weary horse.

'Look,' the drunken steward said, and glanced back at his office at the entrance, a bottle on the table, a short fire in the corner, 'cross the courtyard and then enter through the main doorway. Follow the wide main hallways which shall lead you the chapel. There you will find a canon who can guide you to Abbot Pescall.' He clearly did not wish to lead anyone through the dark and cold abbey. 'You work for Thomas Crumwell? The King's man?'

'Yes, and I can tell the King that the men who work in the abbey are due a pay increase if you wish,' Nicóla said as she pulled away her black riding gloves. 'Or I can also tell my master that my privacy was not respected here.'

The chubby steward gestured for Nicóla to lead on, and she crossed the muddied courtyard and straight in the entranceway of the abbey, lavish stained glass windows dotted around the wooden doors. Vow of poverty indeed. Crumwell had briefed Nicóla before she left London; this abbey was a disgrace to the faith. Inside its thick austere walls and elevated decoration lived 25 canons, only half of whom ever attended services. They were known for leaving the abbey and drinking or hunting at regular intervals, breaking their vow of living a cloistered life. It was the richest monastery in Leicestershire, yet had crippling debts. The abbot and his 24 other canons had no less than 100 servants to serve them and their vow of humility, and yet as Nicóla wandered aimlessly through hallways, some wide, some narrow, all she could hear was the distant sound of the choir perchance coming from the chapel. These monks did not respect the rules of a monastic life under the Rule of Saint Augustine. While their religion dictated this was a time for prayer, the abbot could be anywhere.

Sure enough, after only minutes of searching the enclosed halls of the abbey, Nicóla came up against a monk, the man dressed in his traditional black robes, a white collar around his neck. The monk wore an incredible cross around his neck on a gold chain. The light from a hallway candle flickered and reflected light off the monk's bald head. 'Who are you?' he barked, and Nicóla smelled ale on his breath. 'Are you one of Kingston's guards? You cannot be here. You laymen must stay in your rooms in the outer halls.'

'I come for Abbot Pescall on the word of Thomas Crumwell.'

The frail face of the monk turned to worry. 'Abbot Pescall is perchance in his private rooms. Thomas Crumwell, you say?'

Ah, so all the canons knew of the need to bribe Crumwell to keep living their unholy life here. 'Thomas Crumwell is my master.'

The short monk guided Nicóla through dark hallways, all the wooden doors to private rooms shut away. They stopped at a set of stairs and the monk pointed up. 'The abbot's office is at the top of the stairs. You must knock before you enter.'

Nicóla went up in silence and paused at the door; the space smelled damp, the air thick and cold. She reached for the handle and noticed it was made of silver. The greed of the monastery was there for anyone to see. She listened at the door and heard several voices. Two, perchance three. A loud laugh echoed towards her so Nicóla pushed the door open. Before her lay a magnificent room, warm with a huge fire roaring, extraordinary red and gold tapestries on the walls, soft furnishings, silver plate on the tables, grand carpets on the floor. Close to the fire stood a naked old man, and a much younger man dressed in his hose, sitting at his feet. Another boy sat on a nearby chair, also naked. The three did not move, shocked by the intrusion.

'Who goes there?' the older man growled as he grabbed his robes of white from the floor. Nicóla watched the boy on the floor wipe his mouth and she cringed.

'Abbot Richard Pescall.'

'Get out of my rooms, or God shall strike you down,' the abbot swore as he held his robes over his sagging, hairy skin.

'I come on behalf of Thomas Crumwell,' Nicóla said and took her hood from her head. 'I believe you are well known to my master.'

The man's eyes widened in fear. With a wave to the boys, they collected their clothes and scurried out of the door across the room.

'Who are they?' Nicóla asked, and folded her hands together behind her back.

'They are no one. Simply boys who are educated in the almonry.'

'On what do you educate the boys, Abbot?'

'Please, if Master Crumwell…'

'Put your clothes on,' Nicóla commanded. This feeble old man had no power here. Nicóla was prepared to pull the dagger at her waist if needed but the abbot's own vice seemed weapon enough. Nicóla adverted her gaze as Abbot Pescall struggled to get his white robes on again. The moment he was fittingly covered Nicóla crossed herself and sighed.

'I come on behalf of Thomas Crumwell to deliver a message to Cardinal Wolsey. I understand His Eminence is here in the abbey.'

'Please, Cardinal Wolsey is much ill; he all but fell into my arms on arrival. Wolsey was put straight to bed and is being attended by members of his own household, aided by us in every way possible. Master Crumwell should feel his friend is safe here.'

'I hope Cardinal Wolsey is treated better than the boys you claim to educate in religious life,' Nicóla replied. 'If you allow me to see Cardinal Wolsey, and never speak of this inspection, I can assure you what I have seen shall never be mentioned.'

'You will not tell your master? Please, Master Crumwell is in receivence of my latest incentive.'

'Bribe. You can call it a bribe, Abbot Pescall. Let us not lie in a house of God. Show me to Cardinal Wolsey and your sinfulness shall be silenced to me alone.'

'Cardinal Wolsey is attended by his personal chaplain Edmund Bonner. They have travelled from York together. I must warn you… ah…'

'You have no need of my name,' Nicóla interrupted. 'Warn me.'

'I must warn you Cardinal Wolsey is frail. He does not expect to live beyond the abbey walls.'

That threw Nicóla for a moment. Would it be so bad if Wolsey died? It saved so much debate, ended the risk for Crumwell, but denied the King his justice.

The room the abbot showed Nicóla to bore none of the lavish sins of Pescall's private rooms. Two guards on the door paid no notice of Nicóla's entry with the abbot's permission. The room was lined with windows, but only snow falling against the glass could be seen against the darkness. The wide bed sat in the centre of the room, the head close to the windows. Wolsey lay there, at rest. Bonner lifted his face from the side of the bed where he too rested in slumber, drooped forward in his seat against the bed, his black vestments wrinkled. Bonner looked in surprise as Nicóla undid her riding cloak. On the other side of the bed, George Cavendish stood from his seat.

'Mr. Frescobaldi? I have not seen you since Esher.'

To Nicóla's surprise, Cavendish strode over to her, pain in his bones evident, and drew her into his embrace. His black clothes felt as damp as hers. 'Mr. Cavendish,' she said, relieved when he let go. 'God be with you.'

Chaplain Bonner crossed himself and too embraced Nicóla. Clearly, emotions ran high; the lines under Chaplain Bonner's eyes had grown. 'You have come from London?'

'Yes, direct from Austin Friars.'

'Do you bring word from Thomas?' Cavendish asked. 'Wolsey says every day Thomas will come to him.'

Nicóla looked around the portly chaplain and gaunt Cavendish to the Cardinal in his bed. The blankets were drawn right up to his chin, their grey fur edgings the same shade as Wolsey's skin. He was such a heavy man, yet now his chins sagged back, pulling the skin on his face away from his features. In her pocket, Nicóla carried hemlock seeds, ready to poison him if need be, depending on his mood towards Crumwell. But God looked ready to finish Wolsey. Crumwell had sent her with the wish she talk only with the Cardinal, but they both knew talk may not be enough to silence Wolsey in the Tower. Wolsey could expose Crumwell when he confessed his own crimes.

'Let us pray to the mother Mary for His Eminence's health,' Bonner said and gestured to the seats beside Wolsey's bed. Nicóla sat down with Cavendish and Bonner sat opposite them. She brought her hands together and closed her eyes as Bonner began to speak.

'Maria, gratia plena, quae mater egerem, rogamus attentius eminentiae eius infirmus vester pro mirabilis Dei auxilium petit. Vere pius aegrotorum curam sustinere tua offeres virtutes sanitatum.'

'Amen,' Nicóla and Cavendish muttered and crossed themselves.

With a gentle flutter, Wolsey's eyes opened. He focused on Bonner and then glanced to Cavendish and Nicóla. His eyes regarded nothing but pure sadness. Wolsey did not seem to recognise her for a time, then a smile rippled across his sallow cheeks.

'Nicóla Frescobaldi, have you come with Thomas? I knew Thomas would come.'

'Thomas will be hither soon,' Bonner lied as he held Wolsey's vulnerable hand. 'Like you said, Thomas would never leave you.'

'No, Thomas would never leave me like this,' Wolsey said and coughed, an angry sound from such an infirm man. 'Please tell me, Mr. Frescobaldi, what does Thomas wish to say to me?'

What could Nicóla say? She was not heartless, no matter her mission, no matter all the things she had seen and done. What if her father had ended his days like this, old and sick, alone and far from home? She would have wanted someone to soothe him. 'Your Eminence,' she began and tried to speak louder for the frail man's hearing, 'I come to tell you Thomas wishes to speak with you again. Thomas wants you to know his fealty is always with you. For the past year, Thomas has tried to keep you safe, far from the sinful anger of London.'

'We have the wisest king in the world,' Wolsey coughed. 'Henry will never hurt me.'

Nicóla shared a look with Bonner. The chaplain looked close to tears. They knew Henry not to be the wisest man in the world, perchance once, but no longer. Execution would be the only way for Henry to stay high in Lady Anne's favour. Wolsey ruined Anne's life when she was denied a marriage to Henry Percy as a young woman. Revenge would be had on an executioner's block.

'Tell me, Mr. Frescobaldi, you went back to Rome, did you not? Gardiner got you out of the Tower.'

'Well indeed, Your Eminence.'

'Did you see the Pope?'

'Yes, Your Eminence. His Holiness speaks so highly of you. Pope Clement prays for your soul, prays for you to get through your trials here in England. His Holiness says no prince of the Church such as yourself should ever have to suffer in pain, suffer in poverty or be punished for denying the King what he should never have asked.'

'Henry will not get his annulment,' Wolsey croaked.

'No, Your Eminence. Pope Clement has not swayed in the King's favour. The royal marriage shall be safe.'

'When will Thomas come?'

'Soon, Your Eminence,' Cavendish hushed his longtime friend. 'Thomas will come.'

'Thomas would never leave me like this. Mr. Frescobaldi, I have a box for Thomas. Small, plain dark brown. You must fetch it from my private papers.'

Bonner got up from the bedside and reached for a pearl-lined chest which sat on a table in the far corner of the room. Next to it hung the red cardinal's robes. Bonner opened the chest and took out a thin box; he handed it to Nicóla and she clutched it tight.

'You must give this to Thomas as soon as he arrives,' Wolsey said and opened his eyes again. 'I wish to see him receive it. I want to see him read my words and see the gift which is inside. Please, Mr. Frescobaldi, do this for me. Hand it to Thomas.'

'Of course, Your Eminence,' Nicóla said, ready for tears herself. Crumwell would never come and it was heartbreaking to see such a sick man ache for his lost companion. She watched as the Cardinal fell back towards sleep.

'A letter came by way of the King today,' Bonner almost whispered. 'Kingston's men went through the Cardinal's household at Cawood Castle and found some £1500 to be missing from the inventory. The King wrote to ask about the missing money. Can you believe such a thing? Wolsey is on his sick bed and the King is demanding to question His Eminence's accounts! All Wolsey could say was he needed patience, as he cannot answer while he is so ill.'

'What ails him?' Nicóla asked.

'Wolsey is at the end. The journey was difficult. Wolsey was taken from his home, from his mistress Joan, taken by the Constable of the Tower on the King's orders. The King who Wolsey toiled for all these years. Wolsey is abandoned and perchance God calls him away from this Earth to give him peace.'

'If only peace could be found,' Nicóla whispered.

'I fear there shall never be peace in England again.'

The night dragged on, each hour slower than the one before. Wolsey drifted in and out of sleep, as did the three at the bedside. Just after midnight, Bonner performed the last rites, worried he might not get the chance before Wolsey slipped away. Just as the first sign of morning speared through the window and over Wolsey's bed, there was a bang on the door, which flung open with alarming power.

'Sir William Kingston,' Bonner said, shocked from his sleep. Nicóla stood up as the man entered the room. Both she and Cavendish appeared dazed from dozing in their seats, and Nicóla steadied herself against the bed. Kingston was a man of considerable years, perchance not much younger than Wolsey himself. Kingston regarded the Cardinal in bed and the power he exuded faded away; he could tell as well anyone Wolsey was near the end of his life.

'I have come again to ask about the missing £1500 from Cawood Castle, on the King's orders,' Kingston said, his voice only half as strong as Nicóla expected. The man could plainly understand an answer would not be forthcoming. Wolsey stirred at the movements in the room and opened his eyes at the red and black-dressed Kingston.

'Ah, sir,' he croaked, 'I see you view the matter much worse than you should. How it happened I know not. If I had served God as diligently as I have the King, he would not have abandoned me in old age. Is this my just reward for my worldly diligence to His Majesty, for satisfying his vain pleasure, instead of regarding my Godly duty?'

The three stood in total silence around the bed, and after Wolsey's words, Kingston himself seemed at a loss. Now was not the time to question an old man for the greed of a king.

'Perchance, Sir William, we shall speak outside,' Bonner suggested, and the Constable stepped backward from the room without another word. Cavendish followed Bonner and closed the door.

Wolsey reached out and grabbed Nicóla's hand. 'Thomas would never leave me like this,' he whispered yet again.

'No, Your Eminence.'

'Thomas will be hither.'

'Yes, Your Eminence.'

'I want to go to God, as it is time I serve Him in heaven as I served the King on Earth.'

Nicóla sat down by the bed again, Wolsey's hand still in hers. There was little to say to a dying man. Death would surely come soon.

'Thomas would never leave me like this.'

'Never, Your Eminence.'

'Do what you must, as Thomas would.'

'Cardinal?'

Wolsey turned his head and looked right at her. 'I know you are a woman, Nicóla. I know this because of the love I witness when Thomas sees you. But Thomas would never leave me in this manner.'

Thomas would never leave me like this. Wolsey knew Crumwell was not coming. Wolsey knew Nicóla was sent in Crumwell's place. When he said Crumwell would never leave him, he meant Crumwell would never leave him to the suffering. 'Thomas would never leave me like this, he would help me,' he whispered and closed his eyes.

Nicóla let go of Wolsey's hand and carefully slipped his pillow from under his head. She placed it down on the Cardinal's face and a few moments later he began to cough. She forced her slight weight forward, her arms locked over the pillow as she held him down. 'Thomas would never leave you like this,' she said as he began to fight. It did not take long. Wolsey was already halfway to God; the message already written, Nicóla being only the messenger.

She lifted the dirty white pillow and looked at the cold face before her. Nicóla placed the pillow back under Wolsey's head and closed his brown eyes. In less than a minute she had killed a man who had served God, a king, and most importantly himself, for almost sixty years. 'Glory be to the Father, and to the Son, and to the Holy Spirit. As it was in the beginning, is now, and ever shall be, and for all ages. Amen. Eternal rest, grant Thomas eternal rest, O Lord, and let perpetual light shine upon him. Rest in peace. Amen.'

As the beginning of the sunshine came through the windows, Bonner and Cavendish returned from the conversation in the hallway. In a second they both saw Wolsey was at his end. Bonner rushed to the bedside and grabbed Wolsey's now lifeless hand and repeated the prayer. 'Gloria Patri: Gloria Patri et Filii, et Spiritus Sancti. Sicut erat in princípio, et nunc, et semper, et in saecula saeculorum. Amen. Requiem aeternam dona réquiem Thomas Domine, et lux perpetua luceat eis. Requiesce in pace. Amen.'

Nicóla and Cavendish crossed themselves as tears came to their eyes. It was not Nicóla's first kill, not after the horrors of the sacking of Rome, but this was so much different. Nicóla killed for Crumwell; in his name. The father of her daughter. Her master. Nothing would save her soul now. But the worst part – to take the life of a man of the cloth caused Nicóla no pain, the act not difficult to perform.

Chapter 24 - December 1530
Greenwich Palace and Austin Friars, London

Forswear until coequal thee believeth the seecryt

Crumwell sat rigid in his seat for so long he almost became dizzy from lack of movement. He folded his hands on his lap and blinked a few times to awaken himself. Sat in the presence of the King, his mind lingered far away. Where, even he was not quite sure. The words from Wolsey's letter, of love and forgiveness, stayed in his thoughts. Inside a tiny box was a gold ring, holding a large turquoise stone; now it rested on Crumwell's left forefinger. It was the ring Wolsey always wore, and many spoke of its magical powers, as it could control the King.

George Cavendish sat next to Crumwell, tears in his eyes as he spoke. Every so often, Edmund Bonner, the third in the row, spoke, giving Cavendish a break, who was still distraught from Wolsey's death. The King sat across the table, on a chair taller than the rest, allowing him to look down on the men before him. Both Bonner and Cavendish needed to recall the life and death of Wolsey in custody before the Privy Council, but King Henry had wanted to hear the story first. Crumwell knew it was because Henry did not wish to look upset by the news in public.

'Wolsey was devoid of a cardinal's red vestments when placed in the coffin,' Cavendish said with a sniff. 'Wolsey was given purple, that of a bishop, his own clothes, for his final rest.'

'What type of coffin?' Henry wanted to know the cost.

'It was a plain coffin, Your Majesty,' Cavendish replied. 'Plain wooden board, the simplest which could be arranged in a short time.'

'A far cry from what Wolsey expected, is that precise, Crumwell?'

'Yes, Your Majesty,' Crumwell replied, and brought himself back to the conversation, the same one he had with the two men days ago at Austin Friars. 'Wolsey had planned a magnificent tomb at Windsor, designed by Benedetto da Rovezzano and Giovanni da Maiano. The black sarcophagus and monument are already prepared.'

'Perchance I could be buried there,' Henry scoffed. 'God knows it was my monies which paid for its construction.'

Cavendish waited for a break in the conversation before he continued. 'Wolsey was buried with a gold and white mitre on his head, and a bishop's crosier lay across his body.'

'It is true that his body was viewed by the public?' Henry asked.

'The Mayor of Leicester came, Your Majesty, to view Wolsey in his coffin. Other men also witnessed him lying in state, such as Sir William Kingston, and several of his guard. Several other notable men in the area also came. They wished to confirm Wolsey's death with their own eyes. It was as if no one could truly believe God had called the Cardinal from this Earth.'

'Cardinal Wolsey was buried in the Lady Chapel of St Mary's Abbey in Leicester, Your Majesty,' Bonner added. 'As a thunderstorm passed over the abbey, he was laid to rest, well before dawn, no light visible to be seen.'

A single tear plucked itself from Crumwell's eye and trailed down his freshly shaved cheek. He had already cried to Nicóla when she returned from Leicester and told him the news, with Cavendish and Bonner, now without a master, in tow. Nicóla was present as Wolsey slipped away, just a man at the end of his days. But Crumwell was not there; Crumwell was the loyal servant who did not stay with his master. God forgive him.

Crumwell glanced up from his cold hands and the King stared back at him. Henry, too, had eyes glistening with tears, but he held them back with furious determination. 'Thank you, gentlemen, for your private audience,' Henry said and stood up, which thrust the other three from their seats as well. 'You may go but I shall need to summon you here to also tell the story to the Privy Council upon our next sitting, which will not be until after the Epiphany celebrations.'

'Thank you, Your Majesty,' Bonner and Cavendish said in time and bowed.

'I shall have Mr. Crumwell inform you of what to do next. But first, Crumwell, I wish you to stay.'

The men left, both upset after the difficult conversation, and as the door closed behind them, Crumwell noticed the King wipe his eyes upon his red and gold sleeve. But he forced a fake smile in Crumwell's direction and stood up straight, his hands clasped before him. 'Such a difficult time,' Henry said and wandered over to the fire. A servant stepped forward to offer wine but Henry waved him away. 'I can offer both men work in my household. Cavendish is welcome in my privy chamber.'

'I believe Mr. Cavendish wishes to retire and write, Your Majesty. However, Chaplain Bonner wishes to continue serving Your Majesty.'

'I might send Bonner to Rome, to protect our interests in the Pope's presence.'

'Excellent choice, Your Majesty.' Having faithful Bonner in Rome would make him a helpful spy for Crumwell.

'I have had a complaint about you, Crumwell, from the Lieutenant of Calais, Sir John Wallop.'

Crumwell pursed his lips. He had argued with the high-ranking diplomat just a week ago, over monies changing hands. 'Sir John and I exchanged words over a matter of the late Cardinal. Sir John and I do not share the same views on the life or treatment of Wolsey.'

'I warned Wallop he was not to threaten or insult you,' the King replied, almost as if he was pleased with himself to bestow something so simple on Crumwell. 'I like you, Thomas, I do. You have worked so well for me this past year. Perchance we can, at last, put the issue of Wolsey behind us. I so want to start a new chapter in my life.'

'Of course, Your Majesty,' Crumwell replied, unawares of the point to the conversation.

'I hear your Waif is back in the city.'

What of it? Who spoke of his Nicóla? 'Yes, Your Majesty.'

'For what reason? In what capacity does Frescobaldi presume to be back in England? Also, I hear the Waif brought with him a child, which is living as a bastard in your home. Why would a man of considerable fortune, born in the celebrated city of Florence, the beating heart of art and culture in Italy, be here, in your home, laying bastards at your door?'

Crumwell was so drained, more tired than he had been in some time. He worked constantly both for the King and himself. Also, he would be lying if he confessed to only sleeping next to Nicóla at night. Now, with the added weight of grief, even Crumwell's quick mind dulled, like the weather of the deep English winter.

'Is the child yours, Thomas? A son?'

'No, Your Majesty, the child is a girl.'

'Pity, an extra son is always helpful to a man. I was my father's second son, and here I am, the King of England.'

Crumwell watched the King, his face weakened in spirit, no doubt his mind on Arthur, his older brother, dead at only fifteen of the sweating sickness. 'The late Cardinal, Your Majesty, once told me that when grief steers our hearts, it is because we are adjusting to a new world. God shall show us how to draw strength from the grief, strength from lost loved ones, which can help us carry on.'

Henry half-smiled but did not look at Crumwell. 'Do you miss your wife, Thomas, your daughters?'

'Keenly, Your Majesty.'

'But you have been delivered of a bastard daughter. I hear the child has the golden eyes of the double-minded man, but not your dark hair.'

Crumwell pursed his lips again. Bloody spies. Anyone could be swayed for a few coins. Though he could not judge; he paid staff in every noble household in London, and beyond.

'And the mother, Thomas? Could it be the sister of our Mr. Frescobaldi? I hear that the Pope's secret son, the son of a Moorish servant girl, married a wealthy Florentine girl.'

'Yes, last January, Your Majesty.'

'Her name?'

'Nicóletta Frescobaldi, Your Majesty.'

The King smiled. 'Ever since the Italian's first visit here, Lady Anne was perplexed by the Waif. Anne said Frescobaldi had the ears of a woman, stretched earlobes from when a noble girl has to wear heavy earrings at a young age.'

Crumwell looked up at that comment. It was the same hint that Crumwell first noticed in Nicóla. Lady Anne's mind far exceeded anyone at court. Everyone wondered of the Waif, but no one openly said a word.

'Is this Nicóletta the mother of the child?'

'Yes, Your Majesty.'

'Despite being the Pope's daughter-in-law?'

'The Italians, the Medici family, have a different view of bastard children, Your Majesty. The Pope had a child in his youth and it was raised by his nephew's family. The Pope was already a cardinal and had to deny the child. The mother married an Italian man, and was never a part of the child's life. The boy was raised a Medici, while his father went on to be Pope. The son was married to the sole remaining Frescobaldi daughter in order to gain her fortune, a marriage planned by the Pope.'

'I heard the Emperor wished for his bastard daughter, Margarete of Austria, to marry the bastard Medici boy. This Florentine girl must be special.'

'Mistress Frescobaldi and her brother Nicóla are favourites of the Pope, Your Majesty, rare jewels treasured by an ailing old man.'

'And yet Mr. Frescobaldi is hither, with his sister's child, in your home.'

'Yes, Your Majesty.'

'You think I cannot see that Frescobaldi is a woman? If Lady Anne says it is so, then it must be so. Are you saying my Lady Anne is a fool?'

'No, Your Majesty. I believe the Lady Anne Boleyn to be nothing but highly educated and mannered. I have lost count of the number of men at court who admire her, and the number of ladies who wish to be Lady Anne is extraordinary.'

The King laughed, pleased with the flattery. 'The Pope's own daughter-in-law is in your house right now, dressed as a man under your protection, with the child you have together. I must say, Thomas, you are well placed. You have done rather well for yourself, a bastard child on the Pope's daughter-in-law? And to think Rome judges my living! How angry is the Pope in all this?'

'My belief is that Frescobaldi is free to travel, as the dowry is paid to the Medici family, and the bridegroom has a fertile mistress.'

'Those Italians are so strange. Is there a reason why I ought not to have the Waif tossed in the Tower for violating laws of public order? Why on Earth does the Waif act with such behaviour? How can you allow such behaviour in your home?'

There was no option but to speak the truth. 'Your Majesty, my close friend, Francesco, had five legitimate daughters, and a bastard, Nicóletta. The legitimate daughters perished young, along with their mother. Francesco educated his only living child in the image of a son, as Sir Thomas More does with his daughters. Nicóletta grew to be masterful in languages and accounts, vital to a banker and merchant such as Francesco. If he married off his daughter when she came of age, he then would lose his hard work. If his daughter took on a male identity, she could work for her father, carry the family name, travel with safety. The family is not noble, so no rules were to be broken. She became a bastard male heir, Your Majesty. Frescobaldi is well-read, well-tutored, can ride, hunt, train falcons, do business deals as well as any man. In truth, Your Majesty, while God ordained a female body, God gave a male mind.'

'God gives out no such accidents.'

'God made this decision, Your Majesty, and I feel there is no place in which I can question the Lord's decision.'

'It seems as though the Waif softened for you, Thomas, if you got a child on her.'

'I can but beg forgiveness, Your Majesty.'

'Thomas, a while ago, when I had the Waif in my chambers, beaten by the Duke of Suffolk at Blackfriars, you promised to make me the richest man in England.'

'I intend to do so, Your Majesty.'

'If you can do that, then I can be ignorant of the abomination that is your Waif. I call her such because to the outside world, it looks as if you have a love affair with a man.'

'Frescobaldi came here to seek my protection and protection for the child, Your Majesty. My Waif's new husband is a lewd and depraved man.'

'And you love this woman, you have spoken of love before. And yet Frescobaldi has married, by order of the Pope himself. The same Pope which forces me to stay in an illegitimate marriage with Katherine. Why should I not expose the Italian and toss her in the Tower, less well-kept than last time, as a punishment upon the Pope?'

'Because Frescobaldi has access to the Pope. You know such; for you have exploited it in the past. Frescobaldi is here and is on your side, Your Majesty. My Waif knows as well as you about being in a marriage that does not fit as it should. All the envoys you send to Rome fail. This is an opportunity we can use. As I say, the body of a woman, but the mind of a man. My Waif may be one of God's more curious creatures, but now my creature all the same.'

'I must have my annulment, Thomas.'

'Then let me gain it for you, Your Majesty. I can do both that and make you the richest man in England. After all, it is your rightful place. I have heard most lewd reports of Leicester Abbey, where Wolsey lay. If we root out all the black hearts in the Church and take over the profits of these corrupt men of God, your Exchequer could be full. The Church is recognising not your authority, rather the authority of the Pope. It is the time they swore allegiance to you, paid to you.'

'You have read Tyndale's book, Obedience of a Christian Man?' the King asked. 'Anne gave me the copy she got from your Waif.'

'I find it enlightening, Your Majesty.'

'It says, a king may do right and wrong and shall give an account but to God only. No more begging to Rome, no more writing to Rome, held up by sackings, petitions or any such mess!'

'I have also read A Supplication for the Beggars, by Simon Fish. Fish was a friend of mine, Your Majesty, and Sir Thomas More has arrested him for heresy. Sir Thomas More loves to burn heretics now he is Lord Chancellor.'

'I shall not discuss More's business, Thomas, so ask me not to do so,' the King warned. 'But yes, I too have read Fish's pamphlet. It states that more money ought to be spent on the needs of the poor, rather than clerics becoming fat on the piety of their flock. Fish worries that spirituality has installed its own state in England, an authority as powerful as my own. Both Lady Anne and I much enjoy these new books, and I know you do too, Thomas.'

'All of parliament are on your side, Your Majesty.'

'Thomas, I want you to be a member of my Council. We will not sit until after the Epiphany celebrations in January. You will be a junior member, but the council is small and in need of new ideas. Norfolk, Suffolk, the Boleyns, they know power but do not understand making money, not the way you do. I need you to be the voice of reason.'

'I am ready to serve, Your Majesty.'

'I need my annulment.'

'I shall be your Queenmaker, I swear before God.' Even if only to keep Nicóla safe.

~~~

By the time Crumwell returned home to Austin Friars, he

stumbled as much as any drunkard. Weary humours weighed heavy on his body, grief similar to his soul. Neither Ralph nor Richard were still awake, just a maid at the door when he came in and tossed his coat in her direction. Crumwell pulled himself up the wide staircase to the third floor, keen to see his bed. His fingers trailed along the rich green tapestries of the hallways and stairwells as he made his way to his own rooms. The warmth of his bedroom met him the moment he opened his door, the fire so strong it roared like an animal.

Nicóla sat in one chair close to the fire, dressed in the white nightgown lined with pale brown fur which he had commissioned for her. Nicóla smiled at the sight of him, but it faded as he came close, his feet dragging on the carpets. Nicóla stood up as he approached, just as he fell to his knees.

'Tomassito, what has happened?' she gasped.

Crumwell clung to her, his arms around her waist, his face pressed against the warmth of her stomach. He felt one of her hands in his damp hair, another on his aching back and he finally burst into heavy tears. Nicóla let him cry and did not ask again, did not need to ask; he had to let Wolsey go. Crumwell clung so tightly to her, his arms aching as he held Nicóla's body, his tears free to propel down his cheeks and seep into the fabric of her nightgown while she stroked his hair. He would have fallen in a heap on the carpets without her warm touch to hold him against her.

Crumwell knew not how long he howled before he heard Nicóla's voice again, soft, almost a whisper, a vibration deep in her body. 'Behold us, my beloved Jesus weighed down under the burden of our trials and sufferings, I cast ourselves at Your feet, that You may renew our strength and our courage, while we rest here in Your presence. Permit us to lay down our cross in Your Sacred Heart, for only Your infinite goodness can sustain us; only Your love can help us bear our cross; only Your powerful hand can lighten its weight. Amen.'

'Amen,' Crumwell whispered and felt Nicóla move as she crossed them both.

Crumwell looked up to Nicóla and she wiped his tears away with a single finger and laid a kiss upon his forehead. 'All my fortunes shall come from abandoning Wolsey,' he whispered.

'No, you did not abandon him,' Nicóla whispered. 'You sent me to him and he knew what that meant. Trust me on this. He ruled this nation for twenty years and it was his will that you do the same.'

'Henry has appointed me to his Council.'

Nicóla half-smiled back at him, his eyes still filled with tears, rimmed with the red of anguish. Crumwell blinked a few times and waited for her to speak again. Nicóla could make everything better again. He finally felt improved from all that emotion.

'No one shall make you feel this way ever again, Tomassito.' Nicóla brushed her hands through his hair and cradled his face. 'I swear to God; we shall make sure no one makes you feel this way again. This is an important change.'

'I want to destroy the Catholic Church,' Crumwell muttered and stood up at last. 'Never again will I seek guidance from men in clerical uniform, for they give no forgiveness, no solace. Only God can provide that. The Church needs to be reformed. Damn Rome and all they have done to you! Damn them for causing Wolsey's fall. They use the Lord to create their own wealth and comfort. We sent Cranmer to Rome to persuade the Emperor to endorse an annulment. But even that is not enough; we must reform.'

Nicóla nodded but said nothing, and Crumwell pulled her into his embrace. Finally, there was a way forward; reform would save them. All done with Wolsey's ring on Crumwell's finger.

Chapter 25 - March 1531
Austin Friars, London

Love ceaseth to be revelry if it ceaseth to be seecryt

Nicóla slowly awoke in bed but refused to open her eyes. She felt the cold of the morning on her bare shoulders and searched for the blanket to pull up as high as her chin. It must have already gone dawn, the fire not tended for hours. She put one hand out in a dozing search and found Crumwell facing away from her. Without waking, he turned to her and put his arm around her. Pressed up against him, her head on his shoulder, she felt the cold golden band of the large turquoise ring Crumwell wore, the gift to him from Wolsey. He had read the note from Wolsey, but not shared its words; they were fit for no one but him. The ring he put directly upon his left forefinger. At least now Crumwell could start to execute his own plans, free of Wolsey's shadow.

In the peace, Nicóla drifted back into sleep once more. But time had no wish to stay still. Faint sounds called to Nicóla, who felt far away in her sleepy state. A voice, mayhap more than one person, the sound of banging, mayhap footsteps. None bothered her. Nor did they seem to wake Crumwell, who also made no movement. Nowhere in all of Europe had ever given as much comfort than the warmth under the covers of Crumwell's bed.

The sound of the opening bedroom door brought the world into stark reality in a heartbeat. Both Nicóla and Crumwell jumped in fright at the thought of being found. Crumwell bolted up in bed and pulled the covers over Nicóla's head, but whoever had the audacity to open the bedroom door could see someone was in their master's bed.

'Sorry, Master Crumwell,' Nicóla heard Ralph say. She heard the panic in his tone; Ralph had seen too much and it scared Ralph as much as the pair in the bed. Crumwell was practically Ralph's father, a father in bed with a mistress. 'I… there…'

'What is it, Ralph?' Crumwell interrupted and rubbed his face to wake proper. 'Can a man not oversleep after a late night at court?'

'Yes, of course, but… Master Secretary Gardiner is here, Master Crumwell. He has come urgently to speak with you before proceeding with the King today.'

'Gardiner is the King's secretary, what could he possibly need to know that he does not arrange himself?'

'I know not of his motives, Master Crumwell. But be assured he is anxious to speak with you. He did not even mention the indictments being presented at the King's Bench at Westminster. Gardiner has also noticed one of his lawyers, Thomas Wriothesley, is here, working for us.'

'Let me dress and prepare for my day, Ralph. Tell Gardiner I shall be but minutes.' Crumwell clicked his fingers to dismiss Ralph.

The door closed but Crumwell waited a few moments before he lifted the bed cover from Nicóla's face. She smiled at him, her naked body pressed against his. They both began to laugh at the situation as she crept up his body and kissed his lips, still holding her smile. She loved how he ran his fingers through her short hair when he kissed her, to hold her so close to him. One kiss turned to another and another, warm once again under the bedsheets. The silent rest was long gone, but the duties of the King's secretary waited in the offices.

'You must go to work, my love.'

'Let Gardiner wait,' Crumwell whispered against her skin. 'Let him tarry downstairs while we commit a beautiful sin he will never be able to understand.' Crumwell's kisses returned them both to that warm and safe place Nicóla could only find when protected by him.

Crumwell's cheeks appeared flushed, his white linen shirt still not tucked into his dark hose when he went to speak with Gardiner. Nicóla slipped through the side door into Crumwell's library off the main office, and found Ralph also there, pretending not to listen to the conversation happening between their master and the King's secretary.

'There you be,' Ralph spoke with a wicked smile. 'I could find you not when shaky-hands Gardiner arrived. Richard tried to make conversation with Gardiner, but he was in no mood. Where be you all this while?'

Lies ran so smoothly from her lips. 'Master Crumwella asked me to show another guest from the house,' Nicóla replied in a whisper.

'The mistress in his bed?' Ralph said, his youth showing his curiosity to speak of lovers. 'Master Crumwell has a mistress? I had no idea.'

'I do not wish to speak of it, all I know is that I needed to show a woman the rear exit of the house.' Nicóla held a smile at her own lie. 'I suggest there is no mention of this to Crumwella. What goes here?'

'Come and listen,' Ralph gestured, and the pair stood together behind the open door to the office.

'We simply cannot have indictments sent to the King's Bench, speaking against our bishops and abbots, suggesting they are wrong in supporting papal authority! Of course men of the Church support papal authority, it is our divine calling to do so, Thomas! How can you support such notions?'

'Stephen,' Crumwell tried to reason with Gardiner, 'none of this is new information, I worked quietly on the prelates for months, under our King's instructions. The plan is in Henry's hands, in his head. These men are subject to praemunire. These clerics must be tried for praemunire, for recognising the Pope over our King.' Just as the King wanted. Crumwell had the paperwork ready, months of work done in secret until Henry was ready to be persuaded. All clerics in England would now be breaking the law in recognising the Pope's authority.

'Praemunire suggests that their belief in papal authority is undermining the King and his power. To suggest these fifteen clerics have done so, Thomas, is to suggest ALL the clerics of England believe in the power of the Pope over the power of the King, including me.'

Crumwell threw Gardiner his deeply scornful grin and said nothing.

'What do you hope to achieve, Thomas? To throw every cleric in England in the Tower?'

'It would certainly lower the corruption of the Church, a goal both Lady Anne Boleyn and I share.'

'You have risen so high since Wolsey's fall, Thomas,' Gardiner warned him as he paced back and forth, his white vestments swishing around his heavy waist. 'You have seemingly hoped to swoop in and claim all of Wolsey's power over the King.' Gardiner paused to point at the turquoise ring. 'You have Wolsey's ring on your hand. It is said that ring has magical powers, the power to control the King himself. How could you wear the ring?'

'I wear the ring at Wolsey's request. Jealousy is a sin not attractive to your manner!' Crumwell cried and ran his hands through his dark hair to hold it from his still flushed face. 'I plan on naught but serving our master, King Henry. I think you burdened, Stephen, because you hoped to claim the void left by Wolsey. Wolsey was the man who made us both at court. I have risen and you have the jealous humours I expect from a woman!'

'Good God,' Gardiner spat back. 'I am an archdeacon. I am the King's secretary. I have been sent on diplomatic missions to France, to Rome to see the Pope.'

'As have I, in years past!'

'The King has demanded that I gain a precedent from the University of Cambridge to procure the decision as to the unlawfulness of marriage with a deceased brother's wife.'

'I am awares, Stephen, it is in accordance with the plan for resolving the question of annulment without the Pope's intervention. It is a plan I came up with my own advisors, and suggested to Henry.'

'Which advisors be those?' Gardiner scoffed and crossed his arms. 'That strange Waif creature who seems to be your shadow? Perchance Richard or Ralph? Hardly a qualified council of advisors.'

'Do not profess to understand what I discuss with the King, Stephen. Not everything needs to be dealt with by the limp hand of the Church. Sometimes strong and drastic hands and minds are required,' Crumwell warned his longtime friend. It was plain to see this friendship had come to its natural end, with Crumwell seeking to break the Church's stranglehold over England, and Gardiner as loyal as always to his faith.

'You were not to take Wolsey's place at the King's side,' Gardiner said and stopped pacing. 'You were not to assume our old master's favour.'

'And yet I have done. When I am finished, Stephen, I shall have more power over this country than Wolsey ever had. I am not bound to the Church; I can see what is necessary and what is not, without needing to beg to God for guidance every day.'

'I knew it,' Gardiner cried back. 'I knew all you wanted was Wolsey's power, you heretic! You used the Cardinal as a step into the nobility. You are a commoner, Thomas. You will always be just a commoner. All of the court looks to have you thrown down to whence you came.'

'You are a commoner just the same,' Crumwell laughed. 'I know you claim your mother was the bastard daughter of Jasper Tudor, that you are somehow special, a bastard cousin to the King. I know it to be a lie; Wolsey knew it and told me so. We laughed about it over dinner one evening. If my work has risen me higher in the King's favour than you, then you must regard your own failings.'

Gardiner threw his shaking hands in the air, the Archdeacon at the point of breaking. 'I know that this morning, an urgent message was sent to court, and you were not there to hear the news. The King spoke with me, and you seemed nowhere to be found. The Church's own form of parliament, the Convocation of Canterbury, is coming to the palace to talk with the King. Perchance all this blackmail you had Henry enact upon clerics will soon be over. The King may see sense.'

'If the Archbishop of Canterbury, old Archbishop Warham wants to speak on behalf of those charged with praemunire, he shall have to appear in court at Westminster, not a direct plea to the King. You are a lawyer too, Stephen, you know this. Charges are already laid.'

'You charged Bishop Fisher, Bishop West, Bishop Standish, Archdeacon Travers! How could you do this! All are fine men of the Church.'

'Fine men indeed, but who support Queen Katherine in her stubbornness not to allow an annulment. That drew the King's anger, not mine, Stephen. I do as the King's whims command.'

'The King does whatever the Lady Anne wants. Anne reaches too high, she expects too much.'

'Lady Anne Boleyn can do as she pleases. She is intelligent and has more time with the King than the rest of us together. There is no point in being jealous of the Lady Anne. Why come to me, Stephen? I will be at court with the King today, so what is the rush?'

'The Convocation of Canterbury will give the King £100,000 in order to stop the cases against the clergy. That is what I heard.'

Crumwell coughed a few times. 'You say £100,000? That shows

how guilty they are of choosing the Pope's authority over the King's. We ought to charge the entire clergy and the King's Exchequer shall be filled in no time! Let us hear what Archbishop Warham has to say immediately! Ready the King!'

'Thomas,' Stephen replied with a sigh, 'this is serious. We have the King wanting reform, taking power, letting Protestant thought into England. We have More, the Lord Chancellor, wanting Catholic reform, wanting to burn more heretics, those embracing Protestant reform. Do we need to create a country which will tear itself apart?'

'Go back to court, Stephen, have some ale, pray. The Convocation of Canterbury is exactly what we need. They shall pay the King, and he shall have the praemunire charges dropped against Bishop Fisher and his creatures.'

'And what of you and your creatures, Thomas? Who will stop you?'

'I remember you took the Waif from the Tower, in hopes of using his knowledge. Yet the King took the Waif from you. Judge not my creatures, for I know you are jealous.'

'And what of this mention you took in the Waif's bastard niece?'

'Spies in my house again?'

'Always,' Gardiner grinned.

'Likewise. Sadly no women ever wish to enter your bed, so you lack joy in your life.'

'My man in Sir Thomas More's household tells me More has taken a new mistress.'

'Pious old More? Poor Alice, she deals with enough grief from her changeable husband.'

'But you, Thomas, taking in bastard children, and creatures like the Waif? Are you adding to your collections of party tricks, like your leopard, your beavers in the garden?' Gardiner said with a frown. 'All most strange.'

'Beware of idle rumour, Stephen, for I have plenty I can share,' Crumwell replied.

'Such as?'

Crumwell paused for a moment, a hand over his mouth. He was unsure of an answer. Nicóla stepped from behind the door and into sight. Both men turned to face her, neatly dressed in her Crumwell household livery of black and grey velvet.

'Archdeacon Gardiner,' she said and bowed slightly to

acknowledge him. 'I am sure you do not remember, but when you visited on an envoy to the Pope in 1527, I too was there. You asked for help with an annulment for the King; you appeared not the confident and highly educated man of God you have claimed. Rather than the scholar and diplomat the King thinks you are, I saw you, begging on your knees, crying to Pope Clement that you needed an annulment. You wept like a wounded girl, with no argument that could satisfy His Holiness. Yet you came back to London and proclaimed your intelligent discussions fell on unwise ears in Italy. But in fact, it was you who was unable to aid the King before the Pope, and I do not think King Henry would like to hear such a thing about his secretary, especially at a time when he needs firm guidance.'

Gardiner stood frozen on the spot, just staring back at Nicóla. She held his barbarous gaze and did not move. Crumwell's complexion started to turn red as he held in his laughter. Gardiner finally removed his glare from Nicóla.

'I trust I shall see you in the King's privy chamber this afternoon, Thomas.'

'Stephen,' Crumwell replied politely as Gardiner swept out of the office towards the front door, his robes brushing the stone floors as he left.

'That was simply wonderful,' Ralph marvelled once Gardiner was safely out of Austin Friars. He stepped around the door as Crumwell burst out laughing.

'I wish I had seen Gardiner on his knees, crying like a child,' Crumwell snorted as he imagined the scene.

'Not a word of a lie, either,' Nicóla shrugged. 'Gardiner is the most ineffectual diplomat I ever witnessed before the Pope.'

'But £100,000 to be paid to the King?' Ralph asked as they calmed themselves down again. 'I wonder how the King shall take this new stage.'

'I think His Majesty shall like it very much,' Crumwell grinned. 'I know it is exactly what I wanted when I first drew up charges against the Church.'

'Blackmail can be a beautiful thing,' Nicóla added.

'Ralph, go and prepare a boat, so we can get to court. There is much work to be done,' Crumwell instructed, his face changed to the typical business expression. He clicked his fingers twice and Ralph scattered.

'I think I shall not see you any longer today,' Nicóla said with a pout.

'It is the perils of being court favourite,' Crumwell shrugged. 'If you could stay hither and be of service to Richard with my private business...'

'Of course, Master Crumwella. May I make a suggestion?'

'Naturally.'

'King Henry shall be best pleased with this money. But before he accepts any money from the Convocation, he ought to demand certain things from the Archbishop Warham.'

'Such as?'

'Tomassito, you ought to have the Church write up a new law, stating that the King is the supreme head of the Church in England, not the Pope. The threat of praemunire has frightened the Church, but it will also make them bitter. The time to act is now. Write up a new bill or article stating that Henry is not the only Defender of the Faith, as is already obeyed, but that is the only supreme leader of the Church in England.'

'You are right, as always,' Crumwell said. His mind already moved through the conversation; Nicóla could practically see him working on the paperwork. 'The King must have spiritual jurisdiction in England. The Church must be broken.'

'Yes, precisely. When this money is paid to the Exchequer, they will expect all clergy to be pardoned from the statute of praemunire, and they will want the laity pardoned also. In return, the King ought to ask that the privileges of the Church are upheld only if they do not detract from the royal prerogative and the laws of the realm. The power of the Church can be reined in at this opportunity; the time to exploit the power of the Church is now, Tomassito.' Crumwell headed straight for his library, gently pushing Nicóla through the doorway with him. He shut the door and kissed Nicóla deeply, holding her body tight against his. 'Only you could make the destruction of the Church so enticing.'

'Whatever you need, Master Crumwella.'

'I need to make the King rich.'

'Then you ought to go to court and do so, and we here at Austin Friars can work on making you rich.'

Crumwell let out a wicked laugh as he kissed Nicóla again. 'It is almost too easy to take money from the Church. They are so easily shaken and buckle so easily under pressure. Their corruption has made them soft.'

'They are getting what they deserve. Come and visit baby Jane with me before you leave.'

~~~

Nicóla sat down to her small desk at the corner of Crumwell's library, under the window which overlooked the gardens, and in came Richard, his hands filled with messages.

'You would think it was you who ran all over London with letters, not just our messengers,' Nicóla jested as he sat down at Crumwell's main desk.

'You would think,' Richard replied, his gentle Welsh accent soothing as always to Nicóla. He was Crumwell's nephew and had taken his surname, but he still had the ancestry of his father in him too; an accent was a legacy Nicóla understood.

'Men writing to Crumwella, asking to have their debts extended, I assume?' Nicóla sighed as she regarded her work before her. The accounts filled by the day, almost too much to handle, a situation she felt used to in Florence. But Richard did not say a word.

Nicóla glanced up and saw him holding one letter, the rest tossed on the main desk. At once the large wax seal upon it told her all she needed to know. She rose from her seat in silence and Richard finally looked up.

'Why should the Pope write to you?' he asked.

'You may not believe me if I told you, Richard. My father was close to the Pope's family. You could say I am still close to His Holiness.'

Richard coughed and frowned as he thought of an answer. He handed Nicóla the letter and replied, 'all the spies in England will know that letter is hither. The King himself will know if a letter from the Pope has arrived in England. He worries people are colluding with Pope Clement. Regard what happened to poor Wolsey when he wrote to the Pope.'

'Fear not, Richard. At least this letter appears to still be sealed. The ribbons sealed through the wax are broken not.'

'We ought to send a messenger to the palace, so Master Crumwell knows of the letter. It might play havoc if the King says something and Master Crumwell knows not.'

'Indeed,' Nicóla replied and tore open the letter with the knife on her desk. Just the breaking of the seal and the ribbons made her think of the Pope, of Giulo sitting in session in Rome, writing all his letters, sharing the news with Campeggio, with the others in his confidence.

'Tell Master Crumwella I have received a letter from the Pope, asking about my whereabouts and what news from England. Tell him the Pope wishes to know of my personal movements only.'

'The King might think you a spy.'

'I fear the King thinks such already.'

'It is fortunate that our master is so close to His Majesty's ear. I shall deliver that message personally, Nicóla. I wish not to repeat any of these words to anyone else.'

Richard disappeared and Nicóla sat back at her desk. She unfolded the letter, written in Italian by Giulio's wide scrawling hand.

My capricious daughter

How we do so miss you here in Rome, much woe is brought to us when cast from your company. But thou ought to be removed to the care of your husband in Florence. My son can be something of a candle waster, prone to anger. But the word of God himself has touched you and bestowed upon you our Alessandro, to be your husband. He informed me of your leaving of the family palace, and we gathered you took the blessed Giovanna to England. We understand the pain of a bastard child, sweet Nicóletta, and you are praised by God for bearing such a burden during work for our Lord. Yet you are to be removed to your husband and the marital home upon the receivance of this letter. Your quick wit and gentle intelligence are needed at this time in the new court of Florence, as we once again take control of the city. Alessandro is to be invested to his position as Duke in July and shall need the Duchess at his side. We remember there are to be no legitimate children of this marriage, but the city does require an heir. If you wish to leave the blessed Giovanna in England, we shall understand. But, Nicóletta, you are to return to serve your Medici family, as your father, and God, intended. It is not safe in the court of King Henry at this time. The esteemed Bishop John Fisher has written a great number of times and has also written to Charles, our Holy Roman Emperor. If Charles is to invade England on behalf of his aunt, Queen Katherine, we much fear for your safety, Nicóletta. Please return home to Florence as needed to take your post as Duchess of Florence. It is our sole command at this time.

Pope Clement VII, God's voice upon this Earth

Apostolic Palace, Holy See of Rome, this day XXI MDXXXI

Richard again appeared in the library. 'Are you well, Nicóla? You look most pale.'

'All is well, Richard. The letter is as I said, a personal message.'

'Not many could utter such words, that they gained a personal message from the Pope,' Richard grinned as he tied his black cloak at this throat.

'Not many wish such things upon themselves. Tell me, Richard, do you know where resides the Bishop Fisher?'

'Fisher is often lodged in a private palace close to Westminster.'

'I am asked to deliver upon him a small token, a favour from the Pope, a friendly gesture.'

'I shall convey so to Master Crumwell.'

'No, please do not!' Nicóla cried, and then quieted her tone. 'I am sorry, Richard. Please, I do not wish this to be at court. It is a simple token between friends, a bag of peppercorns traded by the Portuguese. I do not wish it to sound as some sort of message passing, or a sign that the Pope is discussing the royal marriage.'

'Does the Pope make mention of the annulment?'

'No, nothing, all of the business happening with our families in Italy only.'

'I just heard a rumour,' Richard smiled, 'the Lady Boleyn has a new motto, in French. Aisi sera groigne qui groigne.'

'Let them grumble; that is how it is going to be,' Nicóla replied. 'That shall win her no favour.'

'If only she could lay with the King,' Richard laughed. 'At least then Henry could set her aside. Then we could return to the golden days of court.'

'We all wish for thus.'

'Well indeed. Did you know that they are due to burn poor Thomas Benet as a heretic, on Sir Thomas More's orders?'

'Burned for owning books, reading books, reciting books,' Nicóla sighed.

'Heretical texts.'

'Texts we have all over this manor,' Nicóla scoffed. 'That damned More, he does more harm than good. He sentences people to death on a whim. His humanist writings are extraordinary, but his humbleness seems a myth and his mercy is nowhere to be seen.'

'Be careful who hears such words outside these walls, Nicóla,' Richard warned. 'I shall be off to Greenwich. I will return as soon as

I can to assist you with our papers.'

'Take your time, Richard, and I thank you. Master Crumwella does not wish me to be at court. Creatures such as I catch too much attention.'

Nicóla sat back at her desk. Sometimes she felt a bite of regret when she lied so strongly to a man's face. The plan already swarmed her mind; deliver not peppercorns to Bishop Fisher, but the hemlock she possessed, crushed into peppercorn. Bishop Fisher stood in Crumwell's way, so he needed to be poisoned. It seemed unlikely his cook would place pepper in anyone's food but Fisher's own, knowing the price of peppercorns from the spice routes. Pepper was a luxury Fisher had commented on at court when Nicóla once spoke to him during the legatine court hearings. If Fisher was colluding with the Pope, it would enrage the King on a scale that could not be anticipated. Hemlock mixed with pepper could at least make the old man too ill to cause disruption at court. At best, it could be enough to stop Charles the Emperor from planning an invasion of the country. Bloody Bishop Fisher needed to be silenced, much like the cruel Sir Thomas More. She swore no one would crush her darling Crumwell again, and there was no way Nicóla could keep this invasion information private and go home to the new Duke Alessandro. Fisher had to be stopped before the King got any closer to his annulment. Crumwell wanted a new queen, and it would raise him high at court, so Nicóla would do anything to be of service.

Chapter 26 - April 1531
Westminster, London
Keypyng seecryts is four survyval

King Henry sat on his throne, thoroughly drained. The gold cloth of estate hung high over his head, drooping a fraction, and Crumwell could not pick why it irritated him. The cloth seemed to represent the King's mood, despite the fact His Majesty should have appeared buoyant. Crumwell stood to the side of the King, his hands clasped before him, as still as the guards who stood on the opposite side of the room, blocking the closed door. In the centre stood skittish Archbishop William Warham, constantly tugging at his collar. Warham was an old man of more than eighty years, and yet Henry refused to let the purple-clad cleric sit down for the discussion.

'I want to hear no more of the Convocation's discussion,' Henry ordered Warham. 'I care not to have the men of Canterbury stand together and ordain to tell me what I can or cannot do in my own realm. I am weary of the Church creating canon law, creating laws for English people to live by when it is I, my parliament, who should create all laws, not only civil laws.'

'Your Majesty, canon law is decided upon by Convocation, by the men of the Church. Your divine spiritual learnings and…'

'Enough!' Henry barked and raised one hand to the old man. Crumwell felt worried perchance Warham might just fall to the hard floor in the public presence chamber. Henry's mood had lapsed into anger, his eyebrows so furrowed they sat in a V formation. Henry sat up straight, his knees wide apart, and brought the tips of his fingers together.

'After all these discussions, I have decided to accept the Convocation's offer last month of £100,000 in order to pardon the accused clerics of praemunire. In this case, the Convocation has done the right thing. Parliament shall pass a Pardon of Clergy Act and render all charges of praemunire against the clergy dropped, is that not true, Mr. Crumwell?'

'Yes, Your Majesty, it shall be passed with much expedience,' Crumwell replied and smiled as Warham threw him an angered scowl.

'Then, we shall meet with the Convocation, and officially sign the papers stating the deal is done, assuming the articles I wish to add are complete.'

'They are all ready to sign, Your Majesty,' Crumwell added, and again skittish Warham threw him an angry look. The Archbishop truly did not care for Crumwell, but the foolish clergy seldom did.

'I am Defender of the Faith, and I want to be the Supreme Head of the Church of England. I want spiritual jurisdiction over the Church, and the privileges of the Church shall only be upheld if they do not argue with royal prerogative,' Henry said with a true grin.

'But it shall be hard to make such changes, as the Church is free to make its own canon laws,' Warham argued.

'Then Convocation shall have to understand these changes and hold fast to them,' Henry cried and slipped in his seat again. 'Let us head back into the official meeting and then we can sign, and you can make the first payment of the £100,000 you owe, Archbishop Warham.'

'Thank you, Your Majesty.' Warham's voice held all the sincerity Crumwell expected from a snake.

With a dismissive wave, Henry allowed the skittish Archbishop to leave the room. What made the old man smell so horrid? As soon as he had gone, Henry groaned to standing and sighed. 'Ah, Thomas, debating the Convocation is tiresome. I cannot wait to tell my Lady Anne that I plan to make or destroy canon law in England. I will be the Supreme Leader of the Church as far as the law of God allows.'

'I am glad you are seeing progress at long last, Your Majesty.' If anything, Crumwell needed that bribe in the King's Exchequer, but changing Church laws appealed too.

The King nodded and put his hands on his hips. 'Has the Pope sent any more letters to your Waif, since that last one asking her, sorry, him, to return to Florence?'

'No, Your Majesty. Mr. Frescobaldi did, in fact, write back to Rome right away, stating that you forbid travel, but the reply was only sent one week past.'

'You are most welcome, Thomas,' Henry said and slapped Crumwell on the shoulder. 'My royal order means your Italian mistress can stay as long as you like. She is under orders never to leave England unless I grant her safe passage. Your strange little creature born to the wrong body is hidden under my protection.'

'I am humbled by His Majesty's grace,' Crumwell mumbled. He meant it; Nicóla did not wish to return to Italy and the King withholding her saved both she and Crumwell from the reality of her recent marriage. Alessandro de' Medici now had her money, so what more could he want? It was the Pope who wished Nicóla home, and Crumwell did not want those feeble hands on her again. A loud bang echoed across the room, and in ran one of the King's gentleman-ushers, his black livery a size too big on the young lad, the Tudor rose not well sewn on his chest. Definitely new to court.

'Your Majesty, there is news from the home of Bishop John Fisher!'

'Is he dead?' Henry jested and Crumwell snorted.

'There is a rumour of poison, Your Majesty! Last night Bishop Fisher sat at dinner but ate scant. However his guests became ill upon eating a broth and two have since died, and many of his household have taken up ill.'

'Poison?' the King croaked in shock; Henry always worried about poison and had all his food, and Lady Anne's food, tasted before dining. 'Are they quite sure?'

'Yes, Your Majesty. Bishop Fisher ate so little that he is only ill, but fighting with the grace of God. Many are fallen ill in his household. His cook, Richard Roose, is in the Tower and has confessed to adding what he thought was exotic peppercorn to the broth, under the Bishop's request. Perchance he instead put poison.'

'Why would a simple cook decide to do such a thing,' Crumwell stated rather than asked. 'That is not smart thinking.'

'No, perchance the cook was paid, or blackmailed, or threatened,' Henry said. 'Go and alert Archbishop Warham, and get him to uphold the Convocation despite Fisher's absence.'

The boy ran away again and Henry cried out in anger. 'Must God put a block in every road I must walk?' he fumed. 'As soon as everyone hears of this, they will assume the Boleyns poisoned Fisher. Everyone blames my precious Lady Anne when something goes wrong. I have had enough! I shall sign this Convocation, give Anne the wonderful news of the signing, and the news of Fisher's poisoning. I shall inform my wife also. They shall see all much differently.'

Crumwell watched the King pace back and forth, anger showing with interwoven fingers. Now was his time to pounce. 'Your Majesty, now the Convocation is controlled, may I suggest further changes? Ones that shall soothe the Lady Anne of the lengthy delays?'

The King stopped in a moment. 'Go on.'

'We draw up paperwork, detailing abuses of the Church, and submit them to the Convocation. The Convocation must be stripped of all legislative powers if many cases of abuse are being committed. You, Your Majesty, must be the fair judge who punishes abuses, and the Convocation must renounce their power to the State.'

'Can it be done? Can we find enough abuses of power within the Church to support such a change?'

'Well indeed, there shall be no problem. Church corruption spreads far and wide in this country. It will take time but shall work.'

'Do it. I will have Sir Thomas More look into the poisoning of Fisher. I must go to my Lady Anne at once!'

Crumwell bowed as the King rushed away, his guards following close behind, but he could barely contain his excitement. Little by little, the Church came crumbling down. It mattered none to Crumwell who poisoned Bishop Fisher and having the prominent Queen Katherine supporter ill was nothing but helpful.

~~~

As Crumwell strode towards the King's chambers for an early morning meeting, an outpouring of people seemed to be coming in his direction. The hallways shuffled all one-way movement, and as he got closer to the King's rooms, he could hear the reason – King Henry was furious, in one of his angry and vicious tirades, in which few could be spared. People fled in any direction. Today was to be a challenge.

The pompous Duke of Suffolk lumbered towards Crumwell with his head held high, his beard-covered chin jutting upwards, with his group of men trailing him. 'Crumwell,' he said with a sniff as he approached in the wide hallway, 'perchance someone as grim as yourself can handle the King's temper.'

'That depends on what you have done to anger him, Your Grace.'

'I am sent from the privy chamber; Henry shall have no more of me today.'

'Your crime?'

'One moment it was my admiration for Queen Katherine, next it was my lack of admiration for Lady Anne. Yet, he is raving against both women, so I know not the remedy. I am leaving court.'

Crumwell bowed as Suffolk waddled off, and carried on towards the King's rooms. The guards positioned at the main doors were quick to move and allow him through, and he trailed past the public rooms and through into Henry's privy chamber where Sir Thomas More and the Duke of Norfolk stood together like naughty schoolboys caught playing during lessons. The Chamberlain announced Crumwell's appearance, but King Henry stood facing away, looking over the gardens outside his window. He breathed so heavily Crumwell could hear the King's anger from far across the wide room, his breath hot enough to mist the glass.

'Your Majesty.'

The King spun on the spot, his elaborate red overgown swirling about his body. 'Crumwell! Perchance now we shall have sense!'

Both More and Norfolk regarded Crumwell up and down, the pair both showing disdain for his presence.

'Your Majesty, I have here…' Crumwell started and presented his black leather satchel where he kept his papers. The esteemed package had finally arrived from Thomas Cranmer in Rome, months and months of study and debate on the annulment. Cranmer remained in Rome, ambassador to Charles, Holy Roman Emperor, and King of Spain. If Cranmer could convince Charles on the annulment issue, all would be well. While Cranmer toiled, the scholars of Europe were sending back their opinions, at Cranmer's request.

'Ah, more work for me, I see!' the King interrupted and strode across the chamber. He smacked the satchel from Crumwell's hands, papers showering to the floor. 'I have men like you to do all the work on my behalf! I cannot simply do everything at all times! As it is, I have a wife and a wife-to-be constantly bawling me, crying out demands. Now must I suffer more?'

'On the contrary,' Crumwell said, in an attempt to sound unfazed by the shouting and spittle. 'Now that the Convocation of Canterbury is resolved, you have the title and the monies you need from the Church. All signed and complete.'

'But I can be only the Supreme Head of the Church as far as the law of God allows!' the King screamed and threw his hat from his head. He stomped on its velvet as if to make a point Crumwell did not understand. 'Still, the Queen continues to petition the Holy See. If I am the Supreme Head of the Church, no one, even the Queen must not be able to appeal to Rome on any spiritual matter! That stupid, imbecile Pope still believes that I ought to appear in Rome personally and answer to my behaviour, or face excommunication!'

'Pope Clement has threatened you with excommunication for the past two years, Your Majesty. It seems to be something he throws at people when he is in a certain mood,' Crumwell replied and shrugged, a habit he had picked up from Nicóla at home. Nicóla believed Clement could not excommunicate a king; he did not possess the stomach for such dealings.

'You still have the Waif in your manor, do you not?' Henry asked an accusatory finger pointed at him, already knowing the answer.

Crumwell glanced at More and Norfolk, both listening to Crumwell take the burden of the King's anger. 'Yes, Your Majesty. Nicóla Frescobaldi is still residing at Austin Friars at Your Majesty's pleasure and is doing most well helping my nephew Richard in running my finances and legal matters. They just had your Master of the Horse, Nicholas Carew, in my office, begging to borrow funds, after he accrued a great gambling debt.'

Finally, the King's complexion broke into a smile. 'Nicholas Carew, you say? That man has vexed me of late. I hope the Waif posed upon him a great interest rate.'

'Well indeed, Your Majesty.'

The King's anger averted so easily, by talking about other's troubles. 'Have you heard the latest news at court?' the King continued. 'I have the Duchess of Norfolk, merry to tell the court of how the Lady Anne has quarreled with me over a visit by the Princess Mary. My own daughter is ill and Katherine wants Mary brought to us here in London. Lady Anne forbids this. I cannot live with Anne acting in vain jealousy over my own daughter! But I cannot allow Mary to visit, or things shall increase in vexation! How long must I be stuck with the Queen, living this sinful life?'

Crumwell stood straight and tall, hands clasped behind his back, as the King continued to pace and rage. He only ventured answers when Henry stopped to breathe. 'I have heard no rumours from the Duchess of Norfolk, or any other woman, and I have no intention of listening.' Crumwell glanced at Norfolk, whose tortured wife had shared her niece's arguments with the King all over London. Of course Crumwell's creatures had heard, but it was not worth mentioning.

'Your Majesty,' squeaked the voice of beady-eyed Sir Thomas More. 'If you permit so, I am happy to break with Queen Katherine on the subject of…'

'I care none for Katherine's desires! Not for having our daughter at court, not for our marriage, not for my soul to guide itself back to Rome, none of it!' Veins throbbed in Henry's forehead, and Crumwell half-wondered if Henry might drop dead on the spot. Henry stopped and caught his breath and everyone held theirs, ready for the next scream.

'May I collect up my papers, Your Majesty?' Crumwell asked and gestured to the floor. Henry waved a dismissive hand and Crumwell bent down to pick up the important news he had brought to the King.

But just as things looked calmer, the King spun back and pointed at Norfolk. 'You,' Henry yelled, 'I heard that you commented, to the Marquess of Dorset, that only the devil himself might promote a plot such as an annulment! You said it while adoring the Queen's courage! Is this true?'

'Your M-M-Majesty,' Norfolk began, his palms upwards in explanation.

'Out of my sight!' Henry bellowed, and Crumwell's ears stung as he stood up with his satchel. 'And you,' he pointed to More, 'take your stories about Bishop Fisher's health and leave me in peace! I shall deal with that issue on my own. Fisher is naught but a grave thorn pricking at my conscience!'

Both More and the Duke bowed and left the room without a word, probably relieved to have made it out alive. Crumwell stood still as the King rounded upon him again. 'Can you believe More?' the King seethed. 'He came here to tell me how Bishop Fisher is healing after someone tried to poison his broth. If only the fool was not fasting that night! Two of his servants are dead and the rest are still recovering, as is bloody Bishop Fisher! And the world all thinks that it was the Boleyns who poisoned the Bishop. They blame the Lady Anne for bloody anything! Did I not say that exact thing to you just last week, Crumwell?'

'Yes, Your Majesty. I do not suspect the Lady Anne, for she would never do something such as poison a man. Lady Anne is all piety,' Crumwell replied. In truth, he suggested the poisoning to have come from someone acting on behalf of the King himself but would go to the grave with that idea locked in his head.

The cook who did the poisoning, he is arrested and awaiting interrogation in the Tower. I want him condemned by attainder without trial.'

'Attainder without trial is for criminals, Your Majesty, men whose guilt is assured.'

'I do not care for the facts, Crumwell! I want this done!'

'Parliament could pass a law, making murder by poison high treason, regardless of the victim's status. I could write up the paperwork and we could…'

'Write and I shall sign,' the King said, his chubby finger pointed at Crumwell again. 'I am King and can decide on whatever laws I wish. From now on, your plans shall be executed without delay, Crumwell. We must make sure that you can work without impediment on my behalf. Well indeed, make poisoning high treason. The punishment shall be… being boiled to death.'

'Boiled, Your Majesty?' Crumwell swallowed hard; even he felt squeamish over that prospect.

'Yes. I want you to go to the Tower and personally investigate the cook. Get him to confess who asked him to commit the crime, so the Boleyns are cleared. Then, boil him. Do it personally.'

'Yes, Your Majesty,' Crumwell replied slowly, and clutched his leather satchel.

'At least that shall ease one of my burdens. I want your Waif in here. I want him – her – him, to write to the Pope, but I shall tell what is to be written. Still the Waif has heard not from the Pope since she refused to return back to Florence?'

'Not to my knowledge, Your Majesty, and rest assured I would know; for nothing goes in or out of Austin Friars without my knowledge. Not enough time has passed for letters to arrive.'

Henry nodded as he fell into a seat at the long table in the centre of the room. He rested his face in his hands, but Crumwell did not speak. The King had worn himself out now, as would a sleepy child who argued about going to bed. 'How are the changes at York Place coming along, Crumwell? My Lady Anne wishes to live there soon enough.'

'York Place is greatly extended and changed, according to your wishes, Your Majesty.' How well Crumwell knew York Place, Wolsey's old palace. Now it looked totally different, triple the size and a courtyard and garden which had seen many nearby houses knocked down to accommodate. York Place could be a city on its own, hefty enough for thousands of people at court.

'We are to change the name to Whitehall,' the King said, his chin rested in his palm, one elbow on the table edge. 'What do you think?'

'Whitehall is most appropriate, Your Majesty.' Crumwell could still see the shining white hallways of the palace in his mind, with Wolsey's coat of arms painted on the walls. Of course, all gone now.

'I want to do repairs to the Tower of London, Crumwell, the Queen's rooms must be better appointed. I want a new palace for Westminster, by the abbey. We also need additional fortifications in Calais. Can you oversee all of that?'

'Of course, Your Majesty.' It was always better to agree now and worry about the arrangements later. No one could say no to the King.

'Can you continue to oversee the building and preparation of the Henry the Eighth College in Oxford?'

'Naturally, Your Majesty. I was doing just that on Wolsey's behalf.'

'We need larger taxes on wine brought in from the Low Countries.' The King's mind bounced like a cloud on a windy day.

'Consider it done.'

'I want better sewers built in London. Lady Anne says we need better sewers.'

'I quite agree. Leave the details to me, Your Majesty.'

'Why cannot everyone be of service as you help me, Crumwell?'

'Not everyone has the mind to do many tasks at once, Your Majesty. They are of a different time, a different way of learning.'

'If only Gardiner worked as hastily as you. Always too busy itching that long nose of his.'

Crumwell smiled; he had not spoken to Gardiner since March and the Convocation meeting. Gardiner was now in France, acquiring theologians opinions and information for the King's annulment.

'Any chance you can silence my cousin, Reginald Pole?'

Still not calling him Thomas, as Henry normally did, as if he substituted Crumwell for Wolsey. Crumwell was unawares how he felt about that; either way, the King was all about being pleased, none for being denied. 'As it happens, I can.' Crumwell approached the table and Henry sat up straight. Crumwell pulled papers from his satchel, still damaged from their flight to the carpets. 'Your cousin, Reginald Pole, is back in Padua to study, and considers himself in self-imposed exile, as he does not agree with your annulment. Pole has written saying he does not endorse your moves to leave Queen Katherine.'

'I know all of this.'

'But have you heard from Thomas Cranmer in Rome?'

The King grabbed the papers from Crumwell's hand and began to read. 'Thomas Cranmer in Rome, the ambassador to Charles the Emperor under your orders, worked with Edward Foxe, as you requested, and now have completed their Collectanea satis copiosa, the Sufficiently Abundant Collections, which proves no English King has a superior on Earth. Cranmer shall travel back to England to present the work, but he has written, stating his initial findings. Also, other diplomats around Europe are completing their works.'

'And what of the scholars of Europe?' the King asked, his voice light as dawn sunshine, full of hope and calm.

'French scholars believe you are free to marry, as do the German reformers. Reginald Pole may not agree with you, but theologians in Venice, in Florence, Milan, all side with you. The Swiss domains too, and some in the Low Countries.'

'Spain?'

'Spain, naturally, is for the Queen. We shall never get Spain, and Portugal needs to keep the peace with their neighbour.'

'The masculinity of my kingship is being damaged, Thomas.' Now he was calling him Thomas; the King had finally calmed, trust was restored. 'I must have good news. Norfolk, at least, says Katherine cannot have her matter argued in parliament, no matter how much Ambassador Chapuys wants to fight on her behalf. The court shall move to Windsor in the summer, and I shall leave the Queen there and take Lady Anne on progress. That way, Katherine can see the

Princess Mary all she likes, and it will not anger Anne. I need time away from everyone at court, as they do not help me in my cause.'

'As you wish, Your Majesty.'

'Except you, Thomas. I need you. Come to Windsor with us, but then return to London so that affairs can be handled in my absence. Only you can be trusted. I place all the power and the responsibility upon your shoulders.'

Crumwell could never be sure why Henry trusted him so, but the power and privilege fed his vanity so that Crumwell felt he could achieve anything. 'As you wish, Your Majesty,' he repeated, resisting the urge to show off his greed-fuelled grin.

'Boil the cook who tried to kill Bishop Fisher, and then bring me your Waif. I want matters sorted before we leave for Windsor.'

Crumwell bowed and left the room, Henry left to pour over the news from the scholars of Europe. He would get his annulment whatever the cost. And now, Crumwell was be forced to bring Nicóla back to court, somewhere he never wanted to take her.

It took a while for Crumwell to leave the King's chambers, yet Sir Thomas More still waited for him in the hallway. The Lord Chancellor appeared overworked enough to sleep in the window seat where he waited. 'Sit with me, Mr. Crumwell,' More offered.

Ralph appeared still not back from his own tasks, so Crumwell took the moment to sit with the humanist turned heretic burner. 'Are you not busy, Sir Thomas? For when Cardinal Wolsey was Chancellor, he barely got a moment's pause.'

'Always busy. We have not sat at your table and had a mighty dinner party in a while, Crumwell.'

'You are starting to burn men like me, lawyers, thinkers, honest men, just because of the books they have read. I fear we shall not dine together for some time.'

'I only burn heretics who have broken God's laws and spoken out in public places. All had a chance to repent before taking the flame.'

'What of Simon Fish? I hear he is imprisoned for writing a pamphlet on the corruption of the Church. Will you burn him too?'

'If he continues to deny the truth of the Bible, then, yes, perchance I will burn him.'

'Do you desire something, More?' Crumwell sighed, already weary of sitting next to such a fanatic. The man was Henry's longtime companion so More was not about to disappear from the court.

'Did you hear that William Tyndale has published a paper, with talk of disobeying laws I oversee in England? That heretic, telling me what I can and cannot do? That I am wrong in my spiritual learnings? Tyndale also writes against the King's annulment. Henry shall protect Tyndale no more. He shall be punished for his crimes.'

'I know it is your biggest wish to see William Tyndale burned alive, More, but he is an Englishman revered in Europe as a Lutheran, as a reformer of the Church. He translated the Bible into English. I fail to see how this could be such a heinous crime.'

'God's words are to be in Latin, not English. And I know you are a reformer too, Crumwell. You are a heretic.'

'Then burn me, More,' Crumwell sighed. 'Just get the King to sign the paperwork, as he has spiritual jurisdiction now.'

'All thanks to you. You are destroying the power of the Church, do you not see that?'

'I do, and I like it,' Crumwell whispered and threw More a smirk.

'I heard a rumour about you, Crumwell. I heard you still have that Waif creature living in your home.'

'At His Majesty's command.'

'I hear unnatural things.'

Crumwell's face turned to a deep scowl. 'Nicóla Frescobaldi is the son of my Italian master, and a companion of the Pope in Rome. You would be grateful to have such a person in your life, someone so touched by God. You know Mr. Frescobaldi, have spoken with him at length in my home.'

'You see, I am a spiritual man, Crumwell. I have friends in Rome. What I do not understand is the relationship between Nicóla Frescobaldi and Nicóletta Frescobaldi.'

Crumwell swallowed hard and did not move in his seat; how he acted now could have a serious effect later. Not a muscle in his body could give away his worry. 'They are brother and sister.'

'It seems the sister is the new Duchess of Florence. Should not her brother be in Florence with her, rather than here with you?'

'The family's relations are of no consideration.'

'I hear the Pope is most worried for Mr. Frescobaldi here in England. Or is it Nicóletta here in England? The story all seems most confusing.'

'Perchance you ought to have learned better Italian, oh great scholar Sir Thomas More,' Crumwell said and abruptly stood. 'The

King trusts Nicóla Frescobaldi, as do I. Leave your confusion, and leave my companion's sister alone in Florence. You seek to meddle in too many things when you cannot even keep matters here in London under control.'

Crumwell swept away from More and did not look back. If anyone discovered the truth about Nicóla, Crumwell would be shamed out of his favour, even with the King on his side. He could never dispatch Nicóla and baby Jane home to Florence to the depraved Alessandro. More was officially a serious enemy to the Crumwell family.

Chapter 27 - April 1531
Austin Friars and Westminster, London

Seecryts liketh adventures, but art jealous and keep thee high-alone

As usual, the noise coming from the offices at Austin Friars hastened no privacy, no peace. Crumwell hired an additional fifty staff to the house in the time Nicóla lived there, most working in the nearby offices to Crumwell's main library and office. Crumwell, Nicóla, Ralph and Richard all worked in the library and office, jammed together, while the other staff, those drafting papers, their handwriting being used on paperwork, their math skills, not to mention the men who collected debts on behalf of Crumwell, had separate spaces. Spies, Crumwell's creatures, from homeless children to high-ranking men seeking favour, poured in and out through the day, relaying their tales. However, everything constantly mingled, even the sound of Crumwell's constant finger clicking as he gave out instructions. Though, Nicóla could tell her own constant clicking back and forth on her calculation table irritated Ralph, so the long days at Austin Friars harmed everyone's humours.

'Your old friend, Sir John Gage, the Vice-Chamberlain of the King's Household, has asked for a loan,' Ralph said as he opened the newest of the letters received to Austin Friars.

Crumwell smiled but did not look up from his desk. 'Gambling debts, I can be sure of it. Gage was always horrid at cards.'

'Are you any better?' Nicóla said but continued with her calculations. 'I heard Richard Rich regularly takes money from you at cards and dice.'

'Richard Rich is a cheat,' Crumwell added, and Ralph laughed. 'Whatever Sir John needs, give it to him. Nicóla, take the note from Ralph and draw up a contract.'

'There is another from the King's Bench,' Ralph added. 'Sir Christopher Hales, the Attorney General, the judge who oversees much for the King of late. He, too, asks for a loan. He does not specify why, but seems most desperate.'

Now Crumwell looked up from the draft of import taxes. 'The judge, Hales? What does he ask?'

'Hales writes he is in need of £100.'

'What, £100? What could he have done to run up such a debt?'

'I hear his illegitimate son is something of a wastrel,' Richard muttered.

'Was Sir Christopher Hales the judge who prosecuted Wolsey?' Nicóla asked, unsure of the name.

'He did,' Crumwell sighed. 'However, to have a debt over a judge is a benefit to me. Nicóla, write the contract for this also. Increase the interest to be charged, at your discretion.'

'Certainly, Master Crumwella,' Nicóla mumbled.

'Master, may I be excused?' Ralph asked.

'Tarry but a moment.' Crumwell put down his quill and looked at his companions. 'We are to go to Windsor on progress, all of us. Nicóla, you shall act as an informal companion. Ralph, you remain my master secretary. Richard, it is you whom I need to be special.'

'Whatever you need, Master Crumwell,' Richard said, his eyes wide. He looked to Nicóla and Ralph, who felt equally surprised.

'You are my nephew, Richard, and I do not intend for you to be buried here at Austin Friars your whole life. Prepare your amour; I want you to represent us in the King's joust at Windsor. With luck, you shall do well and impress the King. I shall have you on the Privy Council before the year's end.'

'The Privy Council?' Ralph choked.

'It is a place where I need total confidence among the men. Richard, you are the man for the role. Do not think this a smite upon you, Ralph. You too shall be rewarded at the right time.'

'Thank you, uncle,' Richard said; his large hands shook with excitement. Richard on the Privy Council secured Crumwell's position ever more at court. 'Might I go to speak with my wife Frances for a moment? I must thank God for this moment also.'

Crumwell dismissed him with a click of his fingers and Richard disappeared. Ralph then followed after, the door slammed shut. As soon as privacy reigned, Nicóla turned in her chair and faced Crumwell. 'That is quite the honour,' she commented. 'And Richard is a deserving man.'

'Do you suppose Ralph is worried he shall not be elevated?'

'Perchance, but Richard is of age, and Ralph is but a young man. I am sure all will be well. Tomassito, might I also take a break from work? We slept but four hours last night, such is the workload now.'

Just the mention of sleep made Crumwell yawn. 'You are well, no?'

'I am, I just… I just forgot the role Hales played in Wolsey's prosecution! I learned the art of memory in Florence, just the same as you, Tomassito. I forgot something! People like us do not forget anything.'

Crumwell gestured Nicóla to him and she obliged, her feet dragging across the floor. He reached out to her and Nicóla sat down on his lap. 'I am sure your loci tutors taught you how to study your surroundings in order to learn to remember everything you see,' he whispered, and gently tickled the back of her neck with his fingers. 'You know you need an absence of emotion in order to accurately map any situation or equation so you may recall it again in the future. I need to touch your skin in order to remember how soft you feel, how you smile when I tickle you…' Crumwell's voice trailed off as he kissed her base of her neck just above the embroidered edge of her white shirt. 'If I wish to remember how much I take pleasure from kissing you, I must study you, map you…' he teased and kissed her lips, as if enjoying the smile on her face.

'What will this lesson help you recall, Master?' she asked.

'It is always best to go over old lessons, in case more can be learned.'

'I have learned it is most dangerous to act in such ways in your office, Master Crumwella.'

Crumwell sighed with acceptance and Nicóla climbed off his lap.

'With permission, I shall go upstairs to the nursery and visit Jane.'

'Give her a kiss from me,' Crumwell said and sent her on her way. Nicóla left the offices and went towards the servants' stairs to go to the third floor. She weaved through a narrow hallway and past the kitchens to the stairs. But as she passed the entrance to the laundry room she heard a muffled sound. Nicóla paused and poked her head into the steaming laundry room, the laundress girls all hard at work. No, the noise had come from the staircase. Nicóla carried on and almost bumped right into Ralph, preoccupied with one of the laundress girls in his arms.

'Sorry,' Nicóla muttered as Ralph tried his best to hide the young woman behind him, her face hidden under the white cap she wore, all askew, her dark hair dishevelled.

'How do you Italians move so silently?' Ralph admonished, and tried to straighten his hose.

'Be worried not by my eyes,' Nicóla replied and passed the entangled pair. 'I come from a land where passions are neither despised nor discouraged.' Nicóla continued and did not dare look back at her friend.

Once she reached the nursery, she witnessed baby Jane in the centre of the room, sitting on her own on a thick red carpet, two nurses beside her.

'Might I visit Miss Crumwell?' Nicóla asked the two maids.

'Certainly, sir,' one of them replied and Nicóla sat on the floor with her daughter in a moment. It was well known Nicóla constantly visited the nursery. Jane had Nicóla's olive skin and rose-gold hair, but the wide golden eyes of her father. Nicóla sat in silence and baby Jane reached for silver buttons on Nicóla's doublet.

'You are the one who brought the baby here?' the new nurse asked Nicóla.

'Yes, it was me.'

'Where are the parents?'

'Jane was born of my sister. She was unable to keep the child when she remarried.'

'So why did Master Crumwell give the child his surname?' the nurse continued.

'Because my son-in-law is a fine man and a careful master,' came a reply. Nicóla turned to see Mercy, a pile of freshly laundered blankets in her hands. Hopefully, Ralph had the laundry girl whisked away before Mercy caught them. She was one of the most pious women Nicóla had ever encountered, her face lined with age and weary from experience. 'Mr. Frescobaldi, always pleasant to see you in your niece's nursery. Girls, can you excuse us?' Mercy asked.

The two nurses left the room, and Mercy pulled up a chair,

smoothing her black dress and white apron as she sat down. 'Many years ago, I had an older sister,' Mercy began as they both looked to Jane, her rose-gold hair curled atop her head. 'She was not like myself nor my other sisters. My father was to marry my sister to a fine boy where we lived, but she refused and ran away. We heard that she had dared to dress as a man and crossed the channel into Calais. She worked in a bakery. Lord knows how she paid for the journey.' Mercy paused and crossed herself. 'Can you imagine? A woman dressing in a doublet and hose to go on an adventure? What would God say?'

'Mercy, I can imagine,' Nicóla replied.

'My Thomas is a good man, was a fine husband to my daughter, God bless her soul, and a fine master of this house. He took me in when my husband died, and let me stay on after the death of my dear Elizabeth and the girls. I am mistress of his great home and have a baby in the house once more. My new husband works in the stables, merry as ever. So many are touched by Thomas' generosity.'

'Master Crumwella is naught but kind and generous to me also,' Nicóla said as she held Jane's tiny hand in hers.

'I hope he is only kind and gentle.' Mercy stared right at Nicóla.

Mercy Pryor knew the truth. Nicóla often wondered why more people did not work it out; she was a slender girl, her clothes fitted with pads in the shoulders to make her look wider, her features gentle like a woman, her voice not deep, no matter how low she tried to speak.

'The generosity that Master Crumwella has shown me is beyond reproach,' Nicóla said. 'He is kind to me, and indeed soothing as I have grieved for my father these past years. My father taught Master Crumwella so, and that is of great comfort after the loss.'

'I am most glad,' Mercy smiled. 'After the loss of my daughter and young Anne and Grace, I wish the best for Thomas. I hope he too has found comfort.'

Nicóla smiled and Mercy returned the gesture. It was the kind of motherly nurturing which Nicóla had never received, her mother dead in childbirth, her stepmother suffering the same fate years later.

The door to the nursery opened and there stood Crumwell, a letter in his hand, a worried expression furrowing his brow. 'You must excuse me, Nicóla, but we must away to court immediately.'

Mercy took the baby from Nicóla, who quickly got to her feet. 'What news?'

'A letter from the Pope.'

Nicóla took it from Crumwell before she had even left the nursery and her daughter. Out in the hallway, silent on the top level of the house, the gallery below also devoid of people, she took the letter and saw the seal of the Pope. 'It has been opened,' she said.

'It means someone has read it already, perchance many people.'

'It is in Italian, though.'

'The King has spies, the Emperor has spies, the Queen has spies, the Boleyns have spies, Ambassador Chapuys has spies, More has spies, Gardiner has spies…'

'We have spies…' Nicóla cut him off from his worry.

'The first line reads "my daughter-in-law," Crumwell said. 'The first words give away your identity, which I can assume was the Pope's intention.'

La nuora

We are much discontented by your last correspondence, stating that you are in the capital of England and that King Henry has ordained for you to remain in London until His Majesty grants you permission to be dismissed. You are a child of our nation and not of England. You cannot be held there by a king who has lost his way and is in desperate need of guidance. You are hereby ordered by us, by God, to return to your lawfully wedded husband and to leave the illegitimate child behind in a home befitting her situation. As your husband is now Duke of Florence, and the Republic is no more, there are many opposed to Medici rule. Our family is of the land and so is yours, Nicóletta. We continue with the building of the great fort in Florence, in which you can live with the husband God has joined to you. While Italy believes you are in the safety of the Apostolic Palace, other times at a Medici villa in the country, you continuing to live in England so brazenly under your traditional guise is no longer appropriate. You are to return and shed your disguise at once. It was us, as Cardinal all those years ago, which suggested you take the life of a banker like your father, and it is us who now commands you to throw off those shackles and take your place as a true and lawful wife. To defy such an order is to defy God. So unless you are there to remove the King's concubine from this Earth, you are to return home. Pope Clement VII, God's voice upon this Earth Apostolic Palace, Holy See of Rome, this day XIV MDXXXI

Nicóla stared at the shaky signature of the Pope for a moment and then folded the letter again. 'I assume you read all.'

'I did.'

'And we need to hurry to the court why?'

'The King commands you report to him as soon as the Pope writes.'

'If I stay in England, my love, all it shall do is enrage the Pope, and hurt the King's chances of an annulment.'

Crumwell scoffed. 'There is no chance of an annulment, we both know. We would not be asking advice from the theologians of Europe if we thought the Pope accommodating.'

'I cannot leave Jane behind in England!' Nicóla raised her voice without meaning to do so. 'She is my daughter,' she hushed herself. 'But at least if she is here with you, Jane is safe.'

'I refuse to send you home, Nicó. I promise I will not dispatch you to Florence.'

'To my lawful husband. I consented to marry Alessandro.'

'You consented freely?'

'No.'

'Did you consummate the marriage?'

'Lord, no. He had three other women that night, arranged by me.'

'The King may not get an annulment, but you could. Forget the Frescobaldi fortune, stay here with me.'

'Do you want me? It is one thing to have a hidden mistress…'

'That is not how I see you, Nicó.'

'I am so consumed, Tomassito. I have the mind of a man and the body of a woman tucked away. I was accepted as such, spoken to as a man, given a male name. I could travel in safety, I could discuss finance, build a group of merchants, traders… I could live. I have turned away from being the Duchess of Florence to be your, what, attendant? But I am bound by God…'

'If I can break the marriage of a king, I can break your marriage also,' Crumwell interrupted.

'I was married by the Pope himself,' Nicóla replied and felt ready to cry. Her eyes prickled hotly with tears. Should have poisoned the Pope, not Bishop Fisher.

'What if you could live openly as a woman here, and still be in my household? You are more than an attendant, you are my financial advisor, my accountant. Or I can get you a place at court…'

Nicóla scoffed and shook her head. She felt tears spilling from her eyes. 'The mind which is created quickly to love is responsive to everything that is pleasing, soon as by pleasure it is awakened into activity,' she recited. 'Your apprehensive faculty draws an impression from a real object, and unfolds it within you so that it makes the mind turn thereto.'

'And if being turned, it inclines towards it, that inclination is love; that is nature, which through pleasure is bound anew within you,' Crumwell replied. 'Yes, of course I read the works of Florence's greatest poet, Dante Alighieri.'

'If the Pope wishes me to be a Medici, then I shall be a Medici,' Nicóla said and took a deep breath. 'Let us to court.'

~~~

Nicóla followed Crumwell through the palace, her head down as she walked. Not once had she visited the palace since her return five months ago, and only seen by those who came to Austin Friars. Things were certainly different; now as Crumwell walked, people stepped aside, and they all stopped to watch him go by. He was no longer a man who could simply slip between men and go about his dealings; now people actively watched for him. When they got to the King's chambers, Crumwell clicked his fingers twice, and one of the gentlemen-ushers rushed over, sweeping petitioning men aside as Crumwell and Nicóla walked straight through.

Once in the antechamber, it was only a minute before the Chamberlain announced Crumwell into the King's presence in the public presence room. Nicóla knew to stand back, and wait to the side of the doorway as Crumwell went through. She could not help but peek around the red curtains which hung between rooms to see the King and Crumwell together.

'Did you bring what I asked for, Crumwell?'

Crumwell clicked his fingers twice, and Nicóla rushed through the curtains and into the presence of the King. She bowed low, black cap in hand, and held herself there for a moment to show her graciousness to King Henry.

'The Italian Waif,' the King said, his shoulders jostling as he laughed. 'Let me look at you.' Nicóla stood still and silent as the King put his huge hands on her shoulders and stared his blue eyes directly at hers. Crumwell had told Nicóla all about how the King knew she was female, but as the Pope's daughter-in-law, the King found her too curious to be angry or to banish her. 'Mr. Nicóla Frescobaldi… that is quite a name.'

'Nicóla is much easier, Your Majesty.'

'Fear not; for I am a master orator. Welcome back to court. I trust you are well in the care of our Thomas?'

'Well indeed, Your Majesty. The kindness my father once paid to Master Crumwella is paid over and over in his kindness towards me.'

'How charming.' The King found the whole scenario most amusing. 'For the praise of you that I hear from Thomas indicates he most trusts your counsel. I hear your sister married during your trip home to Italy.'

Nicóla threw a look to Crumwell as the King let her go and stepped back. Neither of them could see what the King wanted.

'Spies here tell me that the Pope wrote to you, and somehow the letter got through without being translated. Does the Pope always tell you to burn the letters?'

'Yes, Your Majesty.'

'Why?'

'Privacy. The letter instructed me to return to Florence at once, Your Majesty. I do not wish to return.'

'You wrote back to the Pope, under Thomas' instruction?'

'Yes, Your Majesty. I wrote as Master Crumwella instructed me, that I had to remain in London at His Majesty's pleasure.'

'And you have heard no response?'

'Yes, Your Majesty, this morning I received a second letter from the Pope.'

'Your Majesty,' Crumwell jumped in, 'a letter was received just today at Austin Friars and we came to you as soon as we possibly could. The letter was already open.'

'And you know not whose spy opened the Pope's letter?'

'No, Your Majesty, however, the letter is in Italian, and that may provide some level of discretion if spies had no time to translate.'

'Frescobaldi.' Henry turned his attention back to her. 'Secret letters from the Pope could be seen as a sign of treason. The Pope is well known for his dislike of me. However, as Thomas trusts you, I shall trust you. Thomas would suffer if you lie to me.'

'I shall do nothing to hurt England, or Master Crumwella.'

'As a relative of the Pope, Mr. Frescobaldi, tell me; how much does the Pope hate me?'

'Your Majesty,' Nicóla ordained to lift her gaze from the floor again and looked at the King, 'the Pope harbours no ill will to any of Europe's kings. He considers them all his children and His Holiness their moral compass. He feels His Majesty has strayed too far from the flock and wishes to guide you home. Excommunication threats are the way in which he seeks to guide you home to Rome. But never would Pope Clement have the strength to do such a thing to a Catholic prince such as yourself. You have committed no sin worthy of such punishment. Both I and Cardinal Campeggio have told His Holiness that you have suffered a crisis of faith. I also told the Pope of the Lady Anne's pious and honest nature, regardless of what others should say. I told the Pope you are blessed by God to have both Queen Katherine and Lady Anne as women in your life, as both are esteemed and devout souls.'

'You spoke of the Lady Anne to the Pope?'

'His Holiness questioned me directly, Your Majesty. The Pope has had a great many opinions thrust upon him. It was I whom he sent to London to observe on his behalf, and I reported what I learned. I told him that His Majesty did not seek an annulment because of the Lady Anne, but that if you remarry, your choice is one of piety.'

The King licked his lips a few times. He seemed greatly offended that the Pope even spoke of Anne. But what could be expected? That Rome did not know of his desire to remarry? The great liar Eustace Chapuys surely wrote the Pope and the Emperor daily with reports of "that great whore", as Chapuys called Anne, in ink and in tongue.

'I want you to write again, Mr. Frescobaldi. I want you to tell your Pope that if he excommunicates me, I can never return to Katherine. I want to write out the letter myself, and have you rewrite it in your hand, all under the eyes of Thomas, who shall swear you have not changed or added anything in translation.'

'I swear on my life I can write as you command.' In truth, it mattered none what Nicóla wrote. Now she had defied a request to return home to Florence for Alessandro's dukedom ceremony, the Pope would be angered and too proud to listen to her advice.

'You may remain in England, is that plain, Mr. Frescobaldi?'

'Yes, Your Majesty. I know of a gravest threat to your kingdom, and you must hear all at once.' Now Nicóla had the King's attention.

'What is it?'

'The Pope instructs I am to return home, and live as a woman. For me to revert to a woman will undermine all the fine work from Master Crumwella's offices, as I harm him by association. But that is not all. The Pope plainly states that unless I am hither to kill Anne Boleyn, I have to leave England immediately.'

'Kill Lady Anne!' the King bellowed, the room echoing with his wild tone. 'The Pope truly states this?'

'Very clearly, Your Majesty,' Nicóla replied, knowing the letter was far vaguer than that. 'I believe there may well already be a conspiracy underway to kill Lady Anne Boleyn.'

Nicóla glanced to Crumwell beside her and he stood stunned. Now he knew what she meant when she said "be a Medici." To be ruthless, to cut down your nemesis before they can strike.

'I believe there is a conspiracy going on, and I believe the man they wish to have on their side is Sir Thomas More,' Nicóla added.

Crumwell coughed a few times, no doubt stunned again at Nicóla's lies. But she was right to do it; More was ready to expose her identity.

'Sir Thomas is a life-long friend of mine, Mr. Frescobaldi.'

'More is also a man of fervent faith, with a strong sense that Queen Katherine is your wife now and forever. He believes in the authority of the Pope, and you know all this to be true. I choose not to return to Rome, to a place that would happily see Lady Anne dead just to let them win an argument. I stand hither today and I see no evidence of papal authority, only the authority of His Majesty.'

'At this stage, I have no idea who I can trust,' the King said as he stroked his short orange beard.

'You can trust Master Crumwella, who only has care for both yourself and Lady Anne in his heart and prayers,' Nicóla replied, and stood up as straight as she could, tiny next to Crumwell.

'I understand that Thomas has a great affection for you. Thomas says you received a similar education in Italy as he did himself, both instructed by your father.'

'Yes, Your Majesty. My father was a great man who believed in education.'

'You are lucky, and you know why.'

'The fantastical nature of my birth.'

'Well indeed, the fantastical nature of your birth. I do so find you amusing, Mr. Frescobaldi. We are to go on progress for the summer, first to Windsor and then riding and hunting from there. You and

Crumwell are to attend at Windsor. When we return to London, I wish you to join us at court.'

'Your Majesty?' Nicóla threw a look to Crumwell. She did not want to leave her daughter at Austin Friars! 'I have naught more to offer.'

'Nonsense. My Lady Anne finds great comfort in your company I fear. Anne knows of your... fantastical birth, shall we say. She has the great musician Mark Smeaton, the poet Thomas Wyatt, and a great number of men who visit her rooms during the day to talk and entertain. I am sure she would like the beguilement of an Italian theologian. Is that what you are now, now that the Church has set you free?'

'I am a banker again, Your Majesty, under Master Crumwella's command.'

'You may still work for Thomas hither at court. Thomas, I want you at court constantly as well. I know that may make things difficult for you with your own business, but let us be plain; you are too important to have away from the court of power.'

'As His Majesty wishes,' Crumwell said. 'We shall always be at court once you return from progress.'

'In the meantime, you can continue to work on those papers, citing the abuses of the Church, Thomas. And do not worry; I shall make sure you both have rooms at court which are very close to one another.' The King winked at Crumwell and Nicóla.

'I shall have the words for the Pope prepared, Mr. Frescobaldi,' the King added and headed back to his throne. 'I am expecting you to be my personal link to Rome now.'

'Your Majesty,' Nicóla said and she and Crumwell bowed in time, before turning to make a hasty retreat.

'We are to live at court?' Nicóla almost choked on her own words. 'But what of Jane?'

'Jane can stay at Austin Friars,' Crumwell replied. 'She has nurses and Mercy has much adored her over these past months. Jane is in safe hands.'

'Tomassito, she is our daughter, I will miss her so,' Nicóla whispered, the antechamber filled with men wishing to see the King.

'I know, but we must do as we are bid. My Gregory is away from me so often, so I understand the burden. We shall cope as best as we can. Jane is safe at Austin Friars.'

'And my work for you?' Nicóla asked.

'You work for the King, and me, now.'

Nicóla swallowed hard as Crumwell led the way back out of the King's rooms. The web of the English court only seemed to thicken by the day. The first thing to do was write to Pope Clement and say she intended to stay in London, to wipe the concubine from the Earth. Only that might buy more time.

Chapter 28 - May 1531
Smithfield and Greenwich Palace, London

Thryee may keype a seecryt if two of thym are dead

Nicóla stood perfectly still, the breeze catching the hem of her black overgown. She stood in the courtyard at Austin Friars, beside the horses which waited to take Nicóla and Crumwell to Smithfield. Today would be the day she watched a man boil to death, boiled for the crime of poisoning Bishop Fisher. This was not how she expected her plan to end. She had gone to Bishop Fisher at Lambeth Marsh, told him of her letter from the Pope, how the Pope had sent peppercorns as a gift. The humble Bishop had taken the gift most graciously, assuming his secret messages to the Pope were in Nicóla's knowledge but also her safe-keeping. The hemlock mixed with the pepper was to be put on Fisher's food alone. But the cook, this Richard Roose, had put pepper in the meal for the entire household, not just a garnish on Fisher's meal. Now two people were dead, others ill. And an innocent man, a common man, would be boiled to death for his "crime", in full view of the public. And the King had said Crumwell must stand as a witness and report when it was done.

'Are you quite sure you wish to attend?' Crumwell said as he appeared in the front doorway, dressed as always in black, ready to attend the execution. Nicóla nodded and swallowed hard. Both Ralph and Richard stood behind Crumwell, neither eager to attend today.

Nicóla had barely seen Crumwell recently – he so often stayed at court now, so much to do. He had ordered this innocent cook to be interrogated. The poor man claimed the poisoning was an accident, then a jest, then he tried total ignorance. Crumwell had stood in the Tower, in this innocent man's cell, and hounded him until he accepted his fate. Nothing would work; the King needed Roose dead so people would stop saying that the Boleyn family tried to kill Fisher. No one knew it was Nicóla; not even Crumwell.

The pair mounted their horses and set off for Smithfield, only a mile or so from Austin Friars. As soon as they left the gates of the house, Nicóla guided her horse close to Crumwell's.

'What is it?' Crumwell's huge golden eyes searched for the problem in her expression, genuine worry, despite the fact she had not spoken a word.

'Are you certain this man must die, Tomassito?'

'The King commands it. Poisoning is now high treason, a law I wrote and passed in parliament.'

'And if this man is innocent?'

'He confessed to me, confessed that he was the only one who touched the broth. It is simple.'

'Did you torture him in the Tower?'

'Only a touch; no devices were used. I am not Sir Thomas More.'

'But what if this cook did not know the ingredients were poisoned?'

'It is possible, but Roose has no way of proving his innocence, and the King needs a criminal punished. Why? Are you...?'

Nicóla paused too; they needed to keep their voices low as they made their way through the crowds. 'Am I having the emotions of a woman overcome me?' she asked, her eyebrows raised in surprise. 'Tomassito, you know me better than this.'

'It will not be easy to see a man die in such a state. He will die without the final words of the Lord. This is going to be difficult. It is my duty to observe and report to Henry. It is not your burden.'

'If you must bear it, then I must bear it.'

'Perché, Nicó?' Crumwell changed to Italian for privacy, and Nicóla knew to do the same.

'Have you heard the expression that poison is the weapon of a woman?'

'I have heard poison is the weapon of Italians,' Crumwell replied, his complexion now a little pale.

'I bought a most expensive bag of black peppercorns some weeks ago.'

Crumwell drew is horse even closer to Nicóla and held her reins in his hand. 'You must tell me all, Nicó.'

Nicóla took a deep breath. 'My first letter from the Pope, the one I destroyed… I did destroy it, because of its tale. It said that Bishop Fisher secretly communicated with the Pope and the Emperor in Rome, on behalf of Queen Katherine. There was the talk of war over the annulment. I still had a bag of hemlock seeds, which I had in case I needed to silence Wolsey all that time ago, but never used.'

Crumwell still had no idea of the true ending of Wolsey's life, and she would never tell.

'You put hemlock in black pepper?' Crumwell whispered, still in Italian.

'I once saw Fisher put a great deal of pepper on meat when dining at court. I knew of his fondness. It is so expensive, black peppercorns from the far east. It is traded through Portugal to Antwerp and then London. I knew if I gave Fisher the gift of pepper, it would be he who ate it, not his household, due to the cost. If the Bishop died, then war could be averted, and your place in the King's favour would be safe.'

'You attempted to kill a bishop for me?' Crumwell asked. 'Nicó…'

'For you, and England. For if there is a war between the King of England and the Emperor of Rome, then there might be so much bloodshed, all because Giulio – Pope Clement – will not grant the dissolution of a marriage. Plus, being Italian in London, I would be first to have my head severed. That would leave me unable to protect Jane.'

'Nicó…' Crumwell uttered but said no more. He ran his hand through his hair and swallowed hard.

'And now this man shall be boiled in my place. Something was flawed in my plan. The cook must have shared the pepper among guests and servants alike. The pepper cost me more than a servant earns in a year. I thought only Fisher would die.'

'It is well indeed a great sin to take the life of a prince of the Church.'

'My soul was lost to hell the moment I lay with the Pope as a girl. Confession or repentance is useless to me.'

'It is so ruthless, Nicó.'

'Shall I return to the Apostolic Palace, as the Pope asks, to suffer my punishment from God?'

'My Lord, no.' Crumwell was forced to let go of her reins as the crowd thickened, people heading to Smithfield to see the boiling. Even while speaking in Italian, it was too hard to hear more of Nicóla's fateful words. Nicóla tried to not to cry, relieved Crumwell did not turn her away for her crime. She already had the lives of two innocents on her hands, and now the suffering of this poor servant. Bishop Fisher still had not risen from his bed.

'I came hither two years ago simply to observe Cardinal Campeggio, and look what I have become.'

'I am the man who personally wrote the paperwork for this boiling death to occur,' Crumwell replied. 'I stood there and watched the King sign the attainder and the execution warrant.'

The horses reached the clearing at Smithfield, to see Thomas Boleyn, Earl of Wiltshire dismounting his horse. Anne Boleyn's father was there to watch the boiling too. He was the subject of much suspicion since Fisher fell ill. Perchance he needed to see the boiling for himself. They stood on the top of a slight hill, able to see the crowd below, gathered around a wooden scaffold, an enormous pot being brought to the boil.

'Mr. Crumwell,' Boleyn said as he watched Crumwell and Nicóla dismount. Nicóla fell back a few steps from her master and the Earl, ever the servant.

'My Lord,' Crumwell nodded hello and looked out over the muddy space where the crowd gathered to watch the boiling. Far fewer than a hanging at Tyburn or beheading at the Tower. Even the solid stomachs of London appeared unsure over a boiling. Nicóla looked up over the brim of her wide hat, to see a fire burning, the cauldron atop the flames. The cauldron sat before the wooden scaffold, a pulley set up, presumably for the rope to dip the cook into the water. Hundreds stood nearby, some even seemed to be enjoying the warmth coming from the cauldron's fire.

'I understand you are hither as the King's overseer today,' Thomas Boleyn commented to Crumwell, which caught Nicóla's attention.

'Indeed, my Lord. And yourself?'

'I wanted to see a man deservedly die today. I wished to hear if he makes any kind of confession.'

'Roose made a confession to me, in the Tower. Your appearance may suggest you have guilt over the poison of the Bishop,' Crumwell replied.

'I have no guilt!' Boleyn replied in full force. He clenched his fingers, covered in leather gloves of deep red.

'I am awares, my Lord, your innocence I much believe. Shall you like to come with us? We are to attend the boiling from up close, at the King's command.'

A gesture from Boleyn and his four guards appeared to take the horses and accompany their master. Nicóla followed the Earl and Crumwell down the hill and through the crowd awaiting the execution. She kept her head down as two guards pushed people aside to allow their betters to get through. Nicóla could feel eyes upon her as she moved between people, the smell from the unwashed almost too much to bear. Several people commented on how vile the lords were to condemn a man to boil. They passed the large, dark grey cauldron and Nicóla felt the heat on her cheeks in the cool spring air.

They climbed the scaffold stairs and looked down at the pot of water, large bubbles already simmering along the dirty water's surface. At that moment, Nicóla pulled her rosary beads from her pocket. They were not permitted at Austin Friars; Crumwell thought them useless trinkets of Catholic lies. But Nicóla was raised in Italy, the home of the Holy See. It was not so easy to let go of her faith in place of the reformed ideas.

'Eternal Father,' Nicóla whispered as the crowd cheers rose; the prisoner was being led to the scaffold. 'I offer You the Body and Blood, Soul and Divinity of Your dearly beloved Son, Our Lord Jesus Christ, in atonement for our sins and those of the whole world. For the sake of His sorrowful passion, have mercy on us and on the whole world.'

Nicóla paused again as she saw the cook, Richard Roose at the bottom of the wooden stairs. He was a man of middling years, a plain man, dirty and bloodied from time in the Tower. Were his wounds those caused by Crumwell? 'For the sake of His sorrowful passion, have mercy on us and on the whole world. Holy God, Holy Mighty One, Holy Immortal One, have mercy on us and on the whole world,' she repeated in a whisper.

Crumwell stepped closer to Nicóla, so close their coats sat against one another. The back of his hand sat against the back of hers. That was as close as he could get for any type of comfort. Guards pulled the grey-dressed cook up the stairs, and the crowd cheered louder for the man who came to die. He was not able to say any words, nor repent any sins, nor have the word of God spoken. Nicóla heard the calls of blessings for the man's souls, while others cheered to get the boiling started.

Richard Roose, barefoot, his hands bound with dirty rope, shuffled forward and stopped right before Nicóla. He looked into her green eyes, and Nicóla swore she saw the soul of a man resigned to his fate. She had seen it before, in the eyes of her own father. 'Everlasting Father, for the sake of the love which Thou didst bear to St. Joseph, whom Thou didst chose above all to occupy Thy place on Earth, have mercy on us and on those who are dying. Amen,' Nicóla said, the words so swift Roose barely understood them.

'Thank you,' the man whispered, tears parting the dirt upon his cheeks. Nicóla forced her rosary beads into his grubby short fingers, hidden from view. As the guards shuffled him away, and he sobbed like a starving child, desperate to embrace safety.

Crumwell leaned to whisper in Nicóla's ear. 'You are well to remain silent; this man is not to receive the benefit of clergy. My own law states so.'

'Even I cannot remain silent for this,' Nicóla muttered in return and met his golden glare with her own.

The sound of the crowd melted away as Nicóla watched Roose bound in rope, and hooked to the pulley system. In only a minute he was ready to be lowered to the cauldron, just below the scaffold boards. The rosary beads appeared through his fingers. 'Most Sacred Heart of Jesus, I accept from Your hands whatever kind of death,' Roose uttered, his voice high-pitched and terrified as the weight on the pulley lifted him from his feet and moved to hang him over the steady water. 'It may please You to send me this day with all its pains, penalties and sorrows; in reparation for all of my sins, for the souls in purgatory, for all those who will die today and for Your greater glory. Amen.'

The man seemed to utter no more as the rope started to let him downwards to his death. He started to whimper, then cry, then yell as he got closer to the water, the crowd cheering beyond. Crumwell turned slightly away from Roose towards Nicóla, unable to watch. As they stood slightly overlapped, he grabbed Nicóla's hand inside her long overgown and held it tight. Nicóla could not dare to move away. Boleyn appeared troubled not by the scene, even pleased. Roose cried out as his feet touched the water, and he fought in his ropes. His legs started to dip in and his yell became an anguishing scream. Crumwell held Nicóla's hand even tighter, be damned who might see; no doubt all eyes lay on the fighting man. His screams became higher pitched as the water began to encroach on his body, his legs soaked. The water started to turn an odd colour and Nicóla saw it was skin peeling away from the body. Roose fought the ropes, an instinct to fight the water, and the whole pulley system lurched. It dunked him speedily, totally sinking him into the boiling water. People jumped in fear to avoid the splashing of the scalding liquid, and Nicóla noticed several women faint onto the grass in shock. Nicóla crossed herself and Crumwell did the same.

He let go of her hand, and with a quick confirmation that Roose was in the water, he quickly left the scaffold. Boleyn was fixed on the pot, filled with boiling water, blood and skin, strands of hair, several floating rosary beads and perchance an eye. People in the crowd either fainted or vomited, not just the sight, but the sizzling sound and fetid meat smell that came from the cauldron.

Nicóla ran to catch up with Crumwell as he stalked back to the horses, but he did check she was safe and close behind him, not forgetting her at Smithfield. The moment they mounted, Crumwell spurred the horses on towards the Thames to get the boat to Greenwich. Only once on the boat did Nicóla feel she could speak.

The bobbing over the Thames water did nothing to ease her lurching stomach. 'Machiavelli wrote that reforming a current order is one of the most dangerous and difficult things a prince can do.'

'I have told you before, Nicó, I am not "The Prince" of Machiavelli's writings. Machiavelli also wrote that by rising the easy way, it is not certain such a prince has the skill and strength to stand on his own feet.'

'What we just witnessed was not easy. Remember, Cesare Borgia is an exception. He rose through the blessing of a benefactor, like of you and King Henry, but then held his own power.'

'Then let Borgia be "The Prince." And remember what happened to Borgia. No one visits his grave.'

'We must regard this horrific act as a way of installing yourself in your own power base. The King wanted Roose dead, and you made it so.'

'Machiavelli wrote that a prince should carefully calculate all the wicked deeds he needs to do to make fast his power,' Crumwell replied.

'You have done naught wrong, Tomassito. You have executed the King's orders. I know it is not always simple. Do you think I wished to be there today? To see that?' Nicóla lowered her voice to a whisper. 'After knowing what I know? It ought to be me in that pot.'

'If the King knew what you did for England, Henry might give you a title, not an execution. You acted in the King's name.'

'You are not angry with me? Not after what we just witnessed?'

'No, I am not.' Crumwell glanced away for a moment, out over the dirty brown river, towards houses dotting along the water's edges, the faint sounds of voices in the distance as they headed east towards Greenwich Palace. 'But no matter what we do, I do not wish to witness such acts, even though I have seen men die. I have killed men in battle. To kill or betray gains a man no integrity. There is no virtue in living without mercy or faith or religion. There is no dignity in achieving greatness without these morals. However, it often seems that in order to achieve great power, one must choose these virtues or be cruel.'

'To be cruel like me, to know what I know, and say naught,' Nicóla admitted.

'We must separate our consciences from our actions as we follow orders of our King. We must remember that as we rise in favour.'

Nicóla nodded a touch and sighed. Still, a weight sat in her chest for the death of a man she never knew. 'I shall remember that when I serve my prince. When I serve "The Prince".'

Crumwell threw Nicóla one of his charming half-smiles. 'Machiavelli never wrote of me, Nicó.'

'Oh he did, my prince. You are no ordinary man.'

~~~

Nicóla stood in the antechamber and watched as Crumwell strode into the King's public presence chamber without any announcement. 'Ah, Mr. Crumwell,' the King said when he looked up from a paper in his hand. He tossed it to a gentleman-usher and stepped down from this throne. 'Is it done?'

'Yes, Your Majesty.'

'Did the cook utter any confession, name any conspirator?'

'No, Your Majesty. Uttered naught but words in the wish for God's mercy. Thomas Boleyn also witnessed the boiling. I am afraid we shall never know the full story of what happened at Lambeth Marsh.'

'I am glad it is done. I wish to hear no more words about how Lady Anne tried to kill Bishop Fisher. She has a stable conscience, my Anne. She would never commit a sin against a man of the cloth.'

'I am sure, Your Majesty. There are rumours, from my creatures, that Bishop Fisher writes to the Emperor in Rome, and the Pope.'

'Do you think it is Fisher who wants to see Lady Anne killed? Not just Sir Thomas More?'

'I am unawares, Your Majesty. I fear Fisher prefers war over peace in England.'

The King slapped Crumwell on the shoulder and smiled. 'You did respectable work today, Thomas. Long may you reign.'

Chapter 29 - June 1531
Windsor Palace, Berkshire

Most wondrous pleasure can cometh from having a seecryt

Riding in the country gave Crumwell so much clarity. Moving the royal court thirty miles to Windsor from London was such busy affair; hundreds of people and carts of clothing, jewels, books, and papers had already left by the time the official train with Henry and Anne set off. Even Queen Katherine was sent on early so Katherine and Anne did not travel too closely together. With summer at its height, Crumwell had the rare chance to be away from his offices, away from drafting legislation, from settling accounts, from writing fake letters to the Pope on Nicóla's behalf, claiming she was now an Anne Boleyn assassin-in-waiting. Nicóla was strong these past weeks, proving she was not Crumwell's mistress in need of saving. She was happy to deceive the Pope, pretending to be lying in wait to murder the Lady Anne. It kept Rome at bay for now.

'Master,' Nicóla called to him from her horse next to his, as they rode in the royal procession, 'what makes you dream on this lovely summer's day?'

'I thought how fine it is to not worry for a day.'

'It is a shame that this Windsor Castle is only day's ride from the city. It is also a shame that Ralph has stayed behind at Austin Friars, for I now have no one to race with while we ride.'

'You consider me too old? I was a soldier once.'

'Once,' she chided.

'I suspect Ralph is happy to remain at Austin Friars if only to continue sneaking romantic moments in the laundry room,' Crumwell laughed. He wanted a good marriage for Ralph; the boy deserved to be well-married. But Ralph was young and happy, so Crumwell worried not for his dalliance with Ellen, a young widow Crumwell took in from the streets, two young children attached.

Nicóla sat so comfortably on horseback out in the country. She had cut her hair short once more, and Crumwell could only assume she felt awkward about her identity again. The short style made her look even younger than usual, and dressed in the lighter fabrics of summer, she looked thinner than ever. More feminine than ever. Nicóla looked radiant in the sunshine, even when she laughed and joked about Crumwell's age. This woman put herself into the centre of a fight between the Pope and the ordained King just so she could stay by Crumwell's side. Nicóletta Frescobaldi, whose crown of the Duchy of Florence waited for her back home, instead rode the roads to Windsor because Crumwell needed her. Wanted her.

'My God, Thomas, I swear I have never seen you smile so,' said the voice of King Henry, and Crumwell turned in his saddle to see Henry ride up beside him. 'I never pictured you as much of a rider.'

'You disparage your advisor, Your Majesty,' Nicóla spoke up, quite out of turn. 'Master Crumwella much enjoys riding, and hawking, hunting, falconry, and is quite the shot with a long bow.'

'We shall see at Windsor then,' Henry answered in one of his calm moods.

'I was just saying that I have no one to race my horse with, as Master Crumwella is far too advanced in age,' Nicóla added.

'I think you need your servant whipped, Thomas. Mr. Frescobaldi, if you wish to race…' The King pointed off the path into the distance, across a wide field, a perfect line of trees in the distance at the base of a hill.

'Should I give you both a head start?' Nicóla asked.

With an angry cry, Henry turned his horse and charged off, and Crumwell dared to take on the challenge. But so did Nicóla, much lighter on her horse, a beautiful black animal Crumwell bought for her just a week prior to the progress to Windsor. The three all laughed at the absurdity of racing like children across a dry field somewhere far west of London. By the time they got to the end of the clearing, it was tiny Nicóla who got clear ahead of her betters.

'I do so thank you for the opportunity to ride with you, sirs,'

Nicóla laughed in her victory. 'I am indeed humbled.'

'I only let you win because you are a lady,' Henry replied, panting from the challenge.

'I have no doubt, Your Majesty,' Nicóla said and turned to Crumwell. 'What is your excuse?'

King Henry roared with laughter. 'Thomas, this one has such spirit! A pity you cannot marry her!'

Crumwell cleared his throat, unable to think of anything to say to that.

'Worry not, Mr. Frescobaldi,' Henry added, 'I shall not divulge your secrets to anyone.'

'I trust you completely, Your Majesty,' Nicóla said as the threesome turned to walk their horses back to the train.

King Henry waved out, and Lady Anne waved back across the distance. The King could be hard to understand, so Crumwell never knew when the time to be relaxed might come, but Nicóla seemed adept at being able to laugh and jest with Henry with total ease.

'You ought to come to a party at Austin Friars, Your Majesty.' Nicóla said as they trotted along the field. 'Master Crumwella does throw the most delightful celebrations. Always wonderful entertainment, lively guests, food and wine with no expense spared. Master Crumwella almost has his own court set up when it is time for an evening of diversion. And the animals he keeps in the gardens! Things I have never seen! Have you heard of a beaver, Your Majesty?'

'Indeed, I have not seen one. I shall be delighted to dine at Austin Friars,' Henry said and threw a smile at Crumwell. 'I feel as though perchance I am missing much revelry!'

'We had a dinner party just this week past, for the household. It was the first birthday of the baby Jane, who lives in the manor. Of course, it was the adults who drank to her health.'

'Ah, this is the bastard Frescobaldi child you took in, Crumwell,' Henry replied as they came back to the other riders heading to Windsor. 'Mr. Frescobaldi, I have a task for you.'

'Of course, Your Majesty, I do desire a rematch.'

The King roared with laughter again. 'We will only be at Windsor for a short time before Lady Anne and I go riding together to do some hunting, a small party only. I shall leave Queen Katherine behind at Windsor. Mr. Frescobaldi, speak with Her Majesty before I depart. I would so like to hear what she would say to the relative of the Pope.'

'Certainly, I shall make myself available to Her Majesty as soon as we arrive.' Henry gave Nicóla a nod of thanks and headed further up the train to Lady Anne and the rest of the Boleyns.

'The King certainly likes you,' Crumwell muttered to Nicóla.

'Is that not a good thing? I am here solely to promote you.'

'Sometimes I cannot even think why.'

'God has put us hither, Master Crumwella, for a reason. This is the only place to achieve great power. It is a lie to say we want anything but power.'

~~~

Crumwell stood at the window of his sumptuous room at Windsor Castle. He almost wondered if there was a problem, for him to be provided with such lavish accommodation. The room was enormous, the bed draped in purple and green velvet curtains, the entire room lined with gold among the carved wooden walls. Tapestries of the Apostles hung on the walls, probably from Brussels, given their quality and thread weight, Crumwell's merchant eye questioning them all. The window looked out over the front garden of the castle, a perfect sculpted abundance of greenery. Behind him, Nicóla carried his luggage, one of the strange things about their relationship. As a servant, Crumwell had to let Nicóla do all his arbitrary tasks, to help keep her gender a private matter.

He heard the door close across the bedroom and he said, 'we need to make sure we are doing enough to ensure all the men in parliament are continuing to feel anger towards the clergy. We must press forward with…'

Nicóla's small hands appeared around his waist, and she held on tight as he looked out the window. 'Tomassito, I must ask you to say no more of your work today,' she whispered in his ear, amusing him.

Crumwell turned in Nicóla's arms and embraced her, a strong kiss upon her lips. 'What be my orders, my love?'

'Come.' Nicóla took him by the hands and led him through a smaller side door, which led to a space filled with an enormous bathtub, made of metal, rather than traditional wood. Steam poured off the circle of clean water. 'I want you in there,' she said.

Crumwell could not get his dirty clothes from his body fast enough. He watched Nicóla get into the bath, the tub more than considerable enough for two people. He stepped in after her and she welcomed him into the warmth of the water. He dipped his head under and felt pure relief from the day's riding aches simply melt from his bones. Crumwell sat up again and leaned back against the heat of the metal tub and Nicóla came to sit beside him, to begin a moment of pure love.

~~~

Crumwell awoke the following morning, lying flat on his back, his head propped up on the thick pillows of the bed. The curtains sat already open and he turned to see Nicóla standing close to the window, still naked from the night past. 'Come back to bed,' he muttered.

Nicóla turned with a smile and wandered over to him. She sat on the side of the bed, and Crumwell pulled her into his arms, his hands already drifting to her body. As they kissed he pulled her back under the covers, back underneath the warmth of his body. Windsor felt like a place apart from the world, a scene stolen from another world.

'Why do you seek to leave my bed, Mistress Frescobaldi?'

'I was thinking I must see the Queen today. The King is to set off with Lady Anne on a hunting trip and their date of return is unknown. In case this is the moment that Henry leaves Katherine forever, I must speak with her. She is a good woman, something of another time, the last in a long line of courageous and honourable queens.'

'I thought your mission was to make me the Queenmaker.'

'Indeed, but that does not mean Queen Katherine deserves no respect.'

'Do you wish me to come along to see the Queen?'

'Katherine knows you are Henry's man, my darling. Katherine might not listen to my words if you are present.'

'Let me help you,' he muttered as he brought his lips to her. Either of them could agree to anything inside that room in Windsor Castle.

Up and dressed, Crumwell stalked the wide open galleries of Windsor Castle towards the apartments made ready for the Queen. Nicóla walked one step behind him, as was custom for a servant.

Crumwell wanted to reach out and take her hand, but could not, and she would refuse if he did; Nicóla's disguise was so well practiced that she never slipped from the character.

Directed by one the Yeoman of the Guard, Crumwell found the rooms of the Queen and walked into a huge white and gold decorated room where Katherine's thirty ladies-in-waiting chatted while a lute played across by the window. There sat the dignified Queen Katherine herself, adorned in an elaborate dark blue gown, a book open as she sat in the sun.

'Mr. Crumwell,' Katherine spoke, her robust Spanish accent such a contrast to Nicóla's light flowing Italian. 'This is much of a surprise.'

'Your Majesty,' he replied with a deep bow, as she deserved, and Nicóla copied. 'I bring you Nicóla Frescobaldi. Mr. Frescobaldi…'

'I remember well enough,' Katherine said as she stood, and all her ladies followed. The sun caught the red of her hair, the silvers shining in the sun. Katherine crossed the room and presented her hand to Nicóla, who kissed it, as though she were a man. Queen Katherine knew the truth but played along.

'You travelled with Cardinal Campeggio,' Katherine said and took Nicóla from Crumwell. He was left to stand in the doorway, not far from the ladies-in-waiting as Katherine spirited Nicóla away to the window seat. The conversation appeared hushed, and in Spanish, a language Crumwell had never picked up. He watched the women pray together and felt an immense tinge of sadness; Queen Katherine was to be left at Windsor Castle, just her, her thirty ladies, and only 170 staff. The King was due to ride away with Anne Boleyn and never return to his wife. After two and twenty years of marriage, this is what the Spanish royal received, all because she had aged too much to have a son. Katherine held something magical in her presence; the daughter of two anointed sovereigns, born to be a queen, perfect in every sense. Even with Katherine's stubbornness, her pride getting in the way of an annulment, and even with her fervent Catholic faith, Crumwell had nothing but affection for the Queen.

Watching Nicóla on her knees before the Queen as they prayed together, Crumwell remembered how much Nicóla gave up in becoming a reformer like himself; for Nicóla's Catholic faith, at this moment, seemed as strong as Queen Katherine's.

'Master Crumwell, always a pleasure.'

Without moving a muscle, Crumwell's golden eyes glanced beside him to the distraction, a blonde woman, one of the ladies-in-waiting. Only aged about twenty, dressed in a white gown, like all of Katherine's companions. With his hands clasped before him, Crumwell's eyes stayed on the girl, who insisted on talking more.

'I hear you are much elevated at court, Master Crumwell,' she said.

As she spoke, she moved her shoulders, which made her dress move around her.

Why did she care for his presence? 'And you are?' he muttered, his voice sounding especially deep, as irritation tended to create.

'Lady Anne Stanhope, lady-in-waiting.'

'Lady Stanhope?' he repeated, his thick eyebrows raised now. 'I have heard of you.'

'And what have you heard?' she asked, her fingers toying with the edge of his black velvet sleeve.

'A merchant friend dealt with your father.'

'And?'

'And it was said that you, young Lady Stanhope, are more presumptuous than Lucifer. That stands to reason you are not yet well-married.'

'I shall be,' she replied, her smile still flirting with the thought of entertaining Crumwell. He pulled his sleeve from her fingers. 'One could suggest you are presumptuous, Master Crumwell, a commoner before the Queen of England. Through my mother, I am a descendant of King Edward the Third.'

'Then you shall have no time for the likes of me,' Crumwell said, not even looking at the girl. Nicóla was coming in his direction. The pair made a hasty retreat from the Queen's rooms. With exception to the snobbish Lady Stanhope wrestling for affection, Crumwell knew where he was not welcome.

'So, what did she say?' Crumwell could not help but ask the moment they entered the red and gold gallery which shouldered the beautiful garden outside.

'Do you know that the Queen still makes Henry's shirts? And he happily takes them, even after all that has passed between them?'

'Yes, I do know such. But what of news?'

'Queen Katherine was most entertained to hear I was the wife of Pope Clement's son. Katherine did not believe the rumours that the Pope had a child. I told Katherine I married the Medici boy, and that the Pope was my father-in-law. I told Katherine that the Pope will never give up his fight to save her marriage and the Emperor was her undying support. Katherine will never feel the sting of annulment from the Catholic Church. It seemed to give her much comfort.'

'You cannot say any of this to the King.'

'I will tell the King that Queen Katherine broke with me on the subject of simple conversation. I will say that Katherine knows of my relationship with the Pope, but appears to not be planning anything behind Henry's back. It is true; all Katherine does is wait and pray that one day, Henry will steer himself back onto the path of righteousness.'

'All words Henry has heard before,' Crumwell cautioned.

'I am certain, Tomassito. But Henry needs to hear the same words because Katherine is not speaking with the Pope at the moment, only her nephew the Emperor. Katherine does not want war; Charles' soldiers will never land on English shores.'

'Tell Henry that, make the start of his new life filled with peace.'

'I will tell the King anything that reflects well on you, Tomassito. We are witnessing history; no king has done such a thing to his wife. Mistresses, certainly, but this? Annulment, destroying the Church? I feel closer to God by Katherine's side than I do beside the Pope, and I told her so.'

'We are reforming the Church. I am reforming England and Henry is the tool in which I need to do this.'

'I knew I had picked the real leader of the country,' Nicóla said and looked up to him with a wink.

With Nicóla's by his side, Crumwell felt ready to change the entire world.

Chapter 30 - November 1531
Whitehall Palace, London

Gents shalt consume pain, make seecryts, and argye to God

Crumwell sat at his desk, unable to hear much more than the rain hitting the window behind him. His chambers at Whitehall were far more than he expected; the rooms were spacious enough, his private office big enough for three large desks and many shelves of books. There was a desk against one wall, where he put Nicóla to work on his behalf, and another by the double doorway for Ralph when he visited, where he could keep an eye on the other clerks in other rooms. The main office had an entrance chamber where Crumwell installed two gentleman-ushers to receive guests. A locked private hallway also led off the entranceway, where it went to three separate bedrooms for himself and anyone he wished to house at court. The hallways could also carry on towards the private rooms of the King, making it easier for Crumwell to move around the court without the endless requests from courtiers and the idle talk which flowed its way between the thousands of people housed in the lavish newly-named Whitehall Palace.

Crumwell simply did his best never to think of the palace as York Place when he was with Cardinal Wolsey. The interior was changed anew, rooms even more lavish than before, with Turkish carpets, tapestries from all over Europe, gold and silver plate everywhere, portraits and jewels abound. Lady Anne housed in Wolsey's private rooms, where Crumwell himself seldom visited any longer.

The big news was that the King's progress was over for the

summer and everyone was back in London, but the Queen was not there. Katherine still resided at Windsor, left behind by Henry. The King resolved to never see his wife again. Anne Boleyn was the only woman at Henry's side now, while Queen Katherine stayed at Windsor, visited by her daughter, the Princess Mary. Mary resided at Ludlow Castle, 140 miles northwest in Wales. Mary was now sixteen and had been plagued with illness for some time. Terrible headaches, woman's troubles no one could understand. The stress of her parents' annulment no doubt made things worse. Princess Mary needed her mother, and Henry now saw his own daughter as much of a threat as he did his wife.

Crumwell looked not around his wide desk, piled high with work; he leaned back in his soft high-backed chair and read the book in his hands. He looked for the right wording for the supplication he wrote for the King and parliament. To his left sat Nicóla with her back to him, silent as she calculated payments to dispatch to spies, the creatures needing bribes to keep their alliances and the information coming from various places. Crumwell had recently placed a spy in the friary where Thomas Abel, a chaplain close to Queen Katherine, lived and worked. That way, all correspondence the Queen sent to Charles the Emperor through Abel could be read and reported back to Crumwell directly. It sometimes worried Crumwell how well Nicóla judged what spies deserved in payment, but then Florence was founded upon such a suspicious system.

Crumwell glanced over at Ralph, also hard at work, his fine writing going down upon accounts which needed to be settled for the King. Ralph's blonde hair fell over his expression, his quill twitching while he wrote. The three of them could go for hours without a word, sometimes they talked and laughed and got slight achieved. Tonight, the fire burned steadily in the wide square-shaped room, warming the place, its stone walls all already covered by books or tapestries. The floor was covered in a magnificent rug which Nicóla had gained from a trader she knew in Venice, who had bought it from the Turks, lavish in purple and gold. In the warmth and silence of the office, Crumwell almost confessed to feeling his age, the peace almost putting him to sleep at an early hour, dinner not long dispensed.

'Discord and division have arisen between the clergy and the laity in England, in part because of heretical books, but also upon the merciless behaviour of ordinaries,' Crumwell said out loud.

Both of Crumwell's companions listened to his words; Ralph looked up for a moment and then went back to his writing. Nicóla did not turn in her seat but replied. 'Not merciless, it sounds overly harsh.'

'I am writing a preamble which will state abuses of the Church against the King. When the time comes, Henry shall seek to move upon them and bring reformation in England.'

'You say that as if you know it will soon be upon us, Master,' Ralph said without looking up from his work.

'A good servant has the paperwork ready before his master asks for the task to be performed,' Crumwell replied.

'How are we mere mortals expected to keep ahead of your brilliant mind, Master Crumwella?' Nicóla replied and turned a fraction in her chair, and winked at him.

'I second that,' Ralph said with a gentle laugh, still writing.

'Uncharitable,' Nicóla added. 'Discord and division have arisen between the clergy and the laity in England, in part because of heretical books, but also upon the uncharitable behaviour of ordinaries.'

'Could you write the preamble?' Crumwell offered.

'I was just making a suggestion,' Nicóla replied. 'Do I wish to write up papers which shall strip the clergy of their power in this country? No, that is most certainly not my place, that is yours, Master Crumwella.'

'It is the Statute of Restraint of Appeals, preventing anyone from appealing to Rome on ecclesiastical matters, which will strip the clergies' power,' Crumwell sighed and closed his law book. 'The day we present that to parliament, the King shall become more powerful.'

Behind Ralph in the entrance room, an usher clad in black velvet and satin appeared before the main doorway. 'Master Crumwell,' he panted, 'a message for you from the King.'

Crumwell clicked his fingers twice for the boy to continue. 'The King requests you join him in the public presence room immediately to attend a meeting with Archdeacon Stephen Gardiner.'

Crumwell dismissed the boy with a wave of his hand, and the boy bowed and left. 'Both of you, come with me now,' he ordered, and Nicóla and Ralph dropped everything at his instruction.

Rather than taking the private hallway to the King's privy chamber, the three trailed between chatting courtiers in the vast warren of hallways. Judging by the number of people close to the King's chambers, Lady Anne must have been in attendance. A number of her ladies were present outside, chatting among themselves as a great number of men looked on.

'Perchance you could find yourself a wife,' Nicóla mused to Ralph.

'Do not let Ralph be further distracted by women,' Crumwell replied over his shoulder to his attendants. 'Ralph is but four and twenty years of age.'

'What were you both doing at four and twenty?' Ralph asked they kept their brisk pace.

'I was embraced in the safety of my father's household in Florence, in the arms of chastity,' Nicóla replied.

'I too was living in Florence when I was that young,' Crumwell smiled. 'There was never a shortage of pretty girls.'

'Do tell us more,' Ralph said with a smirk. 'Do you remember him then, Nicóla?'

'No, I was born in the years when my father took in the young English beggar from the streets,' Nicóla replied. 'I was in the nursery still when he chased the skirts of Florence!'

'I need not be reminded of my age!' Crumwell laughed, but the conversation died as they were shown into the King's rooms. In the antechamber stood shaky-hands Stephen Gardiner, his round face flushed pink with excitement.

'Stephen, you have pulled yourself away from your work in France, I see.'

'Some of us need to keep our King's alliances firm,' Gardiner replied and smoothed one hand over his crisp white robes.

'Some of us are too prized to be sent abroad,' Crumwell hit back, and Nicóla and Ralph both tried not to laugh.

'What are you here for, Thomas?' Gardiner asked, ignoring the smirks on the faces of the King's legal advisor and his servants. '

The King asked for me directly. Curious how the King's master secretary does not know that. Oh, that is right, Henry sent you away and deals most well without your guidance.'

Sir Henry Norris called for both Crumwell and Gardiner together. With a double click of his fingers, Nicóla and Ralph knew to follow their master into the public presence room of the King. Henry was not on his throne, though Lady Anne sat in the seat beside the King's, presupposed to be the Queen's. Anne did not give the slightest expression as they filled the small space where Henry regularly met people for an informal audience. Henry stood there, his hands outstretched to greet his secretary.

Gardiner bowed before the King, and Crumwell followed suit. Nicóla and Ralph quickly ushered themselves to one side with Norris, and noticed Anne's longtime friends, Thomas Wyatt and Mark Smeaton both there, presumably to entertain Lady Anne. Also present stood the King's ever-present fool, Will Sommers. Wyatt and Smeaton gave excited waves to see Nicóla back at court but were not allowed to speak.

'Stephen,' Henry said and wrapped his thick arms around his secretary for a moment. 'You have come from Cambridge?'

'Yes, Your Majesty, and I have all you need.'

Crumwell eyed the black satchel in Gardiner's hands.

'Thomas,' the King said and diverted Crumwell's golden gaze. 'I need you hither to witness what Gardiner has brought me. I need your keen eye.'

'Certainly, Your Majesty.'

'I have here,' Gardiner said, his chest almost swelling with pride under his pious white robes, 'the precedent from Cambridge University, their written opinion on the ability of a king to procure the decision on the unlawfulness of marriage with a deceased brother's wife. We unanimously decided in your favour, Your Majesty. Cambridge has concluded that it is unlawful for any man to take the wife of his brother, living or dead.'

The King clapped his hands together with pure unfettered joy, and turned to Lady Anne in her seat, raised higher than the men before her. 'Hear this, my love, another step forward in the progress to make you a queen.'

There it was. Crumwell's eyes met Anne's for a moment. The same look they shared that lonely night in the Grafton House chapel, all that time ago. Anne admitted she was trapped by Henry's faith of love. Anne could not escape. But she could not let her exterior show this. It was so quick, so subtle, Crumwell only noticed because he had seen that look that lonely night in the light of the candles of the altar.

'I thank you wholeheartedly, Archdeacon Gardiner,' Anne said, her voice sweet and silky. Everything about Anne seemed perfect in Crumwell's eyes. For all the world, she was hated as the woman who stole a king. But Anne was a calm and gentle woman, intelligent, witty and charming. The King chased her; as had Henry Percy and Thomas Wyatt before His Majesty. Anne was trained in France and had charm most women in England lacked. Anne was a wonderful ally, but as Nicóla kept reminding him; the moderate man will inherit the kingdom, so Crumwell never openly supported Anne or Katherine.

'Lord Chancellor Sir Thomas More must know of this at once,' Crumwell said, drawing the King back to the conversation. 'More shall need to read this information.'

'It is another step in making certain that the royal marriage is unlawful. The scholars of Cambridge are on my side. Half of Europe's scholars have reported back, claiming support. We must move forward,' the King mused to all.

'We need to undermine the Church,' Crumwell cried out, thinking to the supplication he slowly wrote over months. Not minutes ago had he discussed it in his office, and now the opportunity presented itself.

'Thomas!' Gardiner threw back. 'You forget I am here as a man of the cloth, a scholar, an expert in canon and civil law.'

'And I am here as a lawyer, an expert in civil law only,' Crumwell replied. 'I am not clouded by my religious views, I seek only to be of service to the King. Your Majesty, you asked me to study abuses of the Church many months ago; we could put a supplication to parliament in mere months. The Church ought to clean up its own abuses before it swears it is better to make decisions on marriage ahead of you.'

'You two men are the best I could possibly have before me,' the King said and looked to Anne for approval. She smiled sweetly and said nothing.

'I find I cannot agree with anything Mr. Crumwell says, Your Majesty,' Gardiner said, instantly offended by Crumwell's notion.

'I am glad you argue, Stephen,' Henry replied. 'It shows you are honourable, not simply following my words. Which is why I am making you Bishop of Winchester.'

'Your Majesty?' Gardiner coughed with surprise. His hands began to shake more than usual.

'You are to be Bishop, Stephen. The post is vacant, ever since the death of Cardinal… Wolsey.' The King paused and looked to Crumwell. They shared a single second together at the mention of the name. Crumwell, for that vanishing moment, felt relief Henry still thought of the old Cardinal, as Crumwell often did himself. 'I do not love you less for arguing against me, and this honour should prove this, Stephen,' the King continued.

Gardiner bowed low, down on one knee to the King. 'I thank you, Your Majesty, for an honour I never expected.'

Henry gently pulled Gardiner back to his feet and took the satchel from his hands. 'You have done me proud, Stephen, and I have never felt more confident of the truth of my marriage than I am at this moment. You may go, and spread the word you shall receive your purple bishop's hat immediately.'

'Your Majesty.' Gardiner bowed once again and withdrew formally with a smug grin.

The King handed Crumwell the satchel. 'Go through these papers; make sure everything we need is in here. The precedent set by Cambridge is soothing, but we need laws changed in order to bring down Rome's power over my annulment. Only you can do this, Thomas.'

'Of course, Your Majesty. We will set to work immediately.'

The King looked from Crumwell over to Nicóla and Ralph against the wall. 'Mr. Frescobaldi,' the King said, 'come let me look at you.'

Nicóla stepped forward and bowed low. Her hair, now almost to her shoulders again, brushed her rosy cheeks, and Crumwell had the urge to reach out and touch Nicóla but had learned long ago to suppress his urges. 'Have you settled into life at court yet? I am sure you will be friends with Lady Anne, as you can see both Mr. Smeaton and Mr. Wyatt are.'

'Yes, Your Majesty,' Nicóla replied and glanced to the musician and poet across the room. 'I shall be honoured to make an acquaintance with the Lady Anne.'

'And I shall be flattered by your company,' Anne said as she stepped down from her seat and came to Nicóla. 'We share a great deal. Henry has told me all about you and Master Cremwell in great detail.'

Crumwell tried to keep a straight face. He had a bastard daughter by his "male" servant. Anne knew all. The Boleyn family probably did also, and they were all powerful and well-connected.

'I trust you are a man who can keep a secret, Master Cremwell,' Anne said with a smile.

'Well indeed, my Lady,' he answered the jest as calmly as possible while Anne teased his relationship with Nicóla.

'You have eyes everywhere, I hear, Mr. Cremwell. In my apartments today, I found a drawing left among my things. It was a drawing of the King, the Queen, and myself. Only I lacked my head. Someone came into my room and left it. How do I find out who did such a thing?'

'Your ladies may know,' Crumwell answered.

'Lady Anne Gainsford was in my rooms all day and saw nothing. Do you know Lady Gainsford?'

'No, Your Majesty.'

'Anne is a lady of already two and twenty years and has the most beautiful blonde hair, not rose-gold like your Waif, much brighter. Lady Gainsford is in need of a husband, and has spoken of you many times.'

Crumwell was not sure how to answer. Lady Anne knew of his relationship with Nicóla and yet said such a thing to him. How cruel; how petty. 'I am sure Lady Gainsford wants a man more suited to her in age.'

'Nonsense,' Anne rebutted. 'Age is of no importance. Though, you would need an official post at court. Legal advisor is too… informal. Perchance we could find another role, something more lucrative?' Anne posed to the King.

'Thomas here shall be well rewarded for all his work in good time,' the King replied with a smirk at Anne's teasing.

'I feel the gift of Lady Gainsford is rather too much for me,' Crumwell jested, in an effort to ease the tone. The King and Lady Anne laughed, as did Nicóla. Behind him, Crumwell heard the laughter of Ralph, and Wyatt and Smeaton both.

'I have another lady recently into my household, Lady Margery Horsman. She is of a dark complexion and has also spoken of your place as a husband,' Lady Anne confirmed. 'I am much pleased, Mr. Cremwell, that Queen Katherine is gone from court now. Several of her ladies had an eye upon you, including young Lady Anne Stanhope. She is too much trouble to bear. I should rather give you to Lady Jane Seymour, or her young sister, Elizabeth.'

'I am an old man,' Crumwell said and took a deep breath. He glanced at Nicóla's smile; set, fake before the King and his love.

'Worry not, Thomas,' Henry said and slapped Crumwell's shoulder, so hard Crumwell almost lost his footing against the tall

King. 'There are spoils for everyone at my court; it is a new age.'

'I shall get to work on studying the new Bishop Gardiner's papers,' Crumwell said.

'You shall celebrate Christmas and the giving of gifts at New Year with us, will you not, Thomas?' Henry asked. 'Your whole household will be at court.'

'I am honoured, Your Majesty.'

'Let us leave Mr. Cremwell to his work,' Lady Anne said and placed a gentle hand on Henry's arm.

'As you wish, my love,' Henry replied.

Crumwell bowed along with Nicóla, and as they withdrew, Crumwell noticed Mark Smeaton take occasion to blow Nicóla a kiss and she returned such.

'That was amusing,' Ralph sounded as the group trailed back towards Crumwell's private chambers. 'It is not I who may find a wife at court, it is you, Master Crumwell! Lady Anne has women in her household ready to marry you!'

'Nonsense, Ralph,' Crumwell said over his shoulder. 'It was jest only.'

'These halls hear curious conversations indeed,' Nicóla said with a smile to Ralph, thinking Crumwell did not see.

'Ralph, I need you to go to Gardiner's chambers and ask if he has any other papers pertaining to this precedent. I need to know this immediately,' Crumwell snapped and clicked his fingers twice.

'Yes, Master Crumwell,' Ralph replied and turned on his heel. In a moment he was lost in the warren of alleys in Whitehall.

'Tomassito?' Nicóla asked Crumwell but he did not respond.

Only once they were closed in his chambers again he did turn to Nicóla, who stood before him as he placed Gardiner's satchel on his desk. 'I found that rather less amusing than everyone else,' Crumwell sighed. 'Does everyone forget that I was married once? I had a wife, and two daughters, all taken from me at once. I did not marry only for the position; I greatly respected Elizabeth!'

'I am sorry,' Nicóla muttered, and her gaze fell to the purple carpets beneath their feet. 'Your wife was a fine woman, and gave you a good son.'

'And Elizabeth's mother, Mercy, is now the nurse to your own daughter, Jane!' Crumwell continued and then paused. Why be angry at Nicóla? She had done nothing. Nicóla had to protect her identity, least lose her place at court, lose her place in England, close to him. 'I am sorry. The King and the Lady Anne know of your truth. I told the King more than once how much I loved you.'

'You did?'

'Despair got the best of me on several occasions when you were away from me, Nicó.'

'I accept that you will remarry, Tomassito. I am married, and you shall be also.'

'I will never marry, I swear upon it, before God, that I shall never marry another. Never again.'

Nicóla locked her green eyes on his gaze and he could not dare to understand what she thought. 'I am not yours,' she spoke gently. 'I am not what a man wants in a mistress. No man wishes to undress another man at night when he seeks a woman. He does not seek to work alongside the woman he cares for. He does not seek to discuss business or finance with a woman. It was one reason why I agreed to the marriage with Alessandro. He wanted only my money, my name, for his family. Alessandro does not want me. I am to be for no man, for I love the freedom of being a man. When it comes to love or marriage, women get no choices.'

'No,' Crumwell implored and felt cutting pain in his chest. 'Nicó, no, that is not what I mean. Yes, there are times when I look at other men with their wives or mistresses, dancing after dinner. I see them give and receive favours with the ladies. But as I said, I was married. That is not part of my life any longer. I shall take the company of you, the love of you, over any other.'

But to Crumwell's dismay, none of his words seemed to have the desired effect. Nicóla's face spoke of a broken lover, worse, a forgotten lover. Her eyes moved away from him, no words in response.

There came a loud pounding on the door, and before the gentleman-usher could announce anything, in came Sir Thomas More, his thick black fur coat catching the breeze, such was his speed. 'Is it true?' More commanded and stopped so abruptly before Crumwell and Nicóla that his golden chains of office shook over his shoulders, his usually beady eyes wide in panic.

'Good morrow, Lord Chancellor,' Crumwell said, his mind clouded and prepared not for More. 'Wine?'

'Is it true that Cambridge has set a precedent stating a man cannot marry his brother's wife?'

'It is true. I have not finished with the papers yet, but you may have them when I am done.'

'Damn it, Crumwell, I know you are a Lutheran. You want reform. I am here to save the Catholic Church from heresy, from men such as you.'

'You are here to advise the King,' Crumwell scoffed, 'and on state matters, as Lord Chancellor does. Not cloud His Majesty's opinions on anything else. Do you not think perchance one day that state and religion should be separate?' Crumwell ran his finger on the gold band of the turquoise ring Wolsey had left him, thinking of his words in the letter left behind. Tell the King what he should do, not what he could do. But Crumwell could hear Nicóla's advice also. The moderate man shall inherit the kingdom. There was no point in discussing any more. More said nothing, and Crumwell sighed. 'I am simply reading the papers set out by Gardiner to make sure that legally, they are precise. Whether they are spiritually sound, that shall be at your discretion, Sir Thomas.'

More seemed to relax a little. 'Good. This kingdom is overrun with heresy. It is my job, along with Bishop Fisher and Archbishop Warham, to stamp it out.'

'And now Bishop Gardiner, did you hear? Bishop of Winchester in place of Wolsey.'

More nodded just a touch. 'Gardiner is a sound man, with sound faith. Did you hear the King has permanently banished Queen Katherine from the court? Her Majesty must leave Windsor for The More, one of Wolsey's old country homes.'

'It is a fine manor, I oversaw the renovations and extensions myself,' Crumwell replied. 'It can easy hold a court of well over 200 people, perchance more.'

'The Queen ought to be at the King's side!'

'I only make legal decisions, Sir Thomas.'

'Legal minds can make decisions, dangerous ones. Richard Bayfield did just so.'

'Richard Bayfield was a Benedictine monk and Chamberlain of the Abbey of Bury St. Edmunds, as well as an educated man,' Crumwell countered.

'And a reformer and heretic. Well, Bayfield is back in England, with copies of the New Testament on him, in English! Also works by

Luther, by Zwingli and Melancthon. Bayfield shall be burned at Smithfield in one week, for heresy. It took us ten years to wait for him to return to England after he escaped his fate years ago.'

'In Wolsey's day, men like Bayfield got warned and let go, and yet you are burning educated, learned, pious men, Sir Thomas.'

'Someone must be heavy with heretics. Be grateful you are in favour with the King, Crumwell. For a search of your private home might certainly turn up much evidence for your own burning! The doubleminded man indeed! And that says nothing of this Waif hither.'

'Please leave us to our work, Sir Thomas,' Crumwell replied, his complexion unmoving in expression. Arguments solved nothing, achieved nothing, advanced no one. No one made such threats in Nicóla's presence.

More rushed himself from Crumwell's chambers, and as the heavy main door slammed shut, Nicóla had already returned to her desk to continue work on the accounts. Crumwell stood in silence for a moment, his head filled with many subjects to consider.

'Nicó…'

'Is this right?' Nicóla replied. 'The King is giving £10 to his falconer? On top of his usual salary?'

'Yes, a bonus for something. Nicó…'

But Nicóla said nothing. A jest of marriage by Henry and Anne had put a serious thorn in their relationship, bringing upon conversations which were better left unsaid. And when it came to romance, Crumwell was woeful. He had never romanced Nicóla, they were a meeting of the minds. But as long as being burned by More was a factor to consider, courtly love had to be considered, if only because time left on Earth could be short.

Chapter 31- December 1531
Whitehall Palace and Austin Friars, London

One can learnth to loveth seecryts

'Him.'

Nicóla turned just a fraction but did not regard Crumwell. She stood straight, her hands behind her back, just as her master beside her.

'Which?' she muttered.

'Him.' Crumwell gestured most subtly into the crowd. Christmas, and the opening of the new Whitehall Palace, was in full celebration at court, everyone packed into the main hall together, sitting at tables after dinner, some dancing, all talking and laughing together as the wine flowed freely. As always, Crumwell stood to one side and observed, the way to understand people at court. Nicóla stood one step behind her master, leaning near the wall as the party happened all around them. King Henry sat at the head table on his throne, the Lady Anne by his side in a splendid golden dress, a coronet decorated with pearls perched atop her flowing dark hair. Everyone wanted to be close to the royal pair, deep in conversation with Anne's brother, slippery George Boleyn, and their father, the Earl of Wiltshire, whom Nicóla had not seen since the boiling of Richard Roose some eight months ago. Many whispered this Christmas at court was not as in times past, without the Queen and all her ladies present. It seemed just fine to Nicóla; the place filled with music and wine and laughter, such as Christmas always deserved.

Nicóla locked eyes on the man Crumwell mentioned. He was a

young man, perchance of twenty years, fair hair, perfectly ordinary in every way. 'What of him?'

'He works in George Boleyn's household. We have no eyes there.'

'Do we need an eye in Boleyn's rooms? All Boleyn does is read, drink and bed married women.'

'We need eyes everywhere.' Crumwell's lips barely moved as he spoke.

'You want me to recruit the boy?'

'Use that charm of yours, Nicó.'

'You are the one filled with charm,' Nicóla countered her master.

'I shall accept the compliment.' Crumwell turned and regarded Nicóla up and down. 'You do look especially tempting this evening.'

'You like this, do you?' Nicóla asked, a tiny smile forming on her lips. The last weeks had been awkward and Nicóla could not quite decide upon why. 'My master had this crimson velvet doublet made for me,' she jested, 'and fine crimson satin hose to match. The stockings are so fine and soft. And this beautiful white linen shirt of mine, with these fine gold arm ribbons, in the French fashion...'

'Your master treats you well.'

'He usually commands me to wear all black livery, so this is a pleasant change.'

'Your master may wish to buy you all manner of fine things, but for the fact you wear men's attire.'

'My master has no need,' Nicóla giggled and wondered where her wine glass had gone.

'All you need to do is go over, with a sweet smile, to the young man and suggest in return for any information he wishes to share, he shall receive payment from me,' Crumwell returned to business.

'Are you requesting I speak with the boy because you are too drunk to do so, Master Crumwella?' Nicóla asked.

'Fewer arguments from you, young servant,' Crumwell said with his smug smile and turned to face Nicóla. 'Otherwise, I shall have to take back your fine crimson.'

'Only if you take it from me personally,' Nicóla whispered back, also feeling muddled with mulled wine and Christmas cheer.

'Master Crumwell?'

Crumwell spun around to Lady Bess Holland. She was one of Lady Anne's ladies-in-waiting, young, blonde and attractive, as all of Anne's household. She stood dressed in a lovely green gown, her hair swept back from her face. She smiled sweetly to Crumwell as if one of his friends.

'Lady Holland,' Crumwell said and clasped his hands together. 'May I be of service?'

'I was wondering,' she said with a giggle, 'if you enjoy dancing? Only you never seem to come to the floor during celebrations such as this.'

Nicóla tried her best not to laugh; Tomassito, dancing? Nicóla had known him two years and he only ever danced at Austin Friars' parties. Dancing would only take away time from plotting or working.

'Alas, I seldom find the time, Lady Holland. May I ask why you enquire such a request?'

'I enquire, in case there was such a lady who wished to know you somewhat better, and perchance a chance to dance with you?'

'I know you to be much close to your Lady's uncle, the Duke of Norfolk, Lady Holland. I am certain he shall not like to see you dancing with one as baseborn as myself.'

'I ask on behalf of another, Master Crumwell,' young Bess replied, unfazed by being known as the mistress of a man triple her age.

Nicóla stepped forward into the conversation. 'My Lady, Master Crumwella is a most curious man, and quite a fine dancer indeed. If there is a lady at court who wishes to catch his eye, all you must do is say the word, and he shall sweep her directly to the dance.'

Crumwell threw Nicóla a frown as she snaked away from the pair, and she threw him back a daring smile. It seemed women at court were now regarding Crumwell as a potential suitor, such was his dramatic rise in favour, and not a wife in sight.

The boy from George Boleyn's household had seemingly disappeared. Nicóla stopped between the crowds, nodding hello to people as she went in search of the boy. Instead, she came up against Lady Anne herself. 'I beg your pardon, my Lady,' Nicóla said with a slight bow.

'I was looking for Thomas Wyatt to dance, the wonderful man he is. We used to dance together as children. But I cannot find him anywhere. Do you care for dancing, Mr. Frescobaldi?'

No one could say no to Anne Boleyn, the wittiest woman at court. 'Certainly, my Lady.' Nicóla escorted Anne to the dance floor and took her hand. 'You know how to dance the steps of a man, I hope,' Anne whispered. 'For I do not!'

'Fear not, Lady Anne, I have lived as a man for many years. My appearance never slips.'

They danced together beside the other couples, a gentle tune played by Smeaton on his lute. 'Have you ever considered living as a woman?' Anne asked in Nicóla's ear.

'It occurs to me from time to time, my Lady, however, you know as well as I, the difficulties of our gender.'

'You have certainly caught the eye of many women hither tonight, in your wonderful crimson outfit. How do you fend off all the women who must want a young Italian man in their bed?'

'I lack the tall stature of a man, meaning few women consider me a fair match. Also, I never stand still long enough for any women to catch me,' Nicóla replied, and Anne laughed.

Her laughter caught the attention of the King, who looked over, and Nicóla nodded in respect to His Majesty. 'Do not worry, Mr. Frescobaldi, I shall retain your secret. Henry cares deeply for Master Cremwell, as does my father, so we all keep your secret.'

'I thank you, Lady Anne,' Nicóla said and regarded the pretty woman before her, the same height. 'In Italy, I lived this way, however, I was never in need of secrets, as I was accepted in my man's life, had a man's world, wore men's clothes. It is different hither.'

'The court can be notoriously suffocating,' Anne replied as she regarded the dancers. 'We constantly all praise youth and virtue, but hither, old men are able to prey on the virtue of women with no consequence. We are told to maintain our virtue, yet surrounded by temptation in which to lose it.'

'Take it from me, Lady Anne, once your virtue has been stripped from you, by force or choice, you can never gain the same level of power again. You are forever changed.'

'You know this for certain?'

'Painfully so.'

'Cremwell took your…?'

'No, no,' Nicóla said and Anne laughed in relief. 'The loss of my virtue was what caused me to live the life I do now. There was no room for me to come back from the pain I suffered.'

'I dare not ask,' Anne replied. 'But you send me to bed tonight with good counsel, knowing my virtue, and my power, is safe in my heart.'

The music came to its end, and all applauded Smeaton's beauty. Anne made her way back to Henry, the crowds parting as she made moved through them as light as a golden whisper. Nicóla spotted Crumwell on his own again, and she weaved through the crowd to her master. 'Did the blossoming Lady Holland entice you into anything special, Master Crumwella?'

'Bess Holland is the Duke of Norfolk's whore! I hardly think she is a smart choice. She came to speak to me on behalf of another.'

'Oh, how prosperous,' Nicóla said and rubbed her hands together. 'Tell me, Master, who here at court has her eye on you? Is it Anne Gainsford, as mentioned several weeks ago?'

'No, it is Lady Margaret Douglas.' Crumwell pointed across the hall to a young woman, beautiful with reddish-brown hair. 'The King's niece, the only daughter of Henry's sister, the Dowager Queen Margaret of Scotland. Lady Douglas is young and new to Anne's household and always looking for mischief.'

'You must be triple her age!' Nicóla giggled. 'What a scandal. A lover to offend her family, I admire this girl already. She and Mary Boleyn make quite the pair of troublesome women together.'

'Take those thoughts from your mind,' Crumwell instructed. 'There is but one lady my eyes are drawn to at court. She wears the most beautiful and exquisite crimson. But I fear all this labouring talk of men and women at court only harms my affection for this lady.'

'Some women are prone to fits of jealousy,' Nicóla replied as the pair continued to look out over the party before them. 'Some just wish to be thrown upon a powerful man's desk where he can dispel any notion his golden eyes wander elsewhere.' Nicóla glanced at him out of the corner of her eyes and Crumwell did the same.

Papers scattered from the desk all over the floor with one swipe of Crumwell's arm. He pushed Nicóla down on the desk and she closed her eyes, her mind swimming with wine. Perchance this was to be their golden age, where they rejoiced in their relationship, secret and unofficial in every way.

~~~

A celebration of Christmas at Austin Friars was again a bountiful affair. Nicóla did not leave the court with a feeling of praise for her behaviour, not at all. She may have lived as a man for fifteen years, but never once formed a relationship with anyone. She had chosen celibacy as her partner. Now, still fervently in love with a man, and still hidden away like a harlot, was not a feeling Nicóla could relish. Exciting? Certainly. Lustful? Definitely. In line with her moral core? Never. Life's rules were always so blurred, and now Crumwell continued to rise high in the King's esteem, Nicóla worried her hold upon Crumwell might fade away. Even at the age of seven and forty, Crumwell was a handsome older man, charming, intelligent, and constantly more popular, his golden eyes bewitching more at court than ever. The reality Crumwell may be a fitting match for marriage at court was a reality Nicóla needed to bear, and soon.

Asked to come to the parlour at Austin Friars, where the yule log burned, Nicóla wandered in to find Crumwell there, sitting with his son. Now soon to be twelve years of age, Gregory had been studying at Cambridge, enjoying the benefit of his father's love of education. Also, there was Ralph with Richard and Frances, all standing by the fireplace, laughing with young Gregory. Sat in an armchair was Mercy, with baby Jane on her lap.

'Do I interrupt?' Nicóla asked as she closed the door to the warm room decorated in carved wood overlaid with green and red tapestries.

'Of course not,' Crumwell said as he rose from his seat next to Gregory. 'You must come and join the family.'

Nicóla came in and sat down on the carpets before the fireplace, something the English seldom did. Sitting upon the floor was for peasants. Mercy put Jane on the floor, and the young girl took gentle steps towards her mother to sit on her lap. If Crumwell were to marry, Nicóla might need to take Jane away from her home. They might need to go back to Florence.

'Every year we usually get together and speak of important things,' Crumwell said as he sat down with his son again. 'Last year we did not have much to celebrate in the house, nor the few years prior. But this year I have decided to bring back tradition.'

'So what will we talk about this year, uncle?' Richard asked.

'We have had an ample year,' Crumwell said as he looked around the family. 'Mercy, I cannot thank you enough for being the mistress of the house and being the carer of the baby Jane. It was unexpected we would take in a baby, but again you have done God's work, and I thank you. Your loyalty and love means the world to me, Mercy.'

'You are most welcome, Thomas,' Mercy said with a smile, and she shared a smile with Nicóla who stroked Jane's curly rose-gold hair. 'A home is not complete without a baby.'

'Gregory, I am most proud of your progress at Cambridge, and you shall have another year at the school before you are moved to another tutor closer to home. Soon you can return to Austin Friars and learn the art of business, and then the art of law at Oxford,' Crumwell continued.

'Thank you, Father,' Gregory said with a solemn face. All knew the boy liked not his stern education, more suited to working with his hands, something now forbidden for a Crumwell son. 'Cousin Christopher, and dear Nicholas and I, all love the education you provide us.'

'Ralph,' Crumwell said and raised his silver cup to him. 'You have been the best master secretary I could ask. I have increased the workload so much and you have not faltered. I wish to promote you to the running of Austin Friars and all my private dealings. You will be in charge at Austin Friars from now on.'

'Thank you,' Ralph said, genuinely surprised. 'I had no idea.'

'It will mean you can spend less time at court and more time hither, close to the laundress you are in love with; do not think I did not already know.' Everyone in the room laughed, and Ralph's pale cheeks flushed at the revelry.

'My nephew, Richard. You shall make the leap to the Privy Council of England on the King's orders. Your mother would have been so proud. But it is you, Richard, who shall take the position offered and you excel in your own way. I could not ask for more.'

'I… thank you…' Richard stumbled. His parents had passed three years ago, his mother, Crumwell's sister, first and then his father soon after. Frances gently kissed her husband's surprised cheek.

'Everything is so exciting now,' Gregory commented. 'I hope I can be at court one day.'

'Perchance,' Crumwell replied. 'I have no doubt we can gain you the quick mind needed for the task. And Nicóla…'

'I am no member of your family,' Nicóla said, surprised to even be mentioned.

'Of course, you are,' Ralph replied. 'You live hither with us, Jane is your niece; we all rely on you.'

Nicóla smiled, grateful to be so welcome, but in truth she still knew not her true place at Austin Friars.

'Dovremmo dire loro la verità?' Crumwell asked her. Tell them the truth? About being a woman?

'Che cosa, che sono una donna?'

'Si,' Crumwell replied. 'Se si è pronti.'

But was Nicóla ready to share such news? Were they ready to hear the truth? 'Sono pronti?'

'Siete amati qui, siete al sicuro qui.' You are loved here, you are safe here. But her gender was Nicóla's secret to keep and understand. Why did Crumwell ordain to own her secret?

'No, per favore, ti prego,' Nicóla begged.

'I am sorry, Nicóla, but it is time.' Crumwell paused and regarded his family around him. 'You all know Nicóla has been a wonderful addition to Austin Friars. And you know I was educated by Francesco Frescobaldi. Francesco had five daughters, born while I lived in Florence. But they were the children of his second wife. His first wife, a love match, of which the family did not approve, died in childbirth. Francesco and Nicóletta had a daughter, named Nicóletta after her departed mother, but the girl got hidden away as a bastard when the marriage was declared unlawful. Over the years, Francesco lacked sons, so educated the daughters by his new wife, but he discovered his bastard daughter, Nicóletta, was incredibly intelligent. An extraordinary mind, tutored in mathematics, languages, Ioci – the art of memory, just the same as he taught me – and much more. A man's mind trapped in a woman's frame; a bastard child considered one of God's accidents. Childbirth also took Francesco's second wife and the plague of 1520 stole his five new daughters from him, God bless their souls.' Crumwell paused as everyone crossed themselves. 'Francesco found himself without an heir to give his business and inheritance. But he still had his extraordinary bastard daughter, Nicóletta, who lived separately to her sisters and did not fall ill. A young woman, with the mind of a brilliant man, a true creature of beauty and intelligence. Nicóletta was able to rise in finance and trading at Francesco's side, as she dressed as her father's son, and known in Florence as the bastard son of Francesco Frescobaldi.'

Nicóla kept her eyes on the floor, but she knew all eyes were on her. Mercy already knew the truth but did not know the history. Young Gregory still seemed unsure of the point.

'You are a woman,' Ralph said out loud.

Nicóla glanced up to him, Richard and Frances. They stared back and she just nodded.

'You are a woman?' Gregory asked. 'But you regard yourself as no woman!'

'I have long been regarded as one of God's accidents,' Nicóla explained. 'I have prayed daily for years for God to answer to my questions. Was I not to be born, not to survive? Why would I have a man's mind but the weak frame of a woman? Why must I suffer inside the body of the weaker sex? Or did God have a plan, to show that a woman's mind can match a man's, if nurtured as a son? God has not yet given me an answer. As a bastard child, not regarded as important, I was not given the chance to learn how to be a lady, how to care for beauty, to sew and dance and be gentle. My father loved my mother deeply, and gave me that love, allowing me to be tutored and educated. My father pretended I was a boy, for only a boy could be so intelligent. Father gave me the name Nicóla instead of Nicóletta, cut off my long hair, dressed me in doublet and hose. Father needed a son, so I became a son by hiding the body God gave me in a moment of weakness.'

'But the notion is so greedy, covetous,' Richard muttered. 'And cruel. It is to deny God's will.'

'The Pope himself knows Nicóla and her gender. She is very close to the Medici family in Florence, including the Pope in Rome. They all know and accept Nicóla as a man,' Crumwell said, his tone almost a warning against judgement.

'So, will you marry a man or a woman?' Ralph asked.

'My clothes, education, mannerisms are those of a man, but I can assure you, I have the normal frame of a woman.'

'Is Jane your baby?' Gregory innocently asked Nicóla.

'Indeed. I am Jane's mother, not her uncle, and your father was kind enough to take Jane into Austin Friars, to help keep my secret, and to stop Jane from being awarded my shame.'

'How long have you known?' Ralph asked Crumwell.

'Since Nicóla first came to London with Cardinal Campeggio all those years ago now, when I worked for Wolsey,' Crumwell explained.

'Naught can fool you, uncle,' Richard jested and everyone laughed a little, perhaps to ease the strain placed upon them by the news.

'Tomassito,' Nicóla said to get his attention. She did not want Crumwell to tell them the story of their affair. It was too much to share. 'Per favore, non dire loro che siamo amanti. Please,' she added again.

Crumwell just nodded in reply. 'In Italy, Nicóla was accepted as a bastard son of frail body and voice. Nicóla prefers the same hither in England, to embrace her safety. The secret must be kept.'

'Fear not,' Mercy finally spoke. 'All women have secrets. We all do what we must to survive.'

'You all know how intelligent Nicóla is,' Crumwell continued, his voice still warning his family. 'Nicóla is an asset to us. Now Ralph shall run Austin Friars, Nicóla is to be my master secretary at court. I have long accepted Nicóla's frailties, and I expect you to as well,' Crumwell instructed. 'There can be no betrayal, least lose all you have gained from me.'

'I am most sorry for ever lying to you,' Nicóla added. 'I never wanted to lie, but I know people question my frail outward appearance. Hence the need for bright colours, detailed clothing. My dark skin, strange hair colour, they all point to me being a strange, fragile foreigner, and my secrets remain secret.'

'I have not always spoken the way I ought to have around a lady,' Richard said and covered his mouth for a moment. 'And to think of some of the taverns we have visited together!'

'I do not wish to hear more,' Frances added.

'You must not change,' Nicóla said, relieved some by Richard's calm actions. 'I have been this way for all my life. I understand all of being a man, trust me.'

'I am sorry you needed to lie,' Gregory said. 'But what if you are not an accident of God, but rather a sensible-minded woman?'

'A woman's place is in the home, raising her children and being a pious wife,' Nicóla told the boy. 'I am not an example for anyone.'

Jane began to whimper on Nicóla's lap, weary and ready to sleep. Mercy got up and took the baby. 'Let me take young Jane to bed. Come along, young Gregory, you also.'

Gregory bent down to Nicóla and wrapped his arms around her, to her surprise. 'I know something of not being alike the others,' he whispered in her ear. 'I shall pray for you, as I pray the new learnings shall answer my many frailties.'

Poor young Gregory. Nicóla saw him rarely, but he held similar manners to herself; slight, gentle, of female favour. Gregory would grow not to be a man of his father's standing. A wife would be forced upon him, whether Gregory favoured women or not.

Crumwell farewelled his son and Mercy took her young charges from the parlour. Ralph and Richard stood stiff, neither eager to speak. 'Gentlemen, you have been given such information in order to be part of its protection.'

'I must confess to be in need of time,' Richard replied. 'I cannot yet understand why God would create such a person.'

'I understand,' Nicóla said and stood up at last. 'For it took time for me to understand this also. But I have had the benefit of time and prayers to guide me through such a life.'

'I need much time to reconcile this affront to God!' Ralph burst forth. 'I believe God creates no such accidents! Rather, you are a woman who has defied what God intended and took what belongs to man alone! It sounds almost as witchcraft!'

'Could you please excuse us?' Crumwell asked of Ralph and Richard. 'There is something of importance I need to discuss with Nicóla, and perchance now is not the night for more discussion.'

Ralph stormed from the room without another glance. Richard and Frances followed close behind, their demeanors much calmer. Once they departed, Crumwell got up from his seat and wrapped his arms around Nicóla. 'That went most unwell,' he said over her head.

'Was it necessary? I was to be a man here; you only know the truth by good fortune. For now I can never be Nicóla Frescobaldi, but rather now a bastard creature. You have burdened even more souls with my problem. It is such I have fought with for many years, an issue I cannot settle with God, and yet you set such news upon others. I must confess to much anger.'

Crumwell pulled himself away just enough to look her in the eye, that wild golden stare. 'Nicó, you continue to sell short your importance hither. You sell short your influence at court, and most important, you continue to sell short my love for you.'

Crumwell let her go and reached into his pocket. He produced a gold ring, with a heart-shaped turquoise stone. 'This is for you, to wear if you wish. I have not treated you as I should have treated a lady for which I feel love. Nicó, I wish to rectify thus.'

'You do not need to do so, I promise you.' Nicóla watched him slip the ring onto her left forefinger. It matched the ring Crumwell wore from Wolsey. The ring to control the King. Now Nicóla had the ring to control the Queenmaker.

'I must be more attentive to you.' Crumwell pointed across the room, to where more seats sat in the far corner of the room. A painting hung on the wall, covered in cloth. 'Come and see what I got for you.'

Nicóla followed Crumwell to the painting, and he pulled the black cloth from the frame. Nicóla gasped so much she felt she may die from chest pain. There was a painting of her father, Francesco, exactly as he looked when she was young. The man who made her a creature. Time stared back from her father's green eyes, a time long passed now. 'But how?' Nicóla stumbled.

'I spent some time with the artist Master Holbein at court, and spoke of Francesco, and Holbein created this painting, from my memory of your father.'

'Tomassito, it… it is perfect. You have created an image of my father, from memory, a skill he taught us both.' Nicóla felt her eyes welling up with stinging hot tears. 'I am stunned, it is just incredible. You have captured the golden time in my father's life, a golden time of my own.'

'You like it?' Her father, with his rose-gold hair and green eyes, his broad shoulders and long nose, all perfect.

'Now I may learn to remember my father as this man, and mayhap no longer only my last memory of him.'

'You were there when he died?'

Nicóla nodded. She had never told anyone the story. 'We were at Villa de Medici, just outside Florence. News of the sacking of Rome had come. Men in Florence, opposed to Medici rule, took the chance to also rise up, and take the Republic. They ransacked the Medici villa, and we were the only few there, besides the servants, who were all killed. Men came into the room where Father and I were, men all carrying knives or swords. The room had enormous doors leading out into the forest behind the manor, and we charged for these doors. We could hide in the forest. The looters, they started to destroy the room, the artworks, the furnishings. A man grabbed Father, but Father knocked him down. Another man grabbed me and Father pulled at him, able to get me free. Father cried for me to run and I opened the door and turned back to him, but this crazed man, he, he had a knife to Father's throat. I could not leave Father! But Father again ordered me to run, his last words before the man slit Father's throat. I watched him bleed and die at that moment. I turned and fled into the forest, and hid until darkness. The palace was set alight, so Father's body was burned to nothing, not given the rites or burial a godly man deserves. I was the only survivor at the palace. I left for Rome the next day, nowhere safe in Florence any longer. Giulio always said, even though he was Pope, if I ever needed him, to come to him, and he took me in. But all I see of Father now is his throat being slit, until this, this beautiful painting.'

What came next remained a mystery. Nicóla never thought herself a creature, rather a smart woman, forced to hide in doublet and hose. Yet no man could believe such, rather that God must have committed a mishap. The lies never ceased, all because of the decisions of the man in the painting, who longed for a son, just like King Henry himself. Such was the frailty of human affairs.

Chapter 32 - April 1532
Austin Friars, Whitehall Palace and Westminster, London

I shall giveth more seecryts to thee at whych hour I feeleth lyke
stoppyng myne own heart

'Our creatures in Europe have produced some most excellent news,' Nicóla said as Crumwell watched out the window of his library. He was delighted to see, now winter was over and Easter had come, the building at Austin Friars could begin. And what a change Crumwell planned. Other homes were being torn down; this was Crumwell's part of London now. The house needed to be more than doubled; and with the need for more servants by the day, the work could not be completed with enough haste.

Crumwell turned from the window, the sun hurting his eyes a fraction, and regarded Nicóla. They had been busy planning the Easter procession festivities at court, so more important news would be welcomed. Nicóla stood before him in her new black livery, all the servants upgraded yet again, thanks to prized tidings, silver thread and buttons, pearls on the collar for his favourite creature of all. Nicóla's rose-gold hair now rested once more upon her shoulders, and she seemed to have no desire to cut or pin it, as she had when she first came to England for sanctuary. The whole court whispered of Crumwell's curious Waif, and instead of hiding, now Nicóla seemed to feed their suspicions. Telling Ralph and Richard caused trouble; for Ralph could not speak to Crumwell or Nicóla, Richard seemed blunt but yielding.

Nicóla seemed to challenge everything Crumwell said, and dressed as womanly as possible within the confines of the livery Crumwell provided her. The truth did none good; all it caused was a Crumwell family rift. The past months stretched Nicóla's love for Crumwell, that he felt sure. Since revealing her secret to the family, Nicóla remained quiet, but of a quiet anger.

'Tell me the rumours,' Crumwell said to Nicóla and sat back down at his desk, eager to work.

'Well indeed, I must bypass so many messages for the greatest one of all. Our dear Dr. Thomas Cranmer, sent to be our Imperial ambassador, has visited German nations of the Holy Roman Empire, as the Emperor's progress has stopped in Nuremberg. Cranmer has only gone and married himself to the niece of Andreas Osiander, the creator of Lutheran reformation in the area!'

'What?' Crumwell laughed. 'Cranmer is a priest! How can he marry?' He paused for a moment. 'Cranmer is a reformer, but it seems mayhap he is more Lutheran now, as Lutherans do not expect celibacy from their priests.'

'This message states Cranmer married a girl named Margarete, rather than taking her as a mistress.'

'Cranmer has been married before, but prior to being ordained. We sent him to the Imperial court to help gain an annulment, not take a wife!' Crumwell snorted with laughter.

'Strange things well indeed can happen,' Nicóla said with a beautiful smile as she regarded the correspondence in her hands. As she stood before Crumwell's desk, he noticed Nicóla's posture change; her shoulders drooped, her hands tense as they held the papers.

'What is it?' he asked. 'Sorry news from France?'

'No… no, it is Florence. Duke Alessandro de' Medici has been made a hereditary duke by the Emperor, not a courtesy title any longer. The Pope has paid for this honour. It makes Florence officially part of the Roman Empire, not a Republic.'

Crumwell leaned forward in his seat, his own shoulders drooped. The detail could mean violence in the city they both loved. 'Are you well?'

'Permission to burn this news?'

Crumwell clicked his fingers and Nicóla handed him the letter. He gazed at it and tore it up. 'Say no more.'

'I shall let you read through the rest,' Nicóla mumbled but stopped on another. 'This one is from your man in the Tower. Of a man named James Bainham.'

Crumwell clicked his fingers again and Nicóla handed the whole pile to him. 'James Bainham is a barrister I had cause to know in the past,' Crumwell said as he read the letter, written by a man in his employ, who guarded at the Tower. 'Bainham got arrested months ago for heresy and personally tortured at Sir Thomas More's home, and then put on the rack in the Tower. Now he shall be burned at Smithfield.'

'Can you not save him?'

'Bainham spoke publicly, saying purgatory is not real, only in doctrine so priests can line their pockets with money as the people seek forgiveness.'

'Is that not a cornerstone of the Lutheran beliefs, to deny purgatory's existence?' Nicóla asked. 'Is it not what you believe?'

'It is, but I am in no position to anger Sir Thomas More. What should I do? Go to court and ask More to stop burning men such as myself? More is already suspicious of you, Nicó. We need to be careful.'

'Tomassito, you cannot let this Bainham burn because you want to hide me from Sir Thomas More. If I am exposed, then it is a risk I need to take. I am a woman in your employ, and I need to wear a man's livery. Perchance it is simple; perchance I should be as free with my truth as you are, and tell More everything. The only person I have spoken freely with is Queen Katherine, and she accepted my secret. It is you, Master Crumwella, who is free with my secrets at present.'

'Please be not angered, Nicó. You violate religious conduct being a woman and acting as a man. The Church does not bend; men such as More do not bend. Besides, the Supplication Against the Ordinaries is ready for parliament, and I have written and nursed this legislation for years, since the time of Wolsey. Thus shall irritate More enough. I seek to take away so much of the Church's power. It will not be long before both beady-eyed More and shaky-hands Gardiner bang down our door in hopes of pulling me down.'

'The Convocation of Canterbury has always made canon laws, and parliament creates civil laws,' Nicóla replied. 'You alone cannot be blamed for seeking to strip them of their power. It is the Church which has abused their powers; it is they who need to be controlled by parliament, for the safety of many souls. The King himself said so.'

'No law ought to be made without the blessing of the King; the King ought to have power over the Church and its laws. The fees charged by the clergy to ordinary men must not be so excessive. The way clergymen hold secular offices, their religious views clouding their judgement, along with nepotism of the Church, the wasting of money, the use of fake relics…'

'Tomassito, there is no need to convince me,' Nicóla said with a gentle smile, which soothed Crumwell's rising heart rate. He would pass the Supplication Against the Ordinaries law if it killed him. The Church needed to be reformed.

'Your supplication is sound,' Nicóla continued. 'Both skittish Archbishop Warham and Bishop Gardiner have spoken against your supplication, angering the King. You are only the man to break the Church and give the King absolute power. You are the only one set to give Henry the right to annul and remarry. Stay your course.'

Crumwell smiled up at his companion; in times of feeling so alone in his beliefs, having someone to agree with, even just in his own library, was all he needed. By all accounts, Nicóla did agree; she had not replaced her Catholic rosary beads since giving them away to the boiling Richard Roose a year ago.

'What be the package that arrived earlier?' Crumwell said with a sigh.

'I am so glad you asked,' Nicóla smiled, and pulled the box from her drawer. She opened it to show her master; a new book. 'It is hither at last; behold, "The Prince" by Niccoló Machiavelli. In print for the first time, with the blessing of the Pope.'

'You are not going to suggest I am "the prince" again, are you, Nicó?'

'Everyone sees what you appear to be, few experience what you really are,' Nicóla recited with a smile. 'That sounds as if you first wrote it.'

'Shall I ever convince you?' Crumwell smiled back.

A knock on the door echoed ahead one of Austin Friars' gentlemen-ushers. 'Master Crumwell, a messenger from the court.'

Crumwell clicked his fingers twice and the messenger was sent in, the familiar Tudor rose emblem on the boy's chest. 'I am having but two days back at my home, so why is court summoning me?' he asked the boy, who held a black hat in his hands, and out of breath.

'Sir, the King requests you attend court today, for a special meeting of the Council.'

'Why, what has happened?'

'I was just told to inform you that you need to be at Whitehall at four in the afternoon.'

Crumwell put his hand in his top drawer and tossed a coin to the boy, who happily went on his way with a reward. Men who gained minor favours were more likely to join the league of creatures later. Nicóla always had a drawer in all of Crumwell's desks laden with coins to give messengers.

'I came to spend the day with my daughter,' Crumwell sighed and Nicóla shrugged. 'Could the world give a man a day?'

'You spent time with Jane when you were falconing yesterday, and when those strange German beavers were running around, Jane laughed and played with you.'

'I heard you saying to Jane you wanted to get pavonis living in the canary cage.'

'The name "peacock" sounds improper. But why cannot we have peacocks? We have so many birds, falcons, hawks and sweet yellow canaries. Why not a peacock? You have a leopard, the beavers and the beast at your Stepney house, what is it called?'

'The elk.' Crumwell got up from his seat and rounded his desk, and took occasion to kiss Nicóla's cheek.

'You spent £400 on wine last month,' she mumbled.

'You are starting to sound as a wife,' he teased. 'It was top quality wine from the King's cellar. And Henry was here for dinner; we had to have the best.'

'How do I know you will not serve peacock to the King next time he visits?' she pouted. 'You cooked swans.'

'The King enjoys eating swan. I will tell the chef not to cook peacocks; we will get peacocks for Jane's second birthday. Let us to court.'

'But no more gambling, Tomassito. You lose so much money to Thomas Wriothesley. And Richard Rich. And Thomas Audley. You may love cards and dice but you do not excel.'

'I save my talents for better tasks. You do sound as a wife.'

'An accountant only. Do you wish to lose Gregory's inheritance to playing dice with the King?'

Crumwell took Nicóla in his arms for a long embrace, away from the eyes and murmurs of the court. 'Io confido solo la tua guida.' And Crumwell meant it; Nicóla's guidance was the only one he trusted, no matter how much their relationship had suffered in recent months.

~~~

The palace at Whitehall busied itself as any day, though one Crumwell had hoped to miss. Days at Austin Friars were such a rare occasion now. He sent Nicóla, flanked by guards, to go more often to see Jane, but work for the King now occupied all of Crumwell's time. Parliament was still Crumwell's favourite place, but Henry took so many of Crumwell's days. Henry's marriage never moved itself away from being the lead problem at court. By the time Crumwell entered the public presence chamber, Henry stood talking with the pompous, ever-insufferable Charles Brandon, Duke of Suffolk. Crumwell could never forget the moment Suffolk beat Nicóla at Blackfriars, in a house of God, before the eyes of two cardinals. As long as he lived, Crumwell could never side with Suffolk on anything.

'Crumwell!' the King cheered, almost surprised to see him, as if he had not requested his presence. 'You do appear well this afternoon.'

Crumwell glanced down at his black coat which fell to his feet, its brown fur trim neatly brushed by his maids. 'I thank you for the compliment, Your Majesty.' Crumwell was plainly underdressed in comparison to bejeweled Henry, who climbed the two carpeted steps and sat back on his throne under the cloth of estate. Suffolk turned and stood next to the King.

'Thomas, good morrow and well met. I am contented to see you hither. There is something I need to say. You have been working for me as my parliamentary and legal advisor for more than two years, but you are much more; you are more a secretary to me. You are prized on the Council. Also, you have been creating the paperwork to strip the Church of its power. For thus, I cannot thank you enough. As for Bishop Gardiner, not six months ago we gave him his bishopric, and now he has turned against me, saying the clergy ought to not grant me power over them. And he has plenty to say about you.'

'You do have your enemies, Mr. Crumwell,' Suffolk added.

'I can be certain, Your Majesty,' Crumwell replied. 'Men do adore to tear at one another, even ones as pious as Stephen Gardiner.'

'Gardiner wrote to me and talked of sinister information, sinful labours and persuasions of such persons. Gardiner means you, Thomas. We must crush the Church into giving me power over them. I am their King, and they shall not kneel to Rome any longer, they shall kneel to my authority.'

'You have parliament's support, Your Majesty. I shall do anything I can to be of service.'

'And Sir Thomas More, my own Lord Chancellor, is too busy burning heretics and having "covert" Catholic meetings to be advising at all,' Henry said, throwing his hands in the air with anger. 'More has become extreme in his love for the Pope. You, Thomas, you are the moderate man I have always needed.'

The moderate man shall inherit the kingdom. As always, Nicóla words trotted through Crumwell's mind.

'But enough; I asked you hither to show a sign of goodwill, Thomas. I am making you Master of the Jewel House. It comes with an annual salary of £50 a year, which I am sure you may find generous for the task. The previous master has passed away, and our jewels in the Tower are in need of care and a keen eye for logging and valuing. You are the man for the task.'

An official role under the King's command! All the work Crumwell did before was important but informal. This was established. This was extra income, and not even a hard task.

'Also, a gift.' Henry gestured of one of his gentlemen, Sir Francis Weston, to hand him an item. Henry stepped down and placed a gold link chain over Crumwell's head to rest around his neck. The gold chain was fine interlinked rings of gold, the same as Suffolk wore at this moment, now Crumwell had one too; a symbol of favour with the King. Anne Boleyn's father had been sporting one for months, as it was currently Henry's favourite gift to bestow. 'Much better,' Henry said and held Crumwell by the shoulders, his face wide in a grin. 'You are well respected by me, Thomas. I will not hear anything said against you, not to my ears. Only you can gain the submission of the clergy. Only you can gain me the right to make religious decisions in my own realm.'

'Which is precisely what I plan to do, Your Majesty. The Convocation of Canterbury, at this moment, are in what could be their final meeting before the Church of England is yours.'

~~~

'Well-beloved subjects, we thought that the clergy of our realm had been our subjects wholly, but now we perceive they be but half our subjects, yea, scarce our subjects. All the prelates at their consecration make an oath to the Pope, contrary to the oath that they make to us, so that they seem to be the Pope's subjects, and not ours. The copy of both oaths I deliver to you, requiring you to create order, and show we are not deceived by our spiritual subjects.' Henry spoke with such fervent passion, spittle landed on his chin.

Crumwell sat before him, his hands neatly folded, his heart no doubt beating far slower than the King's. Henry's speech in parliament, fighting the clergy, said everything Crumwell thought of the Church. The Catholic faith needed to be broken. They needed to be humbled, reformed and rebuilt under the King, not under the Pope. Not under the belief that people needed popes and penance and relics and over-stuffed bishops getting rich off the piety of laymen. Henry could stall no longer, despite what skittish Warham and his Convocation of Canterbury wanted.

So here sat Crumwell on the sixteenth day of May, before the King's councillors and the officers of the clergy at Westminster, ready to hear if they signed the three articles Crumwell had so carefully written. Article one - the Church of England could no longer create canon laws without the King's permission and blessing. Article two – the Convocation of Canterbury would have all current canons laws put to a committee of sixteen, picked by the King, and then each suffer scrutiny and possibly be annulled. Article three – the Church must swear alliance to the King, not to the Pope. The King only obeyed God, not any pope in Rome. Henry would control England and religion, not Catholic clergymen. Crumwell had, in his power, the ability to break down the Roman Catholic Church and could rebuild it in his image for the future.

So while he sat there, with his folded scarred hands, his stiff white collar peeking from under his black velvet doublet, his eyes shining gold and staring straight ahead at the King, Crumwell held the power of every man, woman, and child in England. Henry agreed to all. King Henry, Defender of the Faith, the man who once wrote against Luther and idea of reformation and Protestant guidelines, now sat at Westminster and demanded the Church bow down and renounce their power. Just the way Crumwell had written it. Every. Single. Word.

Footsteps from behind; Crumwell did not move a muscle. Along the aisle shuffled the feet of purple-clad Warham, Archbishop of Canterbury, who brought the scroll for which Henry waited. With silence and a stature hunched in submissive agony, Warham handed the over the scroll; the signatures of the Convocation. The Church was broken. Henry could do as he pleased. He could annul his own marriage. The Pope? Just some bishop in Rome, sitting upon a fractured throne. Just like that, God's power had been diverted to a King aged forty, with red hair waiting its descent into greying years, but a mind as sharp as ever. The days of false Catholic idolatry were over. Soon, the way all England worshipped could be changed, from the King all the way to every peasant farmer.

Henry held the signed articles in his hands and looked forward over everyone, all seemingly hunched in submission. There had been threats made over the last few nights; Crumwell had been told to make ready more preparations to have the clergy arrested. Anne Boleyn's family, her father the Earl of Wiltshire and uncle the Duke of Norfolk, had a serious and angered discussion with Warham, to force final signatures. Whispers of hidden dangers and hooded men swirled at court, men wishing to end Crumwell. Guards followed Crumwell's household staff everywhere, especially Nicóla, in case the threat made real. The King would no longer bow to anyone.

Now the King's blue eyes scanned all those before him, to see naught but stone-like complexions, bowed and bent to his will. Henry's eyes fell on Crumwell, and he responded with slight more than a flick of his dark eyebrow, and Henry broke into a wide, clear grin, filled with vain-glory and self-adulation. It was time to make a new queen.

Chapter 33 - May 1532
Whitehall Palace, London

Oft a secret is just knowledge but knowledge can wield such power

Crumwell sat upright in his dining chair, too busy to rest. The meeting room in his court chambers seated only thirty, but a great much more crowded into the room. The seat at the head of the table was Crumwell's own throne, carved and gilded, and he sat with one elbow rested on the cushioned arm. His golden eyes scanned the room; so many had come to celebrate the demise of the Church. More than one hundred people had come to offer their congratulations. Nicóla stood across the wide room with Thomas Wyatt, merry on wine. Mark Smeaton played the lute, his own composition of merry gaiety. Ralph and Richard laughed as they chatted with young lawyer Thomas Wriothesley, a man whom Crumwell often used when he was not under Stephen Gardiner's counsel. Many of Anne Boleyn's household were there, while Anne celebrated privately with the King. Ladies Jane and Elizabeth Seymour were there, as was the King's niece, Margaret Douglas, the dainty young redhead, all now serving Anne Boleyn rather than Queen Katherine. The intolerable Lady Anne Stanhope, also no longer in the Queen's household, kept attempting to gain Crumwell's attention, without success. Lady Anne Gainsford kept throwing gazes at Crumwell too, though he pretended not to notice. But Crumwell noticed everything, everyone. Courtiers who were paid by all various lords were there, eager to revel in success over the Church. The resplendently-dressed Sir Francis Bryan, with his patch over one eye, was loud as always. Several men from the Duke of Suffolk's household talked in the corner with several ladies from Suffolk wife's household, Princess Mary, the King's sister. All these people wanted to be near Crumwell now. Norfolk sent Howard men, including his own son, to pay respect to Crumwell. All these people, people who hated the fact Crumwell was even a presence, now were eager to pay favour.

But when Anne's father, Thomas Boleyn, the Earl of Wilshire, came to the revelry, only then did Crumwell rise from his throne. 'Master Crumwell,' Boleyn said, his eyes glazed with celebration, his shoulders drooped forward as always. He placed one arm around Crumwell's shoulders and squeezed him the way a father might a son.

'My Lord Privy Seal,' Crumwell said, and could not help but smile at this high man eager for Crumwell's favour. Once Boleyn had come to him for money, now he wanted Crumwell in the inner circle around the King. What a fool; Crumwell already had more power than the mistress' father.

'I have heard you host some rather lavish parties at Austin Friars,' Boleyn continued. 'I thought perchance you had returned to your magnificent home.'

'I am too much engaged in the King's business,' Crumwell replied as he clicked his fingers, and had wine brought to Boleyn, whose rich blue coat slipped forward on him, such was his tilted posture. 'This is a mere trivial engagement until I next return home.'

'I heard you have the best wines in the city.' Boleyn sipped from the silver goblet and his eyes lit up. 'From the King's cellar?'

'Always.'

'I heard you are a gambling man, Master Crumwell.'

'Always.'

'Would you care to place a bet on whether Sir Thomas More has a head for much longer?'

'The King could never take the head of Sir Thomas More; they have been allies since the King was young. There is a reason why More can come and go from the palace calling him "Harry." Sir Thomas More wants the King to remain faithful to Katherine, the Pope and the Catholic faith,' Crumwell scoffed.

'I bet you £50 one day, More will be... no more.'

The pair of drunken men laughed at the idea. 'I shall take your bet,' Crumwell said and shook Boleyn's hand. 'How is His Majesty?'

'Henry is most eager to spend time with Anne tonight. As you can imagine, Anne is most pleased with Henry's victory. We have given them some privacy.'

'All are welcome hither in my chambers,' Crumwell said, and Boleyn grinned again. 'Everyone.'

'Even Queen Katherine?' Boleyn snorted. 'Where is she now?'

'Living at The More in Hertfordshire, still.' Crumwell's eyes drifted; he noticed the Imperial Ambassador Eustace Chapuys enter this rooms, his grey furs still over his shoulders even in late spring. Chapuys gazed around, his eyes barely skimming the faces in the joyful room. Only when he spotted Nicóla, seated against Wyatt while they watched Smeaton play, did he move.

'How are you enjoying your role as Master of the Jewel House?' Boleyn continued, snapping Crumwell's fixation on the ambassador.

'In truth, I have done little,' Crumwell sighed, watching Nicóla whisper in the ambassador's ear. Crumwell watched Chapuys lick his lower lip as Nicóla spoke to him, his gaze lingering. It stirred an angry feeling of jealousy inside Crumwell.

'Pray you shall rise higher still, Master Crumwell. Your skills can be applied to so many areas.'

'You know us lawyers and bankers,' Crumwell said, now no longer caring for having Anne Boleyn's father in his company. Now he wanted to know why the Holy Roman Emperor's man in England wished to talk to precious Nicóla. No one could go near Crumwell's precious Nicóla. Not a man who looked at her the way Chapuys did. How had he not noticed this before? Of course, women regarded Nicóla, unawares of the truth, but men, too?

'I shall fetch my son and Norfolk, and we shall come and toast your victory,' Boleyn continued.

'Of course,' Crumwell mumbled and watched Nicóla with her hasty hand movements while she spoke. He could not read her lips – not through all that wine – but Nicóla spoke Italian and she spoke with haste.

'If you ever wish to talk reform of the Church…' Boleyn offered.

Now Boleyn had Crumwell's attention. 'You have plans for reform, my Lord? Are you of the same ideas as your daughter? With dreams of cleaning up abuses of the Church?'

'I would crush the whole damned Church if I had my way,' Boleyn said through gritted teeth, the smile still on his face.

'Then yes, we ought to talk.'

Boleyn slithered away and Crumwell spun back to Nicóla, now in her seat alone, Wyatt talking with Smeaton. Nicóla raised her wine to her lips as she caught Crumwell's golden glare. She gave him one flash of her eyebrow and got up from her seat. She disappeared through a side door which led to the hallway back to the offices.

Crumwell, the care of his behaviour lost to drink, ran out of his own party to meet her. Nicóla stood in the dark, the sound of the party still echoing through the halls, with her arms folded over her chest, eyes cast to the stone floor.

'What?' he asked. 'What did Chapuys want? Do I need him killed?'

Nicóla looked up, a gentle smile. 'That could start a war, Tomassito. Chapuys came to give me news of the Pope. As far as Rome knows, the Convocation is still deciding on the articles of the submission. They will not receive this news for a while yet, God be praised. But, His Holiness has decided to send me a message through the Emperor's man; the Pope is angered I am here and not at home. I must write to the Pope to quell his temper.'

'But no one knows you are his daughter-in-law. Why is the Pope worried? What does it matter? The Medici have your dowry.'

'I am presupposed to be hither as a spy, as a potential assassin. Every time they hear Henry has stepped further from the Church, I fall from favour.'

'You gain favour hither. Soon the King shall be able to annul your marriage!'

'You jest, Tomassito. My marriage was ordained by the Pope in Rome. No signed papers can overthrow God's man on Earth.'

'I bet that is what the slimy Florentine thought when he bedded you as a child!'

Nicóla placed her hands on Crumwell's shoulders, her fingers toying with the chain around his neck. 'I was not a child; I was fit to be his bride, had he not become a bishop. You are drunk, Tomassito.'

'I can handle wine.'

'You are drunk on the power you gain by the day.'

'There is no line I can overstep, there is no issue in which I overreach.'

'Yes, you are drunk, on power and on wine. Take heart, my love, for your creatures are out there, gathering information, gaining strength, everything you need to inherit the kingdom. You must at all times appear moderate. Enjoy your party, enjoy all the courtiers wishing to place their noble lips on your backside.'

'Stay away from Chapuys. He means to have you. You blur the lines of gender and attract even the most pious men.'

'Are you jealous?' she grinned.

'I saw Chapuys gazing at your neck as you spoke, wanting his lips on your skin.'

Crumwell pushed Nicóla against the wall and brought his own lips to the soft skin of her throat. No one would ever take anything from Thomas Crumwell ever again.

~~~

Crumwell moved slightly as he sat at his desk; Nicóla had walked around behind his seat, and he paid no heed. Now she pulled at the collar of his shirt. The party had not seen their beds at all, talking until the sun rose and they needed to attend Mass. Now it was straight back to work; something Crumwell had done many nights prior.

'You are straightening me,' he stated.

'Yes, I am, so you can appear as a royal adviser and not a drunkard,' she said and carried on, back to her nearby desk. No one else was there; all the others out completing tasks.

'Ti comporti come una moglie.' It was true; she did act as a wife.

'Forse lo si desiderata cosi?'

'Yes, I do desire it so.'

Nicóla turned from her work and smiled. But a bang followed by footsteps heralded one of the gentleman-ushers. 'Master Crumwell, a messenger from the King.'

Crumwell clicked his fingers twice, and Sir William Brereton, one of Henry's most trusted courtiers, entered, causing Crumwell to stand at once. 'Crumwell, you are requested in the King's chambers immediately. Henry is most fixed upon anger.'

Crumwell strolled to the King's rooms; nothing was ever as serious as the King cared to think. There were two types of courtiers; the ones who were wastrels who barely lifted a finger and the others who believed the world was a scary place. Crumwell knew neither demeanor would serve in order to find success. Most of these men had never done a real day's work in their lives.

But when Crumwell reached the King's rooms, he was shown into the King's privy chamber. There Henry stood with his feet wide apart, his eyes wet with tears, not unlike the day he learned of Wolsey's death. Just a few steps from the King stood Sir Thomas More, a small wooden box in his hand. More too had the tears of a broken man, his black-clad shoulders drooped; his hands held the box as if it were about to catch fire. They looked to Crumwell with a mixture of surprise and anger. More could not look Crumwell in the eye. The King did not seem to find any words, his bottom lip protruding yet again.

'Your Majesty.' No emotion, no movements, no questions.

'Crumwell, please take the box from Sir Thomas,' the King instructed.

More handed the box to Crumwell and took the weight of it. He dared to peer inside, and recognised it at once; it was the Great Seal of Office. Only the Lord Chancellor of England could bestow the stamp which bore Henry's royal approval. Crumwell had watched on the day the Duke of Norfolk stripped Wolsey of the title and honour, and now the Seal was back in Crumwell's hands, where it belonged. Just the thought back to that day with Wolsey brought an intense pain in his chest. Mayhap the others in the room had similar aches.

'Your Majesty,' More said and bowed low. The King dismissed him and More swept from the room without a beady-eyed glance at Crumwell.

'The Lord Chancellor has resigned, Crumwell. More wishes to restore his health and live a private life with his family.'

Crumwell could not stand cold any longer. More was out of office, out of power! The highest role in the land now lay vacant. The most powerful royal advisor had run away. Shock brought Crumwell to standing straight. 'A surprise, Your Majesty!' Now the King's top post was empty, and Gardiner, the King's master secretary, had fallen from favour. The King was weak and alone without More, a companion and advisor of almost twenty years.

'Crumwell, you keep the Seal until we have found a replacement for the role of Lord Keeper.'

Lord Keeper of the Seal; a position not used for fifteen years. With Wolsey as Lord Chancellor, he kept the Seal. Suddenly, the King was thinking differently. Crumwell had the Seal of the King, the stamp which every paper in the land needed if it was to be petitioned to, or by, the King or parliament.

'Yes, Your Majesty. Is… is there anything else?'

King Henry trailed his fingers along the edge of the table beside him, his blue eyes still wet with worry. 'Twenty years, Thomas.'

Thomas. The King was calming again.

'More has supported me for twenty years. A grand man, a humanist, a layman who understood the Church and all its dealings. But this, my annulment, he will not support. More will not support the submission of the Church to me. He will not acknowledge that I am the head of the Church. More will forever support Queen Katherine.'

'I am sorry, Your Majesty.' More was gone; the evil More, the burner of reformers, was out. No one else would have to be tortured at More's homes, no one else burned alive for their beliefs. All the books Crumwell kept under lock and key at Austin Friars would not see him reduced to meat over a flame.

His golden eyes cast away from Henry's fingers on the wood, along the table, to see the chains of office More wore; the sacred Chain of Esses made to represent the Spiritus Sanctus. How More had coveted that livery collar, how More had wanted to wear it, with its gold Tudor rose pendant. He had left the chains of the office behind with the King. The King had lost another long-time partner, just as he had Wolsey several years before. No doubt Henry would grieve the loss of More's guidance just as he had grieved for Wolsey, no matter the anger he felt.

'You know, Thomas,' the King said and turned to look out the window, 'I know not if I am angry or if I am glad. Should I be pleased I have swept my enemy aside, or feel betrayed by my own friend?'

'I know I found it difficult when…' don't say his name aloud… 'the Cardinal passed away, even though I knew I could no longer be under his patronage, Your Majesty. The situation had changed so much I could not hold on to the past.'

'But we long for the past, do we not?'

'The past is a whole wide world, Your Majesty, filled with so many memories, so many possibilities and wisdom. The present is merely a view of what is in front of us.'

'And the future?'

'Boundless as the seas where the new world was just discovered.'

The King turned back to Crumwell and gave a gentle smile, eyes

still glazed with sadness. He scratched his orange beard and sighed.
'Perchance we stand at the edge of an eminent journey, Thomas.'

'I hope we do, Your Majesty.'

'There is no telling what could be next.'

'Yes, there is, Your Majesty. I can tell you. You are going to marry
the Lady Anne and I am going to plump your Exchequer.'

'I do admire you, Thomas. I know I can trust you.'

And you can make me the next Lord Chancellor, a baseborn man
ready to lead the realm.

Chapter 34 - June 1532
Whitehall Palace, London

Other people's seecryts can beest a business to avail oneself of

Nicóla chased after Crumwell through the hallways at Whitehall while holding his papers and struggled to pin back her ever-growing curls. She pushed her hair into her wide-brim hat but almost tripped on Crumwell's long black coat as she caught up to him.

'Cosa fai?' Crumwell asked over his shoulder, wondering what she was doing.

'Niente, Master Crumwella,' she said, flustered, and straightened herself. Nicóla was not doing anything, other than running late for her tasks, so unlike her. Crumwell walked so fast towards the King's rooms Nicóla could barely keep up with him. Even his walk was serious. The crowds parted, like Moses parting the sea, when Crumwell arrived; no one dared get in the way. It was time for the King to hear petitions and none could be done without Crumwell at his side, and Nicóla at his, writing for her master. Crumwell heard a petition, the King made a suggestion, Crumwell made a solution, and Nicóla readied the paperwork. But no quill could keep up with Crumwell's mind. God bless Ioci - the art of memory. Poor Ralph never quite kept up with Crumwell, even Nicóla struggled at times.

They got to the King's rooms, already flowing with people waiting their turn to speak to the King. Crumwell brushed through them all with Nicóla trailing him, people calling his name, hoping for a favour. Nicóla watched Crumwell stop and gesture to a handful and they followed him; all picked to go first with the King, while Henry's mood was still light, his attention still constant.

'Mr. Thomas Crumwell.'

No sooner than Crumwell's name was introduced, he breezed through the main doors into the King's presence and bowed, Nicóla copying behind him. 'Your Majesty.'

'Thomas,' the King replied and clapped his hands together. 'Tell me, is there much to be done today?'

'Always, Your Majesty, but I am sure we can settle accounts soon enough.'

Crumwell gestured to Nicóla over his shoulder, and she handed him his black leather satchel. With a single click of his fingers, he gestured her to get out of the way, to sit at a desk in the corner by the guards so they could begin.

'How do you do it, Thomas?' Nicóla heard the King mutter. She pretended not to hear a thing, only ready to take notes.

'Precisely what, Your Majesty?'

'Mr. Frescobaldi. Do you not get an earful for treating your secretary so… so…'

Nicóla crept up behind Crumwell, needing to hand him one extra note for the King. 'How you can treat a lover as a servant. I believe that is what His Majesty means,' she said gently to Crumwell. Nicóla could not speak directly to the King without invitation.

'You are glowing, Mr. Frescobaldi,' the King said to her. 'Always a pleasure to see Crumwell's creature.'

'Thank you, Your Majesty, you are so kind to welcome me. It is such a pleasure to be hither. Master Crumwella may speak to me as he pleases, without risk of this "earful" you speak of.'

Crumwell threw her a furrow of his brow; leave. Nicóla scurried to a desk and pulled out the papers. She too had a handful of messages given to her as they left Crumwell's office, several addressed to her. Nicóla pulled open the first one without making any sound; words from a friend who lived in Venice, a spice trader popular with her father years ago.

'Master Crumwella,' she begged as she read. He turned, his eyebrows raised in surprise. She dashed to him and handed him the letter. She watched Crumwell's eyes skim the words from Luca Accardo, hastily written in Italian.

'Ti fidi di questo uomo?' he muttered.

Trust Luca? 'Si, completamente.'

'Your Majesty,' Crumwell said, 'I have hither a note from a foreign creature of… mine… saying there are plans to fortify the city of Venice, as an assault from the Turks is imminent.'

'Terrific news! As long as the Emperor is fighting the Turks, he is less burdened with what happens with my marriage. Excellent work, Thomas. You have so many eyes out there.'

'Anche a Roma sono interessati e preparati,' Nicóla whispered.

'Even Rome is worried and preparing for war, Your Majesty,' Crumwell repeated.

'You are full of good news,' Henry said, and slapped Crumwell on the shoulder, before turning back to this throne under his cloth of estate. 'Thomas, there are several men in the Tower under charges of heresy. I need to assess their guilt and decide on their punishments. I want naught to do with it; More was handling them. Can you decide if they deserve the death penalty or not? They can all be hanged at Tyburn; I have a distaste for burnings and none shall deserve quartering, I suspect. They shall have to be interrogated.'

'Certainly, Your Majesty.'

Nicóla gritted her teeth as she made notes for later. Sending men to their deaths; vile. Crumwell's morals never seemed to follow a similar vein of dread for the subject. But at least Crumwell would refrain from burning anyone for their perceived crimes.

The King gestured for the double doors behind Crumwell to be opened and the noise of the waiting masses echoed into the room. But as Crumwell went to take his place standing by the King's side, he said, 'no, Thomas, please come and stand in front of me.' Crumwell stood before the King, his face a scant anxious, much unlike him. His thumb rubbed the inside of the Wolsey ring on his forefinger, as he did when worried.

'Mr. Thomas Crumwell,' the King said, changing into his more formal tone. Nicóla grabbed her quill as the men in the antechamber silenced and looked on in curiosity. 'I am appointing you the Clerk of the Hanaper of Chancery. It comes with a salary of £60 per year, plus a daily due for expenses.'

A hush of whispers came from the antechamber at the sum. All petitions to the King needed to be placed in the Hanaper basket. Now Crumwell controlled the Hanaper personally. Bribes would flow like a river.

'As you are currently in possession of the Great Seal, you can be the one to decide which papers are legally stamped and you shall be known at court as Royal Keeper of the Great Seal. Men who present papers to you may wish to pay you extra to receive the Royal Seal, pay you a personal financial incentive. This is on top of the Seal fee, and all I ask is that you give the crown ten percent of any incentives.'

'I am deeply grateful to Your Majesty for this role.'

'But I need a special patent written up and it will need the Great Seal, and I ask you do not charge me for the use of your services.'

'It will be a pleasure, Your Majesty.'

'It most certainly will, Mr. Crumwell. I believe you are the only man I can truly trust with this honour. You shall not fail me as Wolsey and More did.'

Crumwell bowed to the King before taking his place by his side. He briefly turned to Nicóla and showed just a second of his smug grin, a flash of his golden eyes, before he could resume his duties.

A young messenger flew into the chamber with the power of a swooping hawk. 'Your Majesty, Your Majesty!' he panted and bowed low, his hat falling from his dark head.

'Pray speak,' Crumwell commanded.

'Your Majesty, I come hither to inform you of the death of the Archbishop of Canterbury. Archbishop Warham died in the night, Your Majesty. Warham went to Kent to visit his nephew, the Archdeacon of Canterbury, and passed away from illness. He seemed unwell for some time, and God has taken him from this Earth.'

Henry made the sign of the cross and everyone obeyed. He dismissed the boy with a distracted wave and leaned back on his throne. Henry glared at Crumwell, the two men just pausing to take in the news. 'After all this time, we get the Church to accept my authority over the Pope, and then Warham goes and drops dead,' the King laughed. 'Does God think this amusing?'

'Warham was such a pliable man, well, until recently. He had prepared to meet his maker, given how overly pious he seemed these last years. Perchance breaking the Church's power was too much for his heart to bear.'

'Now we will need another archbishop,' Henry sighed. 'First, we need to send out an official announcement of Warham's death.'

'Cranmer,' Nicóla coughed.

'There is always Thomas Cranmer, Your Majesty,' Crumwell

presupposed. 'You know Cranmer is most confident of you as Supreme Ruler over the Church of England. In fact, he suggested we make your "Great Matter" a theological one in the first instance.'

'I also sent him to Rome to persuade the Holy Roman Emperor into supporting an annulment, and has found no success.'

'Nessuno può cambiare la mente dell'Imperatore,' Nicóla said, not glancing up from her paperwork.

'No one could change the Emperor's mind, Your Majesty,' Crumwell repeated to the King in Nicóla's place.

'Mr. Frescobaldi,' Henry said and Nicóla jumped to her feet and bowed before him. 'Tell me of the Pope. How are things between him and the Emperor?' The King was kind enough to keep his voice low.

'Relations remain the same, Your Majesty, as far as I am awares. I spoke with Ambassador Chapuys just yesterday, and it seems the Emperor and the Pope have mere triflings to speak of at present. Queen Katherine herself ordered her nephew never to use force against England. They have their own problems in Italy. Rome is a cesspit of vice and corruption. If the Emperor has time to chatter with Chapuys in letters about me being hither at court, then they are not focused on your business. Let them idly talk. Let them be invaded by the Turks. We all know alliances come and go with more fragility than the emotions of a woman.'

Both Henry and Crumwell laughed at the comment. 'The new piece of legislation Master Crumwell prepared,' Nicóla bluffed. She knew Crumwell minded her speaking freely. Their minds were much similar beasts. 'A Statute... of Restraint of Appeals,' she said, giving a name to a law they had only thought of in passing. 'A petition which states no one can appeal to Rome on any spiritual matter under pain of praemunire.' Nicóla gritted her teeth and prayed Crumwell take the lead.

'Tell me more,' the King said to Crumwell. Nicóla watched Crumwell's mind at work, as if planning an entire legislation on the spot. 'England is an empire and ruled under one king, who in one person, rules entirely in both matters of Church and State. The King shall be answerable to no one but God, as he is the ruler of his realm. Your stature shall be dignified and you hold your rightful place in Europe, a supreme leader of men.'

Nicóla could not help but smile as Crumwell explained himself as if he had it in mind for months, but all out of his mind and mouth in a matter of seconds.

'I should decide on the matter of my annulment, the Archbishop of Canterbury should decide, not the Pope. An archbishop we now no longer have.'

'We could write to Thomas Cranmer and recall him from the court of Emperor. After all, England is an empire also, and Cranmer could serve this Imperial crown, not the one of Rome.'

'The Imperial Crown of England,' Henry said, and Nicóla could almost see what Henry imagined; himself as an absolute ruler. 'Make all my decisions for today, I need time to work on my own matters. Send out a message about the death of Archbishop Warham, and then send out a letter to Cranmer; is it time he came home.'

Nicóla again scurried through court as Crumwell returned to his own chambers. People chased after the pair, eager for Crumwell to hear their petition, if the King would not. Several men handed Nicóla letters and she took them as she and Crumwell disappeared inside their own rooms.

'Statute of Restraint of Appeals!' Crumwell cried at her the moment they stood in the offices. Several clerks and accountants peered up from their desks as Crumwell passed them towards the private office, his voice strong as always.

'A vain attempt to win favour?' Nicóla offered as she dropped Crumwell's papers back on his desk. 'Master…'

'All of you! Leave!' Crumwell yelled and the half-dozen clerks all scattered away from his private office. Nicóla stood before him in silence, her hands folded together; how was it to be on the wrong end of Crumwell's temper?

'Your logic is brilliant once again!' Crumwell yelled and clapped his hands together with joy. 'I wish I thought of it myself.'

'You did, or so the King thinks. You are the man who explained it to him.' Nicóla paused as she pulled open the first new letter from her desk, believing him not angry.

'With Warham dead, there is so much possibility ahead. With Cranmer in place, we could get the King his annulment after all. If I do not, I could find my head struck off, or banished such as More. And Lord knows what the King would do to you, Nicó.'

Nicóla paused for a moment as she read. 'I have a letter hither from a man claiming to be Cardinal Wolsey's son, one Thomas

Winter. He asks for a loan of £100, as he is much in trouble and knows you have attained a dignity such you can save your friends as you please.'

Crumwell sank into his chair behind his desk. Nicóla watched him fiddle with his Wolsey ring again. Some wounds could not just heal and disappear; Nicóla knew herself. 'Send him £100 pounds from my personal account. No need for a loan. No, I will write him myself.'

'Of course.' Nicóla let him take a moment and she tore open another letter. 'Word from shaky-hands Gardiner.'

'Is he complaining how much his diocese has to pay the King again? Taxes are taxes.'

'No, he needs your help.'

'He needs me to be of service?' Crumwell snorted. 'God's blood.'

'Gardiner has signed a treaty with France, but it needs the Great Seal. He fears all his work in France shall be undone without the Seal, and seems most worried. He asks you get his commissary, John Oliver, to be present with you before the King when it is presented. It is luck indeed that you are now the Keeper of the Great Seal.'

'Gardiner brags about going to France to sign an aid treaty, a better one than Wolsey ever could commission, and now is running back to me for help?'

Nicóla tossed the paperwork on her desk. 'All this, and now your new promotion to the Hanaper is dismissed.'

'The fees will not be dismissed,' Crumwell said. 'I have the Seal and a lengthy number of legal documents require the Seal. We get to decide who gets the Seal on their patents and their grants. This is power, and comes with side payments to ensure success and speed.'

'You mean bribes going in your pocket.'

'More bribes going in my pocket. As if there are not enough people thinking they can buy my favour.'

'Let them continue to try,' Nicóla replied. 'We shall expand all of Austin Friars and add more properties on bribes alone.'

'It is a golden age, my love. We can have clerks to do the work with the Great Seal, so we get the money and do little in return.'

'I can officiate, Tomassito. It is no worry to dispense precious legality.'

'And let us see what this patent the King requires us to issue on his behalf, all with the Great Seal. Someone is probably going to get a title. It shall be rude of us to charge the King to use his own Seal.'

'Us?' Nicóla asked.

'Us.' Crumwell leaned forward in his seat and looked Nicóla square in the eye. 'Do not think you are sliding away from me, Nicó. I need that fine mind of yours.'

'I am not going anywhere.'

Crumwell jumped from his chair and rounded his desk to Nicóla's. He pulled her into his arms and held her tightly against him. The soft trim of his black coat tickled the tip of her nose. He sighed deeply, his chest rising and falling with her head against it, one hand tight on her back, the other on the back of her head. 'Tutta bene?' she asked.

'Yes, I am all right. We are surrounded by greed and vice. The King talks endlessly about love, yet seems not to understand it. He marries a woman and grows bored. So many men grow bored as they are matched to people for money, not love. They parade around with harlots and talk of lust, and the King lusts for Anne but calls it love. Love is comfort and trust. It is respect and truth and loyalty. I have all those things and I never want to let you go.'

'Praise to God you shall never have to. Let others lose their heads in this battle.'

Chapter 35 -September 1532
Windsor Palace, Berkshire

Seecryts maketh boundaries and only danger cometh to those without boundaries

'Thank you.'

Crumwell turned to Gardiner beside him, one eyebrow raised. 'Excuse me?'

Bishop Gardiner cleared his throat and looked at his feet. He stood in his bishop's purple, his hat perched on his short dark hair, always too far forward on his huge forehead. 'I said, thank you, for your service with the legalities of the French mutual aid treaty. All will be signed and witnessed.'

'I know; I am the one taking care of the signing. You are most welcome, Stephen,' Crumwell said through gritted teeth, not letting his fake smile droop. He clutched patents rolled up in his hands, the wax of the King's Seal still warm. He too bore a new outfit, black as usual, the best satin and velvet he could find at short notice, the fox fur lining cost a small fortune. Nicóla had placed his black square cap on his head so tenderly, as a mother to a child, a smile to show her pride. As his waistline began to catch up with his age, Crumwell often worried Nicóla no longer found any carnal attraction in him. It was a worry for a man half his age.

'You have no need to make a fuss,' Gardiner replied as he regarded the great hall of Windsor Castle, filled with nobility all dressed in their best. Henry and Anne had been at Windsor on progress for much of the summer. 'You have risen quite high at court, but you could fall again at any moment.'

'Unlike you, Stephen; from Wolsey's secretary all the way to bishop and diplomat. You cannot lose your papal skirts... oh, my misstep; you indeed can. Just as Wolsey did when you abandoned him to work for the King.'

'You are no better,' Gardiner muttered through a stiff smile. 'You charged to court the moment Wolsey was banished.'

'At least I cared about Wolsey.'

The conversation broke off at the announcement of the King, who walked the aisle between the standing courtiers, to come to his throne under the gold cloth of estate, where Crumwell and Gardiner stood together. Henry wore clothes of white and red silk, with a golden livery collar with the biggest diamond pendant Crumwell had ever seen, the size of a walnut. Henry took his place standing before his throne and its plush golden cushion, and his accompanying lords stood to one side, all dressed with the crowns of their dukedoms and earldoms. Anne's father Thomas Boleyn, first Earl of Wiltshire stood triumphant, and gave Crumwell a slight gesture of acknowledgment as he lined up. Next to him stood Boleyn's brother-in-law Thomas Howard, the Duke of Norfolk. Crumwell endless nemesis Charles Brandon, the Duke of Suffolk was there, meaning his wife, Henry's sister Mary was nearby. Also up the aisle came Edward Lee, Archbishop of York and John Stokesley, Bishop of London who came to stand next to Gardiner. Everyone of note was present on such a propitious day.

Crumwell skimmed the crowd for a moment and caught sight of Nicóla, Ralph and Richard, all present today. Even though the weather was warm, Nicóla wore the new full-length black coat lined in fox fur with the pearl-studded hat he gifted her, eager to never let it out of her sight. The French ambassador stood close to Nicóla, seeming weary, ready to go home and take up the role of Bishop of Paris, or so Crumwell's creatures told him. As expected, Eustace Chapuys was not present. Neither was Sir Thomas More, both men rumoured to be illegally visiting Queen Katherine.

A double bang for silence and Lady Anne Boleyn's name was announced. She appeared in the entranceway and began her walk, no, her parade, between all those at court. She regarded left and right, making sure everyone important was there. Even the cherished

Princess Mary, the Dowager of Queen of France, Henry's sister and Suffolk's wife attended, and Mary despised Anne. Everyone had to be at court today to see Anne in her splendor. Crumwell could price Anne up, given the amount of cloth she wore; a dress of crimson velvet lined with gold embroidery. Her dark hair flowed freely down her back, all how a queen should appear at her coronation. She was all but a queen today, given the patents Crumwell had just written and sealed on the King's behalf, his "special" patents. Anne made her walk, with her cousin Countess Mary Howard of Derby one step behind. The Howard girl helped Anne kneel before the King in her gown, a knee pillow on the floor for her comfort.

Crumwell handed Gardiner the patents, and everyone wanted to hear Gardiner's pronouncement. The King gestured to the Bishop, who stepped forward.

'On this day, the first day of September 1532, Henry the Eighth, by the grace of God, King of England, Wales and France, Defender of the Faith and Lord of Ireland, today by patents hereby creates Anne Boleyn, daughter of the first Earl of Wiltshire, the Marquess of Pembroke. Also, lands in Wales, to the value of £1,000 per year.'

Mary Howard helped Anne stand, and the King stepped down to place a golden coronet and red mantle on Anne, his smile as strong as the steady gaze on her. He applied the white ermine cloak around her shoulders, to match his own, and those of her father, uncle, and Suffolk. Court rules were clear; only royalty could wear ermine. Anne would be the first woman to be awarded a title in her own right. The title had belonged to none since the death of Jasper Tudor, Henry's great-uncle, forty years ago. It showed how strong Henry's affection was for Anne. In his turbulent mind, Henry thought himself already annulled from Katherine. Crumwell had thought so many a time recently, the way Henry spoke, always hasty, always with a sense of urgency. Anne was noble now; a legitimate option for Queen of England. The court applauded as Henry handed Anne the two patents pertaining her title and lands, and Gardiner slipped away from Crumwell.

'I need to go and officiate Mass for the King,' he muttered, and the Bishops of York and London followed like obedient dogs. They almost moved alike a snake towards prey, much like the movements of Anne's father.

Suffolk coasted towards Crumwell, and Crumwell tried hard not to roll his eyes with irritation. 'Your Grace,' he said, his back straight, his eyes narrow, tone curt.

'You wrote the patents, Crumwell?'

'Yes, I am a lawyer.'

'Is it true Anne's title shall be transferred to her male heirs, whether or not they are born legitimate?'

'Yes, Your Grace, idle rumour does you well.'

'But children must be born legitimate to inherit a noble title.'

'Not this time; the King requested this particular change.'

'Henry means to get a child on Anne at once,' Suffolk said, and sniffed, sounding wet and ill. Crumwell took a step away. 'It also means Henry is not totally certain he can marry Anne yet.'

'The King shall have Anne at once,' Crumwell sighed. 'Now he has thanked her for waiting, I doubt Anne shall hold out on him for much longer. A man such as Henry not satisfied in bed all these years? By God, Anne had better be all Henry hopes.'

'After such a wait, any woman would satisfy. Then mayhap he shall finally give up Anne. Henry always loved the thrill of the chase.'

'Perchance he means to enjoy the thrill of the catch for a change,' Crumwell said and Suffolk scoffed with laughter.

'Has any man enjoyed such?'

'I have,' Crumwell muttered, looking out to see Nicóla, who spoke with Sir Francis Weston, a young man who worked in King Henry's privy chamber. Rumours suggested Weston adored Anne Boleyn, stared at her most often, though so many men at court did, part of what Henry loved about her. Next to Weston stood Sir William Brereton, a boorish man of similar years to Crumwell. Brereton regarded Nicóla up and down constantly and it caused Crumwell's heart to tremor. Nicóla's hair was much long these days, that of a woman. Perchance Brereton felt suspicious, as she appeared more feminine than usual. Mayhap he preferred the company of men. Such happened at court all too often, even in men who claimed to have never tried the "double wick" style of lust.

'You?' Suffolk said, and tried to spot who Crumwell watched in the crowd. 'People talk of your loathing at vice, how virtuous you are, but have you taken a lover, Crumwell?'

'They pronounce me not a man of vice? Sir, I am a banker, a lawyer, a politician. If men did not enjoy vice, I would be out of a job! Speaking of such, one of the men in your household, he has borrowed a sum from me and has not made his payments.'

'Well, do as you must,' Suffolk replied and left the conversation, to attend private Mass with the King and his new Marquess.

A double click of the fingers and Nicóla and Richard all fell into line behind Crumwell, with Ralph trailing behind, still repulsed by Nicóla, though silent, while they made their way from the main hall to their apartments.

'Well, that is one more noble we have sucking off the King's teat,' Crumwell commented as they walked.

'I suspect the King wants Anne sucking off more than the royal teat,' Richard jested.

'Idle talk has its uses,' Crumwell replied. 'What have you heard?'

'I heard there are some peasants on the northern lands getting restless. They do not want their Queen thrown out for a whore such as Anne Boleyn,' Richard replied, his voice low in the crowd.

'Solution?' Crumwell asked the group.

'A travelling company of actors,' Nicóla said slowly, 'and they act out stories written by someone such as Thomas Wyatt, talking of the King's love of his common sweetheart. Everyone enjoys a story of people rising high, do they not?' Nicóla asked.

'I love that idea, and it keeps Wyatt in work. Wyatt does so get long in the face with woe when not writing,' Richard laughed.

'I hear Elizabeth Seymour, one of Anne's ladies, is with child, making Anne anxious about giving the King a son. Lady Elizabeth, now Sir Anthony Ughtred's wife, is less than half Anne's age, only fourteen. Ughtred is more than triple his wife's age. Have Lady Elizabeth removed from court,' Nicóla suggested.

'Marriage can be such an ugly contract,' Crumwell sighed as they went to their chambers. 'There is a boy in Suffolk's household, a groom who has not paid his debts. Suffolk has granted permission for us to be more assertive with the collection.'

'I am merry to go and speak with him,' Nicóla said and rubbed her hands with joy.

'What are you going to do? Talk endlessly with your fine deceptions until his tiny mind bursts?' Ralph teased her.

'Now!' Crumwell snapped at Ralph and stopped, the group forming a tight circle. 'Richard, Ralph, go and see the boy, you know who I mean. Perchance with a twist of his arm, a punch his ribs shall entice him to pay.'

'Why cannot I go and deal with this?' Nicóla said, hands on hips in an attempt to stand as tall as the men around her.

'Because, the entire court of two thousand people is going to France in only a few weeks, and we have to make sure all is ready. You understand preparing ships for transport, which is vital. I need you at work. Men, go and be generous to our non-payer. All of you in return can attend the King's feast tonight.'

Ralph and Richard headed off with happy faces, and Nicóla trailed behind Crumwell to their apartments. Once in their sheltered rooms, with only a few people at work with writing letters, Nicóla let out a sigh.

'What be this?' Crumwell asked. 'You want me to send you out to collect payment?'

'I am not weak, Tomassito! I can fight, I can use a sword, a knife, a bow. Let me do the work of the others.'

'The only weapon you need is in your head.' Crumwell longed to kiss her soft olive cheek, but could not with clerks in the room, so he changed to Italian. 'If you are lucky, one day you can come to the Tower when interrogating someone for the King.'

'Un tale dono,' Nicóla spat.

'Yes, it is such a gift! It is hard enough for me to keep you, Ralph and Richard separated, Nicó.'

'We cannot work together because you ruined everything with the truth, Master Crumwella!'

'That was almost a year ago! When shall you forgive me?'

'When Ralph and Richard accept my frailties!'

Crumwell ran his hand over his mouth and turned back to English. 'Soon we will have our Queen on the throne and shall be so prosperous that we can all reconcile.'

'Perchance, with the Lord's mercy,' Nicóla sighed.

~~~

Crumwell yawned as he made his way back to the King's privy chamber. It was only time for dinner and yet he felt so drained. So much work to do, not enough hours. And being away in France for two weeks was of no use at all. But the King needed to show off his prize – the newly ennobled Anne Boleyn. Crumwell headed into the antechamber, to find Edward Lee, Archbishop of York. Lee had taken up the role when Wolsey died. The two men knew little of one another, though Crumwell knew Lee to be a follower of Queen Katherine, an excellently educated fellow. But Lee approached Crumwell as if they were much allied, which could only mean one thing.

'Master Crumwell,' Lee said, 'you are well met. I am finished with the King.'

Crumwell smiled, his familiar greedy smirk. 'Can I be of service, Archbishop?'

'I was wondering, about the situation with borrowing money… you see, the Archbishop of York is a pleasing role, but sometimes there can be a deficit.'

'Write out your needs, and send it directly to me, Archbishop. Worry no more and repayment shall not be necessary.' Honestly, these men had no sense with money. It made Crumwell's life too easy. 'Perchance you could repay my favour with some advice?'

'Of course.'

'I have a business associate, a man who wishes to marry, however, the woman is already married.'

'In the eyes of God, they are joined for life.'

'Is it difficult to prove nonconsummation for grounds for an annulment?'

'Proof can be difficult. Any children?'

'There are no children between this couple. The woman he wishes to marry has given birth, but through another man.'

'One could argue the child is pre-contract, or proof of prior affinity. All sounds most bawdry. The Pope could issue an annulment.'

'Do we have to ask the Pope this question? Can it not be issued in England?'

'No, without an English cardinal, and after the death poor Wolsey, as you know, we do not have someone capable of this decision in England.'

'Thank you, Archbishop Lee,' Crumwell said and turned to enter the King's rooms. Crumwell already knew all of this, but it never hurt to ask.

A short wait and Crumwell appeared before the King, all ready for the feast, glittering in gold and pearls.

'Ah, Thomas,' Henry said as he signed something at his desk. 'I wanted to thank you for the ceremony today.'

'My pleasure, Your Majesty. It was an honourable occasion.'

'You will join the feast? You are king of parties after all.'

'Thank you, Your Majesty.'

'Bring your Italian Waif and anyone else you wish. You have worked admirably these past months, Thomas. I need your support. How are plans for the trip to France?'

'Going well, Your Majesty. No issues have arisen.'

'Splendid. I wish there was a way I could thank you for your work. All the information you gain from your creatures, all your advice.'

'Well…'

'Name it and it is yours.'

This was Crumwell's chance. 'I am Master of the Jewel House, Your Majesty, and I have gone over the item list.'

'There is something you covet.'

'I shall pay, of course, Your Majesty, the full value. A ruby ring.'

'Did it belong to my mother?'

'No, confiscated from an arrested heretic in the Tower several years ago.'

'If it is not one of my mother's, then take it,' Henry said with a wave of his hand, and then pulled himself up from the desk. 'Have it marked down as a personal gift from me to you. Do the paperwork and sign it all yourself.'

'As I said, Your Majesty…'

'No, no payment; you admire it, so take it. Though, you wear a ruby ring, do you not? The ring you got from Wolsey, the ring which magically controls me?'

'We know better than to believe superstition, Your Majesty. And the ring is turquoise.'

'I like you, Thomas. You have brought my life from the darkness into the light with your ideas and your plots. Soon I shall present Anne to the King of France, and gain his approval of our marriage. I once spoke to you about the ache of having love denied but no more. I hope you are as unburdened from the ache of love denied as I?'

'I am of great cheer, Your Majesty. Also, the jewel-encrusted livery collar which you ordered shall be ready in time for the trip to France.'

'Excellent. We are on the verge of the golden age you spoke of, Thomas. You shall get me a new queen. We will change England.'

Or lose his head if he did not secure said new queen.

Chapter 36 - October 1532
Calais, English territories of France

Oft seecryts provided successes but only at whych hour patience is observed

Nicóla did not visit Calais in the two years since her ship stopped there while ferrying baby Jane to England. The tiny port, a haven of England in France, now held the entire English court. No part of France gained any love from Nicóla. Cold, damp. French people. Eustace Chapuys said the same thing constantly, while always inviting himself to dine with Crumwell. Everyone wanted to dine with Crumwell these days. A whisper in his ear here, a passing of a bag of coins there, a concealed note in every handshake. Such was the life of all those in the Crumwell household now.

Nicóla stayed with Ralph and Richard in Calais when King Henry set off for Boulogne, to meet King Francis. Crumwell had no choice but to accompany the King, for they needed to create deals on the trip, an informal meeting with most formal connotations. Henry needed the support of Francis, another European king pushing at the Pope for an English annulment. What Francis wanted in return, Nicóla knew not.

While suffering a long wet week in Calais, Crumwell and Nicóla drafted a letter to Pope Clement, a "personal note" from Nicóla, requesting the appointment for Thomas Cranmer as Archbishop. Cranmer was appointed and informed, and on a ship back to England. But still, Pope Clement needed to endorse the appointment. Nicóla wrote to the Pope, stating Cranmer was nobody, a nothing, too weak to affect any change in England, and thus shall prevent the King annulling or reforming anything. Nicóla still needed to seem an agreeable spy in the English court in order to stay with Crumwell. The trouble was, lying had become such a way of life. Nicóla understood politics well enough; lying was part of the job. But it was always trying. And Nicóla felt increasingly consumed all the time. She missed baby Jane, not so a baby any longer, back in London. One thing Nicóla much suffered was a sick feeling for her home, and after finding a haven in Austin Friars and the English court, two weeks stuck in Calais did her mood no favours. So tired, French food making her ill, and even lonely, in a court of thousands of witty people eager to see her master, made a worn secretary to the King's advisor.

'Is there something wrong with this wine?' Nicóla wondered.

She sat at a table in Crumwell's rooms, drinking with Ralph and Richard, in need of a break from the work and noise of the trip. Ralph had not spoken to Nicóla for the entire year, work able to separate them. Crumwell left the group with strict orders to stay together in his absence. Even after almost twenty years of caring for Ralph, Crumwell had worn low on patience for Ralph's discomfort around Nicóla.

'It be fine, for French wine,' Ralph mumbled.

'When will you tell Master Crumwell you wish to marry one of his laundress girls?' Richard asked Ralph as he scratched his chin beneath his dark beard.

'I shall pick my moment,' Ralph replied.

'Wait until Anne is presented to King Francis,' Nicóla suggested. 'If all goes well, Master Crumwella will be in a reputable state. If not, it can cheer him, hopefully. Your romance has bloomed this year?'

'I am certain Master Crumwell will be saddened if he cannot marry me to a fitting house. He is as a father to me. I owe Master Crumwell my life,' Ralph argued. 'Already, thanks be to you, Nicóla, I am out of Master Crumwell's favour.'

'You cannot blame Nicóla,' Richard said. 'I am sure, had I not married in my youth, Master Crumwell would seek to marry me off to a noble house as well.'

'I rather think Master Crumwella shall be pleased to have you married to your own choice,' Nicóla said with a yawn. 'It will be young Gregory who is gifted a well-placed marriage.'

'Has Master Crumwell not sought to marry you to someone?' Ralph asked her.

'Who shall have me?' Nicóla shrugged. At least they were speaking. 'No one wishes to marry the Waif, Crumwella's creature.' She paused, thought of home. 'In fact, gentlemen, I have been married. I am your age, Richard. I was betrothed at a young age, but it came to naught. But another offer came up; my father accepted the match. My betrothed was ten years younger than myself, so I needed to wait. My father then died, and I was forced to honour the pre-contract, as my father-in-law gained control of my inheritance.'

'So you are married still?' Ralph frowned.

'Sadly, I am.'

'Does Master Crumwell know?'

'He does.'

'You are estranged?'

'My husband has an amante ufficiale, an official mistress, and bastard children are not shamed in Florence. I was declared a bastard, my husband is a bastard, his father also.'

'Will you ever go home to Italy?' Richard asked. Both men's complexions resembled pies fallen from the kitchen window, such was the surprise of Nicóla's confession to marriage.

'I know not,' Nicóla shrugged and placed her cup on the table. 'I am no different to the Lady Anne, a wife and yet not quite. I am akin to Queen Katherine, a wife, and yet forgotten.'

'Does your husband not wish to see his daughter?' Ralph asked.

'You mean Jane? No, she is not a consequence of marriage. As I said, the Italians do not look so harshly upon bastards. My dowry was so large my husband's family happily overlooked Giovanna, as she is known there.'

'And Master Crumwell knows all of this?' Richard asked.

'Well indeed. Master Crumwella is a decent man and an honest man. He took the time to listen; he understands the climate from which all this occurred.'

'Shall you ever go home, be removed to your husband?'

'If my place hither was no more, perchance. Florence is my home. And my husband is the Duke of Florence.'

Richard spit his wine down his doublet; Ralph's eyes almost fell from his face.

'Oh, Richard, do you know how long it took me to source grey velvet in such a dark shade?' Nicóla chided him. 'At your request!'

'You are the Duchess of Florence?' Ralph asked, suspicious now more than ever. The Duchess of Florence dressed as a man the English court, drank as a man at the English court, gambled as a man at the English court.

'Well indeed. Alessandro was raised the son of Lorenzo de' Medici, the Duke of Urbino, but his real father is his uncle, Pope Clement.'

'The Pope has a son?'

'Yes, His Holiness got a child on a servant girl just as he reached his majority, though he was already destined for the Church. His Holiness had a handsome dark son, and his nephew's family raised the child as a bastard.'

'The Pope is your father-in-law!' Ralph cried.

'Shh,' Nicóla whispered. 'Yes, that is true.'

'Does Master Crumwella know?'

'Yes, so does the King. I am not permitted to leave England; I am not permitted to leave Master Crumwella's sight. Or I shall end my days in the Tower.'

'You are almost a hostage.'

'A merry hostage,' Nicóla shrugged. 'I would rather work for Master Crumwella than return home.'

'You defy the will of God at every turn, Nicóla!' Ralph spat at her. 'You deny God, you deny your husband, you bear bastard children… you drag our master into such vile sin! You deserve to burn, you witch!'

'But,' Richard interrupted, his dark brow furrowed again, 'who is Jane's father?'

The door opened into the room and without a greeting, Crumwell clicked his fingers twice. None were ready for their master's return. 'Ralph, Richard, leave before I disown you both!'

In a second, Richard and Ralph abandoned their wine and Crumwell took a seat next to Nicóla. Ralph threw Nicóla one more angry scowl as the door banged shut. Crumwell waited until their footsteps faded from the door before he kissed his beloved.

'I have a gift for you. A full-length overcoat, in the French fashion with the puffed shoulders. It is the darkest green I have ever sourced, and lined and collared with white lynx fur. But the godless words I heard from Ralph were so harsh that nothing could cheer you now.'

'What cost by the yard for this green fabric?'

Crumwell laughed and kissed her again. 'You are most welcome. Nicó, I need to hear all during my absence. Has Ralph been this awful the whole week? No, first, I am sorry to say I have some difficult news to bear.'

'Did plans with King Francis not go well?'

'Yes and no. King Francis does support Henry's marriage to Lady Anne. He shall send two French cardinals to Rome, to plead on Henry's behalf. The cardinals wish to make fast, for Francis' son, a marriage to Catherine de' Medici.'

'Lorenzo de' Medici's bastard daughter. She is young and beautiful. She was raised alongside Alessandro, as her half-brother.'

'Catherine's marriage is being discussed as we speak. There is the talk of the Pope, King Francis, and King Henry all meeting together in France, to discuss supporting one another's marriage requests.'

'I am so sorry, Tomassito, but I fail to see why this is ruinous news. This is foreign support for the annulment.'

'A party was sent from Italy to talk of Catherine de' Medici's marriage. They are travelling with the French court.'

'You are worried I shall be seen by the envoy?' Nicóla suggested. 'I suppose it is possible, but on pain of death everyone who knows my truth is sworn to secrecy by the Pope. But most people believe Nicóla and Nicóletta to be two different people.'

'The envoy; Catherine de' Medici's brother is in attendance.'

It brought burning to her lungs. Suddenly they acted as if caught under the hooves of a horse. All that awful wine needed to return from her stomach. 'The Duke of Florence is sent to ready the marriage of King Francis' son to Catherine de' Medici?'

'I have already seen Alessandro de' Medici with my own eyes. With skin as dark as his, he is hard to miss. I admit him to be the first dark-skinned noble I have seen.'

'In Christendom, he is probably the first dark-skinned nobleman, hence his nickname.'

'Il Moro. He does not appear Moorish.'

Nicóla just shrugged. 'I do not burden myself with his appearance.' But this was no simple thing; her husband was at the French court. But Alessandro would never unmask her disguise; he would be too ashamed to admit to being married to the creature. 'What be my orders?'

'Orders?' Crumwell asked, and knelt before Nicóla in her chair. 'I will not give you orders. I want you to stay away from the Medici.'

'What if one of the conditions of the marriage… is me?'

Crumwell looked to the floor, his gaze cold, his complexion hard. 'Tell me, Tomassito.'

'Henry already agreed to send you back to Florence. As a gesture of favour to the Pope. Henry will do anything to get his annulment.'

'King Henry is going to give me up, so Francis can get his son married to Catherine de' Medici, and Henry can have Anne.'

'That is part of the deal, yes.'

'So their marriages shall come at the expense of me being handed back to Alessandro de' Medici, the bastard whom nobody ever loved. Wicked and sinful, a devil dressed in fine clothes and touted as a gentleman. Perchance I am well-suited to him, for I am a bastard and wicked through.'

'I must confess not knowing the cure to this yet.'

'It is simple.' Tears came to Nicóla's eyes, the soul sucked from her chest. The day would always come. 'I should go home to Florence. Why should I stay with you and cause you trouble? Tomassito, you are rising fast, even the Pope knows it. You do not need me around your neck like a curse any longer.'

'You would give me up?' Crumwell sat on his knees, every year of his age lined upon his face. He seemed to age before Nicóla's very eyes.

'Only if you desire to be free of me. You are not a man of sin. You are not some foul courtier who gives guards a few coins and goes to plow a girl behind curtains at a court party. You are an unblemished person, and hiding the Waif in your care does you no credit.'

'I could rule the English court without you, Nicó, but I shall be worse for it. I love you.'

'Henry loves Anne, and it is tearing a kingdom to pieces.'

'And I shall rebuild it better. Who knows, perchance we have not many years left. The time for piety, for honesty, for truth have passed us. God has given us both a lashing. Stay.'

'Do we kill Alessandro?'

'Simple solution, but reasonably suspicious.'

'Pity.'

Crumwell jumped and dashed from the room. He returned a moment later and fell to the floor again as Nicóla wiped her tears. 'I have another gift for you, it was presupposed to be for the festivities. But I want to give it to you now.'

Nicóla watched his hand unfurl to reveal her ruby ring. The same one her father gave her just before he died. She had lost it when imprisoned in the Tower. 'Tom...' Again her chest hurt.

'I am Master of the Jewel House. All jewels taken into the King's coffers are listed and under my authority. I checked for rubies collected in the summer of 1529 as soon as I got the chance. I remember your father wearing it on his smallest finger all those years ago.'

'It was Mother's and Father wore it after she died.' Nicóla already wore the turquoise ring Crumwell gave her for Christmas, on her left forefinger just as Crumwell's. Now she had this one too, to be slipped on her ring finger. Nicóla thought her ring gone, a treasure from another world. She looked to Crumwell, and he appeared thoroughly beaten this time.

'I keep thinking, every day which passes, Tomassito, that... that all this will end, and end poorly. There are so many reasons why my lie makes no sense. Every day I could be caught out as a woman, and the English are not known as caring. It could harm your reputation. You have dukes coming to you for advice and help and money. You have reached where you ought to be, beside the King, ruling the parliament, almost ruling a country, and you ought not be weighed down by me. You need not feel obliged because I am the daughter of your old master.'

'I love you, Nicóletta. In my prayers, I thank God for you. You are right; naught makes sense. Yes, things could go wrong. Or we could raise Jane and find success. We could see Gregory grow up with a family, even though his own kin were lost to sweating sickness. We could make England an empire again, and banish the Catholic Church in England forever. We could go in so many ways.'

'It could end with our heads on the block, our necks touched by the edge of an axe.' Nicóla sunk off her seat and wrapped her arms around Crumwell and he began to cry in her embrace. He held her so tight; not even for the Pope was she prepared to go home. She let go of Crumwell and wiped his tears with her fingers and kissed him.

'If I need to kill Alessandro, then I shall. I will not leave you on anyone's orders.'

~~~

Decoration made no matter in Nicóla's mind. All the gold cloth in the world did not catch her eye. The place in which Henry displayed Anne to King Francis was no amazing place; lavish detailing, yes – tapestries, carpets, candles and sparkles and gaiety, but nothing special. Nicóla wore her coat from Crumwell, its rich green sleeves puffed to make her shoulders broader, useful when needing to be a man. Nicóla wore all black but for the coat, her long hair caught under her collar, and a hat she refused to remove. She felt inside her overcoat; her dagger at her waist. Just in case. It was time to make a stop away from the main celebrations at a room easy to find.

Nicóla banged on a door, and a gentleman-usher appeared. Nicóla looked him up and down. French or Italian?

'Io cerci Alessandro de' Medici,' she tried. Yes, Italian.

'Tu sei tu?'

'Nicóla Frescobaldi.' Just the syllables of her name caused a rattle through the apartments.

Heavy footsteps approached the door and Alessandro was there in a second, pushing the boy aside. They stood eye to eye, the wispy Italian dressed all in black, just as his wife. He had aged, no longer the look of youth in his protruding black eyes, now he had long passed twenty years. The loathing in his dark gaze said a lot; his stare said more words than he ever had to his wife. Alessandro dismissed the usher without taking his eyes from her.

'Are you enjoying my fortune?' Nicóla asked.

Alessandro grabbed Nicóla by the arm and pulled her inside. In a second, Nicóla had her dagger ready and thrust at his throat. Alessandro's hands dropped to his sides, fear taking over. He was always so weak; so entitled, so unprepared for life. Alessandro hid behind a lofty name and famed legacy, and Nicóla was a commoner.

'You took a part of my fortune when you disappeared from Rome,' Alessandro said as Nicóla edged him from the door and through another doorway into his dining room, the dagger still pointed at his face. 'I cannot gain the money from Antwerp.'

'I moved a sum and it is in London now. You can keep the rest of it, all my father worked for.'

'Baby Giovanna?'

'Safe in England.'

'The old man? Crumwella?'

Nicóla lowered her blade and watched the sweat drip from

Alessandro's forehead. He cared not if she hurt him. How appropriate. Their marriage formed such a foundation.

'I want an annulment,' Nicóla said to him. 'I am a pawn for Francis' son to get your Catherine married. You know His Holiness cares not if Francis has Henry's support for anything. Noblemen switch alliances so fast it proves naught. Alessandro, you may be here for your sister's marriage, but I am here as my master serves his masters, the King and the Lady Anne.'

'How could you support the whore and the stupidest king in Christendom?' Alessandro spat, his voice still as high-pitched as ever. Nicóla's voice was deeper after her years of lowering her tone.

'You know Machiavelli, Alessandro. You know "The Prince".'

'Is it true? That this Crumwella is "The Prince" of Machiavelli?'

'I believe so. Crumwella possesses a mind, a charm, a wit no one else can hope to ordain.'

'You have picked an unproper man who wants to be a prince, that is for certain. You make His Holiness nervous because you hold yourself to Crumwella. His Holiness fears this Crumwella. I know not why a woman of your wealth should fall upon a man so old. Why be his mistress?'

Nicóla wanted to put the dagger straight into Alessandro's throat, but she would be without a head if he perished. 'Women prefer men to boys. I did not lie with you, but I gave my virtue...' she paused and stepped right against him to whisper in his ear '...to your father.'

Nicóla leaned back and watched the blood drain from Alessandro's distinct dark features and he blinked his beady eyes over and over. 'You have an affinity to my father?' Alessandro cried, and reached out to the wall to steady himself. Always such a weak man with a wicked heart. 'You have committed the most wicked of sins, of the flesh, of, of, incest!'

'Yet it was His Holiness who married us, the man I committed the sin beneath. The Pope used you to gain the money of my father, to help rebuild the Medici empire. So the Medici family could have their city restored. So His Holiness could have another army to back you as you wander around Florence, plowing every daughter in sight.'

'I am in love with Taddea!'

'And her sister?'

'Taddea is having my child. Taddea will give me a son. A Medici son. And yet I am bound to you, the Frescobaldi creature.'

Nicóla took a few steps back. Alessandro despaired as she did. He was a man who taunted stray animals and killed them for pleasure. He was a man who would lay with the daughter at lunch, and lay with the mother at dinner. Alessandro would sleep with his "sister" Catherine if given the chance, said so about five years ago, when she was but eight years old. He made his maids bathe before him. It never occurred to Nicóla that he had feelings for anyone.

'Why not petition an annulment, Alessandro? You consented not to this marriage. I consented not.'

'I do not measure us married, and neither does His Holiness. You abandoned the family, you broke what is sacred of marriage. It is a sin to abandon the family home, it is a sin to not give a husband his dues.' Alessandro's bitter rancor pooled in his voice.

'You made it clear I will never share a bed with you.'

'Yet it is a sin not to; we must consummate the marriage, whether we want to or not.'

'Alessandro, your father has already gained my father's fortune. Let me go. We did not freely consent. We did not consummate the marriage. I abandoned the family home, all grounds for annulment.'

'But it looks terrible for my father, for he is the Pope!'

'The Pope ought to not have a son, so it is too late to look terrible! Annul from me and marry someone more pleasing to the Emperor, such as his bastard daughter.'

'Not an inferior idea. With the Turks pressing upon us, threatening war at any time...'

'Leave Crumwella to present Lady Anne to King Francis. I shall put in a safe word about young Catherine de' Medici to both kings. King Francis can marry his son to Catherine, without us being pawns in a game played by the Pope.'

Nicóla stepped back and Alessandro dropped his raised hands. 'Tell me, Nicóletta, do you truly believe the King shall put a whore on the throne of England?'

'Anne Boleyn is no whore. Sadly, she is also not Katherine of Aragon.'

'Have you truly strayed so far from the Catholic faith, as His Holiness believes?'

'His Holiness already knows of my sins. I shall always have God in my heart and soul, but the Church needs to be destroyed. Without the Church, you and I would not be joined. Think of that.'

Chapter 37 - October 1532
Calais, English territories of France

Every sir might not but hast a hundred seecryts to kept

Decadence. Over-indulgence. The paucity of morality. Any way to word it, the feast, the coming together of the English and French royal courts bore a chaos of lavish and wasteful luxury. Lady Anne Boleyn came in as part of the masque, women dressed as goddesses from Rome, and pulled off her golden feather mask after dancing with King Francis, and everyone pretended they had not recognised her instantly. Everything seemed fine to Crumwell; for £11, Anne's fancy mask seemed to make everyone merry, a bargain at court for a change. The wine flowed as if freshly gathered from the fountain of youth. Everyone laughed and danced while surrounded by cloth sewn in golds and silvers. There was no time to keep still; every time Crumwell turned, another person stood there, ready to be in his favour. Even King Francis was polite, even to the common doubleminded man, who they presupposed wore the turquoise ring which controlled the English king. Tolerance reigned; no wonder everyone claimed no girl raised in the French court could be married a virgin. Given the flirting, the plain openness of teasing, trifling and toying of courtly love going on meant no lady would re-enter England intact at this rate.

Crumwell wanted eyes on one man – Alessandro de' Medici. Be it rational? No. Be it jealousy? Definitely. Be it stupid to want to crush his face? Medici would not be the first man to receive a crushed nose by Crumwell's hand.

Crumwell looked away from the conversation he stood in, hearing yet not listening. He saw Henry enter from a side room where he spoke with his French counterpart; now was the time to attack. Henry had plenty of wine and could be more easily tempted.

'Ah, my dearest Thomas,' King Henry said and threw an arm around Crumwell. 'I do so hope you are having a wonderful time after all your help on this trip?'

'I am, Your Majesty.'

'I know you do not worry yourself with ladies but, surely, even you can esteem the delectable offerings here for men of the court?'

'Everyone does seem best pleased.' Even Thomas Wyatt did for a change; normally Wyatt wandered around the court, brooding over his loss of Anne Boleyn years ago. George Boleyn seemed to be having an enjoyable time; he was an intelligent man, caught in a dull marriage, with the slippery hands of an adulterer. Nicóla danced with Mark Smeaton, the pair filled with cheer, though Crumwell knew Nicóla played a game of pretend. Every man at court seemed captivated by the party.

'The French King is merry,' Henry said, the wine on his breath stinging Crumwell's eyes. 'We have a treaty, but also, we have an agreement. We have done a fine week's work, Thomas. Most satisfactory.'

Now. 'Your Majesty, I know the French King wishes to marry his second son to the Italians. I know the Medici asked King Francis to help get Mr. Frescobaldi back to Italy.'

'Yes, is that not so odd? That your Italian Waif married the brother of the French King's son's betrothed?' Henry paused, replaying his own words in his head to see if he had it right; Henry nodded when he sorted himself.

'Your Majesty,' Crumwell said, their conversation called into each other's ears, the party so loud no one could hear. 'Mr. Frescobaldi wishes for an annulment. It is like your marriage to the Queen; it goes against certain laws of marriage set down by the Church. If a man can freely enter into a pre-contract, which can be binding, then why can a man not decide he is free when the laws are broken?'

Henry hung onto Crumwell's shoulder as Lady Anne wandered over. 'Darling,' Henry said and kissed Anne's cheek, still holding Crumwell. 'Listen to what Thomas has to say. Thomas says if a man can decide himself bound by marriage, such as a pre-contract, surely he can declare himself free when laws of marriage are clearly broken.'

'I think you wear the words of a man with too much cheer in his wine goblet,' Anne giggled. She too put an arm around Crumwell, leaving him caught between the notorious pair.

'You see,' Henry said to Anne, shaky on his feet, 'Thomas, here, wants an annulment for his Italian Waif. What be the grounds?'

'Lack of free consent, non-consummation, and affinity.' God's blood, do not say with the father-in-law. Nicóla's tryst with the Pope could never come to light; that brought no favour.

'With all that, there can be no marriage,' Anne laughed. 'That is every law broken!'

'The Italian Waif is most scandalous, surely not becoming of you, Thomas,' the King laughed.

'I think,' Anne said, still laughing, 'if someone clearly knows the laws of marriage are broken, then a marriage is not lawful! Only God can judge the truth. By such notion, the Waif is free!'

'Then so am I!' Henry said. 'Do not burden yourself, Thomas; I will not send your Waif home to the Pope. I care none for the terms King Francis set out. Frescobaldi is a hostage of my court, linked to the Pope and also to King Francis' son. I would not give away such a prize! Fear not, my man!' the King planted a kiss on Crumwell's cheek and laughed, and Anne copied him.

Crumwell looked up to see Ralph staring back at him. Ralph gestured with a single nod of his head. 'Allow me to burden you no further, Your Majesty,' Crumwell said and slid from between the drunken lovers, who crashed against one another.

He moved between the courtiers towards Ralph, who jostled to the same. 'I spotted him,' Ralph said. 'Richard has eyes on him. Not a curious man; prefers to stand in dark corners. I, then Richard, tried to strike up a conversation in French, but he had none of it.'

'I suspected we would not find a hero, only a coward,' Crumwell muttered. 'Show me.'

Ralph took Crumwell through the party, all along the main hall until they reached a side entrance, covered by falling red banners bearing the French King's royal arms. Then Crumwell saw him, the dark features of Il Moro, the bastard Medici Duke of Florence. Crumwell wanted to feel the desire to slide hands around his throat; strangle the man who kept Nicóla tied to Rome. But… nothing. Crumwell stared at the man, talking to a few others, all looking grim-faced. The new ruler of Florence was little more than a child; short, thin, with a long nose and tiny protruding eyes. He wore fashions which looked twenty years too old; striped hose and an over-puffed cloak. Alessandro de' Medici, the new vicious ruler in Florence was no more than a bastard holding together a fragile family line built on greed and sinful relations.

'Master Crumwell?' Ralph asked, 'are you quite well?' Ralph's complexion resembled Richard's immense worry.

'I am clear-minded,' Crumwell said, even surprising himself. 'All is well. I want naught with this dirty Italian,' Crumwell shrugged and smirked, to himself as much as anyone else.

He turned on the heel of his shining new square-shaped black shoes and headed back towards Nicóla in the midst of the party. The enemy was weak, without importance.

~~~

Many hours had perchance passed when Crumwell woke. Darkness still fell over the court. He lay flat on his back, still clothed on the bed, even his shoes on his feet. Nicóla lay face down next to him, tucked under his arm, as she usually did, curled up like a forsaken animal who sought a warm haven. Ralph stood over the pair, both dulled from too much wine. He frowned, clearly confused at the sight of the pair in the same bed, but made no mention.

'Master,' Ralph said, his voice seeming strangely loud in Crumwell's confusion. 'The King has sent a guard to fetch you. The King commands to see you at once. The guard also says the King and the Lady Anne have yelled most ardently since they returned to their rooms. Now, Henry demands to see you, and also "the Waif".'

Nicóla rolled onto her back, her long hair on her face. 'What an hour to need legal guidance,' she mumbled as she sat up and blinked a few times.

'The perils of the court,' Crumwell said and got to his feet. He put a hand out and pulled Nicóla up too. 'Is there anything else, Ralph?'

'No, the only other thing the King needed was a bible, but he has one now.'

'Wondrous, a theological argument in the middle of the night.'

Crumwell and Nicóla trailed along the hallways in the darkness behind the King's guard. They led through to the lavish rooms of the

King and found no one present but for Henry and Anne, most unlike them, such was their collection of servants. Everyone else was shut away somewhere.

'Your Majesty,' Crumwell bowed, and Nicóla did the same a step behind him. She had only just pulled back her hair and tucked it in the back of her shirt.

Anne had shed tears, her eyes red, her complexion paler than usual. Henry looked weary, as if fresh from battle. Love tended to feel such a way. Crumwell chose to say nothing of these details, the same as the rip in Henry's billowing white sleeve and the scratch on Anne's shoulder. A bible sat on the floor as if thrown down, its pages bent under its own weight.

'I must be the Supreme Head of the Church, Thomas,' Henry said and wiped his nose on his sleeve.

'We have already made it so, Your Majesty. In England, the Church answers to you, not Rome.'

'I want more authority.'

'Thomas Cranmer shall arrive in England soon, to be Archbishop, ready to reform the Church.'

'I want more.'

'We shall finish the Supplication Against the Ordinaries, the theological argument for your annulment, and the decisions of the scholars of Europe.'

'I want your new law, the one where people cannot appeal to Rome for a decision on religious matters.'

'And you shall have it, Your Majesty. Such is the frailty of human affairs that these laws will be passed and enforced to ensure the safety of the Church.'

'Marriage laws must be made by parliament, not the Church.'

'I quite agree. Imagine the world with laws which did not have to be interpreted by clerics, Your Majesty.'

Anne folded her arms over her white nightgown. 'I could be a wife, a mother, a queen.'

'Thomas, I wish to swear an oath, a pre-contract to Lady Anne. I wish to swear we shall be married, and I take her as my wife. I must swear tonight and I wish it legally binding.'

Crumwell looked from the King to Anne and back again. He glanced to Nicóla and she did not express any kind of response. The wine and heady atmosphere must have continued in the King's private rooms. The cheerful Anne and delighted Henry must have fought as the wine wore away. Perchance Anne expected more than to be presented to the French as a trophy. Anne deserved more.

'Very well, Your Majesty.' Crumwell sighed. He wandered to the bible and took it in his hands. Crumwell handed it to Henry, who held it tight. 'By law, you must only pledge to take Anne as your wedded wife and plight one's troth.'

One hand on the bible, the other taking Anne's in his, Henry looked into Anne's black eyes and she grinned. The smile was catching; Henry beamed and Crumwell could not help but do it also. He looked to Nicóla and she smiled too; the secret "marriage" of Henry and Anne.

'On this day, November 14, I, Henry, take thee Anne to my wedded wife and queen and there unto I plight my troth.' Henry handed the bible to Anne and Crumwell noticed a shake of her hand.

'On this day, November 14, I, Anne, take thee Henry to my wedded husband and there unto I plight my troth.'

'Perchance a token or favour to the bride,' Crumwell suggested.

Henry pulled a gold ring from his finger and slipped it upon Anne's. The air filled with silence for a moment, as if time held its breath, no one quite sure what to make of the occasion.

Then Henry turned and looked Crumwell right into his golden eyes. 'Make it so, Thomas.'

Make it so. The King had pledged to God and witnesses to marry Anne Boleyn. Now, Crumwell needed to make it lawful, make it real. Everything Crumwell had worked for since the day Wolsey was pushed from York Place could be taken away. His reputation would be destroyed if he did not now "make it so." It was not an order, more a threat, a premonition of Crumwell's future. Not only did Crumwell need to build an England where the marriage was seen as lawful, he needed to know how to hold the marriage and the country together.

'You ought to marry too,' Henry said to Crumwell and gestured to Nicóla.

'Your Majesty?'

'If you believe me to be Supreme Head of the Church, then I can decide on whether the two of you can marry. Based on your grounds for annulment, I can judge whether or not you can marry your Waif, Thomas. If you believe in the changes created in England, then prove it to me. Pledge to marry Nicóla, here. Anne and I shall bear witness.'

Crumwell looked at Nicóla, her face as blank as his own. It was not just a pledge of marriage... just a pledge of marriage... but also a pledge to prove his belief in the reformation of the Catholic faith in England. It was time for Crumwell to prove his worth, his value, his fealty to Henry, and use Nicóla to do it.

But enticing Nicóla was not necessary. Nicóla stepped forward without delay and took the bible from Lady Anne. Nicóla stood before Crumwell, her face a fraction nervous. She knew the stakes; her brilliant mind assessed it the same way Crumwell just had.

Without any pause, she blurted, in her sweet accent, 'On this day, November 14, I, Nicóletta, take thee Thomas to my wedded husband and there unto I plight my troth.'

Nicóla slipped the bible into Crumwell's hand, holding his fingers in hers. An ordained king demanded so. 'On this day, November 14, I, Thomas, take thee Nicóletta to my wedded wife and their unto I plight my troth.'

The ruby ring Crumwell rescued from the jewel house already rested upon Nicóla's hand; it was done. They were "married." If the Pope had no authority, then he could not ordain a marriage between Nicóla and Alessandro, for she had not freely consented, rather was pushed into a marriage never consummated, never wanted, never truly or faithfully sworn before God.

'If you shall excuse us, Thomas,' Henry said, staring at Anne once more. Tonight Henry sought what he always wanted, Lady Anne in his bed. Crumwell and Nicóla slipped from the room without another word; tonight Henry would conquer all of Anne.

The cold of the unheated hallways stung Crumwell's senses, the darkness only punctuated by the torch which hung next to the door, guarded by two men in Tudor livery. Crumwell took Nicóla's hand as they spirited along the dark hallway together.

'What have we just done?' Nicóla asked.

'We have ensured the King gets what he wants.'

'At what cost? Anne Boleyn's maidenhead was her only card left to play.'

Crumwell pulled Nicóla to him and pressed her against the wall, total darkness around them. 'At the cost of our souls to heaven,' he whispered. 'I have lived my life as a sinner, and so have you. We have denied our stations in life, we have defied the expectations and have broken rules and vows. But if this night cannot hold in its truth, the King will have my head. So, for every day I still have it on my shoulders, I swear I will love you as a wife.'

'I would rather be your master secretary, your counsel, your Waif.'

'Be all of those things.'

Crumwell knew Ralph and Richard to be awake in their rooms, waiting for their master's return. So, just for a moment, Crumwell held his bride against the wall and kissed her as deeply as the King no doubt kissed his Lady Anne tonight.

Chapter 38 - December 1532
Austin Friars, London

A seecryt with a holdout cater-cousins togyther

'This realm of England is an empire, and so hath been accepted in the world, governed by one supreme head and king having the dignity and royal estate of the Imperial Crown of the same, unto whom a body politic compact of all sorts and degrees of people divided in terms and by names of Spirituality and Temporality, be bounden and owe to bear next to God a natural and humble obedience.'

Crumwell sat at the head of his Austin Friars dining table and regarded his guests, who paused to take in his words.

'What do you anticipate?' Thomas Cranmer cleared his throat and smoothed the white linen over his black vestment. 'What I think is, with that one, most long sentence, you shall remove the Pope from English canon and civil law entirely.'

Crumwell put his hands out, palms upwards. 'Is thus not the point of the law I am drafting? To restrict the Church's power, to stop people from appealing to Rome in ecclesiastical matters? When I pass this in parliament, all will be well in England.'

Nicóla cast her eye about the table in at Austin Friars' dining room. Crumwell sat like a king at his table, his back straight in his throne, the shining baubles of Christmas decorations winding up the pillar behind him, dividing the two large windows which looked out onto the garden, all bathed in snow and moonlight. Across from Nicóla sat their special guest, Thomas Cranmer, back from the court of the Emperor, ready to be made Archbishop of Canterbury. He was a small man for someone who claimed such a large presence; a round face, freshly-shaven like Crumwell. His dark hair hung around his face, in need of a tidy after his wanders around Europe. Next to him sat his new wife, Margarete, with curly hair the colour of a sunset and a sweet young face. Cranmer met and married her in Nuremberg while indulging in the glories of German reformation. Margarete spoke poor English, only what Cranmer had taught her, though her Latin was enough to hold a conversation. A glorious sight indeed that Cranmer tossed aside his priestly vow of celibacy; it meant he had become a fully-fledged reformer, a Lutheran. Helpful when needing to break the Catholic Church. An archbishop supporting to Crumwell's ideas would smooth the path to an official Henry and Anne marriage. Only poor Margarete was a secret all needed to keep for now, until clerics in England came to believe the new ways Cranmer so gushed.

The ever present Ralph and Richard sat next to Nicóla, and across from Richard sat lawyer Thomas Wriothesley, lapping up every word his master said. Beside Wriothesley sat courtier Richard Rich, also hanging on Crumwell's every word. At least he was not fleecing Crumwell of money by way of cards or dice again. Nicóla saw the debts in the ledgers; she was fairly sure Rich was a card cheat. Even Crumwell could not lose that often, no one's luck could be that sinful! Something about Rich made Nicóla pause with concern; for within him ran an evil streak, hidden deep for now.

Next to Rich sat Thomas Audley, Crumwell's trusted friend from parliament, and a man who kept his mind on law and never religious matters. Despite being several years younger than Crumwell, Audley seemed worn by life, his waistline ever-expanding as his star raised higher in the King's eyes.

'I feel I have stumbled upon a different England now we are returned,' Cranmer said. 'I knew of the changes being made, of course. The Emperor's ambassador, Chapuys, writes constantly and talks of everything. I feel I watched you all from afar. However, affairs seem to be changing at such pace.'

The rumour is such that King Henry has finally bedded Lady Anne,' Nicóla replied. 'After the visit to France, it is said he appeared from his chambers a new man. It was Anne's sister Mary who claimed so.'

Laughter swirled around the table as Cranmer translated Nicóla's comment to his wife. 'Tell me about this new law you just passed in parliament,' Cranmer asked Crumwell.

'The Act in Conditional Restraint of Annates,' Crumwell explained. 'It was not easy. The King had to appear three times in the House of Lords in order to get it passed. It suspends the payments of annates to Rome. These taxes are so high, they are all but crippling honest laymen who pay for their piety. These payments shall no longer go to Rome. I provided that five percent may still go to Rome, but it was hard to pass by the Commons.'

'It was not easy in the Privy Council either,' Richard added.

'Now the taxes shall go to the King's purse, not the Pope's,' Crumwell continued. 'It is only a suspension of annates payments. The full absolute restraint will take far longer to force through parliament. But once we have this, the Restraint of Appeals to Rome, and give the King the right to appoint bishops and cardinals, then we shall have total authority over the Church in our hands.'

'As Archbishop, I shall take charge of a much-reformed clergy,' Cranmer thought aloud. 'All these changes will have to be explained to both the clergy and the public at length. Much shall change once your law changes reach the people.'

'All for the better,' Crumwell replied. 'We can rid the Catholic Church of all the abuses; the corruption, the taxing; we will have the power. And now we can control canon law, we can rid ourselves of the Catholic lies hidden from view in Latin bibles. It will be English bibles for English readers.'

'As you can see, Dr. Cranmer,' Ralph added, 'Master Crumwell was most busy in your absence.'

'But it is wondrous to have you back,' Crumwell told Cranmer, who gave a gentle smile. 'You were much missed.' He gestured for one of the servants to tend the fire behind Cranmer, another to refill everyone's wine glasses, beautiful sculpted Murano glass from Venice.

'It is as if Austin Friars has become something of a miniature parliament,' Cranmer observed.

'I have fifty people coming to petition tomorrow!' Ralph said. 'Master Crumwell will not even be here, but back to court. That does not count the number of people who simply arrive, or write letters, wanting help or the patronage of Master Crumwell.'

'Also the number of people petitioning the King tomorrow will be immense, and much time shall be lost with the arrival of the newest archbishop at court,' Crumwell gestured to Cranmer.

'The papal bulls are not yet signed and delivered from the Pope,' Cranmer objected.

'I wrote the required paperwork myself,' Crumwell replied. 'Nicóla here wrote personally to the Pope, asking to have you appointed. All will be well.'

'It is a busy Christmas time,' Cranmer said and regarded the beautifully decorated walls. 'And young Ralph, you are to be married!'

'Yes, Ralph promised himself in marriage to Ellen, one of our laundresses,' Crumwell said, his tone verging on disapproval. Nicóla had spent a length calming Crumwell over the marriage after Ralph broke the news. Ralph was desperately in love with the girl, abandoned by her first husband. Ellen was young, with long blonde hair and a gentle voice. It was a love match, for which Crumwell lectured Ralph about; how love could add trouble to a relationship. But still, the marriage was to be; Ralph had already taken Ellen to his bed.

'Perchance Cranmer can officiate your marriage,' Crumwell said to Ralph.

'It would be my pleasure,' Cranmer replied. 'And of the rest of you? All we have spoken of tonight is religion and politics.'

'It is who we are,' Nicóla replied, to a round of nodding.

'My wife, Frances, is not well,' Richard said, in a weary voice. 'Her father, the former Lord Mayor, is most worried, as he has already lost his only son. We shall be at Master Crumwell's Stepney estate, which perchance shall aid Frances' health.'

'Almighty and Eternal God,' Cranmer began, 'You are the everlasting health of those who believe in You. Hear us for Your sick servant Frances, for whom we implore the aid of Your tender mercy, that being restored to bodily health she may give thanks to You in Your Church. Through Christ our Lord. Amen.'

'Amen,' everyone crossed themselves, and Richard gave Cranmer a gesture of thanks. 'And you, Audley, I hear you have been made the King's barrister, along with Speaker of the House of Commons,' Cranmer continued along the guests.

'It was a delight to be able to watch my capable friend receive a knighthood at court,' Crumwell said, and Audley raised his glass in thanks.

'What of you, Master Crumwell?' Cranmer asked. 'Are we to see you as Lord Chancellor of England soon?'

Nicóla watched Crumwell attempt to refrain from his smirk, though no else at the table held back smiles. 'All I wish is to gain some more land from the monasteries in Essex,' Crumwell said and tried to shift the conversation. 'Such is proving difficult. You might think the clergy there should want my patronage, the plotting old men.'

'You seek to buy up all the land around where you were once born?' Cranmer revelled.

'Master Crumwell will own all of Essex before we know it,' Ralph said and everyone laughed again.

'And you, Mr. Frescobaldi? I hear everyone continues to call you "Waif". You are no longer a person of questionable being now you are under the golden eyes of Master Crumwell. Though I must say with your long hair, the questions of your maidenhood could be questioned by someone new to court.' A shrewd laugh echoed at the words. 'In fact,' Cranmer continued, 'my wife did ask me if you were a woman or a man. I hushed her, of course, and said you are a man of female favour.'

Nicóla glanced to Margarete, who sat in silence, unable to understand anyone, though she watched social cues. Latin was the only language Nicóla and Margarete had in common. 'Cur me tot tam inusitatum quam ut tam mulierem quam spectare queant. Tam paruus animus possit. Quisque scire potest abscondere mulieres.'

Margarete giggled; she understood all too well how men's minds could be meek and women must hide any way they can. Poor Margarete was shipped to England in a crate and now lived in Cranmer's home away from the court, hidden from the world.

The door to the dining room opened, and there stood one of the nurses who cared for Jane. The young girl, now aged well past two, stood at her nurse's feet, dressed in a white nightgown. 'Excuse me, Master Crumwell,' the nurse said and curtsied. 'The Mistress Crumwell asked to see all the Christmas decorations around the house before bed. I hoped you would mind not.'

'Of course,' Crumwell said, and Jane and the nurse wandered in. The Christmas tree, at ten feet high, sat in the far corner the dining room, its decorations sparkling off the flames of the fire. Instead of the tree, Jane ran over to her father's open arms. He scooped her up on his lap and she buried her face in his neck. 'Are you merry to see your brother Gregory when he comes tomorrow?' he asked the child.

'This is your niece, Nicóla?' Cranmer asked, and told Margarete in German. 'How sweetly she has taken to you, Thomas, and you call her by the name Crumwell?'

Nicóla reached over and stroked Jane's tight rose-gold ringlets which rolled down her back. Jane turned and flung herself into her mother's arms for a hug also.

'Ea pulchra est,' Margarete said.

'Indeed, she is beautiful, is she not?' Nicóla said as Jane climbed down from her mother, and over to the tree. Giovanna Frescobaldi had lived as Jane Crumwell for two years now, was a true English girl, even with the olive skin and rose-gold hair of her mother.

'Some at court say the child is Crumwell's bastard,' Rich muttered from the end of the table after the nurse took the child up to bed.

Richard caught Nicóla's eye, and never forged an expression. Richard knew, or he thought he knew, whose bastard the child was. Crumwell never established himself as Jane's natural father but spoke of her as an adopted daughter. But with those wide golden eyes, there was no mistaking Jane as a trueborn daughter.

'It is a shame people cannot understand privacy,' Crumwell said.

'Privacy, in the English court?' Nicóla scoffed and everyone laughed in agreement. 'Henry beds his mistress, and in hours, thousands know all about it. No one can keep a secret at court.'

'I am grateful all can be trusted at Austin Friars,' Crumwell replied and raised his glass. Nicóla joined in, toasting the solid group of men ready to reform England, all to cement a king's love in marriage. And now, to make Crumwell Lord Chancellor of England, to rule in Wolsey's place.

Chapter 39 - December 1532
Whitehall Palace and Austin Friars, London

Gents betray their seecryts, tis ladies who wilt beest vigylant

Behind the parties and masques, the power remained. For all the dainty decorations, the golden gifts, the fresh-scented trees, the singing as the yule log was lit, all this sat in the way of anything near important. Christmas had come to court, and while everyone distracted themselves with the coming of the Twelfth Night, the New Year gifts and mulled wine, Crumwell had to keep working. Always working, never getting a break. Gregory was home for the season, but he played under the watchful eye of Ralph at Austin Friars. Crumwell's own home was twisted and bedecked into Christmas heaven, and also for the wedding of Ralph and petite Ellen. Austin Friars was filled to the brim with staff, almost 200 now, plus servants of similar numbers. Crumwell had two children at home for Christmas, he multiplied his new titles at court, and the Catholic Church was about to self-destruct from the weight he applied. Yet, Crumwell felt a need to push even harder; now was the time to create royal supremacy, and sit beside the throne.

Crumwell may not have liked to drink to excess or visit whores, in or outside the court, but gambling… gambling he just could not quell. Sitting around the table in the King's privy chamber, cards in his hands, coins tossed in the centre; this was how business was done. No petitioning during the day, not arguing in parliament, though he loved that, but here, over wine and cards. And losing, most of the time. The King always needed to think he was the most important man in the room. Mayhap once upon a time, before Wolsey's death. Not any longer.

'This time next year, I shall have a wife and a son,' Henry said, his blue eyes full of excitement, paying little heed to the game.

The Duke of Norfolk next to him looked ready to sleep. Cranmer sat next to Crumwell, not playing cards, just listening to the conversation. Cranmer had spent much of the day praying with Lady Anne. Beside the Archbishop-to-be and the King sat George Boleyn, looking half-drunk, a permanent state for a man who was either plotting, taking money from his father, refilling his cup, or chasing the hem of a skirt. In all fairness, George's life was a hard one – he was smart, he was handsome enough, yet his sister was even smarter, and better to look at. He would forever live in Anne's shadow, and his own wife was dull. Still, there were plenty of perks, like cards with the King of England.

'Let me tell you a story, Dr. Cranmer,' the King said as he tossed another few coins on the pile in the middle of the wooden table. 'When at court in France near two months ago, there was a man there. An Italian man. He was the Duke of Florence, bastard brother of Catherine, who proposes to marry the French King's son.'

Crumwell narrowed his eyes, unsure of Henry's point. Henry surely would never betray his trust regarding Nicóla. 'I believe the Duke of Florence married the Waif's sister,' Cranmer replied in innocence and Crumwell nodded.

'Anyway, Medici was at court sharing the festivities and something awful happened,' Henry continued.

'Pray tell, Your Majesty?' Cranmer asked, totally oblivious.

'It was said the Italian got so drunk he slipped at the top of a set of stairs and fell. It is a miracle he did not die, they claim. He has only just set off for his home in Florence now, after needing all this time to recover. The Duke did say, however, he felt he was pushed down the stairs, not that he was too drunk.'

'Why would s-s-someone push some filthy Italian duke d-d-down a flight of stairs?' Norfolk sniffed.

Henry stared straight at Crumwell, who did not dare move. 'What do you believe, Thomas? You are the Italian-Englishman among the court. Why would the Duke say such a thing?'

Crumwell sipped his wine and blinked a few times, slow, measured. 'Did this man see his enemy?'

'No, the Duke saw naught.'

'Then he must have slipped, and claimed the push as a way to cover his drunken manners,' Crumwell stared back at the King.

Neither moved a fraction and Crumwell let the edge of his mouth betray his mood, the tiniest hint of a smile. God bless Richard Rich, and Crumwell's desire to avenge Nicóla just a dash. Rich, so eager to please Crumwell, took the order to push Alessandro down a flight of stairs, and questioned none.

Henry threw down his cards. A pair of queens. 'You lose again, gentlemen.'

Crumwell and Norfolk folded their hands, lost again to the King. As if he needed the money. No one needed the money. The last thing Henry needed was a pair of queens.

'Crowmell,' Norfolk uttered, his throat sounding dry and harsh.

'Crumwell,' he answered.

'This whole b-b-business of you forcing the Church to g-g-give up appeals to Rome, is that not gg-going too far? The Pope is God's man on Earth.'

'Do not question what Thomas puts before parliament. Everyone must bend to whatever Thomas wants,' the King announced.

'My name is Thomas,' Norfolk said.

'So is mine,' Cranmer smiled.

Crumwell leaned back in his chair and eyed the Duke. Thomas Howard, third Duke of Norfolk, had to bow to whatever Crumwell wished, now the King said so.

'What does a man like Thomas Crumwell get for Christmas?' the King asked as he shuffled the cards.

'One of my little creatures is coming back from the Low Countries. An apprentice of Stephen Vaughan, my merchant in Antwerp. Vaughan has just gone on a diplomatic mission for you in Paris, Your Majesty, to see the political situation. Vaughan, he is sending me home a man we have both educated.'

'Another of Crowmell's c-c-creatures sneaking around London,' Norfolk said. 'It n-n-never ends.'

'Crumwell!' he corrected the Duke.

'Perchance it is time for us to retire,' Cranmer said to Crumwell. 'We do have a wedding tomorrow, and I am to officiate at Austin Friars.'

'Send my regards to the bride and groom,' Henry said as the group all stood in respect. 'Is the bride young, graceful?'

'Ellen would not be my first choice as bride, but she's fine enough, fertile and makes my Ralph happy. Ralph and his brother are like children to me. One can become most attached to the wards we take,' Crumwell mused.

'What k-k-kind of woman gains attentions from Thomas Crowmell?' Norfolk asked.

'Crumwell!'

'Mr. Crumwell has someone in mind, I suspect,' Henry laughed. 'Adieu, gentlemen, you may go.'

The barge ride from the palace towards Austin Friars bobbed along in the freezing mist, the water splashing against the hull every so often. Using the King's barge meant they stuck out as they followed the line of the river, all lit up in the darkness of winter. Poor Cranmer looked frozen solid. Crumwell made a note; a gift of new furs for Cranmer once he became an archbishop.

'Do you think the King will accept I have a wife?' Cranmer asked, not facing Crumwell as they sat together drifting along the dank waters of the Thames.

'Oh, I know not his mind. The King believes in celibacy of the clergy. Why? I cannot be sure. Henry is all for reform in some measures, mostly involving gaining power and money. In other things, Henry is very strict. Why did you marry? You are no Lutheran, yet you conformed to their rules and left behind the learnings of the Catholic faith, those which surely have guided your whole life.'

'Once before I married, Thomas. Before I took holy orders, but she died in childbirth. When I met Margarete… I simply cannot explain it.'

'How did you reconcile your soul to God?'

'Why would God send me a love such as Margarete and deny me? A test perchance? I am in no need of being tested by God. Surely He meant for me to have Margarete.'

'You sound similar to Henry and Anne.'

'We deny the King's love at our peril.'

'The King cares too much for love. Can I ask for your guidance?' Crumwell asked.

'Of course. But what can I offer that you know not?'

'You are a man of the cloth, and I am not. You shall be an

archbishop soon enough, so I shall lean on you as we purge the evil and corruption out of the Church in England. It is my soul which asks questions.'

'Have you sinned, my child?' Cranmer smiled.

'Frequently, and I doubt I shall stop. You will soon have the power to rule on Henry's marriage and annulment. Could you rule on other marriages?'

'The rule shall require me to do so,' Cranmer sighed. 'I desire not to end marriages ordained by God.'

'What of a marriage performed outside of England?'

'The Pope rules on annulments now, in countries other than his own. If the reasoning for annulment is strong...'

'Strong indeed,' Crumwell interrupted his friend.

'You speak of someone in particular.'

'My Waif, Nicóla. Married in Rome, under duress, non-consummation. Evidence of abandoning the marital home, and affinity with a family member.'

'If evidence can be produced, or testimony is sound, then yes, I can grant him an annulment.'

'Her,' Crumwell whispered.

'Her?' Cranmer turned from the darkness and faced his friend.

'Please, begin not with the rules of Christian morality in women. Nicóla is like Queen Katherine; nature was cruel in making her body a woman, yet bestowed the mind and courage of a man. God was unjust. Surely your kind soul can understand the need for a saviour.'

'If the papal bulls are signed and I am ordained an archbishop, I shall endeavour to be of service to your... friend. But in doing so, Nicóla's secret would be made public.'

'It shall make you no friends, I warn you now.'

'No matter, for I am here to serve God, to worry on behalf of the men in Rome, with their plump arrogance and their corruption. They make the English court look comparable to a ladies garden party.'

'Any man who leaves Rome with his life is a hero. My Nicóla can swear to thus.'

~~~

Austin Friars was still lit up like the starry night sky upon arrival. Crumwell wandered into the parlour to find Nicóla, chatting with youth Thomas Avery.

'Another young apprentice has returned home!' Crumwell said and wrapped his arms around young Avery. Avery had grown wider in his absence, his complexion now covered in a long fair beard, his hair at least clipped short. He wore fine velvet and pearls; definitely the apprentice of a merchant. Stephen Vaughan in the Low Countries was kind to send Avery back to Crumwell.

'Blessed be to God that I am back at Austin Friars, Master Crumwell,' Avery said, his voice weary from the journey, no doubt. 'Master Vaughan said you are in need of my work and I am merry to be back. Your Mr. Frescobaldi has been most kind in keeping me company.'

Nicóla smiled, but she looked worn, and Crumwell instantly noticed something wrong. 'Tom, for you, I have the most important and pressing task. I am in need of a smart man with a keen eye to go into service for Gertrude Courtenay, the Marchioness of Exeter, the wife of Henry Courtenay, the King's cousin. The King wants eyes on the Marchioness, thanks to her fondness for sorcery and prophesying. Only a good heart and steady mind can take on this task.'

'Never will I let you down, Master Crumwell. I shall scrub your floors if you command me.'

'And weaken the fruits of your mind, Tom? Never. Also, there will be other work to do, letters to read and draft, all paid by me.'

'You are well met, Master Crumwell,' Avery grinned, his dark eyes beaming in delight.

'Go upstairs and sleep, Tom. Tomorrow we have Ralph's wedding and it will be a masterly affair, such as Austin Friars is yet to have.'

'Mr. Frescobaldi was telling me of your new company of actors and musicians for entertainment. Also of the new peacocks in the gardens.'

Crumwell turned to Nicóla. 'Now I have more than one hundred canaries in the aviaries, plus hawks and falcons for us to enjoy every night. But, now, to bed, my boy. Tomorrow we shall be friends over again.'

Crumwell watched Avery disappear through the doorway and onto the main staircase. He turned right back to Nicóla, who still stood, arms crossed over her new grey overgown and red doublet. Her hair pulled tight against her head appeared forced down the back of her high-necked shirt. The recent rings under her eyes looked too heavy to carry.

'Tell me,' Crumwell commanded.

'Perchance somewhere more private?'

Crumwell rushed Nicóla up the stairs to his private rooms, through the presence chamber and into the bedroom, where he closed the door. The maid had already lit the fire and set out wine and cheese.

'Thank you for entertaining Thomas Avery.'

'It is no trouble. Avery is useful, I think. Definitely one of your creatures; intelligent, polite.'

'Are you unwell? Should I call the physician? Is it Gregory? Is it Jane?'

'No, everyone is well. Or, everyone else is well and safe and ready for the wedding. I believe Ralph is still awake in his rooms.'

'None of that, Nicó. You ought to sit down.'

Nicóla perched half on the edge of his bed and Crumwell sat down next to her. He slowly pulled her hair from the back of her shirt and laid it over her overgown. Nicóla placed her hands between her knees but said nothing.

'Please do not say you are leaving, Nicó.'

'What?' Nicóla turned and faced Crumwell, her green eyes looking right into his. 'Tomassito, no!'

Crumwell's heart continued its incessant pattering. 'Then what is wrong? I can be known as the fixer for every man at court, surely I can fix anything for you, my love.'

'Learn to remember I am sorry.'

'For?'

'For I am with child again.'

A wide grin spread across Crumwell's complexion, such as a butterfly opening its wings for the first time. A baby. Nothing could replace Anne and Grace, of course. But a baby. He had missed Jane's birth, and Gregory was now twelve. A baby. 'Sorry?'

'How shall I hide this at court?' Nicóla whispered. 'How am I to be your master secretary, your counsel, when I am with child? And my years; I am two and thirty years old! I am too old to be having children.'

'It can be done, for it is believed my mother was two and fifty years at my birth. It will be done, Nicó. Forget to be at court, I shall keep you hither and take Ralph to court.'

'This was not to happen if I am to live as a man, not as a wife.'

'Did you not pledge yourself to me before God and the King? Do you not have the blessing of the future Archbishop of Canterbury to live as you do, and to gain an annulment?'

'What?' Nicóla frowned. 'You told Thomas Cranmer of me?' Nicóla quickly crossed herself.

'It is beneficial, Nicó, I promise. As for a baby, well, it is unavoidable I believe, given how much I love you. You make me young again. I will rule England a year hence, so have nothing to fear.'

'You must be careful what you say, Tomassito. To imagine the world without the King is treason. You do not want to follow your heretic friends to the burning stake.'

'True power is behind the throne, you know thus, I know thus. Soon we shall be able to live as we please.'

'Yet it pleases me to be a man.'

'You shall have the baby and he will go into the nursery with Jane. All will be well.'

'He? Shall I bear you a son? Another bastard?'

'Tonight you give me the greatest gift. Tomorrow I shall act as the father at the wedding of Ralph and Ellen and know I am true to be a father again. If you want to be acknowledged as a woman at court and yet work and dress as a man, then you shall. I have all the power, Nicó, for I own the King and the Archbishop. Rome's rules no longer matter.'

Chapter 40 - January 1533
Whitehall Palace, London

If true thee loveth in seecryt, thee may dyd hurte in silence

'You could send Gregory to Antwerp,' Nicóla muttered and did not look up from her corner desk to speak. The ledgers looked immaculate, but it never hurt to check. 'Now Stephen Vaughan has given over Thomas Avery to you, perchance Vaughan has a place in his household for Gregory. We both know the time in a merchant's home is the best of educations.'

Crumwell did not respond and Nicóla turned in her chair and looked back to him, sitting at his desk, head in a book. His golden eyes moved back and forth, the only person Nicóla knew who could read faster than herself. Gregory, home for the season, appeared distraught to return to his studies. Ever more feminine, delicate young Gregory's pained heart moved Nicóla to speak for him.

Without stopping his reading, he mumbled, 'is it wrong to say I do not wish to have Gregory so far from home?'

'Of course not, for Gregory is your only son. I was educated by tutors at home, and in the offices of my father, except for the years when I was sent by the Medici to Florence University in Pisa. It seemed a lonely four years.'

Crumwell sighed. 'Gregory's time in Cambridge is not serving a noble purpose and I fear Gregory, while a good boy, shall never be a great scholar. Perchance he is better under Ralph's instruction at Austin Friars.'

'All I know of languages, mathematics, and accounts came by

simply being at Frescobaldi manor. I learned English and Flemish from my father, French from my governess, Latin and Spanish from tutors. I must confess my Greek never flourished, as I preferred numbers. Numbers pray speak to me.'

Crumwell jested, a gentle smile appearing. 'Indeed, I quite agree.'

'Are you certain we can lose Thomas Avery to the Marquess of Exeter's horrid wife? Avery's book work is excellent, his ability to account for funds is wonderful. If you need a spy in Exeter's household, surely you know we have hundreds of creatures in our employ.'

'We have, and I know the names of every one,' Crumwell replied and looked up at last. 'And yes, Avery must work in an established household for a year or so. It is the custom here. Then I will take Avery back in after he has done all he can for Henry's cousin. For you need not Avery, you have twenty accountants already, Nicó.'

'Indeed, and I know the names of every one,' she teased. 'It is after midnight, Tomassito.'

'What is that to me?'

Nicóla gestured through the double doors to the main offices of the Crumwell chambers. Eight clerks still worked away. 'They may be the bees of your hive, but even they must sleep.'

Crumwell clicked his fingers twice and all looked up. Nicóla wandered into the doorway and yawned. All the men at their desks waited for instruction. 'Gentlemen, you may all leave for the night.'

They all packed away their things, muttering goodnights as they left and through the open main entrance came one of the night guards in a hurry. 'Pray, a messenger for Master Crumwell.'

Over her shoulder, Nicóla heard the double click of Crumwell's fingers, and led him into the private office. 'Master Crumwell,' the boy said and swooped his black hat from his head. Nicóla sat in her chair as the boy caught his breath.

'Pray speak.'

'Thomas Cranmer has just received a message from Rome, confirming he shall be accepted as Archbishop by Pope Clement. The papal bulls shall be drawn up and sent with haste. Dr. Cranmer requests you inform the King at once.'

Crumwell pounded his fist on the desk as he stood up, so merry he looked ready to kiss the poor boy delivering the words. 'By God's mercy, we shall save England's soul yet!'

Nicóla stood and gave the boy a coin for his trouble and showed him out. As soon as she closed the door, Crumwell grabbed her and spun her in his arms, her feet leaving the ground. Crumwell kissed her deeply, his hands on her cheeks.

'We have it,' he said, his hands on her shoulders. 'We shall reform England. We shall create Queen Anne. We shall forever be in the King's favour.'

'Suddenly it is Thomas Crumwella, the dreamer.'

'Let us inform the King at once. The letter you wrote to the Pope, it must have convinced him to ordain Cranmer. You and I are to have our best wine tonight!' he cried as he sat down.

It was if God reached down at that moment. Nicóla felt it, beneath her loose doublet. The quickening of her child, the stirring of the life inside her. The first quickening of her new baby. Nicóla gasped at the feeling, and it snapped Crumwell from his daze.

'What?'

Nicóla held her stomach, still totally flat, her eyes wide with surprise. 'The baby.'

Crumwell burst from his chair again to guide her into his arms. 'What is wrong?'

'Nothing, but the baby is moving.'

'The baby is quickening already?' Crumwell asked. 'How soon will he be born?'

'Soon, before summer perchance.'

'It is already almost February,' Crumwell said with a smile and placed a hand on her stomach. 'God wishes us to be merry.'

'Life is indeed a mystery.'

They stood together in the office in silence, nothing but the crackle of the fire. Another knock at the door and the pair groaned in time.

'Come!' Crumwell called out and let go of Nicóla.

'Master Crumwell.' This time, black livery, the Tudor rose at his chest. 'The King has requested you to his privy chamber at once. His Majesty is urgent and cannot wait.'

'Come with me,' Crumwell uttered and Nicóla fell into line behind him as they accompanied the gentleman-usher to the King's rooms. They breezed through the empty meeting rooms and presence chambers, until they came to the door of the King's privy chamber and could hear Henry's deep voice on the other side.

'Wait here,' Crumwell instructed Nicóla. 'You know what to do.'

Nicóla nodded and stood back to the wall, hands clasped. Wait. Watch. Listen. Say nothing of anyone. Observing spoke, people lied. But no need. The door was left open, such was the confidence of no one getting this close to the privy chamber at this hour. Nicóla kept her eyes to the ground, much like the black-clad guard seated by the door. The boy looked so worn, ready to fall asleep in the chair.

'Your Majesty.'

'Thomas, come, I have some grand news.'

'Has His Majesty heard Thomas Cranmer is accepted as the Archbishop by the Pope?'

'No, I had not heard! Good God, Thomas, more immense news. It could not come at a better time. Lady Anne has informed me that she has missed her courses.'

'Courses?'

'Courses, Thomas! Anne is with child! My child!'

'Your Majesty, forgive me, it has taken me by surprise.'

'Well indeed, Anne has taken us all by surprise. Ever since that night in France when we took vows before God, we have engaged in a …' Nicóla covered her ears for that part of the conversation. She was no stranger, but still, had no desire to hear what the King did to Anne Boleyn. As she covered her ears, she noticed the guard had succumbed to sleep. After a minute or so, Nicóla removed her hands, the conversation changed.

'Thomas, I can't bear to have this baby born illegitimate. There can be no questions over whether my son is the heir to the throne. Anne and I must formally marry. Now.'

'Your Majesty, Archbishop Cranmer is preparing to solve the issue of annulment, but it could be months…'

'No. Now. Tonight. It must be hither at the palace, somewhere totally private. Is Rowland Lee here, or should we use a royal chaplain?'

'Dr. Lee is hither in the palace, Your Majesty.'

'Excellent. Wake Lee and bring him to me and make sure he swears to secrecy.'

'Your Majesty, Lee shall need to see a licence which says the Pope allows you to remarry.'

'Worry not, I shall pray speak to Lee. Thomas, I can take care of one priest. I shall need witnesses; I shall get the grooms in my privy

FRAILTY OF HUMAN AFFAIRS

chamber… William Brereton, Henry Norris, Thomas Heneage... no, Heneage is ill. Francis Weston. Anne can bring one of her ladies with her. That makes four witnesses. They could make fine witnesses, could they not, Thomas?'

'Yes, Your Majesty.'

'Can you please stand outside, guard the room as we marry, Thomas? While we do the official business I need to know you are overseeing everything.'

'It would be an honour, Your Majesty. May I suggest a place? The Holbein Gate over Whitehall Road is newly completed. It is beautiful and the third floor is totally empty. No one shall look for you there, and your marriage could be a private opening of the gate to the palace, a totally secret marriage.'

'Perfect, Thomas. Bring your Waif with you. We shall marry before dawn, and then we can head straight to morning Mass.'

'Thank you, Your Majesty.'

'What an evening. A wedding, a son and heir on the way, Cranmer ordained Archbishop. Oh, I almost forgot, I was speaking with your friend Sir Thomas Audley earlier. Audley is promoted from parliament speaker to be my new Lord Chancellor. You may give him the Great Seal once he is sworn to the task.'

Silence. Nicóla held her breath and desperately wanted to peer around the door into the privy chamber. Crumwell had to reply, perchance choosing his words. Lord Chancellor had been Wolsey's position. Sir Thomas More had been brought down, forced from the role. Now, instead of giving it to Crumwell, the King had gone and given it to Sir Thomas Audley? Audley?

'Sir Thomas Audley is a fine lawyer, Your Majesty. He is both intelligent and honourable. We did much work together for the late Cardinal. Audley shall do you proud as Lord Chancellor,' Crumwell answered.

Nicóla knew Crumwell's tone. Measured. Even. The words formed but the mind did not engage. All this work, and now Audley was to be Lord Chancellor? Audley was to now control the Great Seal?

'Thomas, get a guard to fetch Rowland Lee from his bed and brought here. I shall meet you at Holbein Gate at five o'clock, before the sunrise.'

Crumwell stormed from the privy chamber, and Nicóla scurried behind him. She dared not speak a word, and the long determined strides he made back to chambers made it plain Crumwell would not speak a word. Only once they embraced the safety of the private office did he howl at the top of his lungs. After letting out the noise, which sent the guards running into the office in panic, did Crumwell finally sit down and take a few deep breaths. Nicóla dismissed the guards out again and sat down on the chair across the desk, so she was not looking down upon him; he needed no judgement.

'This night shall never end,' Crumwell began, his hand rested against his forehead, his elbow on the red cushioned arm of the chair. 'How many more things could possibly go wrong? We had it; we got so close. There is to be a queen I made, through my laws. Anne to have a son, whom I shall make legitimate. The archbishop, which I have installed, is to reign. My law changes irritated Sir Thomas More so much he left office. And yet, what am I? I am nothing in the court of Henry!'

Nicóla said nothing, allowed him to rage. Crumwell was right; he had destroyed a queen and created another, and yet he stood now with just a handful of titles in court and chambers in each palace. Many courtiers could say the same. He still had his position in parliament, but then, so did many others. Crumwell had time with the King, but at any rate, that seemed to mean scant little. All those days, all those nights! Crumwell could be blamed not for being angry. He expected not to be handed a role; he worked for it. Every day. But one thing waved in Nicóla's mind.

'My love,' she said gently, 'I have a question. Henry is to get married, with three men from his privy chamber. Not his closest friends, such as Charles Brandon or Francis Bryan. Anne is to be attended by one of her ladies, not her father, brother, sister. You, the man Henry trusts more than anyone, has to wait outside the door. Henry could have Thomas Cranmer officiate, but chose Rowland Lee; a smart man, but no one of skillful importance. It is as if Henry is doing this ceremony and yet does not believe in its lawfulness. All the people who will be present are unimportant, people whose voices mean naught. This worries me.'

'Why?' Crumwell asked, his eyes scowling, his hand over his mouth, as he did in times of worry. His golden eyes looked ready to catch fire upon anything he looked.

'Mayhap I am wrong, Tomassito. It just feels, if at a later date,

Henry were to pull out of this grand plot with Lady Anne, he could because the only people who witnessed the marriage are people who can be easily banished from court. Perchance that is why he chose to leave you outside the door. Perchance that is why he picked Audley as Lord Chancellor; because Audley knows so damned little about all these plans. Audley has not heard the details of Henry's love for Anne. Henry and Anne married that night in secret, in Calais. We were the witnesses. You and I also married that night, and Henry deems it real in the eyes of God. This is a ceremony to placate the Lady Anne, as they are simply saying the words we did in Calais. But a rushed secret union? After all these seven years of courting? I feel as if something is missing, as if Henry is planning an escape.'

'Henry might tell me if he was,' Crumwell replied. 'By Christ, the King spared me no detail of what it is to make love to the Lady Anne.'

'I blocked my ears.'

'Wise decision.'

'Are they as skilled at love as us?'

Crumwell finally cracked a half-smile under the hand on his lips. 'Never.'

'None of this is real until Cranmer is officially consecrated by His Holiness, and you know how the Pope is with paperwork. We have months to form a plan.'

'But Audley is still appointed. He will be Lord Chancellor from tomorrow. Audley followed the same career path as More, being the parliamentary speaker, and the Chancellor to the Lancaster duchy. Never was I going to gain those positions, not being low born. To think I abandoned Wolsey to do this work! I left him to die in his sickbed and took all the trappings of office! And for what?'

Nicóla rounded the desk to Crumwell and he pulled her onto his lap. He clung to her tightly, his head resting on her shoulder. Nicóla expected him to cry, but he refrained.

'So many people know my desire to be Chancellor,' Crumwell whispered. 'My closest friends.'

'Well indeed, your closest friends,' Nicóla affirmed as she stroked his dark hair. 'They will never break your confidence.'

'Where have I gone wrong, Nicó? How can I lose now, after forcing Queen Katherine from her throne, and pushing the Pope's power from England? Has God forsaken me?'

'Permission to be ruthless?'

'Granted,' Crumwell said with a slight smile.

'Leave to me the changes needed. We shall go and be prized guards upon this secret wedding at dawn, and keep moving. As long as I am not showing the baby under my clothes, I will be working to be of service to you. Let us not lose all courage.'

Chapter 41 - April 1533
Whitehall Palace and Austin Friars, London

Keepyng a seecryt can taketh a toll, a pryce thee cannot payeth

'Master Crumwell, there is talk.'

'Well, far be it from me to stop the talk. What is the talk, Mr. Wriothesley? Am I taxing babies? Am I controlling the King with my turquoise ring? Am I hiding chests of gold and jewels inside Austin Friars? Am I performing witchcraft on peasants?'

'Oh, all of those things, all made up by Ambassador Chapuys. There is also talk there is a sort of affair between you and George Boleyn's wife, Jane.'

Crumwell burst into laughter and leaned back in his chair. Wriothesley across his desk did the same. 'That meek thing?' Crumwell scoffed. 'Does she even speak?'

'Well indeed she does, of her adoration of you, Master Crumwell. As does Mary Boleyn. And Anne Gainsford, Margaret Douglas, Margery Horsman, Jane Seymour. You have every eager young thing at court casting her eye. You could make a fine husband.'

'Folly, Wriothesley.'

'Do you ever mean to take a wife?'

'Never. What of business, Wriothesley, the real news?'

'The commoners are talking about you.'

'Remember I am one of the commoners.'

'Not any longer, Master Crumwell.'

Crumwell looked to Wriothesley on the other side of the desk. He had come to collect letters to be taken to the Lord Privy Seal Thomas

Boleyn for approval before being sent across the country. Wriothesley stood there, with a stupid white feather floating out of his black hat. Wriothesley was a smart lawyer, but suffered from too much confidence. Still, he was useful to have in service. Wriothesley lacked morals, which often sped up work.

'What is wrong? Wriothesley, just spit it out.'

'There is talk you are lining your own pockets, not just the King's. Much of the court is talking about you, about how much money has flooded into the King's Exchequer since you claimed the taxes from churches away from Rome and into accounts of the King.'

'So the commoners worry I make too much money, and the nobles worry about how much money I am making for the King. I shall add those to the list of crimes against my name. Along with the issue of bedding George Boleyn's timid wife.'

'There is the issue of coin clipping, and how you have made it illegal, and of how harsh the penalty for coin clipping and counterfeiting is now.'

Crumwell put his quill back in its gold holder and touched its cold base for a moment; a gift from Nicóla. 'Wolsey approved of coin clipping. I see the value in taking gold and silver coin, clipping bits off, and melting it to make more coins. But the reasoning of the original coin is reduced. We need to make sure Europe sees our currency as worth its face value. It is essential for trade; merchants and shippers need to know they are being paid fairly.'

'To the common man, this means nothing. They meddle not with foreigners or trading.'

'Then the commoners can leave the King's coins in the value they find them, and have no reason to worry themselves.' Crumwell gave Wriothesley a fake smirk.

'We miss you at Austin Friars,' Wriothesley tried to change the subject from the popular dislike for his master. 'It has been some time since you made it home. Ralph is busy, and with Richard away working for the Privy Council now that his wife is well again… but there are suspicions Ellen is with child.'

'Ralph will be a father soon?' Crumwell said, and his bad mood lifted for a moment. It was but four months since Ralph's wedding. 'More babies at Austin Friars. Wonderful.'

'Ralph is worried he will have to leave Austin Friars to set up home with his wife.'

'Nonsense, it is a home for life for all, including the Sadler children. How… how is Nicóla? He is most unwell.'

'In truth, I barely see him. In bed most of the time, though that is the point of leaving the court when ill.'

Crumwell nodded and thought of Nicóla. She bore Crumwell's bad demeanour and anger over the Lord Chancellor position. For months she worked day and night on anything Crumwell asked. Nicóla carried his baby and had to bind her stomach to hide it under her doublet. But when Nicóla suggested she take to her bed well before her confinement, Crumwell was stunned. It was not like Nicóla at all. Now she was but three miles away at Austin Friars, but it felt a thousand miles, given Crumwell's workload at Whitehall Palace.

'Do you know your Gregory writes to Nicóla?' Wriothesley asked.

'No. Gregory barely writes anything. His Latin is average at best.'

'Master Gregory wrote to Nicóla, in English. He seems to greatly admire the Waif. Gregory said he wishes to come home from Cambridge permanently. He is disliked by other students, and the workload does not suit.'

'With admittance, I too am not happy with Gregory there, the progress on his education is slow.'

'Nicóla was talking with Ralph and Ellen about Gregory over dinner. Nicóla worried Gregory struggled because of your high expectations, and Ralph agreed. The other Cambridge students cast him out because his father is the all-powerful Thomas Crumwell at the King's court.'

'Seems I can do no right by anyone.'

'Nicóla wrote Gregory, provided some solace. Nicóla was to suggest you find the creditors of the Cambridge students' parents, and then financially destroy them by recalling their debts.'

Crumwell could not help but laugh. Nicóla knew no form of parental responsibility. 'That is a very Italian thing to say.'

'Nicóla is not well, Master Crumwell. Ralph and I discussed it several times. I know not the rift which sits between Ralph and Nicóla. They avoid keeping company. But Ralph said you ought to know how ill Nicóla has become, but did not specify why.'

Wriothesley did not know the truth of Nicóla. Ralph did not know of the baby. At least Ralph and Nicóla were speaking a little at Austin Friars. Ralph had thawed in recent months in relation to Nicóla's secret, but would never consider her kin again. The thought of Nicóla with child by Crumwell would send Ralph away from the family and Austin Friars, Crumwell felt sure. Richard felt safe in Nicóla's company now, his heart more patient than in times past. In his current angered state, Crumwell half-thought of telling the world Nicóla was a woman, that she was with child, that Nicóla married Crumwell before the King and his Anne, in Calais. The world did not know Henry and Anne were married in England either, many months after the union. The weight of the court sat on Crumwell's shoulders.

Behind Wriothesley, one of the King's gentleman-ushers appeared. Crumwell beckoned him through the other clerks and into the private office. 'To work, Mr. Wriothesley, for the King's work never stops.'

Wriothesley bowed politely and left, leaving the usher to step forward. 'Let me guess, the King needs me.'

'Yes, Master Crumwell, immediately.'

'His mood?'

'Well enough, Master Crumwell. His Majesty is due in the presence chamber in a moment, and needs your assistance.'

'The presence chamber?' Crumwell asked as he jumped from his seat; the King was not seeing anyone today. 'Has something happened?'

'There are a handful of men who are permitted to listen to the King. Most of his council are arriving, but the King said you must be present before anything can be done.'

The presence chamber, with Henry's throne under his cloth of estate, remained mostly empty. But present were Anne's family, both her brother George, now called Lord Rochford by all, and her father Thomas, Earl of Wiltshire. Perchance they learned Anne had married in secret. Surely so. Wiltshire glanced over and gave Crumwell a nod of hello, in conversation with the difficult Charles Brandon, the pompous Duke of Suffolk. Shaky-hands Gardiner was there, talking with Thomas Howard, Duke of Norfolk. Sir Thomas Audley was there too, with a smile as he spoke with Thomas Cranmer, now in purple bishop's robes. Their conversation quickly broke off when Cranmer saw Crumwell enter.

'A hearty congratulations is in order,' Cranmer said and shook Crumwell's hand.

'It is you being consecrated as the Archbishop,' Crumwell replied. He made sure Gardiner heard his voice; Gardiner could never be an archbishop now; he had risen as high as he ever could. Pious Catholic Gardiner would never gain the King's favour again, not as long as Crumwell kept the King's mind towards reformation and Gardiner continued to oppose the notion.

'Thomas, I hear the Restraint of Appeals has just passed in parliament and is now law. The King shall make all final decisions over the Church, and no one can ask the Pope to sit in judgement on anything,' Cranmer said, loud enough for all to hear.

'Oh, yes. Yes, it passed on the sixth of the month.' This law was one of Crumwell's finest moments, yet after missing out on Lord Chancellor, and Nicóla away ill, the joy was taken from it. There should be parties to celebrate, but Crumwell did not even leave his desk. 'It is a huge step forward, and no doubt will provide you, Archbishop Cranmer, with many matters to settle now the Pope and his weakness, his idolatry, his greedy and spoiled mind can no longer make decisions.'

Both Gardiner and Norfolk looked at Crumwell with frowns, both still so fervently Catholic. Lucky Sir Thomas More was not there; otherwise he may have burst into flame upon Crumwell's words.

'Congratulations on passing the Restraint of Appeals,' Audley said to Crumwell and shook his hand. 'Already I miss parliament, but this new job shall keep me busy.'

'Well indeed it shall,' Crumwell said and dared not grit his teeth, least show his grievance. He did not blame Audley for his appointment as Lord Chancellor; he was a friend and fine gentleman. But it hurt all the same.

'Have you read any of the new published works Sir Thomas More has written? Five new publications, all supporting the Catholic faith, Queen Katherine, and Rome for preventing the annulment.'

'More is lucky he does not lose his head,' Crumwell muttered. 'He resigns as Chancellor to live quietly and pray. He has done slight more than try to raise hell. More and Bishop Fisher need to be far more careful.' Crumwell still feared More, even with More banished far from court.

The doors to the King's privy chamber opened and a bejeweled Henry bounded out, a wide smile on his complexion. Everyone bowed in time as Henry stepped up to his throne, and crossed his legs, the smile remaining. A happily married man, dressed in gold and jewels. Ready to take on life. In his hands he held the chains of office, the one all adored. The Chain of Esses. The golden SS Spiritus Sanctus symbols weaved over and over around the chain, with the Tudor rose pendant in the middle. More had worn it for almost ten years before resigning. Crumwell sighed; was it to be Audley's now? Logic suggested so.

'Gentlemen,' Henry announced as they all stood together in line before the King. 'We have a grand many things to discuss. But I have things I must do, so we shall make this meeting brief. You have all no doubt heard of Crumwell's most grand victory in parliament, passing the Restraint of Appeals Act, meaning Katherine cannot appeal to Rome on our annulment any longer. As soon as we have received the papal bulls from Rome, Dr. Cranmer shall be formally consecrated as Archbishop, and he shall complete my annulment. Without you, Mr. Crumwell, none of this would be real. The Acts you have pushed through parliament are enabling my new marriage, and also filling my Exchequer. We ought to be grateful.'

Everyone gave applause but Crumwell could not raise a smile. Yes, he found success, but for every move he made, every secret he heard, another issue just landed in his lap.

'Mr. Crumwell,' the King continued, 'now we have all the power we need from the Church to reform it and have my marriage annulled. You have plainly excelled even yourself. But now, we must also have the legal means to make marriage to Lady Anne lawful.'

Crumwell sighed; indeed, another request, one he had foreseen months ago. 'Your Majesty, I have two new bills to put before parliament, and both compromise not. The first shall call a special meeting of the clerical Convocation, to sit in judgement on the annulment. As soon-to-be Archbishop Cranmer will have ruled the marriage unlawful, the Convocation shall be forced to pass a canon law stating to that effect. As Supreme Head of the Church, Your Majesty shall pass judgement on the ruling, and thus, legally your first marriage shall be annulled. The second bill shall also be presented, stating Queen Katherine shall be styled as Princess Dowager of Wales, and your daughter, Princess Mary, will no longer be legitimate. Only the children of your second marriage can ascend to the throne.'

'Do these laws have to be presented to the Convocation? Is not the Restraint of Appeals already law? Is Katherine not yet fully defeated?' Henry asked, frown ready to strike.

'Your Majesty,' Cranmer parleyed. 'These issues must be arranged.

All the work Mr. Crumwell has done…'

'Let us worry not about the details, I shall leave it in the hands of you both. We must move to another issue,' Henry interrupted. Crumwell wondered if the King were to announce his secret marriage and the baby. Rumour swirled around court already. Lady Anne had mentioned pregnancy to Thomas Wyatt months ago. Ambassador Chapuys oozed with idle talk, much of it of his own making. If all were public knowledge, the weight on Crumwell's shoulders may ease. But instead, the King held up the Chain of Esses.

'Mr. Crumwell.' The King gestured for him to step forward. Crumwell did so with confusion; was he forced to adorn Audley with the chains as well as be passed over? Oh, to have Nicóla's guidance, her comfort at this time. 'So many things are done officially here at court, as you expect. Roles and posts are created and held for centuries. But sometimes, a king feels the need to create different roles, such as different men require. So with that in mind, Mr. Crumwell, I am making you, with no precedent needed, the King's Chief Minister. This shall be the most important role at court, standing above the Privy Council, above parliament, above the Lord Chancellor. You are to take orders from no one but me, and you are to work with Archbishop Cranmer on all spiritual matters. You shall be something of a Secretary of State. National security in both legal and spiritual matters shall fall upon your shoulders. Such is your role hither these past years you have indeed worked in no official capacity, and have taken such a wide role in court. It is now you must have an official title and role here, so we can continue to exploit all your merits. Naturally you shall also receive money and noble lands to match your new state.'

The King stepped down from his throne and Crumwell bowed, on his knees before his sovereign. The double-minded man had no words to utter. Henry placed the Chain of Esses around Crumwell's shoulders, sitting the gold on his grey overgown, lined with black fox fur. As the title weighed upon Crumwell, so did the pure gold.

'Thank you, Your Majesty does me a celebrated honour,' Crumwell said, his eyebrows high to match his total surprise.

Henry raised him to his feet and Crumwell stepped back to see wide smiles from Cranmer and Audley. Wiltshire and his son Rochford looked much pleased, such was their fealty. The two dukes and Gardiner frowned with curiosity and suspicion. 'Now we enjoy such a level of success, I must depart for the afternoon with Lady Anne. Wiltshire, Rochford, let us depart.'

As the group dispersed from the King's company, Crumwell charged back to his offices. As soon as word of this got out, every man at court, and many ladies as well, would knock upon his door, asking for favours. This was his one chance to leave Whitehall.

~~~

The barge took him downriver and a quick walk saw him to Austin Friars in the middle of the winter's day. Peter, at the steward's room, opened the gates with absolute joy to see his generous master at home. It was Ralph who came to the door, his eyes lighting up at the sight of the Chain of Esses.

'By God, Master Crumwell, did you rob the King?'

'I am the King's Chief Minister. The official title for official work. Better than Lord Chancellor now.'

'Congratulations,' Ralph replied. But his eyes spoke of no happiness, no genuine praise.

'What is it, Ralph?'

'Indeed, I was to send a messenger to you. Have you spoken with Wriothesley? Is that why you came?'

'Yes, I have spoken to him, but came after meeting with the King.'

'You come just in time.' Ralph and Crumwell walked further into the house, and in the private library, Ralph shut the door on the clerks in the other rooms. 'Master, it is Nicóla. She... he... is most unwell. Ellen, of course, knows the truth about Nicóla, but do not worry, she is private. Perchance women make sense of such witchcraft with ease.'

'No matter, I know I can trust your wife, Ralph. It is you who vexes me on that subject. What is wrong?'

'Both Ellen and Mercy have been with Nicóla for the best part of the day. They are all on the third floor and no one has come in or out. Now I know nothing of women's business...'

Crumwell sighed heavily again. Every time something went well, another weight was added to his shoulders. 'Has the physician been sent for?' Instantly the Chain of Esses meant nothing. If Nicóla was half as ill as Elizabeth became, God forbid.

'How would a doctor understand the abomination hidden in our home?' Ralph spat. 'Mercy has been in charge. Ellen went to aid, and never returned.'

'Ralph, Nicóla is with child.'

'You knew, and said nothing? God's blood, how are we going to hide a baby? What happened?'

'I got the baby on her.'

Ralph's eyes grew so wide they almost fell from his face.

'Baby Jane is also mine.' Crumwell paused as Ralph coughed from the shock. 'This is to be private. It is my own life.'

'What a secret to keep!'

'Trust me, the weight was worn us both.'

'This is an affront to God!' Ralph cried and crossed himself. 'We are all deceived!'

'Nicóla is with child and deathly ill,' Crumwell burned with anger, his deep voice quiet yet profound. 'It is time you paid more heed to your words, Ralph. You shall defy me not, for I am commander of England. I wished you not to marry my laundress, but I relented. You have used all my patience and love for you.'

Ralph swallowed hard and his eyes dropped to the carpets beneath their feet. 'I would have sent a messenger to you much sooner, had I known of a child,' Ralph said. 'Mercy and Ellen have been bolted in Nicóla's rooms all day. Everyone has kept away, even the nurses with Jane.'

The door to the library burst opened, and there stood Ellen. Crumwell looked at Ellen's tiny hands; she had recently wiped them clean. Blood still rimmed her short fingernails. Her eyes appeared reddened, her skin pale. God have mercy.

'Master Crumwell, thank the Lord you are here,' Ellen wept as she stepped forward to Ralph. 'Moments ago I was ready to send a messenger to the palace. Oh, Master Crumwell, I am so sorry!'

Crumwell ran past Ellen and galloped straight up the stairs. He shoved the bedroom door open, to find Nicóla curled up on her bed, blood splattered all over the sheets. Mercy stood next to her, washing the blood from her hands in a pewter bowl.

'Oh, Tom,' Mercy wept, 'I am so sorry. We could do nothing, only the Lord could decide.'

Crumwell's golden eyes tried to take in everything; beside Mercy was a white blanket, soaked in blood; the baby. He did his best to look not and knelt down on the floor beside Nicóla's face. Again.

Crumwell felt the pounding of his heart, in his throat choking him, in his ears deafening him. Nicóla looked so pale, almost yellow in her sickness. Her hair, chopped short in haste, clung to her, sweat covering very inch of her sallow skin. Nicóla had said she did not feel right; Crumwell had sent her to Austin Friars and continued working, not knowing the truth. Crumwell could breathe not as he looked upon Nicóla's white nightgown, stained with blood from the waist down, her legs curled up under the wet fabric. Tears ran down his tired cheeks, his sight blurred in the horror. Crumwell touched her precious face and her green eyes opened just a fraction. Nicóla was still alive; this time he was not too late. Crumwell clutched her hand to his chest as her eyes fluttered, unable to stay open.

'Almighty and Eternal God, You are the everlasting health of those who believe in You,' he prayed, gasped as he fought his emotions. 'Hear us for Your sick servant Nicóletta, for whom we implore the aid of Your tender mercy, that being restored to bodily health, she may give thanks to You in Your Church. Through Christ our Lord. Amen.' Crumwell kissed her hand and held it to his tear-sodden cheek.

Nicóla looked at him and opened her lips to speak, but no sound came forth. 'Pray speak not, my love,' he whispered. 'You are in safe hands.'

Nicóla's eyes drifted to the chain over his clothes, Crumwell watched her eyes shape their way around the gold. 'Think now of nothing,' he said in reply. He glanced up at Mercy.

'Sorry, Tom,' Mercy said again. 'About an hour ago, the labour came on quickly and ended just as hasty. A boy, about seven months along. Too small for life, stillborn I am afraid. We had no time to call for a priest.'

'No, I shall send for Cranmer. He knows all and we shall be able to pray in safety and without judgement.' Crumwell got up and went to Mercy, who hugged him tightly. The pair suffered so much loss together. Mercy unwrapped the cloth on the table beside the bowl to reveal a tiny child, a boy. Too small for life indeed; no bigger than one hand. A son, not longed for this world, in heaven with Grace and Anne, and two stillborn sons Elizabeth bore years ago.

'I shall let you send for Cranmer. We all need to pray,' Mercy said and wrapped the baby up again before leaving the bedroom, no doubt to let her own emotions drain. Crumwell returned to the bedside and Nicóla opened her eyes again, this time wider, more alert.

'You are going to be well, Nicó, for I will get the best physician in London to you. I shall request Dr. William Butts, the King's physician. Butts is close with Cranmer, we shall be able to trust him.'

'No need,' she whispered, her mouth dry, her lips white and parched.

'The doctor can be of service. Elizabeth, God rest her soul, miscarried our first two sons before Gregory came along. We must be sure you are well.'

'Pray speak,' Nicóla whispered, 'speak of something else. Anything but this.'

Crumwell's mind fell blank, a rare happening. 'The King titled me the King Chief's Minister.'

'Thank the Lord for something fine,' she whispered. 'For I am at my limit, with life and God.'

Crumwell kissed her thin cheek, his arms around her, blood soaked everywhere. God was angry at Crumwell's changes to the Church and had taken an innocent life as payment.

Chapter 42 - May 1533
Whitehall Palace, London

A seecryt revealed can cureth all ills

It felt desirable to be back at court. To be around people again. In the antechamber, the room of pause while waiting to enter the King's presence chamber, was always a prized place to sit in the corner and listen. That is what Thomas Wyatt did most often, and Mark Smeaton often joined. Sitting there, in a plain room, men milled in groups, whispered and brought much entertainment. Through the wide doorway, left open with guards posted either side, Nicóla heard the voices of the King and Crumwell as they spoke informally with whoever stood before them. Something, anything to block out the thoughts of her stillbirth five weeks ago. No one had any idea, so mourning in public was no option. Baby Thomas was gone from this world, and Nicóla dared not speak the truth; she needed the past months to be forgotten.

'You are well met, Nicóla,' Smeaton said with his wide grin. He had gone and had his curly dark hair cut since Nicóla saw him last, now clipped short like the King himself. 'We worried about you being gone from the court for so long. Not even visitors to Austin Friars?'

'Quite,' Wyatt added.

'We worried you had the sweating sickness or plague, but as the illness dragged on, we knew you suffered neither. What can make a person sick for more than two months?'

'Bad luck?' Nicóla shrugged and the men both nodded. 'Indeed I know not, as the physicians were of no use. The women of the house, though, tended to me and I am healthy.'

'God bless every woman,' Smeaton replied, looking around the room. 'Not that we ever get many in here.'

His eyes ran up and down Nicóla, and she smiled. He knew. Wyatt knew. They just never said anything, they played the game and kept the Waif's secret, just as many back in Italy. Nicóla often felt surprised the game had lasted this long.

'Venetian Ambassador Carlo Capelli,' came Crumwell's voice through the doorway, and an Italian shuffled to meet the King.

'I do loathe that man,' Nicóla commented to her friends, all sitting together huddled in the corner, as if naughty children. 'Capelli spent time in Florence with my father. He is a man whose hands wished to wander.'

'Is that not every man at court?' Smeaton teased, and they all laughed.

'If the ambassador thinks he shall get any help from England as the Turks prepare to invade Venice, Capelli is sorely wrong,' Wyatt mused.

'England is an empire unto herself now, thanks to Master Crumwella. The English Empire has no need for the fealty or protection of the Holy Roman Emperor or his men,' Nicóla replied.

The muffled voice of the King flew through the doorway, and the ambassador was dispatched at once. 'God, that was fast,' Smeaton commented as the older man left the King's rooms entirely.

Again Crumwell's voice called from the doorway, where men stood papers in hand, hoping to hear their name. 'Master secretary to the King's Chief Minister, Nicóla Frescobaldi.'

Nicóla sat upright, surprised to hear her name. She got up gently from her seat and smoothed her long black doublet she had made while recovering. 'What have I done?' she whispered to her friends.

'You have a title and the King commands to see you,' Smeaton said and nudged her shoulder with his. 'Indeed I have found the right friend at court.'

'All part of being one of Master Crumwella's creatures. We can all enjoy such a role,' Nicóla whispered with a saucy grin and scuttled between men to find her way to Crumwell. He led her through the doorway, a narrow smile on his face. No need to panic then.

'Your Majesty.' Nicóla bowed low, relieved to feel no pain in her stomach at last. She stood tall, hands clasped together before the King on his throne under his cloth of estate. Crumwell stood to her right, facing her, smile now gone.

'Welcome back to court, Mr. Frescobaldi,' the King said with a smile. 'I do believe you have been away for some time, most ill.'

'Well indeed, I was much ill, but I am recovered. I cannot thank His Majesty enough for the kind use of his physician.'

'When Mr. Crumwell said you fell ill, I thought there was no other option. It is a shame you were not hither while Mr. Crumwell was elevated in status.'

'Well indeed, but the work has brought me much pleasure as my master rises, Your Majesty.'

'Master,' the King muttered and nodded to Crumwell. 'If only I could order a bride as you can order Mr. Frescobaldi.' He winked to Crumwell, who did not acknowledge the jest. 'Has Mr. Crumwell brought you to rights on all our changes?'

'Naturally, Your Majesty.' The royal baby was still a secret. The fact the secret wedding happened at all was only a rumour. Anne Boleyn must have been ready to burst with her success, though surely the Boleyn clan also knew. She must have said something to Wyatt because he seemed to think Anne pregnant. Cranmer had nearly fainted when he heard of the secret wedding, weeks after the fact. But the King seemed to think the whole world was at his feet, months after the wedding.

'Worry not, Mr. Frescobaldi, my physician is a discreet man. Surprised, but discreet. I understand the illness you have borne, and it is a vast pain to carry. It is an illness that can I understand more than I wish.'

Nicóla glanced to Crumwell, and he nodded once. The King knew she had lost a son, just as Queen Katherine lost five children. 'Thank you, Your Majesty.'

'Let us discuss better tidings. You attended the consecration of Archbishop Cranmer at St. Stephens Chapel at Westminster?'

'Yes, Your Majesty. It was an honour to see Archbishop Cranmer consecrated, and presented new holy purple robes and mitre hat.' The same attire poor old Wolsey got buried in, rather than the scarlet robes of a cardinal. Nicóla dared not regard the King or Crumwell when she thought of old Wolsey.

'It was a marvellous occasion indeed, to pray with the new

Archbishop of Canterbury at Westminster, was it not?' Henry continued.

'Well indeed, Your Majesty. Archbishop Cranmer is an astute and intelligent man, full of heart and praise for the Church and the realm. His mind is clear and open, yet filled with love.' Cranmer also had an illegal wife hidden away, her belly full with child, but no one could know. Margarete was still brought to Austin Friars for dinner in a crate like books being delivered. A crate for a pregnant woman in a foreign land. No wonder Nicóla wished for a man's life.

'You were hither not when we received the nine papal bulls, signed by Pope Clement, approving our choice of Archbishop. I know you and the Pope talked on the subject…'

'I did write to Pope Clement, Your Majesty, when in Calais. However, I have not received any reply.' A lie direct to the King, of sorts. No word had come to England, but Nicóla had written the Pope again, to let him know of her baby and her loss. Now her baby's soul could be mentioned in the Holy See. It would also go a long way in explaining why she had still not returned to Italy.

'Do you not find this lack of correspondence curious?' Henry asked. 'You are hither as the… contact to the Pope. Does Campeggio still advise the Pope?'

'I am certain, Your Majesty. I once lived in the holy embrace of the Apostolic Palace, where no one wishes to leave. To pray in the Sistine Chapel, to live in the Raphael Rooms, walk the abandoned Borgia Apartments, it is all a deeply spiritual place.' For a second, Nicóla felt the familiar pain of being far from home. Those walls inside the papal palace offered such refuge after the murder of her father. Now the same people who once housed Nicóla were her enemies, those who fought to take her from Crumwell.

'It is almost as if you wish to return to the Papal States,' the King said. 'Is that the case?'

'Never on my life or upon my honour, Your Majesty. To be in Your Majesty's presence is a joy, as if walking into the sun after a long winter. I do not wish myself away for anything in the world. You bring new life to your realm, your empire comes into the light, and your people shall be better for it. You shall unbind them from the superstition and idolatry of the Catholic Church, and let them understand true worship.'

'You sound so much like my Anne.'

'I fear I deserve no praise as high, Your Majesty.'

The King gave a slight nod to Crumwell and he smiled. Nicóla said all the right things; the things the King enjoyed hearing. Surely after more than twenty years on the throne, Henry knew when a person spoke in flattering tones. Mayhap his indulgence prevented Henry from being able to appraise anyone.

'Well, I am pleased you recovered, and I thought you may wish to hear some things I have to say to Mr. Crumwell,' the King replied. Henry did so see Nicóla as a fool in his court, a token of diversion for his entertainment. Will Sommers may have been Henry's official court fool, but Nicóla was a novelty to play with at leisure. Nicóla bowed again and stood to the far left, where a few people stood, Anne Boleyn's father being one of them, only now listening to the conversation.

Crumwell took the spot before the King, his black journal in his hands, ready as ever to serve the King. 'Mr. Crumwell, you sent the licence to Lambeth Palace, to Archbishop Cranmer, so he can set up an ecclesiastical court and decide on my marriage once and for all. What progress?'

'Archbishop Cranmer has already made arrangement for the Court of Bishops to sit at Dunstable in Bedfordshire. We thought it better to avoid the crowds of London.'

'Indeed. The last thing we need is a riot.'

'Also, I have written two new bills to put through parliament. The first bill went unchallenged. The second; anyone who fails to pass this law shall be removed from office and imprisoned.'

'Excellent. You are learning how to use your power as Chief Minister, Mr. Crumwell. What be these bills?'

'The first you know, that the Convocation of Canterbury must sit in judgement on the opinion of your marriage and its annulment. As you know, they are already meeting at St Paul's at Westminster, at this very moment. The second bill is to create a licence stating you are free to marry at any time, once the Convocation and the ecclesiastical court have ruled.'

'Ruled in my favour.'

'In your favour, Your Majesty. Legally, all is arranged. Now we wait for the Archbishop's ruling, and also the Convocation passing the canon law, with your approval, of course.'

'And what of Sir Thomas More? Is he still writing against me?'

Crumwell looked to Nicóla for a moment, and then back to the King. 'Yes, More is still writing you must remain married, and is publishing his pamphlets on the subject.'

'More was my friend,' Henry said, slipping on his throne. 'For twenty years he has been a guiding light, a humanist, a man of great learning, and now he goes against me, even after swearing to live quietly. Never mind, I have not said what I wish to say. As you will know, John Bouchier, the second Baron Berners, Chancellor of the Exchequer, died in Calais not a month ago. We must fill the role, as what is going into the royal accounts, and more importantly, going out, needs to be carefully watched. It cannot be unguarded, not now we are finally filling the coffers again. Mr. Crumwell, I want you to be Chancellor of the Exchequer. After all, you are the one filling my accounts with taxes from the churches and monasteries.'

Nicóla felt a pain her chest, but of excitement. Official control over the royal accounts and expenses. Master of the Jewel House, Clerkship of the Hanaper, Master of the King's Wards, King's Chief Minister, Secretary of State, and now Chancellor of the Exchequer. Crumwell now held almost all the important posts in the kingdom. Not being appointed Lord Chancellor still stung, but Audley could never wield much power, not while Crumwell served the court.

Crumwell got down on one knee, his head bowed. 'I cannot thank you enough for the trust Your Majesty places in me.'

Henry got down from his throne and guided Crumwell to stand again. 'Thomas, you are the only friend I can truly trust. You have no fealty to any noble house, you have no daughter you seek to marry me to, God be praised. You do not dangle mistresses before me. You do not lie to me. You are quite unlike anyone who has served me. Your honesty and your incredible work ethic are without equal. Lady Anne speaks of you and calls you "her man" now, such is her trust that you can make her a queen. You are the only man I trust with the Exchequer.'

'Your Majesty,' Crumwell bowed his head once more. The King's ring-laden hands rested upon Crumwell's shoulders, on the Chain of Esses.

'Let us miss the rest of the petitioners for the day. Let us celebrate your fortunes. Bring your Waif, if you desire.' Henry looked to Nicóla and winked.

'Your Majesty,' came an anxious voice from the antechamber.

Crumwell turned and found the man, a messenger eager to enter. 'A message from Westminster.'

Henry gestured for the boy to enter and he bowed, trying to catch his breath.

'Speak,' Crumwell ordered.

'Your Majesty is to be informed that the Convocation of Canterbury, upon their meeting on St. Paul's Cathedral, have voted in the case of your annulment to Queen Katherine. They have voted His Majesty's marriage to Katherine was impeded by divine law, and the Pope cannot alter this fact. The King's marriage to Princess Katherine of Aragon is ruled unlawful.' The boy held out papers as he spoke, and Crumwell snatched them from his grubby hands.

'By God's grace!' the King yelled at the loudest of his deep voice, which echoed around the rooms. It brought all to a halt, shocked by the news. The Convocation of Canterbury, under Cranmer, had finally yielded. Divorce was now possible. Ever since first asking about annulment in 1527, now it was possible. After seven years of waiting for Anne Boleyn, Henry could be free. Thomas Boleyn ran out of the room, no doubt to tell his daughter the news. Crumwell dismissed the messenger boy with a coin, only to see his own spy at the Convocation, Ralph, enter the antechamber. He clicked his fingers twice and Ralph ushered into the presence chamber and bowed, skidding on the floor in his rush.

'Tell us all,' Crumwell urged as Nicóla stepped forward to be included.

'The Convocation set themselves to a vote and Cranmer stated anyone who did not place a vote meant to consent to the annulment,' Ralph explained to the King. 'Most men stayed silent, others openly stated they approved the decision and the annulment. But 25 clerics openly voted against the decision to grant an annulment.'

'Let me guess,' the King said, 'Bishop Fisher.'

'Yes, Your Majesty,' Ralph muttered.

'If only Fisher had died during his poisoning,' the King replied.

Nicóla glanced to Crumwell who widened his golden eyes in agreement with the King.

'Your Majesty,' Nicóla spoke out, hoping she did not talk out of turn. 'From Italy I heard that Bishop Fisher conspired with the Pope and the Holy Roman Emperor for several years. Fisher and Sir Thomas More talk regularly. Bishop Fisher should not be on the ecclesiastical panel with Archbishop Cranmer, for his influence could stop Cranmer from making the final crucial papers about your annulment.'

'Bloody Bishop Fisher,' Henry growled, his happiness already lost in favour of anger.

'You could arrest Bishop Fisher,' Nicóla suggested, unsure of the theory herself. It just flew from her mouth and Crumwell glared at her, Ralph stunned in surprise. 'If you arrest Fisher, hold him in the Tower long enough that he cannot vote on the ecclesiastical court, or see you crown Lady Anne, then he shall not impede you. You could then release him after the coronation.'

The King just looked to Crumwell, who nodded gently in agreement. 'Issue the arrest of Bishop John Fisher, Mr. Crumwell, on the King's orders. No charges to be laid against him at this time. We shall wait and see what happens next.'

~~~

Once back in the Crumwell chambers, Ralph shut the door to the private office, rarely closed. Nicóla sat in the chair at her desk, her back sore, while Crumwell paced back and forth. Ralph's eyes followed his master but chose not to comment. Crumwell considered Ralph his son. The anger and confusion caused by Nicóla's gender put that relationship to dust. They seldom spoke, messages sent in place of words. But Nicóla decided to end the silence.

'Ralph, how is Ellen and her child?'

Ralph faltered for a moment; he wished not to say.

'Has she felt the quickening of the child?' Nicóla pushed.

'She has, Nicóla. Ellen is nervous. Of course, her first husband gave her two children, so she is well versed on the subject. But...'

But Ellen saw Nicóla bleed out and lose a precious son. 'Both you and Archbishop Cranmer shall have summer children. Praise God gives you healthy sons.'

'Thank you,' Ralph murmured.

'Ralph,' Crumwell said and stopped pacing, 'whatever you think of Nicóla or indeed myself, please set all aside and do something important for me. I need you to go fetch papers needed to issue the arrest warrant for Fisher. Also, make a list of names of all who did not vote for the annulment. We shall need eyes on every one until Lady Anne is crowned.'

'Yes, right away, Master Crumwell,' Ralph responded, his voice flat. 'But first…I wish to say I am sorry, Master Crumwell. I am to gain a son just as you lose one. Ellen has forced me to take pity on the situation. I cannot play foolish and treat Nicóla with such disrespect. With patience and God's word, I hope we can one day reconcile.'

'Thank you, Ralph,' Crumwell said slowly.

Without another word, Ralph turned and disappeared from the main office, the door closed tight again. Crumwell fell to his knees before Nicóla and placed his head on her lap. In silence, she kissed his smooth cheek and ran her hands through his dark hair. The pain of the baby appeared whenever least expected, and there were no words. Crumwell just needed to be there with Nicóla, for that moment. Maybe the Crumwell family could heal after all. Because soon enough the world would be on fire, and a new queen crowned. Once reform laws were set upon the English people, thousands would be calling for Crumwell's head.

Chapter 43- June 1533
Westminster and Whitehall Palace, London

Allow thy seecryts breath and batheth in green air, to beest free

From the day the dispatch came from the hand of Archbishop Cranmer to Crumwell, stating the ecclesiastical court had once and for all declared the King's marriage unlawful, Crumwell had barely seen the ground, for all the papers thrust before his face. A whirlwind of activity, the thrill of happiness from success, gifts pouring to Crumwell, thanking him for all his work. Not that he had time to celebrate. His son, Gregory, was home from Cambridge, and this time was permanent, but Crumwell never once got to Austin Friars to see him. Between May 23, when Cranmer's letter came rushing to London, and five days later when Cranmer arrived back at Lambeth Palace, the coronation preparations became a sea of plans and arrangements, accounts and questions to be answered by Crumwell.

Every day, every minute, the King thought of something more he wanted for his delightful wife Anne Boleyn. The secret – the marriage in January - became public knowledge, and on May 28, Archbishop Cranmer finally confirmed the marriage as true. As for the son and heir, Anne's blossoming waist could no longer hide the truth. Crumwell had already spent months planning the renovations to the Queen's Apartments in the Tower of London, where all queens stayed before coronation. The rooms were ready on time for the four days of celebrations Henry demanded. Anne awaited at Greenwich, and Henry had her delivered to the Tower on a barge covered in new cloth of gold, with a procession of barges four miles long around her.

Crumwell swore he saw Nicóla's eyes water with alarm as she put together the accounts just for the procession. That was to say nothing of the cost of one thousand guns fired from the Tower when Lady Anne arrived to stay the night.

It was the procession through the city which caused the most grievance. The constables required to line the streets were a nightmare to pull together; poor Ralph spent an age sending and receiving letters, ordering people to the job. The plain houses in Cheapside needed to be decorated with golden cloth and velvet. Both Gracechurch Street and Cornhill Street had carpets laid, with tapestries hung all in shades of red, as the King demanded. Crumwell emptied out supplies from almost every merchant in London to get it done in time. Anne always loved the French, so Crumwell had the French ambassadors lead her procession, and all twelve expected new outfits, blue velvet with yellow sleeves. The hats needed large white feathers. The horses needed livery to match. At least the gentlemen of the English royal households had their own liveries; Crumwell was not paying for them, nor the procession of judges, the entire English government, or even the Privy Council. Crumwell wore his own livery, of all black, the softest velvet and satin Nicóla could source, embroidered with a golden thread with the King's blessing. Fat, old, pompous Suffolk looked shabby in compare.

The King wanted Lady Anne in white and gold, for her purity and his wealth. She was carried along the procession route in a white and gold litter, a cloth of gold over her. She wore a white gown even Nicóla thought highly esteemed, and gowns were something Nicóla never considered. Naturally, Anne wore a gold coronet in her flowing dark hair. Carriages carried Anne's ladies, who all demanded red dresses for the occasion. How many ladies-in-waiting did one woman need? Even Nicóla could not answer the question. Nicóla priced the new queen by the yard with her white dress, as large as it was, unable to hide the fact her belly held a child of six months now, almost the same age as baby Thomas when God took him to punish Crumwell's sins.

But trouble abounded; Crumwell could create all of this for Anne Boleyn, but he could not make the crowds adore her. They loved their queen – Katherine of Aragon. Crumwell ordered anyone crying out Katherine's name be beaten and have their ears nailed to the King's standard; that would silence Londoners. The procession gave people so little to cheer about, despite its opulent beauty. No one wanted a new queen but knew to keep their mouths shut. A few lost ears, but nothing severe. Crumwell did not tell Nicóla that detail; she might not approve.

Anne waved to her subjects, though few waved back; few bowed, few called to her. The new emblems, which cost a pretty penny to be made in a hurry, with an H for Henry and A for Anne, led people to call ha-ha as she passed. People could grumble all they liked; the K of Katherine would not be seen in public again, just like Katherine herself. It was only once the crown was placed on the long dark hair of Anne Boleyn that Crumwell felt success. He had made a queen. Henry may have wanted Anne, for his heart, for his equal, for his bed, for her womb, but it was Crumwell who created the queen. Crumwell took over and changed laws which allowed the marriage. He had broken the hold of the Catholic Church in England, paving the way for reformation the likes of which England had never seen. Crumwell would not stop until he had changed the lives of every man, woman and child, to bring them into the light of Protestant reform. That started with putting a new queen on the throne, and that queen called Crumwell "her man" to anyone who listened. The costs mattered none as Crumwell sat in Westminster Abbey, holding Nicóla's hand out of sight of other guests. He sat pride of place at the front with Nicóla, where noblemen sat.

At 9 o'clock on June 1, Whitsunday, Anne Boleyn walked down the aisle and sat at the altar in robes of purple velvet, the very best, trimmed with pure white ermine, her coronet gold, as Crumwell's queen deserved. Anne would not be anointed just as a wife of a king. Henry thought of her as an equal. The Lord Great Chamberlain produced the crown of St. Edward, meant only for true-born monarchs. Yet, after being prayed over and anointed by Archbishop Cranmer, Anne sat in St. Edmonds chair, given the crown, the scepter and orb. Even the commanding Katherine had not worn St. Edmonds crown. Nicóla muttered it looked as if the crown, gold and laden with magnificent rubies, diamonds and emeralds, would fall off Anne's tiny head, and Crumwell gave a smothered laugh in the cathedral, not just at the comment, but with jubilation. Jubilation at their success, happiness to see Nicóla well again, and enjoying all which creating a queen provided.

The marriage of Henry and Anne was real, and soon Cranmer

393

could make sure Crumwell's marriage to Nicóla could be, too. Crumwell felt for Anne, so heavy in her pregnancy. He thought of Nicóla, the same time along with her child, and how stress put enough pressure to send the child to God. Yet, Anne sat through her late evening coronation banquet, seated only with Cranmer, while the King entertained the French and Venetian ambassadors across the room. While Nicóla danced merrily in the centre of the banquet with the dainty Mark Smeaton, the pair something of a diversion at court, Crumwell wandered over to Anne and Cranmer.

'Ah, my man, Mr. Crumwell,' Anne said as he bowed deeply.

'Your Majesty,' he replied and watched the smirk grow on her lips, 'I trust you and the future heir to the throne are well?'

'Indeed we are,' Anne said, and rubbed her belly. She paused; she knew what had occurred with Nicóla's child, but said nothing. But it crossed Queen Anne's mind, Crumwell could tell, such was the sadness in her gaze. 'Is this not the most lavish, ornate festivity you have ever witnessed?'

'Indeed I hope so, for I have not slept in three weeks, all trying to bring together a glorious coronation.'

'You have done your utmost and the effort clearly shows,' Cranmer added, a man who always had a kind a word for anyone.

'We still have so much more to come, Your Majesty,' Crumwell told Anne. 'Tomorrow there are jousts, a ball and another banquet.'

'How much have you spent from the King's accounts for this?' Anne asked.

'Does it matter, Your Majesty? For the King said there was to be no expense spared.'

'No, it matters none; but if people are to talk, they may as well have the right figure in mind.'

'The city of London has paid around £45,000, Your Majesty, and the King personally, about £20,000.'

Archbishop Cranmer choked on his wine as if it had lumps of solid gold in it. For the price, it may have.

'For all the waiting,' Anne sighed, 'seven, eight years I have been the object of the King's affection. So much seemed to stand in the way, and yet, suddenly, the path cleared all at once. Is that not strange, Mr. Crumwell?'

Crumwell just shrugged. 'Your Majesty, it is all down to timing. Once old Warham died and we could install Cranmer, life became far simpler with his sound mind and education. It was like His Majesty's father when he won the crown from Richard the Third. He had battled in obscurity all his life, and then, one by one, his enemies died and Henry the Seventh ascended the throne. God clears the path when the time is right.'

'Do you remember, Mr. Crumwell, the night in the chapel at Grafton House? You spoke of love akin to a blind man. A blind man can smell a rose and think it lovely but could smell a poisonous plant as well, such is his inability to tell the difference?'

'Of course, Your Majesty. You also spoke of how the flower had no choice in the matter of the man's affection for its sweetness.' Crumwell knew Anne did not love Henry as he loved her. Anne did love the throne of England though; the reward for being the object the King craved for so long. The throne was thrust upon Anne, but she was intelligent enough to make considerable use of her status.

Queen Anne nodded, the skin beneath her eyes sagging with tiredness. 'All of Europe is talking about you, Mr. Crumwell,' Anne changed the subject, and Cranmer nodded in agreement. 'The Scottish say you are the ear and mind of the King. The Emperor in Rome is told you are the most worthy advisor in England. The French are amazed by your skills, as they are in the Low Countries. The Germans are amazed by the strides you have made with the reformation in England. It is almost as if Europe wishes to put a crown on your head.'

Good. About time. All this work, and now Crumwell had his King and his Queen. He had the top job. He could save the English from the Catholic Church. Crumwell had the Chain of Esses around his shoulders and had Nicóla safely in his life. Ralph, God be praised, would understand in time. Gregory loved Nicóla and lived safe and healthy at Austin Friars with Jane.

Once Crumwell extracted himself from Queen Anne, he wandered back to the party, to the good wishes of everyone at court. They did not esteem him, they feared him, but everyone needed to be in the mind and heart of Thomas Crumwell. He came to Nicóla, who had sat down with Wyatt while Smeaton went back to playing the lute. Nicóla stood up again when he approached, the others still talking.

'Nicó,' he said in Nicóla's ear as she leaned close towards him, 'Mark Smeaton is in love with you.'

Nicóla faced him with a smile. 'Hardly, for I am not certain he perceives to enjoy boys or girls.'

'Luckily you are my Waif and neither boy nor girl.'

'Your Waif, am I?'

Crumwell nodded and gestured for Nicóla to follow him. He led Nicóla from the banquet, down the hallways leading back to the chambers. Out of sight, Crumwell pushed her against the wall and kissed her, keen to have his own wife with him after years of worrying about the King's needs.

'What is all this?' Nicóla asked, breathless from his kiss. 'As I relish it, you are forceful all at once.'

'We work too much. We need to stop, we need to go to Austin Friars with Gregory and Jane. We need to visit the new houses I am building. We also need to make final peace with Ralph, and spend some time with Richard and Frances.'

'I prefer this idea.'

'For once we return, all the more work shall come. Sir Thomas More did not come today. The King is furious, We need to take down Sir Thomas More, and Bishop Fisher – for good.'

'All in good time, my Queenmaker.' Nicóla grabbed Crumwell's black doublet and pulled his lips to hers one more time.

Chapter 44 - June 1533
Greenwich Palace, downstream London

A sir's seecryt and a sir's weakness art the same beaste London

'Please, learn to remember this,' Nicóla said in a raised voice to the eight clerks in one of Crumwell's offices, 'all the letters you edit in preparation for the birth of the royal heir, where written the 'birth of a prince', you must leave a small space in case we need to make alterations. All the physicians and astrologists confirm the baby in Queen Anne's belly is male, but we must be prudent. Everything shall go to the printing press before the baby is born, but we must be prepared for a princess also.'

'Is that not treason, to suggest the royal heir may be female?'

Nicóla turned to the voice and there stood Thomas Wyatt, leaning on the doorway. 'Mr. Wyatt, I can assure you that I desperately desire the baby to be male,' she smiled.

'As does the entire court,' Wyatt said as they wandered from the room through another office of men busy at their desks. 'Praise God peace may reign over England when a boy is born.'

'Are you still in love with Anne?'

'No, I lost Anne to the King a long time ago. But alas, I must be content to simply be close to her.'

Nicóla nodded with a sigh as they crossed the hallway into the main offices.

'Is our patron hither?' Wyatt asked.

'Yes; parliament is not in session.'

'Am I important enough to be in his company?'

'No, but I shall allow you anyway,' Nicóla jested. They crossed the main attendant office and through the wide doorway to where Thomas Crumwell sat, his golden eyes down at his desk, his quill furiously brushing the parchment before him. 'Master Crumwella, Thomas Wyatt to see you.'

Crumwell looked up, eyebrows high with surprise. 'Thomas Wyatt!'

'Master Crumwell, good day and well met.'

Nicóla sat down at her desk against the wall as Wyatt sat across from Crumwell.

'What be these?' Wyatt inquired.

'The Act for the Punishment of the Vice of Buggery.'

'Right,' Wyatt said slowly. 'Should that not be dealt with by canon law, by order of the Convocation?'

'Yes, ecclesiastical courts also deal with such. But now buggery has criminal punishment as well as religious sin.'

'The ever-moral Crumwell strikes again.'

'The laws I am instructed to pass always fall between civil and canon law.'

'What is classed as buggery in 1533?'

'An unnatural sexual act against the will of God and man. The King wishes it to be vague, so can be used to throw at anyone we must execute. The same way heresy and treason are also loosely defined. Buggery laws were used 200 years ago in the same manner; as it is hard to prove or disprove, it can be easily used to slander. I seek not to control the bedrooms of men in this land, I only seek to easily slander men the King commands so.'

'What the King wants, I suppose…'

'Always what His Majesty wants, Mr. Wyatt. There are many ways to control the people, and at the moment, we need all the aid we can find. I am reforming the Church, and cannot turn a blind eye to immoral practices, of any kind.'

'Do you not keep mistresses, Master Crumwell? We have all done such practices. I myself have not seen my wife in seven years, nor ever plan to do so.'

Nicóla did not turn to face the pair. Such was her constancy of hearing people talk about Crumwell and other women she no longer worried.

'No, I keep no mistress,' Crumwell told Wyatt, 'and while I am no man free of sin, I am truly clean of conscience, and have always taken marriage seriously.'

'Perchance your time in Italy and the Low Countries was filled with beautiful women? I am sure there are plenty of young Crumwell's out there.'

'Pray, I do hope not. What brings you to my office, Mr. Wyatt? I am sure it is not my long dance with sinning.'

'Indeed no, though sinning is many parts of my news.' Now Nicóla turned in her chair and brought herself into the conversation. All talk was useful. 'It is the Holy Maid, Elizabeth Barton,' Wyatt continued. 'Have you met her?'

'Oh yes,' Crumwell said and sat back in his chair. 'I first met Barton in 1528, when Wolsey and I interviewed her. She had long claimed religious prophesies. Her claims of writhing on the ground, falling into trances and talking with God already suffered from the exploits of monks at Canterbury Priory when Wolsey spoke to her. Sir Thomas More, Bishop Fisher, and even old Archbishop Warham had all seen her by the time she gained an audience with us. A Dominican Friar, Edward Bocking, is her spiritual director, her exploiter. Bocking pulls her out of the nunnery and states she speaks to God about the King's annulment and Queen Anne, and about how heretics shall destroy the world. You heard what she said of King Henry early in the year, that he would die seven months after marrying Anne. Here we are, Henry still breathing, the royal heir safe in the womb.'

'Barton is speaking again, calling the King the great infidel of England. She is speaking with those close to the former Queen Katherine, claiming God is on Katherine's side, that she is truly a queen still. That the vengeance of God shall vex Henry, that he will die a villain's death. Barton claims she has a letter written in heaven by Mary Magdalene, evidence of her claims that God hates the King.'

Crumwell just sighed. 'Words which are treason. This is why we need to break the Catholic Church; people are abused with lies of this nature. Was a letter written by Mary Magdalene? More like written by Bocking to enhance revenues from poor pious commoners seeking Barton's advice. Everywhere people turn, there are relics and fake stories being peddled for money. This is not even about religion any longer, it has taken a political turn.'

'You must arrest Elizabeth Barton, throw her in the Tower, and those who abuse her,' Nicóla said and both men turned to her. 'As long as people continue to exploit religion to share their political beliefs, every man and woman in England shall be used for the gain of a few. We are the power in England; the only people who tell peasants who to trust is us.'

'Such confidence is admirable,' Wyatt smiled.

'You be right,' Crumwell said, pointing a finger at Nicóla. 'Mr. Wyatt, send word to Sir Christopher Hales in Canterbury urgently. Ride there yourself if needed. Have Barton and the four monks who 'advise' her brought to the Tower and I shall interrogate them myself.'

'That shall not make Hales popular in Kent.'

'If Hales wants to keep his place in parliament, he has no choice. Remember I am the power; men shall do as I please. If every person who claims to have revelations from God is free, and there are many, how shall we control the order of the kingdom?'

'Barton has just published her writing, the Nun's Book, 700 copies,' Nicóla added.

'How do you find such things?' Wyatt scoffed.

'Listening,' Crumwell smirked and Nicóla copied.

'All copies must be rounded up and burned. Pay any man who brings forth a copy,' Nicóla continued, and Crumwell nodded clearly.

'Henry Courtenay's wife, the Marchioness Gertrude of Exeter, speaks with Barton,' Wyatt said.

Crumwell rested his face in his hand. 'And I have a man, Thomas Avery, in her household precisely for things such as this. I shall have him come to me at once. The Marchioness, no doubt, knows her husband, Henry's cousin, could take the throne upon the King's death. This is turning sinister, fast.'

'Do you mean to kill Barton and the others?' Wyatt asked.

'Does it matter?' Crumwell cried.

'No, I just...'

'It would be wrong to kill them,' Nicóla said for Wyatt. 'Perchance Elizabeth Barton simply needs to be seen as a woman of no value.'

'But how?' Wyatt asked.

'She is a woman,' Nicóla shrugged, 'it is so easy. Say Barton is a whore. A woman without virtue is barely a person. Every woman knows this; why else is a lady so protective of her honour? Say Barton is a whore, say her precious priests and monks use her. Watch how fast all shall distance themselves from her in order to be considered clean against the complexion of sin. If Barton and the others do not repent, then perchance a civil law, rather than religious punishment, can be used. There are people always speaking out; we must punish every one.'

'We only just let Bishop Fisher out of the Tower,' Crumwell mused. 'That puts us in better standing with the people, at least for now.'

'What shall you do, have every man, woman, and child in England swear they support Queen Anne?' Wyatt scoffed.

Nicóla looked to Crumwell and he stared back. 'An Act of Supremacy,' she said and he widened his eyes as he thought of it. 'Everyone swears an oath Henry is the supreme leader, political and religious, and that Anne is the lawful queen, their children the lawful heirs to the throne.'

'Be prudent, Master Crumwell,' Wyatt warned, 'soon you will have more power over the realm than the King himself.'

Nicóla held Crumwell's gaze. That was the plan all along. If Crumwell had to live with letting Wolsey die alone, then there had to be more reward, and it had to be huge.

~~~

It was Sir Francis Bryan who brought the news to court. Nicóla sat in the antechamber outside King Henry's presence chamber, watching and listening while Crumwell helped the King with his daily tasks with petitioners. Bryan, with his eye patch, his bright clothing, "the vicar from hell" as Wolsey always called him, strode through the mass of men waiting, straight in without being introduced into the presence chamber. Bryan had a kind of character about him; with his unfailing truth and his lack of propriety made him one of Henry's favourites. But today he bought the most serious news.

'Your Majesty,' Bryan said as he bowed, breathing heavily from his walk. Nicóla slipped between quiet courtiers to stand close enough to hear what was happening. Crumwell had stopped close to Bryan, which he only did when he knew something appeared severe. Normally he stood totally indifferent to the men who petitioned the King.

'News from Westhorpe Hall,' Bryan said as he stood up straight.

'Your Majesty, I am sorry to inform you that your sister, Princess Mary, Dowager Queen of France and Duchess of Suffolk, has died of illness. Her Grace is to be interred at Bury St. Edmunds Abbey, at her husband, the Duke of Suffolk's, behest.'

King Henry and death never went well together. Henry sat firmly in his chair, though the pain of the news began to pinch his face, his eyes twitching, his mouth much the same. Mary had not attended the coronation; she hated Anne Boleyn. But her claim of illness was not as stretched as Henry thought; now his beloved favourite sister was dead. They had been so important in each other's lives; Mary had married his best friend, as angered as Henry was about the union.

'Charles Brandon?' the King asked. 'The Duke is at Westhorpe Hall, Your Majesty,' Bryan replied. 'He has gone into mourning.'

Henry stood up and Nicóla watched his eyes glisten over, even from the distance she stood, in a room now filled with stunned silence, the pain eating the King so evident.

'Mr. Crumwell, please ensure a formal announcement is released. Thank you, Sir Francis, you may be dismissed.'

Without another word, the King turned and disappeared into his privy chamber. 'I suppose he will go to Queen Anne now,' Bryan commented to Crumwell.

'He does little else these days,' Crumwell sighed.

Nicóla stayed as the antechamber emptied; no one would see the King now, not for days.

'Is it true you personally arrested Fisher and threw him in the Tower?' Bryan said to Crumwell, the pair not in conversation often.

'Yes, though Fisher is free for now. We held him in comfort, simply to keep him aside.'

'And Sir Thomas More, shall you make sure he is fallen also? More speaks much against the King's decisions these days. Did not even enjoy the wedding.'

'Not attending the King's wedding is not a treasonable offence.'

'Change the law, Master Crumwell, is that not what you do? Soon you shall supplant me as the King's top henchman.'

'Never, Sir Francis, no one could ever hope to take such a prize from you. You know my old master Wolsey hated you and your lewd behaviour.'

'Ha! Yes, I remember well. Had me banished from the King's privy chamber for tumbling with too many maids. Sometimes, Mr.

Crumwell, I do believe the golden days are well over.'

'Fret not, Sir Francis, there are always pleasant girls to be chased and money to be made. Mark my word.'

Bryan left Crumwell with a brief nod of acknowledgement and Nicóla wandered to her master. 'Indeed I truly feel for the King,' she muttered. 'I watched all five of my sisters die, and we were not half as close as Henry was to Mary. Henry's daughter was named for her.'

'We can expect seldom to be done for a while.'

'Shall the King attend the funeral in Suffolk?'

'No, there is no chance Henry could bear such a public appearance, not in the face of loss,' Crumwell said. 'Plus it is eighty miles from London, too much work involved. If I bring any law to Henry now, he shall refuse it. Bringing in More on bribery charges, or anything shall be not be heeded. Now is not the time to strike against anyone.'

~~~

Crumwell was right; the next days and weeks proved most idle for the King. But the kingdom still needed to be led; which meant Crumwell sitting at the head of the council meetings, giving out instructions, the Duke of Suffolk not present either. The Crumwell chambers of the court never ceased, always people there, around the clock, Crumwell and Nicóla barely seeing their beds. Ralph stayed at Austin Friars, he too rushed to the point of no sleep. The house had 300 staff now, almost its own government building, on top of countless clerks at court. Running a kingdom never came easy.

Ambassador Eustace Chapuys crept into the Crumwell chambers late at night, a face not seen recently, such was his hatred of Queen Anne and open love for Katherine. Nicóla found the ambassador and led him straight to Crumwell, who was furiously working on drafts for another parliament sitting.

'Master Crumwella, Eustace Chapuys.'

Crumwell gestured Chapuys to sit while Nicóla poured the wine for the men on a hot summer's night. With the Queen so heavily pregnant and about to go into confinement, the court could not leave the hot London area. They resided at the light and airy Greenwich palace, not Whitehall right in the city, but still, the heat burned everyone alike, and while Austin Friars was only five miles away, baby Jane seemed so far away, Gregory also.

'Ambassador,' Crumwell said and sipped the wine in his silver goblet, 'how may I be of service? You come more seldom these days. I thought you better suited to speak rumours about me rather than discussion to my face.'

Nicóla grinned as she stood nearby, not asked to leave. Crumwell never asked her to leave. Chapuys looked to Nicóla and back to Crumwell. 'Mr. Frescobaldi, I find your new master to be in a foul mood.'

'Master Crumwella is far from my new master,' Nicóla replied.

'Compared to your old master, the Pope, Crumwell is new. Or is your new master your husband in Florence?'

Crumwell bounded from his seat in a moment, towering over Chapuys, who sat there layered in grey velvet, a fur around his shoulders, looking rough, as if he had found it on the roadside, strange for an ambassador. But it was whispered Chapuys sent all his money to relieve Queen Katherine's poverty.

'You think I know not the truth?' Chapuys said up to Crumwell. 'Remember I am the trusted ear of the Holy Roman Emperor. Everyone knows of the favourite courtier Pope Clement kept, a petite young man, effeminate and gentle, welcome even in the Pope's bedroom. You have the Duchess of Florence hither working as your secretary, and as a man. It is so strange that I understand none of it.'

Nicóla strode over to Chapuys and sat on the edge of the desk, manners be damned. 'Understand this, Ambassador,' she said, her olive face still and measured, 'I am Nicóla Frescobaldi, master secretary to Thomas Crumwella, the King's Chief Minister. You may know the Pope has a bastard son, but it is not well known in Italy. Less well known is the Frescobaldi family kept in the Pope's employ. But I had no official title there; I had no official posting to Florence, no official connection with Alessandro de' Medici.'

'Nicóletta Frescobaldi married Alessandro de' Medici.'

'My sister.'

'There is only one living Frescobaldi child.'

'I am the bastard Frescobaldi,' Nicóla replied, relieved at that truth. The most convincing lies were close to the truth. 'Do not presume to understand my arrangement with His Holiness, nor my sister's life with His Holiness' bastard son. To fall foul of me or my sister is to fall foul of the entire Medici dynasty. Indeed, to fall foul of the Pope, even God himself.'

'To fall foul of King Henry's most trusted minister,' Crumwell added. 'In case the Pope feels far away.'

'Did you hear Alessandro de' Medici, hereditary Duke of Florence now, has recently been delivered of a healthy baby boy?'

No, Nicóla did not know. She had not heard from Alessandro, nor Pope Clement since Calais. No wonder she heard nothing; Alessandro gained a bastard son. The Medici cared nothing for legitimacy, as long as there was offspring. No wonder things seemed so quiet. A new Medici was born. What a relief; new offspring meant Nicóla was no longer needed. 'Yes, I am awares, for my sister is the Duchess of Florence,' Nicóla replied, her expression not allowed to show her mind.

'I heard that the Medici baby is a bastard, got on a mistress, not on the Duchess herself. Indeed, Duchess Nicóletta has not been seen in Florence,' Chapuys teased, his confidence not yet damaged.

'Duchess Nicóletta lives not in Florence. Have you come hither to threaten or speak?' Crumwell demanded.

Chapuys looked from Crumwell to Nicóla and back again. 'I come to talk about Queen Katherine.' Chapuys moved awkwardly; he meant to use his knowledge of Nicóla to gain something, but instead he angered England's most powerful man.

'You mean Katherine, Dowager Princess of Wales,' Crumwell corrected him.

'Katherine is moved to Ampthill in Bedfordshire, with a much-reduced household.'

'Indeed, Chapuys, for I was the one who ordered such.' Crumwell folded his arms and did not sit. Eustace Chapuys was a friend no longer. Everyone ever called a friend slowly turned foe. 'You also sent a member of the Council to speak with Katherine, and found her in bed, ill. Still, Katherine was questioned about whether she has accepted her new title, as the widow of Prince Arthur, the King's brother. She denied it all, of course.'

Crumwell smiled. 'Nature ought to have made Katherine a man; her strength, and that of her mother, would have made Katherine a hero of history.'

'Oh, so you do have emotion,' Chapuys commented, looking at Crumwell's smile. 'Does the King know Katherine is much unhappy?'

'The King is still mourning his sister Mary, as I am sure Katherine is, as they lived together in their youth. The King ordered me to move Katherine, so she should not be unhappy in Bedfordshire much longer. He has ordered Katherine to Buckden Palace in Cambridgeshire, with an even smaller household staff.'

'You mean to make Katherine's life worse, Crumwell? How could you?' Chapuys demanded.

'Not I, but the King.'

'Did you also know the Pope has ruled on the King's annulment at last?' Chapuys said and glanced at Nicóla.

Pope Clement made a decision? Nicóla thought of Giulio, much aged, no longer the man she once loved and adored, surrounded by corrupt men, pressing him into decisions. He would never give an annulment; Nicóla knew it deep in her heart.

'The Pope has sent off the papal command, stating Henry is still married to Katherine. Henry has until September to go back to his lawful wife,' Chapuys said, with smugness in his tone.

'The royal heir shall be born in September and the King will never see Katherine again,' Crumwell said and clicked his fingers twice.

Nicóla grabbed Chapuys by the collar and pulled the man to his feet. Chapuys knew Nicóla was a woman and would not fight. 'Hear this,' Nicóla said in Chapuys' ear, 'you may serve the Emperor in Rome, but we serve the King in England. You are but a mouthpiece, and we bow to no one. The King knows everything of me and indeed of my sister, so you need not threaten us. Henry shall not turn his heart back to Rome, not now, not ever. The tide has changed, Ambassador, so you ought to get on board with us, lest you shall surely drown.'

Chapuys pulled himself away from Nicóla and stormed from the office. Nicóla grabbed his wine goblet, untouched, and took a sip. 'All we need now is Anne's baby to be born male, and you will have everything you need, Tomassito.'

'Long may the Protestant reformation of England reign,' Crumwell said and picked up his own goblet.

'We are doing the right thing, are we not? I am free of the Pope, and the King is free of Katherine, can we halt now? Before we create new enemies?'

'Why? All of England needs to be free, as free as we are.'

Nicóla raised her goblet and Crumwell responded with his. The Queenmaker shall rule the kingdom.

Chapter 45 - September 1533
Greenwich Palace and Austin Friars, London

Seecrycy is the fyrst essyntyal in affayrs of the stayte

'What did you name your stillborn son, Thomas?'

Crumwell glanced up from his scarred hands on the King's table. A silver candlestick partially blocked his view of Henry, sitting drooped at the head of the table, his white shirt collar crooked under his golden doublet. Henry's blue eyes did not look back; they sat somewhere between life and fantasy, caught in a dream during the day. Crumwell did not reply, and Henry snapped from his dream. 'But I should not ask,' Henry added.

'No, Your Majesty, you could never cause offence. The baby was to be named for me.'

'You could have more sons, could you not?'

'I am older than His Majesty.'

'And you have a healthy son by your first wife.'

'Yes, and I have my daughter, young Jane. Who knows, perchance Jane shall grow up to be some sort of grand scholar, setting the world on fire.'

'The world cannot be run by women, we both know this. By God, the pain I went through to gain a son.'

The pain he went through? What of Katherine, loyal and submissive for over twenty years, only to be turned out, as if a servant? Or of Henry's learned daughter, now no longer a princess but the Lady Mary, shoved aside and forgotten in Wales? Not to mention the King's bastard son, born of Bessie Blount some fifteen years ago. Or the countless others cast aside along the way, like old Wolsey, all in pursuit of a son. The young and beloved Henry Fitzroy, bastard though he was, was now Lord High Admiral of England, Lord President of the Council of the North, and Warden of the Marches towards Scotland. Perchance Blount's son was worthy of the throne.

'Do you ever wonder if we have done the right thing?' the King asked, his eyes drifting back into his fantasies.

'We, Your Majesty? I am sure you have done the right thing. You had the scholars of Europe and the clergy of England question your marriage, to ensure it was right and legal, on this Earth and in God's realm. How could you not do so?'

The endless flattery made Crumwell's bones ache. It was only early afternoon. But not any afternoon. Queen Anne had been in her confinement for two weeks, her rooms at Greenwich all laid out as per the specific instructions of the King's grandmother, Margaret Beaufort. Peaceful and graceful tapestries hung over all the walls and the ceiling, pleasant yet beautiful patterns sewn in gold and silver thread, and the floor coated in thick carpets. Not an ounce of light got into the room, though Anne was said to let a window open a little sometimes, which allowed light. Nothing could disturb Anne, nothing could be imagined, lest the baby be deformed. All had to be perfect. Henry had not seen Anne in two weeks; she was presupposed to be in confinement for six weeks, but today Anne was in labour, had been all day. Gold and silver had been rushed from the jewel house, ready for once the next King of England was born. He would be born into a room filled with crucifixes, candles and religious images at an altar.

First, the King paced around the palace, all work cancelled for the day. Then he took to jumping about, preparing the jousts and festivities, which Crumwell and Nicóla had laid out for the birth. Cranmer, secretly a new father himself, was on hand, ready to bless the child, and the christening in the Church of Observant Friars at Greenwich all prepared.

Crumwell turned to the King again, who had the face of a lost boy, not a man of more than forty, about to gain his heart's desire. 'When you see your healthy son, Your Majesty, all shall seem worth its fight.'

'So much fight is taken from me, Thomas,' the King sighed. 'It has cost so much and more to make Anne my Queen. But I wanted this for years, and it has worn me. I have ridden into battle at the head of an army and come out less spent.'

'You took on the Church which bowed to powers other than yourself, Your Majesty. You have helped speed the reformation of the Church in England, which will be of service to the lives of all your subjects.'

'Subjects who hate me, subjects who hate their new Queen.'

'They are of narrow learning, Your Majesty. You will be the saviour of their souls.'

The King smiled, loving the flattery. 'Your new plan, the Act of Supremacy, the swearing of the oath, will make them see sense. Even men such as Sir Thomas More shall bend to my will.'

'As they should, Your Majesty.'

'How long, Thomas, since your Waif heard from the Pope?'

'Not all year. Nothing.'

'Not even when His Holiness wrote to me, ordering me to return to Katherine or face excommunication?'

'Not even then.'

'Do you think the Waif still holds sway with the Pope?'

Crumwell rubbed his forehead, his dark, greying hair tickling the skin. 'May I speak plainly, Your Majesty?'

'Always, Thomas, you above all others.'

'My fear is, if for some reason, Nicóla was to go back to Italy, the Pope might take one look at her, and welcome her back as the prize of Christendom. The amount of love Pope Clement bore Nicóla hurts me deep in my soul. Even Nicóla does not know thus. I fear the Medici family shall welcome Nicóla home to Florence, their base of supremacy, where she could sit with the duchy crown on her rose-gold hair, all while they revere her for the prize she is; a female beauty with the mind of a man. Nicóla is a creature hither, but a treated as a miracle back home.'

'You fear the Medici will steal the Waif from you?'

'Every moment I fear she will change her mind about serving the court hither and go home. Nicóla is still young and still beautiful, like your Queen Anne.'

'And yet the Waif has lived hither for years now, Thomas. Why worry so?'

'All I have worked for would be for nothing if I did not have

Nicóla. Why be hither without her? What good would I be alone?'

'The same way I have ruled since the age of seventeen and yet, without a son, it is all for nothing.'

The two men dropped back in their seats, alone with their burdens. 'Do you ever feel lonely, Your Majesty?' Crumwell asked, his eyes fixed on the blue summer sky through the nearest window.

'Always, I have always felt lonely, ever since my mother died. Then I was not yet a boy of twelve, and she lay in her bed in the Tower, the Queen's rooms, dead after giving birth. Childbed fever took away the greatest white rose of York forever. That is why the rooms sat in disarray for so long; I cannot bear to visit. Still I had my sisters, Margaret and Mary, much like our mother, but it was never the same again. I married Katherine because my mother approved of her. My mother praised Katherine so, I remember as a boy of ten. But I must save my realm now, I must serve the Tudor name with a son; I have no choice. Why else was my mother having a child after the death of Arthur? Because I became the only living Tudor boy. Mother had a girl, named for Katherine, only to die, the baby along with her. My younger brother Edmund died at birth some six years before we lost Mother. In the end, nothing matters more than the birth of a son. Without a son, the kingdom will fall into war again, just as when my father won his crown from the Yorkists. This fear has weighed upon my shoulders since the day Arthur died more than thirty years ago.'

'Is a lucky thing indeed women give birth, Your Majesty. For as they toil with the creation with life, we break down over the past. The creation of life is best left to women.' King Henry raised a smile, his eyes on the wooden detail of his table. 'Thomas, I think you right. My whole life, Wolsey bore the weight of the throne for me. Now you do the same in his place. And yet my shoulders still droop under the pressure, and I would not wish this life on an ordinary man.'

'It is not for us to question why God has placed us where we are; we can but serve Him as best we can.'

Henry nodded slowly, his eyes wide as he thought. 'I do love Anne, in my own way. Does one ever truly understand love? I was in love with Katherine when they brought her from Spain and she married my brother. All those years, seven I think it was, she lived in poverty in London after Arthur died, not wanted by my father or her own. I married her because Arthur had done so, for the kingdom. I married Katherine because she was my childhood dream. It was right for me and for England, though I loved her, I truly did. But there are so many charming girls and Katherine lost so many babies. Love cannot surpass all. All these women, I could have all I wanted, so I took advantage, but Katherine was always my wife. There was no question. Then Anne Boleyn came home from France and refused my advances. Never had a woman seemed so eager to protect her honour, not since Katherine all those years ago. It is akin to hunting, is it not? To obtain what is denied you? And Anne has done her duty; she conceived after only a few weeks. Perchance I can have many children by her, Thomas. But this pregnancy is so difficult for her. God, I would not want a child if it meant it would take Anne from me, as death stole my mother in childbirth.'

'You speak of true love, Your Majesty. Anne can give you a son, the thing you have craved your whole life. But you would wish it away to save Anne from the pain and agony she has endured of late? You ask if it was all worth it? When you love so heartily?'

'You have a way with words, Thomas. You ought to have no fear of losing your Waif to the Italians. Only a fool would leave you now.'

'You are a kind prince, Your Majesty, as Cranmer always says.'

'We shall have another of those parties you host, as you are the rival to my crown in giving great festivities, once the baby is born and all is well. If you desire, Thomas, I can order your Waif to live as a woman, so you can have the mistress you deserve.'

'Please forgive me, I am merry as I am, Your Majesty. We fit together in a certain fashion, one which gives Nicóla comfort after a difficult start to life. Also, being who she is, I think Nicóla means to honour the wishes of her father, an admirable man.'

'Your secret shall always be safe with me, Thomas. You continue to give me all I want, with reforms in parliament, and I have no need to betray your confidence.' The words appeared kind, but a hint of threat lurked beneath.

'Have you picked a name for your son, Your Majesty?' Nicóla out of the conversation made Crumwell's heart beat a little gentler.

'I have not decided. Perchance Henry for my father, or Edward. There have been celebrated reigns under kings of the name Edward, including my mother's father, and of course her poor younger brother.'

Young King Edward the Fifth, King but two months and trapped in the Tower of London, and disappeared, presumed murdered with his younger brother, Richard. Crumwell always harboured the thought it was Henry's father who had those royal boys killed, to make way for himself on the throne, which came to pass after the battle of Bosworth. Perchance the Prince never died at all. But it was indeed eerie for Henry to want his son named after Edward, any of them, after so many Edwards caused pain to the Tudors.

The door to the privy chamber burst open and both men twirled in their seats. A guard stood at the door as Jane Boleyn, Lady Rochford swirled into the room holding her dress so she could move fast enough. 'Your Majesty,' she panted and bowed so fast she must have made herself dizzy. She stopped short when she saw Crumwell, and she smiled a fraction. Oh yes, court talk stated she wished for some sort of affair with Crumwell. Indeed no.

'Your Majesty, I am to inform you that Her Majesty has delivered of a healthy baby girl.'

The King slowly rose from his seat and Crumwell stumbled on doing the same. A girl. A baby girl, not the son and heir England needed. Crumwell had installed a queen to hold the country and allow the reformation to flourish. All Anne needed to do in return was give birth to a son. And yet the cry of a baby girl flowed from the Queen's chamber, not that of the son to create a stable country. A son in the cradle was God's approval of Anne's place, which was what Nicóla said a few nights ago. God was not smiling now, just as Pope Clement warned.

'Much congratulations to you, Your Majesty,' Crumwell said and bowed. 'God has praised you with a healthy child.'

The King still did not utter a word or move a muscle, his face returned to the boy who lost his mother on the childbirth bed. Lady Rochford stood still, her eyelashes fluttering as they always did around Crumwell. Lady Jane was married to George Boleyn; what did she ever think might happen between the pair? A kingdom was in crisis, for God's sake!

'What was it you said about your daughter, Thomas?' Henry mumbled, and half-turned in Crumwell's direction, his arms stiff at his sides. 'Mayhap she shall grow to be a great scholar and set the world on fire?'

'Precisely, Your Majesty. You have a healthy child. May I suggest Elizabeth, after your mother?'

'The child is of red hair, alike His Majesty,' Jane Boleyn continued. 'She is of fair skin but the black eyes of her mother, and strong and healthy. Her Majesty has also come through the ordeal with great strength.'

Crumwell waited for Henry to respond, stunned by the news. 'You are both young, Your Majesty,' he praised. 'A healthy daughter is born; now sons shall surely follow.'

Henry nodded, still slow in his movements. His heart was crushed. All Henry had gone through, for nothing. The son England needed did not prevail. 'I shall say those words to Anne, in comfort for this shock. Lady Rochford, call the child Elizabeth, tell Anne this is my order. Thomas, cancel the jousts, cancel the festivities. We shall go and pray for Elizabeth, and perform a Te Deum in the chapel at once. Fetch Cranmer.'

Crumwell and Jane left the King's rooms together. 'We ought to fetch Charles, the Duke of Suffolk, to console the King,' Lady Jane said to Crumwell, holding her splendid golden gown so she could keep up with him.

'We cannot, for today, the Duke, a man of fifty years, is marrying his fourteen-year-old ward, Catherine. His wife, the King's sister, is dead but three months, and here Suffolk is marrying on the day of the princess' birth.'

'Anne is beside herself. Her father might be furious and I am to tell the Earl next.'

'I have an entire kingdom to inform,' Crumwell said and peeled away from Lady Jane towards his chambers, now in a run. Oh dear Lord, why do this? Just when everything could, at last, come together, for the Queen to deliver of a girl?

Crumwell burst forth into his chambers at great speed, shocking all the clerks at work. Nicóla appeared from through the double doorway into his office. 'We must announce at once the birth of the Princess Elizabeth,' he called so everyone could hear through the rooms. 'Cancel all the festivities. Make sure the news spreads at once! Get the church bells ringing!'

The chambers fell into a hive of activity, all informed of their duties. Crumwell fled through into his office and closed his doors behind him. He fell to his knees, his hands clutched tight around Nicóla's waist. She held his head in her hands as he took few deep breaths to calm himself.

'My love, you must be of good cheer. The child is born. The Queen you installed has survived the most dangerous act a woman thinks to involve herself, so cry not,' Nicóla said, her fingers in his hair.

'Pray for me,' he said, his voice high-pitched, ready for tears to flow. 'Pray we shall not lose all we have earned due to this most harsh disaster.'

'O my God, relying upon Thine almighty power and Thine infinite mercy and goodness, and because Thou art faithful to Thy promises, I trust in Thee that Thou wilt grant me forgiveness of my sins, through the merits of Jesus Christ Thy Son; and that Thou wilt give me the assistance of Thy Grace, with which I may labour to continue to the end in the diligent exercise of all good works, and may deserve to obtain the glory which Thou hast promised in heaven. Amen.'

'Amen,' Crumwell said as he stood up, tears on his cheeks. 'Oh, Nicó, please promise me you shall never leave me.' He held Nicóla's cheeks in his hands, watching her frightened green eyes try to take in his angry words. 'For if I cannot keep this new kingdom together, I shall fall so far I may never recover.'

Nicóla covered his hands with her own, her eyes on his. 'I swear to God and all the world, I am not going to leave you, Tomassito, not now or ever. I promise you, in the sight of God, no matter what happens, the last thing you shall see on the Earth shall be me. If I am called to God first, all I shall call for is you.'

Crumwell kissed Nicóla, his tears on their lips, struggling to pull himself together. Fierce kisses were given and received, lips pushed together in desperation for comfort. Crumwell pulled Nicóla into his embrace and felt her petite hands on his chest.

'Tomassito, tell me, what is wrong? If Queen Anne has delivered of a girl, she is not a disaster as you think. We can keep your queen on the throne. Anne can conceive again. The king has not looked to another woman during Anne's pregnancy. Your queen is still in play. The country can still be saved. We can create a world where this princess can rule if we must, or marry her to the right suitor. Your enemies have not won, my love. Do not think your work all in vain for this.'

'We are to join the King to pray for the Princess, with Cranmer in the royal chapel at once.' Crumwell took a few deep breaths, and Nicóla wiped his tears with her soft fingers.

'Why then all this worry?' Nicóla asked, still in his arms.

'What if it is Wolsey all over again? Wolsey could not make fast a queen and he was destroyed. Now I cannot secure a son. What if I am next to fall? I could not save Wolsey; how could I save myself?'

Nicóla held her tongue, and Crumwell knew she agreed. 'Then we shall have to do whatever is necessary. Wolsey did not see his destruction coming, and we do. Perchance we shall have to use some less polite ideas from my homeland. More under-hand if necessary. Queen Anne has given birth to a healthy child. Anne can do it once more. You are as high in favour as you could imagine being now. Ralph has a healthy son, named after you, at Austin Friars. Our daughter Jane is well. Your son Gregory is safe in the home you have built for him, where he will one day succeed you. Much is to be celebrated.'

Crumwell shook his head and pulled himself together. 'I am sorry; I shall get to work at once.'

'Never excuse yourself for your honesty, for there is so little of it at court. Is the King much angered to have a daughter again?'

'Henry is stunned and ordered me out as I suggested the child be Elizabeth for his mother.'

'Then let us back to work to prepare papers to parliament stating this tiny Elizabeth is heir to the throne. We can make the country stable while we wait for a prince.'

'The King's devastation,' Crumwell said, his hands now sat his sides, his shoulders drooped. 'Oh, Nicó, to see him so close to his heart's desire and have it taken away…'

'God is trying to tell us something, yet we hear it not. We must wait.'

Crumwell took Nicóla's hand and kissed it. 'Know that I do not feel the same sadness with our daughter.'

'I never suspected you did, my darling.' Nicóla brought his hand to her lips and kissed him in return. She seemed so warm and smooth against the temerity of the world.

Crumwell glanced over Nicóla's shoulder at her desk, a huge letter unfolded on top of her correspondence. The papal seal abounded. 'The Pope writes?'

'Well indeed, but worry not, Tomassito, nothing bad comes from the writing. Giulio, he is not well of late, the perils of the papacy do not treat him kindly. He is not of a strong mind, and when his health falters, all is difficult. He writes of Alessandro in Florence, of the Medicis' growing power once more. Alessandro's mistress has delivered a healthy son, named Giulio after his grandfather, making the family most happy. The Pope is to meet the French King in a month, and approve the marriage of his niece Catherine to the French prince. The Pope shall be allied with the French King and the Emperor of Rome, so let us just work on nothing but securing King Henry's power. Henry's enemies are allying themselves. We have less control in Europe than we wish to believe. Let us build the England we can with a princess until a son arrives.'

~~~

Crumwell stood in the chapel of the Observant Friars with Nicóla sat his side, their gloved hands laced together as Princess Elizabeth was brought to her christening. The halls of the palace and the chapel decorated with green carpets on the floor and tapestries and canopies all the way from nursery to altar. Everyone was in place, the pompous Duke of Suffolk and his child bride, and the Duke of Norfolk and his wife. Gentlemen, chaplains, squires, aldermen, and all the members of the Privy Council. The Boleyn family looked most pleased with themselves. At the altar where Cranmer stood in his purple robes and archbishop's mitre hat atop dark hair, stood the silver font, where the holy water dripped upon the infant's red hair. A purified crimson cloth of estate hung over the baby girl, the canopy held aloft by George Boleyn himself. Anne's grandmother, Agnes Howard, the Dowager Duchess of Norfolk, played godmother, and carried the infant on a cushion of purple velvet. Thomas Boleyn followed, carrying the child's long train, along with Elizabeth's other godmothers Margaret Grey, Marchioness of Dorset, and Gertrude Courtenay, Marchioness of Exeter, the lover of the heretical Elizabeth Barton. Crumwell still had to settle that mess.

Words uttered, gifts offered, trumpets blown; as if a baby might enjoy such things! Cranmer performed the christening before a collection of thousands, all there for the occasion, but Crumwell focused on the warmth of Nicóla's hand in his in the front row. Crumwell needed to get Cranmer to annul Nicóla's marriage to the Medici bastard and declare theirs lawful. Cranmer had done so for the King, and it was time for Crumwell to make himself merry. The future no longer held the confidence it did when Queen Anne nursed her pregnant belly. Crumwell felt almost as bad as when he lost his own son, and almost Nicóla too, in childbirth; that was the pain of this girl being born.

~~~

Austin Friars brought such relief. Return of the grand parties once more; meals of swan and oysters, pheasant, venison and cod. Artichokes from the garden of Hampton Court, the palace built by Wolsey not so long ago. Cherries and marzipan, especially because Nicóla loved them. The hawks got let out to fly at dusk, the canaries chirped in the fading summer warmth, Gregory learned the art of falconing from Crumwell in the gardens. Even the most powerful men in the kingdom needed to be at home. All moved so gently at Austin Friars. Ralph and Ellen had their infant son Thomas to dote upon, though the child was kept away from Nicóla. Nicóla returned to wearing the bright new fashions from France, doublets so long they resembled dresses tied with a satin sash at the waist, almost dressed as a woman, slowly moving between the genders every day. Gregory adored Nicóla's company, and wished to dress just like her. Nicóla ran and laughed with Jane, now three years old, the pair with long rose-gold hair, and watched the beavers play in their cages. Crumwell thought to bring the leopard from his country home to London again, to scare all the guests who came by the house. All the creatures of Crumwell, placed in every house in England and abroad, came and went, sharing their stories and rumours, as if everything was normal. Everything was, yet Crumwell could not gain the future for the country he created. The reformation must gain strength, the Church had to break further. Crumwell had saved Nicóla from the clutches of the Catholic faith, and now everyone else could be saved from Catholicism too.

A letter arrived from the palace, ordering Crumwell home to court after only a month of relaxation. A new honour – Steward of Westminster. His tenth official role for the King, adding them all the time, just like Wolsey. Cardinal Wolsey, the man Crumwell always trusted but no longer wished to emulate. Crumwell did not do his job to be rich, to claim to have the power, like Wolsey. Crumwell wanted a better England, for everyone. The turquoise ring on his finger had no need to control the King; Crumwell already had the kingdom in his palm.

Crumwell wandered to Nicóla, standing in the darkness, throwing pieces of bread to her peacocks, which bobbed about at her feet. He stood behind her, placing his arms around her waist. He kissed her cheek and she laughed and raised a hand to his face. Just for now, all seemed well. Crumwell could not bear to tell Nicóla the news heard from Thomas Avery at the household of the Marquess and Marchioness of Exeter. The Holy Maid, Elizabeth Barton, had claimed that God told her that an evil foreign woman had invaded court and hid in plain sight. Crumwell believed not in superstition, but this news, these whisperings, threatened to harm his peace. Also, Alessandro de' Medici had written, but Crumwell opened Nicóla's mail while she played with Jane. Alessandro begged for Nicóla's return, as the Pope was terribly ill, some presupposed poisoned, and the Pope needed Nicóla at his side. For the man who controlled a kingdom, storms kept sweeping upon Crumwell's shore.

'We are summoned back to court,' Crumwell mumbled.

'I saw the letter; you are named Steward of Westminster!'

'One of the first things to prepare for at Westminster Abbey; the wedding of the King's bastard son Henry Fitzroy, Duke of Richmond. He is to marry stuttering old Norfolk's daughter, Lady Mary Howard. The King's illegitimate son married to Anne Boleyn's cousin.'

'Quite the power play. It is time for you to rule your kingdom, Master Crumwella.'

'Things are not to going to be easy now; we have to denounce people, perchance execute people. I foresee far fewer heads in England in coming years.'

'As long as your head stays on your shoulders, my love. Whether I write your letters or interrogate your victims, as long as you are safe, I am ready to go back to court.'

'I thought the destruction the old England would be the hard part, but we have done it.'

'You have done it, Tomassito. For I am only your master secretary.'

'No, we have done it. Now we must rebuild a better country with a reformed Church. We will destroy anyone who gets in our way, starting with Sir Thomas More. No man is safe from us now. More needs to die, along with Bishop Fisher, and that heretic Elizabeth Barton. And countless more clergymen.'

'You make it sound like war.'

'With the Pope and the Catholic faith as our enemy, it shall be war, Nicó. We have taken the country, but now we have to hold it.'

'Heads are going to be lost, are they not?'

'Either we take heads, or ours will be taken.'

'Such is the frailty of human affairs. Then let us shake the throne, without mercy for traitors, until you are master of the realm. As Machiavelli wrote; since love and fear can hardly exist together, if we must choose between them, it is far safer to be feared than loved.'

'Nicó…'

'Even if you claim not to be "The Prince", you are my prince. You are the true ruler of this realm.'

To be continued…

PART II OF THE QUEENMAKER SERIES:
SHAKING THE THRONE

The moderate man shall inherit the kingdom.
That man needs to be the Queenmaker.

November 1533 – Thomas Cromwell and Nicóla Frescobaldi have their queen on the throne. The Catholic Church is being destroyed as the Reformation looms over England. Cromwell has total power at court and in parliament, while Frescobaldi wins favour with the king's illegitimate son, Henry Fitzroy.

But England's fate is uncertain. The nobles still despise Cromwell and his Italian creature. Anne has not given the king a son. Queen Katherine refuses to give up her title, and Thomas More and Bishop Fisher defy their king. The final Plantagenets think they should hold the throne while the Catholics want Princess Mary named as heir.

England can be reformed, but Cromwell must dissolve all the monasteries and abbeys, and with the king on his side, the plan to change religion will sever heads. Queen Anne is losing Henry's love, but Cromwell could suffer if Anne loses her crown. Frescobaldi creates a daring plan to replace Anne and regain the Pope's favour, but Cromwell must execute the plans on his own. Schemes will go astray and the wrong heads will be severed to satisfy a vengeful sovereign.

Kings will rise, queens shall fall, children will perish, and the people of England will march in a pilgrimage to take Cromwell's head, while Frescobaldi will have to make the ultimate sacrifice.

PART III OF THE QUEENMAKER SERIES:
NO ARMOUR AGAINST FATE

The moderate man shall inherit the kingdom.
That man needs to be the Queenmaker.

London, January 1537 – Thomas Cromwell is in deep mourning. His new queen is on the throne at King Henry's command, but the personal cost is too high. Nicòla Frescobaldi is lying dead inside the Medici tomb in Florence, and Cromwell's only daughter Jane is missing. Now, the people of England have rebelled against their king, marching to London to start a civil war. The Pilgrimage of Grace has two demands: remove all the Reformation changes from religion and cut off Cromwell's head.

Cromwell needs his friends, allies and the king's favour more than ever, but he can do nothing when Queen Jane dies giving England its son and heir. Cromwell's son has married the Queen's sister, but the Seymours will disappear from favour if Cromwell does not eliminate all those able to take their place. There is only one solution; become Queenmaker yet again and find a foreign princess for Henry, one to seal religious change and create stability in the war of Catholic against Protestant.

Nicòla Frescobaldi may be dead, but Duchess Nicòletta of Florence is not, so Cromwell and his creature can rule politics again to control England and Ireland. But when war with the Holy Roman Empire threatens, all of Cromwell's powers, titles and schemes cannot save him from his oldest enemy in England, and a betrayal deep in the heart of the powerful Cromwellian faction.

There will be blood…

ALSO BY CAROLINE ANGUS

The Thomas Cromwell Queenmaker Series
Frailty of Human Affairs
Shaking the Throne
No Armour Against Fate

**My Hearty Commendations:
The Letters and Remembrances of
Thomas Cromwell** – *non-fiction*

The Secrets of Spain Series
Blood in the Valencian Soil
Vengeance in the Valencian Water
Death in the Valencian Dust
also available as a complete set

The Canna Medici Series
Night Wants to Forget
Violent Daylight
Luminous Colours of Dusk
Cries of Midnight

Intense Professional Countess

Available soon –

Hatred Gained by Good Works:
Thomas Cromwell in Florence

The Private Life of Cromwell – *non-fiction*

The Indulgent Nursery of King
Henry VIII – *non-fiction*

Printed in Poland
by Amazon Fulfillment
Poland Sp. z o.o., Wrocław
05 January 2022

fa0b8ce9-17c9-4b2e-ab09-a4700acdd61aR01